Downing Street Diary

The Macmillan years
1957–1963

Harold Evans

HODDER AND STOUGHTON
LONDON SYDNEY AUCKLAND TORONTO

British Library Cataloguing in Publication Data

Evans, *Sir* Harold, *bart, b. 1911*
  Downing Street diary.
  1. Great Britain – Politics and government –
  1945–1964
  I. Title
  941.085′6′0924   DA592

  ISBN 0-340-25897-7

WATERFORD

Downing Street Diary

Also by Harold Evans

To Betty and Annabel
who for seven years had
to play second fiddle to
No. 10

Contents

Illustrations

between pages 160 and 161

Through the garden gate[1]
A Garden Rooms girl is a very special person[1]
No. 10 Private Secretaries[1]
Lady Dorothy with Australian friend[1]
'Why can't they do that in England?'[1]
High wind in Bermuda
A helicopter for James Hagerty[2]
Working with Charles Hill carried the bonus of laughter[3]
The joint Macmillan and Eisenhower television broadcast[4]
In Accra with Robert Manning[5]
Prime Ministerial time checks with the author[6]
  and with President Kennedy[7]
With Pierre Salinger aboard *Honey Fitz*
The Macmillans at home[1]

CREDITS

1 From colour photographs by Harold Evans
2 The Air Ministry
3 Department of Information, Nairobi
4 Associated Press
5 Ghana Information Services, Accra
6 Keystone Press Agency Ltd
7 Popperfoto

In Explanation

Without quite knowing how it had happened I found myself drafted into 10 Downing Street in 1957 as the Prime Minister's Adviser on Public Relations, which was a rather grand way of designating his Press Secretary. It further happened that I stayed there for seven years, an exceptionally long time for anyone to work at No. 10 in a senior appointment. Moreover, the Prime Minister I served for all but six months of that time was Harold Macmillan – probably the last British Prime Minister to exercise a significant influence in the direction of world affairs and widely recognised as a man of outstanding intellect, humanity and style. They were years of crucial change for the British people in both domestic and foreign affairs, and much that was done then set the pattern for matters as they now are.

With the good fortune (though it did not always seem so at the time) to be closely involved in all these developments, I began to jot down a record of them, as and when I could find a moment. These were hasty notes, sometimes scribbled at the end of a long day, more usually at weekends, occasionally with a long gap between them. There was nothing systematic about them, and they represented a highly personal view, from a particular angle, of what was happening when it was happening.

I did not see them as material for publication, and in any event the publication of memoirs by civil servants then stood under so many prohibitions and restrictions that the possibility of publication seemed too remote to be thought about seriously. I kept them because I am an inveterate scribbler, because life at No. 10 was endlessly fascinating, and because I felt they might help to keep me amused in my old age.

Having reached old age (but not liking to be reminded of it), I began to look at them again, and to wonder whether they might amuse others as well as myself. Colourful footnotes, perhaps, to a colourful premiership? New light on the rough and tumble – and fun – beneath the surface of great events? An insight into the

9

delicate and often abrasive relationship between Prime Minister and Press? Certainly they could not be much more than this. The story of the Macmillan premiership has been told from many angles, notably in the autobiographies of most of its leading characters, and most notably of all, of course, by Harold Macmillan himself. His memoirs, so comprehensive and so lucid, are a remarkable legacy to historians.

In fact, it was not for me to agonise about the interest and readability of my own recollections. That could be left to the judgment of publishers. Given a willingness to publish, the way ahead had now been cleared by the findings of a committee of Privy Councillors, under Lord Radcliffe, which in 1976 examined the issues involved in the publication of memoirs by Ministers of the Crown and by civil servants.

The problem remained of giving the diaries coherent form. Diaries so often make difficult reading for the uninitiated – all those names one finds so hard to identify and to relate to each other and to the flow of events. Even the flow of events is not easy to understand when so much background is assumed.

So I decided to cast this book into two parts. The first is introductory in the sense of setting the scene from several aspects, though it could, I hope, stand on its own. The second, much the longer, comprises the diaries. They cover (though not comprehensively) the years 1960 to 1963. This was the period of the second Macmillan administration. My regret is that during the first administration – the years of almost unbroken success – I kept only desultory records.

Three final points. Diaries are inevitably egotistical, and if their human interest is usually greater because of that, they are not to be accepted as anything but a partial view. Secondly, they see events only from a particular angle at a particular moment in time (without advantage of hindsight) and therefore, once again, the view is only partial. Thirdly, in the heat of the moment, some exasperation with others will be apparent here and there, but there is no malice. Second thoughts would probably be kinder. But what would diaries be without a little spice?

HAROLD EVANS
ROTTINGDEAN

Part One

1 Prelude to No. 10

When the invitation reached me to become spokesman at 10 Downing Street I was in New York, seconded briefly from the Colonial Office to the British Delegation to the United Nations. Before leaving London early in January 1957 I knew that I was regarded as a strong candidate and that an early decision was likely, but events had to take their course and in the meantime I had an exceptionally interesting assignment.

In fact, events in London took a dramatic turn shortly after I left. On January 9th Anthony Eden suddenly resigned from the premiership on grounds of ill-health. From New York it was difficult to follow the processes which threw up Harold Macmillan rather than Rab Butler as the new Prime Minister, but Macmillan it was and I could only speculate about the difference, if any, that this would make to the search for a spokesman.

The search had been made necessary by the resignation of William Clark in November 1956. He had felt deeply disturbed by the handling of the Suez affair, and though he stayed in post until the worst of the turmoil had subsided he then made his own views plain and resigned. The task of finding a successor was handed to Dr. Charles Hill who, in the aftermath of Suez, had been called into the Cabinet as Chancellor of the Duchy of Lancaster to co-ordinate the official information services, both home and overseas. As ever, a failure in policy was being attributed to a failure in communication.

In his memoirs he says that in seeking to fill the No. 10 vacancy he began by consulting the Lobby correspondents about the kind of appointment they would like to see. Should it be someone from Fleet Street, like William Clark, or a professional from the official information services? Lobby opinion favoured a civil servant, partly on the grounds that in this way they were more likely to get news and background delivered objectively, and partly because they felt that a civil servant could probably press the buttons in Whitehall more effectively. The possibility remained that the new Prime

Minister might prefer to appoint someone already close to him personally and politically, as Mr. Attlee had done in selecting Francis Williams, and as Mr. Wilson was later to do in appointing Joe Haines. This was not the Macmillan view, however, and so Charles Hill went ahead with finding someone from among Whitehall's chief information officers.

He had seen me before my departure for New York. In *Both Sides of the Hill* he writes, 'When I interviewed him, he did all he could to discourage me from selecting him. Sandy-haired, spruce in his blue suit, he almost scowled at me, answering most of my questions with a disconcerting economy of words, telling me more of his shortcomings than his virtues.' Sandy-haired? I hadn't thought so. Spruce? Possibly, since in 1965 the Clothing Manufacturers' Federation were to name me as one of Britain's ten best-dressed men for that year (and how that rocked the family!). Scowling? Well, certainly I did not want him to have any illusions about my suitability for No. 10.

Quite simply, I doubted if in temperament and experience I was the right man. My early background was journalism. I had moved into the Civil Service during the war by accident and not design. I was more interested in the written word than the spoken word, and considered myself neither articulate enough, nor extrovert enough, nor sophisticated enough for the No. 10 appointment. Nor had I much knowledge and experience in the political and parliamentary arena, where the Prime Minister's spokesman operated. I had been close to two Cabinet Ministers – Alan Lennox-Boyd as Secretary of State for the Colonies and Lord Swinton as Resident Minister in West Africa – but my work for them had involved little contact with the political journalists. Primarily I had been an adviser, an organiser, an administrator and a writer. At the Colonial Office, though I was ultimately responsible for Press relations, I considered that this responsibility was best discharged by making sure we had a first-class Press Officer. The daily hurly-burly of Press relations work was therefore something in which I had no great experience. Nor was I sure that I would find it congenial. Moreover, there would be little in it financially.

On the other side of the coin was the prestige and excitement of the No. 10 appointment. Over the years I had also learned that if the finger of Fate beckons it is usually wise to go. A further factor existed. At that time I was still in a state of emotional shock from the sudden death of my six-year-old son, Timothy, while we were on holiday in Italy in 1955. The effect was to move me towards accepting this opportunity to escape into a new and dominating environment. It also made me less apprehensive than I might have been about the hazards and uncertainties of No. 10. All things in life had acquired a new perspective. The worst had happened: there was nothing left to fear. Nevertheless, I felt that I must leave Charles Hill in no doubt about my own doubts, and that was how the matter stood when I left for New York.

This was my second visit to New York, but the first had been fleeting and in very different circumstances. When war broke out in 1939 I was at sea on a small tanker, trying to see the world by working as a member of the crew – a hard way of doing it but the only way since I had only sixpence in my pocket when I climbed to the deck of the *Laristan* in Falmouth Roads. We loaded oil at Aruba, in the Dutch West Indies, but then, instead of bringing it back to Europe, we were ordered to discharge it in New York in order to fill in time as usefully as possible while the first transatlantic convoy was being organised from Jamaica. The *Laristan* berthed at Staten Island after dark on a very wet September night, without any sight of Manhattan. Next morning autumnal mists shrouded the harbour, but I had shore leave and took a ferry to Manhattan. Half way across we emerged from the mist and there, due ahead in the brilliant morning sunshine, stood the clustered skyscrapers of New York, rising unevenly like bars of gold from the white mist. The exhilaration of that moment has always remained with me, and presumably explains why I have never found it possible to share jaundiced views about New York.

In fact, I saw almost nothing of the city because I immediately took the subway to the World Fair, my first priority. Of the Fair, I have two principal memories – Ripley's two-headed cow (one head chewing the cud, the other apparently dozing), and the half-finished Czechoslovak national pavilion, symbolising the Nazi invasion and the fact that a world war was just beginning.

On the 1957 visit I was perhaps still wearing rose-tinted spectacles, aided no doubt by being cosseted as a Delegation official (though the cosseting fell short of an adequate subsistence allowance and I did much of my feeding on stools in drug stores and coffee shops). Working hours were chiefly spent in the U.N. building on the waterfront, where I was in part fascinated and in part disillusioned by this close-up view of U.N. procedures and bloc politics.

My principal concern lay in the Fourth Committee, nominally responsible for Trusteeship affairs but being used as a base from which to harass and condemn Britain as a colonial power. This was what had brought me to New York. Most of the major British colonial territories were already far on the way to self-government or had achieved it. The door was open. But it suited too many interests to pretend that the door had to be battered down – politicians in the territories themselves (most of them educated in Britain), eager for power, absolute if possible; the United States still emotionally imprisoned by its own remote colonial past; and the Soviet bloc, seeking to disrupt western unity and to recruit the Third World. The trouble with battering doors down, however, is that a lot of people get hurt and a lot of time and effort is needed to repair the damage. My task was to see if the United Kingdom Delegation could be given a fuller and faster service of information and guidance on colonial affairs so that it could move quickly to counter the flow of misrepresentation. Improvements were certainly possible, and I made recommendations accordingly, but it could never be more than a rearguard action.

Away from the U.N. I set out systematically to sample the sights and sounds of New York. The sounds included the clang of snow shovels in the canyon of Madison Avenue. The sights included Sir Ralph Richardson, playing to perfection the role of famous British actor-manager walking in Central Park, New York – long overcoat with fur collar, walking stick, brown soft trilby with narrow brim turned up all the way round, stately gait and a look of wide-eyed incredulity as he surveyed the American scene.

But in 1957, as in 1939, what one really remembered was the warmth and generosity of American people (surliness of New York officialdom apart), so that at the end of it all you felt that the Americans and the British were just one big happy family – only to be brought sharply back to earth, alas, when a black chambermaid, seeing me leave my hotel room, called down the corridor to my own chambermaid, 'Ida, yer foreign man's gone out.'

So back to London went Ida's foreign man, with instructions to call on the Secretary of the Cabinet and the Prime Minister immediately on return.

The Secretary of the Cabinet was Sir Norman Brook, an Olympian figure whose aloof demeanour only partly concealed an amiable disposition and a dry sense of humour. Like all the mandarins he was Oxbridge, but unlike many of them he came, not from Eton, Harrow or Winchester, but from Wolverhampton Grammar School. As a grammar school boy myself I found this reassuring (the public school gulf being what it is), especially since my own grammar school at Stourbridge, a venerable King Edward VI foundation, was only ten miles from Wolverhampton, and the two schools were on each other's fixture lists. Perhaps this helped to make for an easy relationship, to which could be added a common birthday (though he was some years ahead of me), jointly celebrated in 1962 at Rideau Hall, the Governor-General's house in Ottawa, during one of the Prime Minister's flying visits. Brook went on many of the Macmillan trips overseas, and on another transatlantic occasion we also had in the aircraft Sir Richard Powell, Permanent Secretary of the Ministry of Defence: he, I discovered, was an old boy of Queen Mary's Grammar School, Walsall, so that within that small Prime Ministerial entourage were represented three grammar schools located within a ten-mile triangle of the West Midlands.

I can't think that this proves anything, except possibly that the Whitehall Establishment was less exclusively public school than commonly believed, though still an Oxbridge near-monopoly. Being neither public school nor Oxbridge I was always a joker in the pack, but this is inevitably the role of the Whitehall spokesman. He is within the Establishment but not of it. His position is exceptional in that normally he has direct access to Ministers, sees the whole panorama of the department's affairs, and is caught up in the handling of major issues. Sometimes it works comfortably enough, sometimes not, depending on the interplay of personalities at the top, and particularly the personality and attitudes of the Permanent Secretary. It is in the nature of administrative civil servants to believe that publicity, especially premature publicity generated in the Press and Parliament, is detrimental to the efficient conduct of official business, and to regard official spokesmen as, at best, an inescapable evil.

The spokesman can therefore have a very poor time of it. Whatever support he gets from Ministers (in itself variable), Ministers are birds of passage and top civil servants permanent, and it is the top civil servants who dictate his career prospects.

At No. 10 I was to find the position different only in degree. If the Prime Minister of the day attaches importance to the activities of his spokesman, he will ensure that adequate support is given by the administrative staff. Also No. 10 is so small and compact that close proximity alone means that all the staff must function as a team to be efficient. Furthermore, the Private Office is customarily staffed by three or four administrative civil servants of middle rank, identified as potential flyers for whom a stint at No. 10 will provide a rewarding experience. Being both young and agile-minded, they are apt to have greater awareness of the role of the spokesman and the nature of his problems, and to be prepared to co-operate with him without coercion. It remains a fact, however, that if the spokesman is an established civil servant his career after leaving No. 10 will be determined by mandarin judgment, and his performance at No. 10, however much it may have pleased the Prime Minister, will not necessarily be to his advantage.

In my own instance, I was fortunate in my colleagues in the Private Office, but at the end of the day, meaning seven years later, when the mandarin judgment came to be rendered, it was another matter. The attitude was bleak, and I had no difficulty in deciding that it would be better to take advantage of early retirement terms and pursue my career elsewhere. Two of the long-serving private secretaries did the same. The trouble was that we had been too long at No. 10 and become too much identified as Macmillan men.

Back in 1957, however, it had seemed that the life of the Macmillan administration was likely to be measured in months rather than years. In his memoirs Harold Macmillan wrote, 'I had only promised the Queen six weeks' (of which, with a twinkle, she was to remind him six years later). This possibility of a short-lived tenure he mentioned at my first meeting with him at No. 10. Oddly, I remember very little of what was said except that he warned me, rather gloomily, that he was too old to learn new publicity tricks and would do nothing out of character. Goodness knows what kind of spokesman he thought he had been given, and possibly he did not think it mattered very much given the prospect of a brief adminis-tration. Yet in a way it was flattering to be seen as a thrusting P.R. man, bristling with tricks of the trade, instead of the dull dog I really was.

Though he did not remember it, or at any rate did not mention it, we had met once before, during the war when for a time he was Under-Secretary of State for the Colonies. At that time I was on the staff of Lord Swinton, recently appointed as Resident Minister in West Africa, and the R.A.F. had flown me home on a quick visit, hopefully to set in train various desirable courses of action. Among other things I had been instructed to call on Harold Macmillan to see if he could coax one of the Press lords to take an interest in West African newspapers, then much in need of aid – financial, technical and journalistic training. Nothing positive resulted at the time, but later the *Mirror* group were to play a powerful part in developing newspapers in West Africa.

Though that was my first Macmillan meeting I had seen him at close quarters once before. Early in 1940 I had volunteered with a few score other would-be heroes to serve with the Finnish Army, then fighting so desperately to stem the Russian invasion which followed the Soviet-Nazi pact. The volunteers were recruited by the

Finnish Aid Bureau in London, and while waiting to depart we were given a number of pep talks by those thought capable of informing and inspiring us. Among them was Harold Macmillan, a member of the aid committee, who had returned from Finland a few days earlier. He spoke with emotion, telling graphic stories of Finnish endurance and heroism, and I for one was duly inspired.

What he did not tell us, and in the circumstances could not tell us, was that the cause was already lost and that recruiting and sending volunteers was no more than a gesture for public opinion. A bit hard on the starry-eyed as they set off by boat and train to cross Norway and Sweden, 'disguised' as tourists by virtue of wearing fur-collared coats and carrying skis.

Well, none of them died on a Finnish battlefield, but most had a rough time after they became stranded in Finland by the German invasion of Norway in March 1940. For my part I was one of a small group which made a dash by rail for northern Norway, travelling in closed wagons heated by charcoal stoves, in the hope of getting away by sea before the German grip closed. It was too late, however, and we were turned back at Rovaniemi on the Arctic Circle.

Then, for me, came one of those unpredictable twists of fortune which transform a situation overnight. The Legation in Helsinki felt it should try to hold the propaganda front by publishing a daily news sheet in English, Finnish and Swedish. But who could compile and edit it? Well, why not this fellow Evans in the volunteers, allegedly a journalist? So Evans it was, and almost overnight I found myself whisked from barrack life amid the lakes and forests of central Finland to a flat in Helsinki, with a congenial job, a modest salary (better, at any rate, than two shillings a day with the volunteers), and rations supplemented by diplomatic concessions.

On the long summer evenings I could drink ersatz coffee under the trees in the Esplanade while the band played excerpts from *Cavaliera Rusticana*, or, if I felt in need of sterner stuff, listen to *Finlandia* at the Conservatoire. In the spring Finnish friends took me mushrooming in the forests, and in the winter on Sunday skiing expeditions – and all this while in the west the war ceased to be phoney, Dunkirk unfolded and Britain began the struggle for survival against the bombs and the U-boats. So much for the too eager. I had left a phoney war to seek a battlefield; instead I was now a civilian in one of the few European countries at peace, however transitory.

This strange interlude was to last a year until July 1941. Then, with the western allies held in baulk, the Germans invaded Russia.

Seeing an opportunity to win back Karelia the Finns joined in. So once more Russian bombs fell on Helsinki, though in no great profusion. From one of them I had my narrowest escape of the war. It fell in the early hours of the morning, slicing apart the block of flats next door. Without benefit of sirens I wakened violently into an inferno of noise, vibration, smoke, dust and the stink of cordite – in a blue funk but unscathed. At least I had a bomb story to ease feelings of guilt about remoteness from the London blitz.

The political situation had now been turned upside down. In British eyes the roles of Finland and Russia had been reversed. No longer was it a matter of sending help to gallant little Finland, but of severing diplomatic relations with a Nazi ally.

To implement the severance was more difficult than to announce it. A venue had to be found for the exchange of diplomatic staffs – the Finns from London and the British from Helsinki. With Germany astride all the lines of communication – the whole of western Europe occupied except Spain and Portugal – it could be achieved only with a German safe conduct. The possibilities were limited. Even so Lisbon seemed an improbable choice, involving as it did a long rail journey across enemy Germany and occupied France. But Lisbon it was, and so on a day in September the Legation staff (plus a number of British subjects on an approved list) found itself crossing the Baltic on a Finnish steamer under German naval 'protection'. From Hamburg we went southwards by train through countryside looking alarmingly normal, given reports of intensive British bombing. Then into occupied France and so, via Paris and Bordeaux, to Irun on the Spanish frontier.

After eighteen grim months inside Fortress Europe we rumbled across the bridge at Irun into a bewildering world of colour, bright lights, hot sunshine, oranges, bananas and relative plenty.

As a souvenir of that improbable journey I still have a passport stamped at Saarbrücken on September 8th, 1941 with a Nazi swastika.

Harold Macmillan also had a souvenir of his Finnish connection – the white fur hat he later wore, to the joy of photographers and cartoonists, during his visit to the Soviet Union in 1959 as Prime Minister.

2 Scenario and Players

My stint at No. 10 began on February 7th, 1957, just a week after returning from New York. Since the job was virtually round-the-clock I could no longer commute from my home on the Sussex coast, and a *pied-à-terre* had to be found within walking distance of Downing Street. To this end I was given a special allowance of £250 per annum, which was adequate at the time. I started in a small flat in Horseferry Road, moved to Artillery Mansions in Victoria Street, and wound up with a modest apartment in a small house in Petty France (since demolished). It was efficiently run by a pleasant Scottish lady, whose other tenants included Ted Heath, then Chief Whip, with an office at 12 Downing Street. As one of the Prime Minister's principal advisers and confidantes he was constantly in and out of No. 10 via the connecting halls of Nos. 10, 11 and 12.

All these *pied-à-terre* addresses meant an agreeable walk through St. James's Park, that lovely breathing space in the heart of Westminster, with its enticement to dally and watch the waterfowl on the lake, especially those solemn comedians, the pelicans.

At least I was now freed from the daily journey to and from Brighton – on a rough calculation a year's commuting equalled once round the world – but, of course, our home life was destroyed. I could not even count on weekends. Fortunately my wife had a major preoccupation of her own in our ten-months-old daughter, Annabel. As time went on there was also the compensation of taking part in some of the social life built round No. 10, not least Lady Dorothy's parties for her grandchildren and other No. 10 offspring at Christmas and for the Trooping.

This mixture of office and family life was to prove an agreeable feature of Macmillan's No. 10. A Prime Minister need not 'live over the shop' (if, for example, he has his own house in London and prefers to live there), but if he opts for No. 10 then its way of life will be largely determined, not only by his own temperament and working habits, but also by the personality of his wife and the extent to which a family exists and is on the scene. If family and staff live

21

cheek by jowl the ambience is likely to be either cheerful or abrasive. The Macmillans made sure it was cheerful. It could hardly have been otherwise with Lady Dorothy's bustling presence, her robust and down-to-earth comments on the passing scene, and above all, her deep interest in people in whatever role she encountered them.

The Macmillans' own home was in the countryside of East Sussex, not far from East Grinstead. To an extent life there also became caught up in official affairs, notably when President Kennedy and General de Gaulle came to Birch Grove as house guests. In addition, Chequers was available. Mainly it was used for weekend meetings of Ministers, when sessions of informal talks could be leavened with croquet, walking and attendance at Sunday morning divine service with the Prime Minister.

The working style of Macmillan's No. 10 was quickly established when he pinned up on the green baize door between the Cabinet room and the Private Office a quotation from *The Gondoliers* copied in his own handwriting. It said, 'Quiet, calm deliberation disentangles every knot.'

Since every political crisis, national and international, and every major political issue, comes into No. 10, it is all too easy in the rush of demands and events to get caught up in a frenzy of activity without making time for 'quiet, calm deliberation'. It was thus a salutary reminder.

From my point of view it was a welcome indication of attitude, especially since it reinforced the lesson I had learnt painfully over the years – that excitability gets you nowhere. An outwardly relaxed and unhurried manner is a necessary part of the equipment of a spokesman, whose demeanour, no less than his words (sometimes more than his words) comes under close scrutiny by professional observers. A poker face is part of the business – or what Harold Macmillan dubbed my 'Lobby face'. In the Press Office, too, I tried to induce calm, however fast we might be working, and customarily had my feet on the desk (a particularly good posture if you have to spend a lot of time on the phone). Later, when Pierre Salinger appeared on the scene as President Kennedy's Press Secretary I was gratified to find that he, too, was a feet-on-the-desk man, though I could not boast the big cigars and very hairy legs which, reported *The Observer*, were other Salinger hallmarks.

The world thinks of No. 10 as the small terraced house in Downing Street, with its famous front door, but behind the terraced house is a mansion with a garden. Both house and mansion were built in the late seventeenth century on Crown land, at one time the site of a Tudor brewhouse and inn, and still earlier of a great Saxon hall. By royal dispensation the mansion was occupied for some time by the Lichfield family. In the 1730s, however, George II gave them both to Robert Walpole for his own use and that of succeeding chief ministers, and the two were joined together by the simple expedient of a connecting corridor.

The terraced house at that time formed part of a small square built as a speculative venture some forty or fifty years earlier by George Downing. Because Downing oscillated in his loyalties between Cromwell and the Crown, Pepys dismissed him as 'a perfidious rogue' and 'a most ungrateful villain'. Downing was also castigated nearly 300 years later by Winston Churchill. No. 10 he described as 'shaky and lightly built', which might seem a harsh judgment on a house which had stood so long (and survived a near-miss in the blitz).

In fact, it was built on marshy ground which covered much of the early Westminster, and bundles of rushes and timber baulks formed part of the foundations. During the Macmillan administration it was found that the foundations had almost disintegrated so that, to exaggerate a little, the house remained standing only by virtue of the walls leaning against each other. A major reconstruction was therefore necessary, and the Prime Minister's office had to remove itself to Admiralty House in the opposite corner of Horse Guards – a hardly less desirable residence, though possessing only a tiny garden. Here it remained for three years, returning in 1963 to a rejuvenated No. 10 – looking much the same, but safer, brighter and a little more spacious.

As not least of the improvements, the Press Secretary's room at the corner with Treasury Passage had been fitted with a handsome bow window. Sitting with my back to it, I felt rather more vulnerable than before to the odd half-brick from aggrieved citizens on the Downing Street pavement. In fact, in my day, no missiles ever came through the windows, the preferred target being the front door and the preferred weapon a milk bottle.

For the Press Secretary to have his quarters near the front door made sense, given the frequency with which he had to receive visitors, including a daily call by the Lobby correspondents group. Nor did it divorce him from the rest of the office – a few seconds' walk along the crimson-carpeted corridor into the Lichfield mansion. The corridor leads to the Cabinet room and to the two adjoining rooms, occupied by the private secretaries. All three rooms have windows overlooking the garden, Horse Guards and St. James's Park.

At No. 10, as in love, proximity is everything – that and the instinct that takes you to the right place at the right time.

What is perhaps not generally realised is that the garden stands at a lower level than Downing Street itself. This means that below the Cabinet room and the Private Office is a suite of rooms at garden level. Here the filing and shorthand typing staff have their home, a location which has given them the collective title of the Garden Room girls. A Garden Room girl is a very special person. Not only does she have to be totally competent at her job, but also the possessor of poise and personality. Moreover, it always seems to happen that she is delightful to the eye. Collectively and individually they adorn the No. 10 scene. So, too, when the Prime Minister travelled overseas two or three of the young ladies would be in the party, working very long hours in conditions which were often makeshift and onerous, but never losing their poise. In whatever part of the world they appeared they could be guaranteed to attract admiring attention as they emerged from the aircraft – with no harm at all done to the British image.

As permanent staff, the Garden Room girls may well overlap administrations and are then in a position to make comparisons. The Macmillan administration rated highly with them for its relaxed friendliness and civilised procedures – though civilised procedures had to encompass dictation from the Prime Minister at unusual hours.

At least with Harold Macmillan they did not have to cope with eccentricities as great as those of Winston Churchill, particularly at the time when Toby the budgerigar was frequently his companion.

One girl tells graphically of being summoned to the great man's presence when he was hunched up in bed, surrounded by dispatch boxes, puffing at the inevitable cigar and sipping the inevitable whisky. To these disconcerting dimensions Toby had to be added. He enjoyed perching on the Prime Minister's bald head, which was harmless enough until he found it necessary to perform acts of nature. For protection the Prime Minister favoured a large, square sponge which he placed on top of his bald patch. So the young lady had somehow to retain her composure while taking dictation on matters of state from the Prime Minister of the United Kingdom in bed with a sponge balanced on the top of his head and a budgerigar balanced on the sponge.

Another of No. 10's young ladies, similarly confronted, found herself in even worse case. Toby's attention was drawn by the gleam of her hair pins and he abandoned the Prime Minister's head for her's in order to pick them out. As her hair slowly cascaded over her face and neck, the Prime Minister continued to dictate, pretending not to notice but inwardly delighting in her brave fight against the odds.

But most alarming of all, perhaps, was travelling with the Prime Minister in the back of his car in order to take dictation. Then, in this very confined space, the selected young lady had to cope, not only with Toby, but also with Rufus the poodle. With Rufus on her lap and Toby on her hat life became very fraught. At least she would be wearing a hat because Winston insisted that the young ladies should be 'properly' dressed, by which he meant shoes, not boots, and a hat. Since most of them did not normally wear a hat, the equipment of the Garden Rooms had to include, within instant reach, a 'summer hat' and a 'winter hat'.

In charge of the services represented by the Garden Room girls and the clerical staff is customarily one of their number who has elected to remain at No. 10 as a career civil servant. These leading ladies have a crucial presence in the hierarchy of No. 10 – especially because of the continuity they provide from one administration to the next – and the smooth running of the machine depends a good deal upon them. When I arrived at Downing Street the role was being filled with an impressive combination of elegance, charm and firmness by 'Mags' Stenhouse, whose 'first' Prime Minister was Lloyd George. She was succeeded by Sheila Minto, who had come to No. 10 in Stanley Baldwin's day and ruled with equal firmness without diminishing by one whit the affection inspired by her splendidly extrovert and friendly personality. She did, however, cause No. 10 one period of strain and tension. This was when she was preparing for her driving test. It had us all on tenterhooks, and a collective sigh of relief could be heard echoing along Downing Street when she returned in triumph.

The spokesman's office is largely self-contained. In my day it comprised a deputy and three young ladies who between them looked after the filing, dictation, typing, and phone, while also helping generally as ears and eyes for the Press Office. Since then, I am told, the numbers have doubled, but I like to think that, small as we were (and possibly because we *were* so compact), we operated with speed and efficiency in all essentials. Let the names of Doris Knight, Esme James and May Whittam be duly inscribed on the battle honours.

In seven years I had four deputies. When I arrived Alfred Richardson was holding the fort. He had been William Clark's deputy and, for my money, could have succeeded him perfectly well. He and I knew each other well for he had worked with me at the Colonial Office as Chief Press Officer, and I admired his quick intelligence, his astuteness and his tireless energy. These qualities carried with them some intolerance when confronted with lack of them in others. It was a stock joke at No. 10 that the telephone engineers had to be called in once a week to repair the springs of his telephone, put into disarray by the frequency and force with which he slammed down the receiver in exasperation. This canard he enjoyed as much as anyone else. Having decided that he would not be asked to succeed William Clark he bent his energies to lobbying on my behalf, chiefly by saying frequently to the hierarchy in No. 10 that the chap they ought to get was Evans – 'but, of course, he won't come'. Nothing was more likely to spur them to action, he believed, than to suggest that they might be rebuffed. During my first six months at No. 10, when I was feeling almost despairingly out of my depth, it was he who kept me afloat and I owe much to his impatient patience.

Following Alfred Richardson came Charles Birdsall, Jimmy Miller and John Groves, diverse in character and experience but with the same total dedication to No. 10's demands. All three were drawn from the official information services, though John Groves had been recruited from *The Times*, where he had operated on the other side of the fence as a Lobby man.

To work with Charles Birdsall could be exhausting for he was a pocket dynamo of a man, restlessly and unremittingly energetic. Never did a promise to ring back a journalist remain unfulfilled, even when remorseless ferreting had failed to produce the required rabbit. His particular patch of Whitehall had been the Ministry of Labour so that he knew the industrial correspondents no less well than he did the Lobby men, a significant bonus.

Jimmy Miller's style was totally different – deliberate and un-flurried, though this external calm and good humour often hid internal stress for he was conscientious in the extreme and could not readily shrug off the anxieties inevitably part of the spokesman's lot. He had worked with me at the Colonial Office and I admired his loyalty and sturdy common sense.

John Groves carried the aura of a *Times* man augmented by Treasury experience – thoughtful, authoritative and slightly aloof – and his first-hand knowledge of how the Lobby worked and thought, individually and collectively, was invaluable. He was still at No. 10 when I left, staying there until the end of the Douglas-Home regime, and in subsequent years heading public relations at the Ministry of Defence before becoming Director-General of the Central Office of Information.

For a spokesman at No. 10 to flourish, his knowledge of events happening and impending must be complete. Almost without thinking he must be able to relate events to the background of pressures and personalities that produces them. Rarely is it a matter of providing a previously agreed and authorised form of words, but more the need to respond instantly and sensibly to skilled questioning. Obviously an understanding as complete as this can be acquired only in time. Obviously, too, the spokesman must have constant and immediate access to prime sources.

At No. 10 this begins with knowing the mind of the Prime Minister. Again the process requires time – time and the spokesman's ability to win the trust of the Prime Minister. This trust is vital. For the Prime Minister the way his policies and thinking are presented must be of first importance. He must do most of it himself – in the House, in public appearances and speeches, and on television. Yet he cannot do it all. His time is heavily mortgaged. There is hour by hour pressure on No. 10 for information, guidance and elucidation. How the spokesman responds to this pressure is therefore significant. He must have the confidence of the Prime Minister and must know his mind.

This I realised was my first task and I expected it to be difficult. Without ever being less than courteous and amiable Harold Macmillan held people at arm's length until they had proved themselves. Nor did he hide a scepticism about the value of official public relations activity. Charles Hill recalls in his autobiography that, on joining the Macmillan Cabinet, 'I gathered that he was not enamoured of the techniques of public relations – he made it pretty plain that he had never used them himself and, despite that, he had become Prime Minister.' He had said much the same to me, 'I didn't seek the job yet here I am.'

This was possibly a little disingenuous given that in all his post-war ministerial appointments – Housing, Defence, Foreign Office, Treasury – he had been backed by large departmental information services. Nor could it really be said that he did not understand and use 'techniques of public relations'. In my experience he was always completely alert to the niceties of presentation, whether in content, style or timing. He thought about them deeply and was usually a jump ahead of the rest of us. Perhaps it was precisely because of this instinctive feel for public relations that he had misgivings about vicarious presentation.

Whatever his scepticism, however, he was prepared to give me a run for my money. From the start he was approachable. It was rarely a matter of formal briefing but simply an understanding that if I wanted a 'gossip' I should seek to insert myself into his presence – not always easy given the state of his diary. One stratagem was to arrive earlier at No. 10 than anyone else and ring him to seek a bedside audience. At nine he would probably still be in bed, wearing a brown cardigan over his pyjamas and surrounded by dispatch boxes, having begun work on official papers several hours earlier.

So one sat at his bedside and trailed any problems that were currently worrying. I say trailed because these were always 'gossips', ranging widely. Nothing so crude as explicit questions and answers would be expected. Their purpose would be to ensure that I knew how he was thinking, having already acquired a knowledge of the underlying facts. This factual information I obtained from access to papers, going through the common 'dip' in the Private Office, plus access to the private secretaries under a general mandate to 'let Evans know'.

I recollect only one occasion – early on – when we specifically discussed the Macmillan 'image'. Under pressure, he then said that the difficulty lay in the fact that he lacked a flamboyant personality. The Macmillans were not 'smart'. They were hard-working, home-loving people with a strong family sense. They had been brought up to work hard, and to respect truth, honour and other old-fashioned virtues. To illustrate this he quoted a letter from the Macmillan firm to a young Scot who sought employment with them in September 1849. It said, 'We shall expect you always to do the day's work in a day.'[1] As to the Cavendishes, it was true that they brought an entirely different strain into the family, but even so the Cavendishes were better known as quiet, hard-working people than as 'smart' people. Also as one got older, one's interests became more and more focused on home and books and grandchildren. He used to be a rebel, and to some extent still was, but essentially these were now his interests.

Much in No. 10 depended on the attitude of the Principal Private Secretary. Customarily he is in very close relationship to the Prime Minister. 'Except in the marital state,' wrote Disraeli, 'there is none in which so great a confidence is involved, in which more fore-

[1] Thomas Hughes Q.C. (author of *Tom Brown's Schooldays*), *Memoir of Daniel Macmillan* (London, 1882).

bearance ought to be exercised, or more sympathy ought to exist.' Certainly the two who held this appointment during the six and a half years of the Macmillan premiership – Freddie Bishop and Tim Bligh – enjoyed this relationship with him. And I was fortunate to enjoy a good relationship with them.

Temperamentally they stood far apart. Freddie Bishop, slim and remarkably boyish in appearance, tended to be dry and precise on duty, though off duty ready to slip into lightheartedness. Tim Bligh buccaneered. It needed little imagination to visualise him captaining small boats on cut and thrust raids in the Mediterranean – exploits which had brought him a succession of gallantry awards.

Freddie Bishop went to No. 10 in 1955 during the Eden premiership and was 'inherited' by Harold Macmillan. By 1959 the mandarins felt that his career prospects called for a move upwards. 'Buggins's turn' was never a motive to recommend itself to the Prime Minister and he resented the loss of a man who, in his own words, had been 'a tower of strength' in the early, difficult days of his administration. As a result Tim Bligh at first found the succession hard going. In time, however, he played himself in, and became no less close to the Prime Minister – too close, it may have been felt by the mandarins, and his knighthood in the 1963 Dissolution Honours upset those engaged in the measured processes by which civil servants receive awards. He left the Civil Service shortly afterwards to join the Thomson Organisation, but died tragically from cancer in 1969 when he was still only fifty-one.

Though Freddie Bishop held senior appointments in Whitehall after leaving No. 10 he, too, took advantage of early retirement terms and joined Lord Cowdray's industrial empire. Later he became Director-General of the National Trust and was knighted in 1975.

The Principal Private Secretary at No. 10 is customarily supported by two or three private secretaries drawn from the Whitehall departments. They include one from the Foreign Office who is given particular responsibility for assisting the Prime Minister in his foreign affairs activities. The extent of these activities will vary from Prime Minister to Prime Minister, but some involvement is inescapable.

'Each Prime Minister,' it has been said, 'thinks that he alone is capable of representing his country's policy. Each Foreign Secretary thinks that the Prime Minister knows nothing of diplomacy. Each Ambassador thinks the same about the Foreign Secretary.'

For Harold Macmillan foreign affairs were a central preoccupation – inevitably so given his experience in North Africa, Italy and Greece during the war, his friendships with Eisenhower and de Gaulle, his own tenure of office as Foreign Secretary, the critical balance between East and West, the Soviet threats on Berlin, and the urgent need for Britain to find a new place and role in the pattern of world affairs. Possibly, the fact that he had an American mother also had something to do with it.

In these circumstances the Prime Minister's relationship with the Foreign Secretary could have been abrasive, but with first Selwyn Lloyd and then Alec Douglas-Home as Foreign Secretary the relationship was essentially harmonious. This in turn minimised the traditional friction between No. 10 and the Foreign Office at the official level.

The foreign affairs private secretary at No. 10 was Philip de Zulueta, still in his early thirties and relatively junior in the foreign service. Young and junior, perhaps, but possessing a formidable array of gifts and talents – intellectual agility, charm, self-confidence to the point of arrogance and a readiness to be ruthless. Even the Prime Minister could be heard speaking jokingly of 'that bully Philip'. His influence was further enhanced by exceptionally long service at No. 10. He joined the staff in 1955 to serve with Anthony Eden, stayed throughout the Macmillan era and was with Sir Alec Douglas-Home until the general election of 1964. Whether the Foreign Office would then have welcomed him back with open arms was perhaps open to doubt, but he spared them any agonising by opting for a career in the City. From my point of view he was never anything but helpful and considerate.

One private secretary normally took responsibility for marshalling answers to parliamentary questions to the Prime Minister – a twice-weekly exercise, on Tuesdays and Thursdays. This was a chore calling for wit and a lively mind, as well as political *nous* and an understanding of the ways of the House. Neil Cairncross, Tony Phelps and Philip Woodfield successively undertook the task during my day, performing it with notable skill. Cairncross and Woodfield were Home Office men and Phelps came from the Treasury. All three returned to departments in the fullness of time, and progressed into the Civil Service stratosphere.

Again I could count on their ready co-operation. Neil Cairncross, small in stature and deliberate in speech, allied a brooding sense of humour with a nice sense of words.

Then there was John Wyndham, later Lord Egremont, born of a long line of eccentric English aristocrats, and himself an eccentric of no mean stature. Reputedly immensely rich (though with the family fortune heavily depleted by death duties), he lived at Petworth and owned large slices of Sussex and Cumberland. Physically he might have been invented by P. G. Wodehouse – tall, willowy, stooping, and peering through spectacles with exceptionally thick lenses.

In 1899, in a book of *Collections and Recollections*, an anonymous author wrote, 'Much of a Minister's comfort and success depends upon the Private Secretary. Some Ministers import for this function a young gentleman of fashion whom they know at home – a picturesque butterfly who flits gaily through the dusty air of the office, making, by the splendour of his minuet, sunshine in its shady places, and daintily passing on the work to unrecognised and unrewarded clerks.'

To an extent this was John Wyndham, though there was never any question of passing on the work. He more than pulled his weight in a role difficult to define – a combination of A.D.C., observer and commentator, contact man, cheerful but determined 'fixer', good companion and court jester.

Prime Ministers are condemned to the loneliness of the summit, and many have had near to them as confidantes able men without political ambition. They have been described by Sir Charles Petrie in *The Powers Behind the Prime Ministers*. The pairings he lists include Disraeli and Monty Corry, Gladstone and Sir Algernon West, Lloyd George and Tom Jones, Macdonald and Rose Rosenburg and Baldwin and J. C. C. Davidson. In most instances 'powers' perhaps overstates their influence on the conduct of affairs, and John Wyndham strenuously rebutted any suggestion that he exerted any significant influence.

There can be no doubt, however, that he enlivened life at No. 10, with 'japes' and a flow of anecdotes and salty comment. When he joined the No. 10 staff as an unpaid temporary civil servant he was duly subjected to positive vetting, a process beginning with completion of a form asking direct personal questions. One, he recalled, asked 'Are you in debt?' with a supplementary 'If so, how much?' To the first he replied 'Yes' and to the supplementary 'About £1 million'. A few days later a pained official arrived in his room, waving the form, and expostulating, 'Now look, old man, there's no need to take it like this. They're questions we all have to answer.' In fact, the answers were precise – at that moment John Wyndham was negotiating about death duty claims on his uncle's estate.

In his autobiography *Wyndham and Children First* he gives a racy account of life with Macmillan, beginning in the Ministry of Supply during the war. The book ends with a brief chapter on 'The Luck of the Wyndhams' in which he describes how he first went salmon fishing – reluctantly – and caught a sixteen-pound fish with his first cast. 'Such luck,' he writes, 'makes one almost afraid.' This was surely prophetic for three years later, at the age of fifty-two, he died of cancer, as Tim Bligh had done.

Also within the No. 10 organisation was the Secretary for Appointments, a post rendered necessary by the many appointments that lay within the gift of the Prime Minister as a legacy from the past. They included at that time the selection of bishops and deans, and this involved much delicate consultation and sounding of opinion. Asquith wrote of a Prime Minister's ecclesiastical patronage, 'This has always been an anxious and sometimes a troublesome function.' During the Macmillan administration ecclesiastical appointments included recommendations to the Queen in respect of both the Archbishop of Canterbury and the Archbishop of York.

The job of Secretary for Appointments thus called for exceptional tact, discernment and administrative thoroughness, and during my years at No. 10 these qualities were displayed by first David Stephens and then John Hewitt. After his stint at No. 10 David Stephens was to become Clerk to the House of Lords. From their particular stance they must have felt a certain reticence about doing business with anyone so crude as an official spokesman, but they both showed me unfailing courtesy. Their chores extended to some responsibilities for the management of No. 10 as a building, and I had to work hard on David Stephens, without much success, when it came to the allocation of accommodation for the Press Office in Admiralty House during the reconstruction of No. 10. When the reconstruction was completed I thought that it would make sense to provide a facility for the Press to see what had been achieved. Neither John Hewitt nor the Ministry of Works had any enthusiasm for this proposal, but they conceded with good grace and the facility worked well.

The Prime Minister's Parliamentary Private Secretary also figured on the No. 10 scene, though more of his time was spent in the House. Robert Allan, a former naval commander and later a pillar of the City, was first in a sequence of three, being succeeded in turn by Anthony Barber and Samuel Knox Cunningham. Each was ready with friendly co-operation. Knox Cunningham, an amiable mountain of a man, was an Ulster M.P. and in earlier days an amateur boxer of some note. I had rather more contact with Tony Barber than the others, partly because he came on the Prime Minister's visit to the Soviet Union, and also because his later ministerial appointments included a hand in information co-ordination (in the Heath administration he was to become Chancellor of the Exchequer). He had a notable ability to remain relaxed in the most difficult of situations, an art developed no doubt when he was a prisoner of war in Germany and, after escaping in Poland, a prisoner of the Russians.

If the Private Office was the fountainhead of information in No. 10, I had access also to other sources. If need arose I could consult the Chief Whip – first Ted Heath and then Martin Redmayne – a process facilitated by their proximity in No. 12. But first and foremost I had the great advantage of being adviser, not only to the Prime Minister, but also to Charles Hill who, as Chancellor of the Duchy of Lancaster, had co-ordination of the official information services as his main duty. As a member of the Cabinet he had his finger on the collective ministerial pulse, and knew a good deal also about thinking on the back benches. He also presided over a weekly meeting of Whitehall's chief information officers when forthcoming events and publications would be tabled and discussed.

Working with Charles Hill carried the bonus of laughter. The pugnacious good humour, the witticisms delivered in that deep, fruity voice, the splendid common sense – all were endearing characteristics, and I counted it a privilege to become his friend as well as his official adviser.

Being the Radio Doctor had first established him as a public figure – that and the 'Chuck it, Priestley' broadcast – but his remarkable career had many facets: ship's doctor, medical officer of health, secretary of the B.M.A. during the years when the National Health Service was being set up, Fleet Street columnist, a National Liberal Member of Parliament, junior Minister at Food, Post-Master General, and now a Cabinet Minister – and all this from modest Islington origins. He further demonstrated his versatility after leaving politics in 1964 by becoming successively Chairman of the Independent Television Authority, Chairman of the B.B.C. (and how that upset the applecart in Broadcasting House), chairman of an industrial company and chairman of a building society. Moreover, with a seat in Lords, he maintained his links with Parliament and politics.

He and I were able to cement our friendship through the tours he took overseas to see if improvements could be made in the work of projecting the British image. This was the task, not only of the official information services, but also the British Council and the B.B.C. Overseas Services since both were financed by government grants though operating with a large degree of autonomy. It was a field of activity in which I had been closely involved for many years, both in London and overseas, so that I could contribute usefully, or thought I could, to his reports and recommendations.

Fitting these tours into No. 10 requirements (including the Prime Minister's own extensive overseas travels) was not always easy, but usually we arranged them during parliamentary recesses, and anyhow it was good experience for my deputies to hold the Downing Street fort.

We made four tours – in 1958 to the Horn of Africa, Aden, India and Pakistan; in 1959 eastwards round the world, taking in Ceylon, Singapore (for a conference of British ambassadors, high commissioners and colonial governors), Hong Kong, Tokyo, Honolulu, the United States and Canada; in 1960 to nine South American countries; and in 1961 through middle Europe (including Warsaw and Berlin).

Some of these calling points I had known from my Colonial Office days. Not least, in the late 1940s, I had looked at everything from fishing co-operatives in Hong Kong to asylums in North Borneo in preparing a Blue Book on post-war developments in the British territories in the Far East.[2] Nevertheless, the tours with Charles Hill provided many fascinating new experiences as well as opportunities for then-and-now comparisons.

In Addis Ababa we were received in audience by the Emperor Haile Selassie, regally attired in full military uniform, and then entertained to afternoon tea in a salon reminiscent of Versailles. We had gold teaspoons and cake forks, and footmen in knee breeches served wafer-thin sandwiches and cream cakes. Since it was a formal occasion he spoke through an interpreter, recalling his years of exile in England. At one time, he said, the snow had been so heavy that it 'broke down the branches of the trees in my compound at Bath'. Withdrawing backwards from the presence, as one had to do, bowing three times on the way, required a steady nerve, for lurking unseen in one's path were fixed obstacles like footstools and mobile obstacles in the form of the Emperor's pugs. However, we managed without mishap, and so escaped being thrown to the young lion patrolling the steps of the palace.

Not many travelling bureaucrats, it was my boast, had in attendance their own medical adviser. In fact, I had to call on the Radio Doctor for diagnosis and treatment only once. It happened in Santiago. Diagnosis was not difficult since I had an attack of acute food poisoning. We were staying with the ambassador and, on a tight schedule, were due to catch an aircraft to Bogota at 1100

[2] Cmd. 7709, *British Dependencies in the Far East 1945–49* (H.M.S.O.)

hours. He arrived in my bedroom at 0900 hours to find me prostrate and groaning, capable only of gasping, 'You must go on alone. I'll catch up somehow.' 'Let me see your tongue,' he said solicitously. Dutifully I opened wide. The next moment two stubby fingers, reeking of Gallaher's Rich Dark Honeydew, were thrust down my throat. Never was a human being more comprehensively sick. Two hours later we were on the aircraft to Bogota.

Another Minister I saw with some regularity was Rab Butler. In his capacity for a time as Leader of the House (he was then also Home Secretary) he saw the Lobby correspondents each Thursday afternoon after announcing in the House the following week's parliamentary business.

The Lobby relished these encounters with Rab, for he was ready to range over almost any political topic and to do so with insight, wit and measured indiscretion. His verbal felicities, delivered with a chuckle, they enjoyed no less. Asked about the progress in Lords of a Bill on gambling, he replied, 'Oh, I think we shall get it quite quickly. After rabbits there is nothing their Lordships enjoy more than betting shops.' Of Question Time in the House he said, 'It's like the jungle. If they see you limping they are after you.' One government statement he described as so eloquent that 'it had tears streaming down the cheeks of even the most thin-lipped civil servants at the Home Office.' Asked to comment on a policy pronouncement by the Conservative Bow Group he replied affably, 'They have not yet contributed to the great corpus of Conservative opinion. When they do I will send you a postcard. I am all in favour of groups being busy.'

Before the Lobby meetings I would give him a written brief, telling him what was currently engaging the Lobby's interest, the kind of questions he might expect, the existing state of knowledge on these topics in the Lobby, the information and guidance they had so far been given, possible impending developments, and the kind of answers he might like to give. On many issues, of course, he needed no briefing at all, but on others it was important that he should know how things stood, and in particular, where the pitfalls lay.

This weekly exercise paved the way for occasional telephone calls, usually late in the evening, sometimes to check on a specific point, sometimes to put a toe in the No. 10 water, and sometimes – so far as I could see – out of sheer amiability. Once when I was crossing Palace Yard a shout echoed round the venerable precincts – 'Evans! Evans!' Its source, look as I might, I could not find, but again it came. This time, looking upwards, I spied Rab leaning out

35

of one of the innumerable mullioned windows and waving with both arms. He had no message for me. He wanted nothing from me. He had simply been looking out of the window of his room, spotted me, and decided it would be nice to open the window, lean out and wave a greeting.

In a man capable of warm gestures it was odd to find also a capacity for upsetting colleagues with public and semi-public asides which were often all the more wounding for being so precisely aimed. Probably they came to his tongue spontaneously and irresistibly rather than from malice, but always, of course, they were repeated back to the victim and stored in the memory. One I remember arose when a Lobby man complained that a certain White Paper was so turgid as to be almost unreadable. 'Yes,' agreed Rab sympathetically, 'it might have been written by Lord Mills, don't you think?' Since everyone liked Percy Mills it probably didn't matter, but inevitably it went the rounds. Of course, the one that really hit the headlines was the reference to Anthony Eden as 'the best Prime Minister we have'.

A great deal of paper has been used in writing about R. A. Butler, and in particular how he succeeded in almost everything except becoming Prime Minister. Perhaps the answer lies in the title of his own highly readable autobiography – *The Art of the Possible*. When a crunch came he was likely to see it in terms of compromise, what was 'possible'. But what is 'possible' often involves a subjective judgment, and others perhaps pushed the boundaries of the possible farther than he was prepared to do.

Working contact with other Ministers proved necessary only occasionally, though the Prime Minister's incursions into foreign and commonwealth affairs led to some involvement with Selwyn Lloyd, Alec Douglas-Home and Duncan Sandys. Soon after I went to No. 10 it was suggested that I ought to make my number with Lord Hailsham, who had become Lord President of the Council. I went to see him in his office in the Old Treasury, through a communicating door from No. 10. He didn't really know what to make of me, and I felt out of my intellectual depth with him. The impasse might be resolved, he felt, by telling me the story of the flustered new privy councillor who, on taking the oath, fell on his knees, not before the Queen, but before the Lord Chancellor. The error being pointed out, he then became even more flustered and shuffled across the room, still on his knees, to the required spot. A good enough story in itself, but enhanced on this occasion by a complete re-enactment, with the Lord Hailsham shuffling across the carpet on his knees from his chair to mine.

For a time Lord Hailsham was the Tory Party's bell-ringing, taking-a-dip-at-Brighton chairman. A good deal of care was taken to preserve the Civil Service status of the No. 10 staff, and the dividing line between their responsibilities and those of the Conservative Central Office was well defined. Whenever the Prime Minister made a speech from a Party platform, or a Party political broadcast, the Central Office took responsibility for the arrangements. No member of the No. 10 staff would be seen at the annual Party conference (or any other Party meeting).

This meant that I had only occasional and casual contact with Central Office staff. George Christ was the official most likely to come my way, partly because he did much of the drafting for the Prime Minister's Party speeches, and also because he spent time in the Press Gallery making himself available to the Lobby correspondents. A small, dapper man, with neat black moustache, his geniality and readiness to help made him well-liked in the Gallery, not excluding those with opposing political sympathies. George Hutchinson I also saw from time to time when he became the Party's head of publicity: earlier he had been the *Evening Standard*'s Lobby man, and a very capable one, too.

Initially the division worked without any great problems, but when the political going became rough in 1962 and 1963, the Central Office began to show signs of wishing, if not to take over the No. 10 machine, at least to exercise a greater influence in arranging and organising the Prime Minister's activities and in drafting his speeches.

In my sphere this first became apparent with the appointment of W. F. Deedes to succeed Charles Hill as the Minister in the Cabinet responsible for co-ordinating the official information services – with the distinction that the mandate now covered the home information services only (no votes overseas). With Charles Hill I had worked very closely, but now it was a different matter. There was a perfectly good personal relationship, but Bill Deedes seemed to prefer to operate independently as much as possible. He was both a strong Party man and a distinguished journalist, high in the *Daily Telegraph* hierarchy and subsequently to be its editor. On both counts he possibly felt little need for a rapport with a spokesman at No. 10 who was non-aligned.

Oliver Poole, the Party chairman, also began pressing the Prime Minister to hold regular open Press and television conferences in the Kennedy manner, on the grounds mainly that he was at his best in question-and-answer encounters. There are all kinds of objections to such conferences. Unlike the President, the Prime

37

Minister is first and foremost beholden to the legislature. He is expected to make statements of policy in the House and to answer questions there. In open Press conferences he is therefore in danger of affronting either Parliament by giving the Press first bite of the cherry, or the Press by giving them nothing new on which to bite. Problems also arise from the rivalry of Press and television, with newspapermen disinclined to act as extras in a television jamboree. The idea, not a new one, was eventually dropped, but later Ted Heath, as Prime Minister, was to experiment with two 'presidential-style' Press conferences. They had mixed fortunes and were not continued.

Also eventually dropped was a proposition which would have meant a fundamental upheaval in the No. 10 organisation. This was to bring in a senior politician as a kind of chief of staff. The name canvassed was Enoch Powell. Again, on closer consideration, the advantages were seen to be outweighed by the disadvantages. A variation on the theme happened in the Wilson administrations when Marcia Williams, though neither a Minister nor a Party official, played a decisive role in the conduct of No. 10's affairs. Contrasting accounts of how this arrangement worked are given by Marcia Williams in her book *Inside No. 10* and by Joe Haines in *The Politics of Power*.

The Conservative Central Office further felt the Prime Minister's public utterances needed to be given a sharper political edge, and to this end appointed two speech writers, one of whom was Eldon Griffiths, then London correspondent of the American magazine *Newsweek*. For a British journalist to represent an American news magazine was an unusual achievement but Eldon was an unusual man. From a Cambridge–Yale educational background, and from a substantial stint in Anglo-American journalism (both in the States and Britain), he went on to demonstrate his versatility by taking up pig-farming in Sussex, becoming a Member of Parliament and a Minister in the Heath Government. Whether, in the circumstances of the time, it was sensible to make him a speech writer for Harold Macmillan, while still representing *Newsweek*, was perhaps another matter.

In this country there is a coyness about admitting that speeches are written by anyone but the great man who delivers them. In the United States nothing odd is seen in this happening, and speech writers are as clearly identified as any other official. This is surely the more sensible attitude. A Prime Minister or a President obviously does not have time to write all the speeches he is called upon to make any more than he has time to write all the letters he has to sign. Briefs and drafts must be prepared and then, depending on the pressures of the moment, the Prime Minister will add, subtract, re-write and breathe his own personality into the draft. But even if he does not have time to do this, and accepts the draft as it stands, it is still his speech and no one else's. In these circumstances the Prime Minister may well make changes on his feet if he finds there is something in fact or phrasing that he suspects or dislikes. Certainly an accomplished speaker, like Harold Macmillan, will always, by asides or extempore passages, insert some magic into even the dullest text put into his hands.

Alas, he did not always reap due reward. To help the Press (who are no longer as adept as they used to be as shorthand writers), and to ensure that an official text is on record, the usual practice is for the text to be issued to the Press in advance, with a time embargo and 'For checking against delivery'. In practice, though the time embargo is likely to be observed, the checking against delivery is usually perfunctory, and the issued text appears in newspapers (to the extent it is considered newsworthy) without the benefit of any running amendments made by the speaker.

A good example is the slogan 'Exporting is fun', with which Harold Macmillan had to live though he did not say it. What actually happened was amusingly described in retrospect by Lawrence Thompson in *The Guardian*.

The Prime Minister rose, acknowledging the dutiful applause with world-weary elegance, and began to pick his way delicately, if with apparent distaste, through the inevitable balance of payments statistics. Suddenly there came a scarcely perceptible lift of those eloquent eyebrows, a distension of the nostrils, a momentary hesitation as if a thoroughbred running in the Derby saw looming before him the unanticipated horror of Bechers' Brook. And as any sensible thoroughbred, in the circumstances, the Prime Minister ran out. He did not say 'Exporting is fun'. He passed majestically round the obstacle, and started the race again on the other side. Once a legend of this kind begins, the very power of the mass media ensures that it is kept alive, repeated and multiplied.

Perhaps better known is 'You've never had it so good.' (The phrase about never having it so good had been used by the *Daily Express* some time earlier.) In this instance the words were used but then wrenched so totally out of context as to turn them upside down. The passage in which they appeared ran like this:

Let's be frank about it; most of our people have never had it so good. Go round the country, go to the industrial towns, go to the farms, and you will see a state of prosperity such as we have never had in my lifetime – nor indeed ever in the history of this country. What is beginning to worry some of us is 'Is it too good to be true?', or perhaps I should say 'Is it too good to last?' For, amidst all this prosperity, there is one problem that has troubled us – in one way or another – ever since the war. It's the problem of rising prices. Our constant concern today is – can prices be steadied while at the same time we maintain full employment in an expanding economy? Can we control inflation? This is the problem of our time.

Though necessarily having to use other people's drafts – to an extent – Harold Macmillan's major speeches were always given the hallmarks of his own thinking, his own feeling for words, and his own skill in delivery. Work on such speeches would usually proceed for a long time in advance, and could cause agonies before they were completed.

At the outset he would prescribe the themes he wished to develop. He would listen also to other people's suggestions. Research would then go ahead, followed by drafting, perhaps by several hands, each on a particular topic, the whole thing being brought together (in the case of Prime Ministerial as distinct from Party speeches) by one of the private secretaries. A first draft thus became available to stimulate further thought and discussion. At this stage he would suddenly say, 'I'd like to dictate. Ask one of the girls to come in.' His dictation would be a tour de force, combining passages from the existing draft with new passages and putting it all into a coherent sequence. Now he had a draft which was close to what he wanted. After further titivation the instruction would come: 'Put it into psalm form' (not more than a hundred words in large typeface on a small page). Even then, almost to the point of walking on stage, there would come amendments, deletions and additions – though these could be handled fairly easily by retyping whichever pages were affected.

In this process I was expected to play a part, taking the lead when drafts were required for speeches or statements for Press or similar occasions. Since during my newspaper days I had acquired some experience of writing in a light-hearted vein I enjoyed such opportunities as occurred to do it again. Sometimes it came out right.

The most notable occasion was when the Prime Minister was

invited to be the guest of honour at a dinner to mark the twenty-fifth anniversary of B.B.C. Television. He was under heavy pressure at the time and barely glanced at the draft before saying, 'Put it into psalm form.' In the car he was rather gloomy about it, not thinking this was his kind of occasion and (since he never watched television) not understanding some of the allusions, but after asking a few questions like 'Who is Lenny the Lion?' he metaphorically shrugged and we talked about other things.

The text opened by describing the ordeal of arriving tired out at Heathrow after summitry, going into the Press room, immediately finding yourself under a barrage of television arc lights, putting up your arm to shield your eyes, and then seeing your photograph in all the newspapers next day under headlines like 'Weary Mac' and captions saying 'Looking old and haggard, the Prime Minister . . .'

This was a sequence he understood only too well and he acted it out to perfection. The audience responded with delight. You could almost see him light up. The rest of the speech was delivered with impeccable timing, precisely the right alternation of light and shade, telling gestures and several rich embellishments of his own off the cuff. In short, he brought the house down.

Not only was it all seen by many millions of viewers but the Press also wrote it up in a big way the next day. He was frankly astounded. It was odd that someone so sensitive to public reactions should not have realised the importance of letting his sense of fun go on display from time to time. No one really warms to the politician who is perpetually solemn, declamatory and pontifical. With his usual generosity he sent me a note. It said, 'It is a sobering thought for the vainest of politicians that all their most successful speeches are written by somebody else. I really feel very embarrassed by the tributes that have been reaching me about the television broadcast. Your jokes were much more successful than any I have ever been able to devise.'

Subsequently, though with a smaller television audience, the formula was effectively repeated. One especially rewarding occasion was a Variety Club luncheon in May 1963, with an audience of tycoons and stars from the entertainment world. It was the day on which, in the afternoon, he was to open a debate in the House on the Vassall affair. At the luncheon he had laughs all the way, and at the end a standing ovation. The gossip writers, who attend these show-business functions, were enchanted.

'That incredible performing Prime Minister of ours, he's master of the lot of them,' wrote Charles Greville in the *Mail*. 'It was a comedy turn which intrigued me. His timing is superb. Then, somewhere between the back door of the Dorchester and the front door of the House of Commons, he slipped into high statesmanship and let off a speech on the Vassall tribunal which positively boomed with Gladstonian severity.'

These, of course, were televised occasions as distinct from television broadcasts.

In the perspective of time, opinion seems to have become convinced that Macmillan was a master of television – an opinion fed by those splendidly philosophical and retrospective interviews with Robert Mackenzie when he had reached his eighties. During his premiership, however, it did not always seem like that, and he had to learn by trial and error.

In the solo performance to camera – which is at times inescapable for a Prime Minister – he recognised that the secret lay in thinking of your audience, not as millions, but as two or three people in the living room of their home. Even so it is not easy to write and speak a script to catch the mood. Too often – however well done – it still sounds condescending, plummy and artificially matey. Persistent facial close-ups, moreover, are likely to be less than endearing.

One answer lay in creating a 'stand-up' setting, in which the camera could vary its shots. As Chancellor of the Exchequer Macmillan used this kind of device in a budget broadcast, when the opening shot showed him standing at the fireplace in his office. From that stance he introduced a number of people, sitting round the fireplace in armchairs, who were to question him about the budget. For the questioning session he himself sat in an armchair. In this way he was combining the advantages of standing up and of armchair discussion in which he felt so completely at ease.

In the 1959 pre-election broadcast – on the advice of Norman Collins[3] – he spoke while standing beside a globe of the world which also provided a useful visual aid for some of the points he wished to make. This was generally regarded as a highly effective broadcast. The risk in this kind of device is that it can seem too contrived. As a variation on the theme, I caused one broadcast to open with a shot of the room at No. 10 in which it was taking place, complete with the Prime Minister at his desk, surrounded by lights and cameras, so that the viewing public could not only be aware of the No. 10 setting but could also appreciate the pressures under which these broadcasts take place. It seemed to make the desired impression, though one political correspondent made precisely the criticism that it seemed

---

[3] A leading figure in British television, and a prolific author, whose books included *London Belongs to Me*.

too 'mannered'. However, in a television broadcast one is addressing not political correspondents, but people in their homes.

Other successful occasions included a joint broadcast with President Eisenhower from the armchaired comfort of a No. 10 drawing room in 1959. This was criticised from the political left as a pre-election gimmick, but it originated during a discussion between Jim Hagerty and myself about how a television appearance by the President might be organised to best effect. To the best of my knowledge, this was the first occasion on which anything of this kind had been attempted. I believe that whatever political bonus may have accrued to the Prime Minister, it served essentially to symbolise for people in Britain the restoration after Suez of the Anglo-American 'special relationship' – and to do so in a way that compelled attention and interest. It was, in short, good viewing, and that was in general how the Press wrote it up.

Whatever might be done to make solo television appearances effective, one always came back to the fact that Harold Macmillan was a supreme conversationalist. In an armchair, talking to two or three intelligent and sympathetic companions, he could fascinate and stimulate as few other men. That it could be translated to television we found from an interview he gave in 1960 to Edward R. Murrow and Charles Collingwood of the American C.B.S. network. Ed Murrow was, of course, a natural broadcaster in his own right, and his vivid broadcasts from London during the blitz are part of history. But he was also an interviewer of rare skill, having the gift to draw out unobtrusively all that was interesting in the person he was interviewing. British interviewers at that time did not generally have this approach, preferring a confrontation technique, perhaps because they were as much concerned with establishing their own images as with establishing the views and personality of their 'victims'. I hasten to add that the aggressive technique has its place. Certainly no politician, especially a Minister, should be afraid of the technique. He will know – or ought to know – more about his subject than the interrogator, by the nature of his profession he should be quick-witted and quick-tongued, he can count on the sympathy of the viewers if it seems that he is being hectored, he can make sure that a few essential points are firmly put across whatever line the interviewer may be trying to pursue, and if the worst comes to the worst he can pay back in the same coin.

The Murrow–Collingwood interview, though designed for an American audience, found its way onto the British television screen, and one seasoned political observer (and practitioner), Charles Curran, believed that this was the moment when Harold

Macmillan became 'visible'. 'For the first time the man in the street saw and heard the real Macmillan – not the comic Edwardian dandy of the caricatures but the masterful, dominating, self-confident statesman.'

Probably the programme also helped to encourage a less abrasive form of interviewing on British television, and interviewers like Robert Mackenzie and Kenneth Harris were seen more and more frequently. Even so, the requirements of political impartiality did not lend themselves to programmes exploring in depth a Prime Minister's character and thinking, and no enthusiasm was apparent in the broadcasting services for the Murrow type of presentation. For these reasons also the advocates of a regular series of television 'reports to the nation', using the fireside chat technique, were always fighting a losing battle.

The fact remains that television does provide a Prime Minister with the opportunity to establish his personality with the public at large, and that this can stand him in good stead (assuming, of course, that the public like what they see) when the political going gets rough and he is under harassment by the Press. For Harold Macmillan this was probably true during the long, hot summer of 1963, when the Profumo affair was raging and everything seemed to be going wrong. Nearly all the Fleet Street newspapers were assailing him violently, but his public appearances during this period were significant for warm demonstrations of sympathy and support. The general public, it seemed, had come to regard him as a man they liked and respected – an impression which must have been formed in part at least by seeing him on television – and had no time for the excesses of his critics. This was noted ruefully by Peregrine Worsthorne who wrote one week in the *Sunday Telegraph* about the need for Macmillan to go, and the next to concede that the Prime Minister had been sagacious and subtle in his judgment of the country's mood.

3   The Fourth Estate

If he wished to tease me, as on occasion he did, Harold Macmillan would argue within hearing range that there was really no need for an official spokesman to say anything at all. It could all be left to Question Time in the House and to parliamentary statements and debates. 'After all, we politicians are trained in the art of evasion.'

Since real life was nothing like that – and he knew it as well as I did – I didn't have to feel too cut up. The fact was that successive Prime Ministers since the war had felt it necessary to appoint a spokesman – with one notable exception. Winston Churchill, not surprisingly, thought it was all a great nonsense to suggest that anyone could speak for him, and no appointment was made when he took office in 1951. In little more than six months the pressures had so built up – from the Press in general and the Lobby in particular and from within the Government – that a face-saving device had to be found. Lord Swinton (then Chancellor of the Duchy of Lancaster but soon to become Commonwealth Relations Secretary) was asked to co-ordinate the home information services, and to this end Tom Fife Clark was appointed as his adviser on public relations. In practice Fife Clark also became the No. 10 spokesman from 1952 to 1955.

Even before the war the need had begun to be recognised. In 1932 an official called a Press Liaison Officer was introduced into No. 10 but he had to double the role with that of Press Officer to the Treasury and his scope was strictly limited.

Guy Eden of the *Express* told me of an occasion when late at night he met a Cabinet Minister leaving the House. 'Did you know that Kingsley Wood died this evening?' said the Minister. Kingsley Wood was then Chancellor of the Exchequer. Knowing that he probably had a scoop, but feeling that he ought to check, Eden rang No. 10. In great agitation the spokesman told him 'Yes, it's true but you can't use it. It's not official yet.'

Whatever Harold Macmillan's teasing, he set out in his memoirs the position as he saw it on taking office in 1957. Describing the appointment of a public relations adviser he said:

> My Victorian predecessors would indeed have been puzzled and shocked by such an idea. In the first years of this century the post was not officially recognised whatever methods may have been used to secure the end in view. Today, with the vast extension of news – through the British, Commonwealth and Foreign Press, and through the new media of radio and television – it is important that those employed in these multifarious tasks should at least be given the facts. Propaganda is best left to Party organisations. But a Government has a right, as well as a duty, to secure that accurate information should be constantly available.

Exactly how a spokesman works will vary from administration to administration. In part it depends on whether he is a permanent civil servant or someone brought in with the appropriate political sympathies. In part it is a matter of his own outlook, style and method of working. But above all it will be determined by the attitude of the Prime Minister. It is, in short, based on a personal relationship. How that relationship worked during the Macmillan years is best illustrated in the diaries.

The working day went far into the evening and beyond midnight if the need existed. Mornings and afternoons were spent reading documents, checking, drafting, internal meetings and discussions, and briefings for the Lobby and other Press groups. Evenings were when the telephone kept ringing. Even when you left No. 10 your home number remained available. With the House usually sitting until ten at least, anything could happen. Calls up to midnight could certainly be expected. Occasionally I had them as late (or early) as four a.m., when last editions were going to press. Then, of course, London's night is other people's working day, and events are likely to be happening round the world which will cause some night-duty reporter to feel that he must 'get a reaction from No. 10'.

Nor could there be any question of comfortable weekends at home when you re-charged your batteries. If the need existed you stayed in London, but even at home the calls continued to come in, especially on Sunday afternoons when the Lobby men were starting a new week. The switchboard girls at No. 10 – marvellously efficient, delightfully pleasant – had always to know where you were in case a crisis developed or the Prime Minister wished to speak to you. Not for him to know where you were. 'Mr. Evans, please' and very quickly Mr. Evans would be at the other end of the line no matter where he happened to be – even in a pub in Brighton, wondering what the Prime Minister would make of the cheerful uproar in the background.

The normal pattern of activity was built round daily meetings with the Lobby correspondents, and weekly meetings with 'inner' groups of American, Commonwealth and European correspondents based in London: plus the constant inflow of Press enquiries. But there was much besides – advising on requests for interviews (Press and television) and putting up briefs if they went ahead: briefing the Prime Minister for Press conferences (the art being to anticipate any question that might be asked and suggest the line that might be taken – with a dunce's cap if you missed a question): handling Press arrangements and briefings during overseas tours and visits: handling arrangements for broadcasts (other than Party political): and helping to write speeches and broadcasts (except those on a Party platform).

To an extent all this activity represented a response to external pressures, but obviously much thought had to go into planning the occasions and timing of the Prime Minister's public appearances, broadcasts and meetings with the Press. Also I expected to have my voice heard on developing issues if I thought that a significant public relations aspect was in danger of being overlooked.

At the heart of it all – in the domestic context – were the Lobby journalists.

As an organised group, they have been on the parliamentary scene for nearly a century, the first Lobby list having been compiled in 1885. Named representatives of certain national newspapers were then given the privilege – a privilege, not a right – to frequent the Lobby used by Members of Parliament entering and leaving the chamber. They thus had an easy and convenient means of contacting Members and talking to them – assuming that the Member was prepared to accept the approach.

Since those early days, and especially since the second world war, the number of Lobby correspondents has grown enormously, and the facilities provided for them have also greatly increased, though not pro rata to numbers. Now represented are not only the national daily papers, but also the provincial dailies, evening newspapers, Sunday newspapers (on a restricted basis), the broadcasting news services and the main British news agencies (Press Association, Exchange Telegraph and Reuters). Moreover, because of the developing load of work, the case for an alternate representative has been accepted in many instances so that the Lobby list, even in my day, had grown to over ninety.

In his book *The Press, Politics and People*, Colin Seymour-Ure describes the Lobby journalist's main function as 'to keep in close touch with Government and Party activities behind the scenes so that he can explain and amplify matters of both politics and personalities to his readers'. He also spends a good deal of time 'analysing and recording the details of Bills, White Papers and all other types of Government and Party documents'. It is *not* his task to report and describe what happens on the floor of the House. This is the work of the reporters in the Press Gallery and the sketch writers (a talented breed, of whom I remember with particular admiration Norman Shrapnel of *The Guardian*).

In recent years the role and usefulness of the Lobby has frequently been put under the microscope. In particular, some of the political commentators writing from outside the Lobby, and with an admitted competitive interest, have argued that the system establishes a too cosy relationship between Lobby men and Ministers, thus making it possible for Ministers to manipulate news and comment. The position is aggravated, the argument further runs, by the 'non-attribution' basis on which the Lobby man writes. He has the run of the place, so to speak, on the understanding that he does not report verbatim and with attribution anything that is said to him in the Palace of Westminster, whether in reasoned argument or in idle comment. He can make deductions from what he is told and what he hears, but he must write it in the context of his own conclusions. Only very general attribution is permissible, such as 'sources close to the Prime Minister', 'some backbench opinion' or even the hackneyed 'well-informed circles'. This convention about non-attribution is at root designed to protect the privilege of the House, but it also ensures a much livelier give-and-take between politicians and Lobby men than would be the case if every word had to be weighed. 'On the record', of course, there is a great outpouring from the politicians – on the floor of the House and in the spate of White Papers and other documents.

The allegation about a too cosy relationship has always puzzled me. In my experience, the Lobby journalists can be very rough indeed, not least with Prime Ministers of whom they have become tired, as any reference to cuttings over a period will show.

On first taking office a Prime Minister is likely to be given a short honeymoon period (in the House as well as in the Press), but after that anything goes. The Lobby journalists, it must be remembered, are regularly talking not only to Ministers and to the No. 10 spokesman but also to the Leader of the Opposition and shadow ministers, as well as backbenchers on both sides of the House and to the Party organisations. Nor as individuals are they likely to be anything less than sturdily independent. Consciously or unconsciously they may be influenced in what they write by the political complexion of the paper for which they work, by their own political sympathies (not necessarily the same), or by their personal like or dislike for particular politicians, but only in a few instances are they likely to be working to a specific political directive (and that would almost certainly not be conducive to a cosy relationship with Ministers, especially Tory Ministers).

My own belief is that the lobby system has evolved sensibly, works well and broadly achieves the purpose of providing an insight into political affairs. In conjunction with the writing of commentators outside the Lobby, and with television and radio reporting and discussion, it ensures that the great British public is comprehensively and rapidly informed about political developments and thinking – to the extent, of course, that the great British public has a wish to be informed. It is all there for the taking, though to get the balance right you will have to discard some of the competitive excitability, read more than one newspaper, watch more than one television programme and listen to more than one Question Time.

This is not to conclude that the Lobby is without its frailties.

Working day in and day out in the hot-house of Westminster the Lobby journalists quickly catch whatever fever is running round the place. Probably they will help to raise the temperature themselves. Writing about politics is how they earn their living and it is a competitive living. If one of their number has a story which seems to be new or novel they are at once under pressure (not least from their offices in Fleet Street) to expand it, embroider it and find a new angle to it. Even when they know the foundation is flimsy they are under compulsion to write, so that within very short order a story which may have been based on little more than a rumour or a piece of speculation can be blown up into dramatic headlines.

Nor does it stop there. Foreign correspondents in London, finding the same story with variations in five or six newspapers, will almost certainly regurgitate it in cables. It then echoes back, with the embellishment of reaction from half a dozen capitals, and so the excitement feeds on itself until the most sceptical concludes that 'there must be something in it'.

Not a little of the time of the No. 10 spokesman is spent discouraging flights of fancy. But he has to make sure that they *are* flights of fancy. Even the most extravagant sometimes turns out to have taken to the air from a firm launching pad. It is his job to discover quickly what the facts really are and to put them into circulation.

Whether shooting down flights of fancy, trimming them down to size or giving them the right proportions – a spoilsport occupation, alas – he will be effective only to the extent that the Lobby feel that they can rely on him, both for accuracy of information and accuracy of guidance. If they feel they can turn to him as a completely reliable source, which also responds quickly, then they will value him and cherish him, and for his part he will be doing the job as it should be done.

This was a reputation I sought to earn, and happily it seemed to turn out that way. At any rate when I left No. 10, the Lobby gave me a valedictory silver dish with an inscription which said, 'From the Lobby Journalists to Harold Evans, for seven years the flawless voice of 10 Downing Street.' To get the balance right I should add that for Hannen Swaffer I was 'Macmillan's dope pedlar', while Cyril Ray, in the *Spectator*, dismissed me as 'pink and archidiaconal'.

I remember no serious disagreement between the Lobby group and myself during those seven years. From time to time I might think that there had been technical transgressions of the rules by individual journalists, for example in relation to publication of White Papers which, as a sensible privilege, the Lobby received forty-eight hours in advance of publication under all kinds of embargo. But with the Lobby as anxious as anyone else that there should be no transgressions leading to loss of the privilege, my representations were always taken seriously and the transgressor reprimanded if found at fault. Only once was the rule about non-attribution broken so far as I was concerned. There was no repetition though I don't think the culprit ever forgave me for making a complaint.

These good relations with the Lobby did not mean, of course, that I liked everything they wrote. Their interpretation of what was said in guidance, taken in conjunction with information from other sources and with the pressures under which they were working, might well produce pieces which I felt had got the balance wrong or did not give the Prime Minister a fair crack of the whip. But what they wrote was their business. My business was to play it straight down the middle with information and guidance.

A too blinkered view, the Party stalwarts no doubt considered, but this was the system we had adopted under the Prime Minister's authority, and in any event the Conservative Central Office had its own channels to the Lobby. Occasionally, if things were not going well for the Government, a Tory backbencher would write to *The*

Times to place the blame on public relations at No. 10. If that happened I could expect very shortly afterwards some gesture of confidence and friendship from the Prime Minister.

In only a few instances did I know where the political sympathies of a particular journalist lay. Peter Zinkin, the *Daily Worker*'s man in the Lobby, was obviously one. No doubt he disapproved of everything I represented but he hid it well. He was liked by his colleagues and in due course was elected to do a stint as Lobby chairman. Joe Haines, destined to be Harold Wilson's Press Secretary, was then a member of the Lobby and his Labour sympathies were roundly declared as a London borough councillor. I sometimes felt that he was regarding me with a sardonic eye, but after his own spell in Downing Street he went out of his way to pay me a generous compliment in an interview with Robin Day on *Panorama*.

The degree of contact I had with individual Lobby men depended mainly on the kind of work they were doing (the requirements of a Fleet Street heavy differ considerably from those of, say, the agencies or a provincial daily), but also on how they chose to develop the relationship. Some more than others regarded me as a valuable source and as a sounding board. I did no 'wooing' myself. Over the years several firm friendships were built up, and remained even after I left the scene, though this personal friendship never prejudiced their writing.

The heavies, as might be expected, had powerful representatives in the Lobby. For the *Telegraph* it was Harry Boyne, later Sir Harry, a proud Scot with a shrewd mind, handsome presence and flowing pen, who had been a major in the Black Watch during the war. Francis Boyd was *The Guardian* man, a Yorkshireman built like an international rugby forward but a gentle and serious giant, universally liked and respected and author of a biography of R. A. Butler. His work, too, was recognised with a knighthood. Often seen in his company was Ronald Butt, then with the *Financial Times* but later a *Sunday Times* writer and a political columnist for *The Times*. His approach was intellectual, and he carried conscientiousness to the point of masochism. His scholarly book *The Power of Parliament* is an important work in its field.

Then there was James Margach, another Scot, whose skill and distinction led the *Sunday Times* to use his photograph in display advertisements, complete with briefcase and umbrella and Big Ben as background. Though soft-voiced and gently courteous, he probed with delicate and unerring precision, and then fed what he had learned into a prodigious memory bank. Few books about

Prime Ministers are more readable than *The Abuse of Power*, published in 1978 after he had retired (Harold Macmillan he assesses as 'second only to Baldwin as the country's most successful and impressive peace-time Prime Minister').

Also an effective Lobby man – thoughtful, thorough and sceptical – was Ian Waller who became the *Sunday Telegraph*'s first representative in the Lobby.

The heavy I have not so far mentioned is the heaviest of them all, *The Times*. The stately veteran Max Mason was their Lobby senior when I appeared on the scene in 1957. He was succeeded by David Wood who began abrasively, with seeming contempt for official spokesmen and also for some of the traditional Lobby conventions (though later he was to say in a broadcast that he knew of no group of journalists who 'aimed more consistently at high standards'). Of his professional competence there could be no doubt, and long after I left No. 10 I continued to read him with enjoyment and profit. But at times he seemed highly prickly and we walked round each other warily.

Though I did not realise it at the time he harboured resentment against No. 10 for the line taken when he wrote his famous 'enough is enough' story about Selwyn Lloyd's tenure of office as Foreign Secretary. Indeed, he felt so strongly that he was still writing about it seventeen years later.

The original story was published in *The Times* on June 1st, 1959, with pride of place on the main news page under a double column heading. It said, 'We may safely accept that Mr. Macmillan has lately taken Mr. Selwyn Lloyd's arm in a paternal grip, led him to one side and spoken from the heart. Mr. Macmillan has let Mr. Selwyn Lloyd know that at the Foreign Office, in these troubled times, enough is enough.'

At that moment Selwyn Lloyd was attending a Foreign Ministers' conference in Geneva, and the report caused an explosion of excitement and speculation in the diplomatic and political worlds – not simply because of what it said but also because it came out of the blue, because of its timing, because of the authority of *The Times* and because of the prominence given to it by *The Times*.

No. 10 was immediately inundated with calls from the domestic and foreign Press, demanding to know if it was true that Mr. Selwyn Lloyd was about to be replaced – or 'sacked' to use the word more commonly used. The answer was an unequivocal 'No'. Following a question in the House the Prime Minister said, 'The Foreign Secretary and I hope to carry on our work together for a very long time to come.'

Not only did David Wood find his story shot down but also himself in dispute with his colleagues. 'Silly officials of the parliamentary Lobby,' he wrote, 'solemnly considered whether their offending colleague should continue to be considered as *persona grata*.'

Well, how did it all happen? David Wood's own account, set out in an article published in 1976, said that, at a reception given by the Whips for the Lobby journalists, 'Mr. Heath, as Government Chief Whip, said the Prime Minister wished to see me and led me to him. Mr. Macmillan was on the crest of form. Being Prime Minister, he said, was like being a publisher, a man with time on his side, whereas being Foreign Secretary – the most disagreeable few months he had ever spent – was like running a daily newspaper, with urgent telegrams flying in for twenty-four hours a day. Poor Selwyn: he'd stuck it so long and so doggedly. But he had told him there would be a change.'

There is no reason to doubt that this was correct in essence. But neither can there be much doubt that David Wood read more into it than was intended. He concluded that he had been deliberately singled out on this social occasion to receive a piece of Prime Ministerial thinking in order to make it into a hard news story. What he could not know was that this was a favourite conversational theme with the Prime Minister[1] – the killing load on a Foreign Secretary (look at Ernie Bevin, look at Anthony Eden), the length of time it had been borne by Selwyn Lloyd and the consequent desirability of finding him some new field of endeavour in due course.

In relation to the No. 10 denial everything hinged on 'When?' The Press at large assumed that a move was imminent. The Wood story spoke of a move being possibly 'several months ahead'. The hard fact which No. 10 had to make plain was that no move was on the cards in the foreseeable future. In short, Selwyn Lloyd was *not* about to be moved, whatever might happen when next there was a Cabinet re-shuffle. The story was published in June 1959. In October there was a general election and the Tories were returned to power. In the new administration Selwyn Lloyd remained Foreign Secretary. Not until a re-shuffle at the end of July 1960 did he become Chancellor of the Exchequer on the retirement of Heathcoat Amory. David Wood decided that a move over a year later was sufficient to justify an attack on 'the Press Officers of 10 Downing Street' for the denial in June 1959.

[1] Also a recurring theme. See p. 289.

As to the 'silly officials' of the Lobby, the convention they were seeking to uphold was that a social function arranged for the Lobby journalists by the Whips, by the Prime Minister or by anyone else was an off-duty occasion, and that anything said conversationally on such occasions was not for anything but storing in the memory as background.

A sad affair – and no doubt for the Prime Minister a reminder that the function of the Press is to publish and be damned.

Though politics received treatment in greater depth in the heavies, the political vigour of the mass-circulation dailies was plain to see. They went in for dramatic headlines, posed problems in terms of personalities and eschewed 'the retinue of finer shades', but it was politics for the market place and they could get things right (or wrong) just as readily as Printing House Square. Nor did it mean that they had less than first-class Lobby men.

While I was there the main figures were Tommy Thompson for the *Mail* (to be followed by Walter Terry), Douglas Clark for the *Express* (with a toe also in the diplomatic water) and William Grieg for the *Mirror*. It was easy to be on good terms with all of them for they were friendly and considerate people.

Tommy Thompson came into the Lobby at much the same time as I went to No. 10 so that, to an extent, we had the same political learning curve. He had previously been the *Mail*'s air correspondent. No one worried harder at a news bone than Tommy. He had an almost intimidating tenacity and rarely failed to find the marrow. Perhaps more than any other Lobby man he regarded me as a source to be exploited, and exploit me he did, though the process was without pain, including as it did lunches at the Boulestin or at the Ritz, when he brought his editor, William Hardcastle. We established a good relationship early on when he was one of the Press party from London covering the Prime Minister's tour in Commonwealth countries in Asia and Australasia in 1958. Sharing the vicissitudes and fun of a tour like that inevitably meant getting to know your travelling companions more quickly and more thoroughly than would otherwise be possible. Tommy later left Fleet Street to become a tycoon, setting up an opinion research company which quickly shot to the top of the business as O.R.C.

Bill Grieg also had a touch of the tycoon in him since, in addition to being the *Mirror*'s political correspondent, he had a stake in a chain of launderettes in London. A calm tycoon, it should be said, almost studious in manner and exhibiting none of the violent fervour of his paper's political campaigning. One sometimes wondered what he made of the virulence of Hugh Cudlipp and Cassandra.

No one in the Lobby had more sensitive political antennae than Douglas Clark who revelled in the drama and intrigue and interplay of personalities at Westminster and was the complete Beaverbrook man. At various times he worked for both the daily and the Sunday paper, and as 'Crossbencher' for a period in the *Sunday Express* he made Sunday a day of either trepidation or delight for a good many politicians. In his eagerness, however, he sometimes cut corners, and he did not emerge well from the Radcliffe Report which investigated the Vassall affair. I felt sad about this because he was a warm person and a good companion, as I discovered on several of the Prime Minister's tours.

He was also a good raconteur. I remember his story of Beaverbrook, at a moment of concern for the workers, asking him about his daily routine. How did he come to the office, asked Beaverbrook. By Underground, said Douglas. 'What do you do on the journey?' persisted the great man. 'Oh, I read,' Douglas told him. 'Good Lord!' exclaimed Beaverbrook incredulously. 'Can you really see to read down there?'

Though lacking the platform of a national newspaper, many of the Lobby correspondents of the provincial papers also had a strong presence. Sometimes, not being in rivalry, they hunted in pairs. A particularly formidable combination was formed by Douglas Haig of the *Birmingham Post* and Trevor Lloyd Hughes of the *Liverpool Post*. Their carefully planned and competently executed pincer movements often put them at the head of the pack. Later Trevor Lloyd Hughes was to go to No. 10 as Harold Wilson's first spokesman.

Several of the provincial men held office as chairman of the Lobby journalists and did so with distinction – Barney Keelan, of the *Eastern Daily Press*, for example, a brilliant speaker in lighter vein, J. E. D. Hall (*Northern Echo*) and Leslie Way (*Western Morning News*). 'Jed' Hall and Leslie Way, apart from being close friends, had also become in-laws. All three had effective broadcasting styles and appeared with some regularity in B.B.C. radio services. Another sturdy presence was that of Drew Webster, who later became London editor of the United Newspapers group.

One of the Lobby's elder statesmen was Graham Cawthorne, also a provincial man, and we had a common interest in the *Sheffield Daily Telegraph* (later the *Morning Telegraph*) which he represented and I had once served. Before coming into the Lobby he was a pillar of the Press Gallery, being at various times its honorary secretary and chairman. His long experience in Westminster became translated into books and booklets, including *Mr.*

Speaker, Sir, A Visit to Parliament and *A Visitor's Guide to Winston Churchill*.

Because of his frequent television and radio appearances the Lobby newspaperman perhaps becoming best known to the general public was Robert Carvel, representing the *Star* and, after its demise, the *Evening Standard*. He was born into the business of political reporting and commentating, for his father was a journalist who also spent most of his career at Westminster – a man remembered with respect and affection among journalists. Carvel senior made headlines himself when he was involved in the Budget leak in 1947. On his way into the House, the Chancellor, Hugh Dalton, told Carvel the central features of his Budget, and these duly appeared as stop-press items before they had been announced in the House. A Select Committee investigated the breach of privilege – no great mystery about it – and though Dalton resigned, the Committee recognised that there had been no breach of Lobby rules.

Carvel junior, blessed with a perceptive sense of humour and a quick tongue, often enlivened morning Lobby meetings in a cross-talk act with his arch-rival and close friend, John Dickinson, of the *Evening News*, a man similarly blessed. With John Dickinson I had fellow feelings for we both hailed from the West Midlands and had worked on newspapers there.

One was also inclined to think of the two domestic agency men – Spencer Shew (Extel) and E. P. Stacpoole (Press Association) – as a double act, though again they were in competition with each other. What they wrote was important because it appeared very quickly on tapes (not only in newspaper offices but also in clubs and commercial organisations), concentrated on the root facts rather than comment, and complemented the interpretative pieces received by newspapers from their own Lobby men.

Since he was honorary secretary of the Lobby journalists throughout my period at No. 10, 'Spenny' Shew figured largely in my daily schedule. It was more than making Lobby arrangements with him, however, for he helped me enormously from his fund of experience and wisdom. I had a deep affection for him, and it was always reassuring to see that stoutish figure ambling along a Commons corridor. Mostly he wore voluminous blue suits (the capacious pockets serving as his filing system), and inevitably the front of the jacket would be smothered in cigarette ash, reminding me of the first editor for whom I worked whose lapels were similarly garnished with snuff. Spenny had a hobby which one might not have suspected – the study of crime. His books on the subject included *A Com-*

panion to Murder, published in two volumes. He sent me copies inscribed 'as a wildly inappropriate souvenir of an association which, seen from my side of the fence, has been entirely delightful'. From mine, too.

E. P. Stacpoole – 'Staccy' – was also a venerated Lobby personality, seemingly shy and retiring, with white hair and open countenance and looking like everyone's favourite uncle. He, too, showed me much kindness. When I left he sent me the nicest of letters. 'I can't remember you ever bowling us a googly,' he wrote. 'Indeed, all through the Profumo affair (for instance) I had a tremendous reputation for rightness and sagacity simply because I went by you.'

Third of the Lobby news agency men was Fraser Wighton, who carried the Reuter banner with the expertise born of long experience. One had never to be deceived by his harassed air. It was essentially through him that Reuters told the world beyond Britain about the decisions and antics of Westminster. He also came on many of the Prime Minister's overseas visits so that I got to know him well and to count him as a friend.

Though my own relations with the Lobby might be good it did not follow that they always loved the Prime Minister. In general, Prime Ministers do not see the Lobby as a group with any regularity. It is largely the Lobby's choice. By convention you are invited to Lobby meetings. In practice if a Prime Minister said that he would like to come and see the Lobby it was unlikely that they would say 'No', though if he came with any frequency and told them nothing worthwhile it might be another matter.

Harold Macmillan went to see them infrequently – usually if he had made a statement in the House which seemed to need further background. Customarily, however, he invited them to No. 10 for an annual drinks party, when all was sweetness and light and both he and they seemed to enjoy themselves. On one occasion he spoke of the relationship between No. 10 and the Lobby. 'We don't try to be clever . . . just try to help you . . . and tell you the truth . . . within reason, of course!'

At one Lobby meeting, however, he seriously upset them (or some of them) – quite without intention – and I do not recollect that he saw them again for briefing purposes, though the annual drinks parties at No. 10 and the Whips Office continued pleasantly enough. It happened fairly late in his premiership, in August 1961, after he had announced in the House the Government's intention to apply for E.E.C. membership. He arrived in the Lobby room before they had fully assembled, and while they were drifting in he took the opportunity, half seriously, half cheerfully, to reproach Douglas Clark for a piece just published in the *Daily Express* which he regarded as misleading and inaccurate. Douglas took deep umbrage – none quicker to cry 'Foul' than the critic criticised. Afterwards I had a letter of protest from Spencer Shew, as secretary of the Lobby Association. He told me, however, that it was not a formal protest and advised that I should simply acknowledge it.

Whether it did any real harm in creating a resentful attitude, conscious or unconscious, in parts of the Lobby is a matter for conjecture, but it can't have helped because it happened at a time when the Government in general, and the Macmillan leadership in particular, was beginning to come under fire. Moreover, events were impending when friends would be needed.

Only occasionally would one of the leading political columnists (as distinct from the Lobby men) seek to see the Prime Minister. Their concern was with trends and political philosophy rather than daily politics. They had more time to think and write, and the best of them wrote with elegance and force. Whether they got things right was another matter, but their importance lay in the contributions they made to thought and debate.

At that time Henry Fairlie was among the giants – highly readable and stimulating though spurning consistency. Peregrine Worsthorne, already attached to a bow tie, was beginning to make his name, and was also prepared to walk in the common mud by joining the caravan accompanying the Prime Minister on his African tour. William Rees-Mogg, destined to become editor of *The Times*, was then with the *Sunday Times*, and saw the Prime Minister from time to time. Strongly on the left were people like Anthony Howard, who would not expect or seek to establish a rapport with a Tory Prime Minister, though he did on one occasion, when working on a book, come to see me to talk about the organisation and working methods of No. 10. His verdict: 'Pretty lightweight.'

I imagine that to these intellectually sophisticated operators I must have seemed to have straw in my hair, but this was perhaps also their view of the Lobby journalists. Certainly no love was lost between the two groups. From the Lobby they in turn were regarded as dilettantes and theorists, out of touch with the nitty-gritty and what really made the world go round.

Then there was Randolph Churchill, that perpetually rumbling and frequently erupting volcano in political journalism. For a man so highly accomplished in his own right it must have been galling still to be recognised primarily as his father's son, especially since his own political ambitions remained largely frustrated. Whatever the cause, his public behaviour was notoriously unrestrained. One of his delights was to bait official spokesmen at international Press conferences. Primarily the Foreign Office spokesmen had to face this crudely offensive barrage, and they acquired some skill in doing it, especially given that the Head of News Department was likely to be a man of strong personality on his way to an ambassadorship. In my day they included John Russell, later ambassador in Ethiopia and Spain, while second-in-command was Donald Maitland who subsequently became ambassador in Libya, Ted Heath's spokesman at No. 10 and most recently permanent under-secretary in the Ministry of Energy. Nor did the international Press corps always take kindly to Randolph's outbursts and on occasion they shouted him down.

As I moved into this arena from the mostly cloistered calm of the Lobby, I did not relish the prospect of public brawling with Randolph. But it never happened. On the contrary he became my friend and supporter, feeding in questions to which he knew I could offer positive answers and even uttering parliamentary 'hear, hears'.

Obviously it helped that he was strongly pro-Macmillan, but I like to think that the origin of this benevolence lay in an incident during the Prime Minister's visit to Moscow.

Randolph had arrived in advance and made contact with the defector, Guy Burgess, an Eton contemporary. Burgess, who had been for some years in Russia, now wanted to visit his mother in England and sought whatever protection might be necessary against detention. Randolph thought the visit should be allowed as an act of magnanimity. To set the wheels in motion he rang me at the Sovietskaya Hotel, where I was staying with most of the entourage (the Prime Minister had been allocated a guest house). Could I come and see him forthwith and he would give me lunch. Despite a very heavy schedule I had to eat. I also felt that if Randolph had a bee buzzing in his bonnet I had better find out what it was.

At one o'clock, the appointed time, I arrived at the National Hotel and was ushered into what in Czarist days must have been equivalent to the royal suite – exuding a musty elegance compounded of red velvet and a profusion of gilt-framed mirrors. It had been commandeered by Randolph on the grounds that his father had once stayed in it. He was still in pyjamas and dressing gown, both flung carelessly open to reveal a manly chest. At a table in the middle of this long salon sat a dumpy Intourist girl attempting to take dictation – 'attempting' because Randolph was striding majestically round and round the table, catching many-angled glimpses of himself in the long mirrors, and punctuating his dictation with diatribes against the Soviet political system. This tableau I was permitted to enjoy for almost an hour, getting more and more hungry but with no signs of lunch.

At last Lydia was waved away and the question of lunch arose – well, he was going to have omelettes, whisky and black coffee, and no doubt I would like that too? So over omelettes and whisky he explained to me the overwhelming public relations importance of speeding Burgess on his way to England, home and beauty – temporarily at any rate. This thinking I undertook to transmit to the Prime Minister – given a suitable opportunity – and in fact did so later in the day. But there were more important things to think about, of course, and it had to take its place towards the bottom of the queue.

I got to bed well after midnight and had lapsed into the sleep of total exhaustion when at two o'clock the phone began to ring. It was Randolph, of course. Why, he demanded ferociously, had I done nothing about Burgess? If I didn't produce results smartly he would send off a piece condemning the Prime Minister for inhumanity and there'd be a goddam awful public row: I'd better get moving or else!

This was too much. Overboard went my never-lose-your-temper routine. The Prime Minister was not in Moscow to dish out favours to defectors, I shouted back. The great British public didn't give a damn about Burgess. All this rot about an anti-Macmillan piece cut no ice. He wouldn't write it anyhow because he was a Macmillan man, and he could go to hell.

That was virtually the end of the matter, but I then had the surprising legacy of finding Randolph not a formidable enemy but prepared to take me to his bosom – and his championship was worth having. I was among those he consulted when he was preparing his book *The Fight for the Tory Leadership* and was rewarded with an inscribed copy. A book of 'essays by his friends', including a tribute by Harold Macmillan, was published after his death in 1968, and helps to a better understanding of this complex and gifted man who could be so intolerably rude and arrogant.

Anthony Sampson was another of the non-Lobby journalists who kept a close eye on No. 10, to the extent indeed of representing *The Observer* on the first of the major Macmillan tours – to India, Pakistan, Ceylon, New Zealand and Australia – and later on the African tour. In southern Africa he was on familiar ground from his editorship of the magazine *Drum*, published in Johannesburg and championing the coloured people. With me he had a half-friendly, half-abrasive relationship. His *Anatomy* books came later, as did a highly discerning biography of Harold Macmillan, which he sub-titled 'A study in ambiguity'.

The British political writers apart, I had frequent encounters with foreign and Commonwealth correspondents in London – or at any rate those who had formed themselves into small groups prepared to offer contact on 'Lobby terms'. Going into No. 10 I inherited three such groups – American, European and Commonwealth. The Commonwealth group had four members only, and the European six, but between them they covered key papers or agencies in France, Germany, Italy, Sweden, Canada, South Africa, Australia and New Zealand. The American group was larger, varying around ten. All three groups came to see me once a week, and severally or individually they would cross-examine me further at lunch in London's more expensive eating places, from the White Tower to the Connaught (an American V.I.P. stronghold).

I enjoyed talking to all three groups. Whatever they gained from me I gained a good deal from them. At that time London ranked as an important and desirable posting, and the men who came were not only skilled professional observers but also, more likely than not, men of strong personality and intelligence. With them one could explore a subject in depth since they were more interested in analysing situations and trends than in day-to-day news. Also, of course, they were taking a rather cooler and more distant view of things British. Through them it was possible to discern how developing situations in Britain were likely to be viewed in other capitals, and also to detect strands of thinking there. Many of them remained in post throughout my No. 10 service so that with several I was able to establish genuine friendship. The *persona* of each group was distinct – the Europeans polite and formal, the Commonwealth four 'matey', and the Americans cousinly, though on occasion astringent.

The American group was led for most of my seven years by Drew Middleton, whose personal reputation allied to that of his paper, the *New York Times*, made him an important figure in international journalism. He had become imbedded in the British Establishment to the extent of being accepted for membership of the Garrick – his spiritual home, said some of his colleagues. When Drew left London he was succeeded as leader of the group by Joe Fromm, representing the weekly magazine *U.S. News and World Report*, as sharp and cheerful as a fox terrier, and as shrewd as the best of journalists should be, but amiable with it and a lively companion.

   On occasions the American group and I had to differ. At the time of C.N.D. and the Aldermaston marches they became convinced that Britain was going neutralist and anti-American. I suggested that they should stop sitting in London, reading the Fleet Street headlines, and do some listening in the pubs north of Luton. Joe Fromm told me later that he did precisely this and came back with quite different perspectives.

4   When Things went Wrong

In his memoirs Harold Macmillan says of his relations with the Press, 'I have generally got on well with proprietors, editors and individual journalists. One must get used to being lauded one day and defamed the next. Perhaps the most trying experience is being preached at.'

His feelings towards the Press bore signs of ambivalence. Perhaps he would not have gone all the way with Macaulay – 'In the Reporters' gallery yonder there sit the Fourth Estate, more important than all' – but he freely recognised the cardinal role of the Press even though at times he did not much admire the manner of its performance. He could wax philosophical about it – 'They can hardly avoid behaving as they do. It is the same with painters. Unless their work is controversial, exaggerated, distorted, they arouse no interest' – but he often found it distasteful all the same and at times made no effort to hide his distaste.

He also resented the amount of time and effort he was called upon to give in dealing with Press demands, and with situations resulting from Press reporting and comment. 'They are making it impossible for us to do any business,' he complained to me once. So, too, with Press conferences. 'Why do you make me do these things?' was an almost standard flash of annoyance before a conference. Afterwards he would apologise and explain, 'If I didn't feel like that beforehand I probably wouldn't do it very well.' It was fair enough. Not least of the privileges of those serving a great man is to act as a lightning conductor – within reason, of course!

Fairly regularly a proprietor or editor was lunched at No. 10 at a small party which would usually include one or two Ministers and myself. In turn the Prime Minister might be invited to lunch with a newspaper's top editorial and management team. These were always agreeable occasions but what impact they had on established Fleet Street attitudes is open to question. If those present happened to include a leader writer something may have been gained in understanding, but I would not put it higher than that.

Whatever Harold Macmillan might feel about getting on well with proprietors and editors, it was not difficult to identify some who were far from loving him. In the *Daily Mirror* and its associated papers this was to be expected, though at times the virulence of the personal abuse he had to endure (notably from Cassandra) reached astonishing crescendos. Even at the other end of the political spectrum, the *Daily Telegraph*, such support as he might receive often seemed grudging, possibly reflecting the dislike reputedly felt for him by the Berrys. Nor did it seem that *The Times* had much regard for him. Sir William Haley, he notes in his diaries, 'lectures us daily in the best grandmotherly style.' In June 1963, at the height of the Profumo affair, Pendennis in *The Observer* compiled a list of 'the enemies of Macmillan'. Among the Press he identified *The Times* as the chief enemy, 'holding him responsible for a weakening in the nation's moral fibre'. 'Unlike most newspapers,' wrote Pendennis, 'the proprietors of *The Times* leave their editor to do the editing; and Sir William Haley hasn't needed any prodding. For months past he has been saying that people needed to make less money and do more work; and the Profumo affair has been the spark that has really set his sense of moral outrage alight.' *The Times*'s malevolence extended to a leader detracting from the Macmillan achievement in engineering the nuclear test ban treaty between East and West, to the extent indeed of not publishing the letter in which President Kennedy so warmly praised the Macmillan role.

In his book *The Westminster Lobby Correspondents*, Jeremy Tunstall quotes one of them as saying, 'I think political correspondents' criticism of Macmillan brought about his end as P.M.' This is perhaps an isolated view, and certainly it does not stand up to close examination. Whatever the upheavals in the summer of 1963 he was sufficiently confident of Party and public support in the early autumn to have decided to lead the Conservatives into the next election. It was illness alone that prevented this.

In the early years of the Macmillan premiership, as he went from success to success and even the economic scene seemed sunny, the Press in general admired and applauded. Efforts on the left to prick this bubble of approval made little impact. The *New Statesman* commented sourly, 'Already decent Tories hang around outside Number Ten Downing Street hoping that Mr. Harold Macmillan will touch them and cure their warts, and soon they will be thinking of him, not as a human being at all, but as a spirit, dwelling on some height.' In the same vein Vicky created in his cartoons in the *Evening Standard* the image of Supermac, intended to debunk but serving in fact to provide further impetus to his public reputation.

Not for three years was there a serious check to the Macmillan run of success. The collapse of the East-West summit in Paris in May 1960 represented the first serious setback. Others were to follow (but successes, too), and doubts and criticisms began to gain currency on the Tory backbenches and in the Press. The Opposition at last had something to exploit, especially when it became necessary in mid-1961 to introduce a pay pause. It was also at this time that the satirical revue *Beyond the Fringe* began its systematic denigration of the affluent society in general and of Harold Macmillan in particular, echoed on television in *That Was The Week That Was*.

This mood of unease was the setting for a series of spy scandals. 1961 saw the exposure of a spy ring at the Portland naval establishment, and of another spy, George Blake, who was an employee of the security services. Then in the autumn of 1962 came the Vassall case, when William Vassall, a spy in the Admiralty acting on behalf of the Soviet Union, was brought to justice.

The case engendered great excitement in the Press, and some newspapers set out to identify the culprits for failures in the security services. Since the Prime Minister has ultimate responsibility for these services any failures are laid on his doorstep, including even failures to report particular developments to him. A little odd, Harold Macmillan was to comment, that success in unveiling spies should be regarded as failures in security. In their anxiety to probe the Vassall affair as deeply as possible some newspapers published reports which implied a relationship between Vassall and the Civil Lord of the Admiralty, Thomas Galbraith, going beyond what was appropriate between a Minister and a junior civil servant in his Private Office. It was then reported in the *Daily Express* by Percy Hoskins, the crime reporter, that rumours were circulating that the First Lord of the Admiralty (Lord Carrington) had been aware for eighteen months that a spy was operating within the Admiralty and had not reported it to the Prime Minister. On the following day Douglas Clark, as political correspondent, wr.te, 'The First Lord's position is now very delicate. Yesterday on a sudden summons he hurried across to the House to see Mr. Macmillan. The reason: the revelation by Percy Hoskins in yesterday's *Daily Express*.'

Since all these reports were false, the Prime Minister felt deeply incensed. The whole matter, he now decided, must go to a judicial tribunal, charged to investigate both Admiralty security and the specific allegations made against Mr. Galbraith and Lord Carrington. 'I felt strongly that not only should the truth be searched out, but also that the purveyors of lies should be punished,' he records in his memoirs. This attitude he also declared in the House in moving that the tribunal be set up. 'I have a feeling,' he said, 'that the time has come for men of propriety and decency not to tolerate the growth of what I can only call the spirit of Titus Oates and Senator McCarthy.'

In the House the Leader of the Opposition, Hugh Gaitskell, had reacted by saying that the purpose of the enquiry ought not to be to save the reputation of the government but to promote the security of the nation. This, as might be expected, was also the reaction in Fleet Street, though in general editorial comment was restrained, especially in contrast to the headlines.

In the *Mail*, for example, Walter Terry reported, under banner headlines, 'The uproar over Britain's security weaknesses switched dramatically last night into a massive row involving newspapers, their right to attack, and the Prime Minister's determination to protect his Ministers.' The adjoining Comment column, however, while emphasising that 'security comes first', agreed that the allegations against the Lords of the Admiralty 'deserve wider investigation'. It went on to say, however, that there might be difficulties under the tribunal method of investigation. 'The reluctance of journalists to disclose the source of their information may be one.'

This was prophetic, for Press anger rose sharply when in March 1963 the Radcliffe tribunal committed to prison two journalists, one reporting for the *Mail* and the other the *Sketch*, for precisely this reason. A refusal to reveal sources has no basis in law and the arguments are finely balanced. A newspaper's ability to obtain news and to probe may well be prejudiced if it is unable to protect its sources: on the other hand, with no obligation to disclose sources, a journalist is in a position to write a story which is almost entirely deduction and speculation and has no true source except in his own mind. Cross-examination of journalists by the tribunal revealed, indeed, the extent to which a 'source' could be no more than a report in another newspaper. The tribunal concluded that reports in several newspapers had been 'fabricated', and that the allegations about Lord Carrington in the *Daily Express* were unfounded (the allegations were withdrawn during the tribunal's hearings and apologies submitted). The tribunal further considered that a report in the *Sunday Telegraph* had posed as fact when it was no more than speculation.

Fleet Street thus emerged from the tribunal in a battered state, with two journalists imprisoned, several shown to have written stories without adequate foundation, and an exposure of the frailty of some of the sources on which reports were based.

In editorials anger and resentment was mixed with heart searching. Anger was deepened in some newspaper offices by an article by Paul Johnson in the *New Statesman*, written after imprisonment of the two journalists. 'I wonder if Mr. Macmillan understands what he has let himself in for?' he asked, and then provided the answer as he saw it. 'Between now and polling day political news reporting (and, of course, the slanting of news) will be heavily pro-Labour. At the same time any Tory Minister or M.P. (or for that matter, judge or barrister) who gets involved in a scandal during the next year or so must expect – I regret to say – the full treatment.'

The *Daily Mirror* took him strongly to task. 'It is hard to believe that Mr. Johnson was feeling well when he wrote his sickening piece.' The notion about meting out the full treatment, said the *Mirror*, was preposterous.

Well, it was soon to be put to the test. The *Mirror* leader appeared a few days after the Secretary of State for War, John Profumo, had denied in the House rumours linking him with Christine Keeler and had threatened that he would take legal action if these rumours were repeated outside the House. The House and the Press appeared to accept this assurance. *The Observer*, for example, commented, 'Mr. Profumo has denied any improper relationship with Miss Keeler and his denial must be accepted,' adding, 'There is always something abhorrent about a public outcry over somebody's private life.' Less than three months later, early in June, in a letter to the Prime Minister, Profumo admitted that he had lied about his relationship with Christine Keeler and submitted his resignation.

Here was sensation by any standard, more perhaps in the lies to colleagues and the House than in the sexual misdemeanour itself, though it had been linked through Christine Keeler with the Soviet naval attaché. Dramatic front-page headlines were accompanied by lengthy inside-page inquests into the whole affair. On June 8th Dr. Stephen Ward, the sinister figure at the centre of it all, was arrested and charged with living 'wholly or in part on the earnings of prostitution'. On June 9th the *News of the World* published the 'confessions' of Christine Keeler (bought, it was said, for £23,000[1]). On the same day the *Sunday Mirror* published a photostat of a

---

[1] Clive Irving, Ron Hall, Jeremy Wallington, *Scandal '63* (Heinemann, 1963).

letter from Profumo beginning 'Darling' and ending 'Love, J' (also bought from Christine Keeler). Rumours multiplied alleging the involvement of other Ministers, and these spilled out to the Argyll divorce case, with the name of yet another Minister bandied about.

The Prime Minister had little option but to set up yet another enquiry. Lord Denning agreed to undertake it, with specific reference to the operation of the security service, though he was asked also to investigate the rumours about Ministers arising directly or indirectly out of the Profumo affair. He began work on June 24th and his report was published on September 26th.

In the meantime, Fleet Street had turned its spotlight on the future of Harold Macmillan as Prime Minister, spurred on by stories of a Cabinet and backbench revolt against him. The alleged division in the Cabinet was quickly shown not to exist when the Ministers said to be in revolt made statements denying it. The story originated, it seemed, from a Tory backbencher who made no secret of his dislike of Harold Macmillan. Certainly on the backbenches there were dissident voices – to the extent of twenty-seven Tory abstentions in a vote of confidence – not enough to bring down the government, but undoubtedly disturbing.

In *The Times* Sir William Haley had now begun to denounce like a Knox from the pulpit. 'Eleven years of Conservative rule have brought the nation psychologically and spiritually to a low ebb,' he thundered. He awakened echoes in several unexpected places. The *News of the World* declared that in the end Mr. Macmillan 'must take full responsibility for the dishonour which has fallen on Britain through the Profumo scandal.' 'What can you expect,' the *Sunday Citizen* asked, 'when a nation is debauched in this way? You can expect what we have now got – a Profumo.' The *Mirror* declared, 'Under Mr. Macmillan's leadership – and he must take the blame – the Affluent Society has become the Effluent Society.' Even *The Observer* got round to saying that Mr. Macmillan had 'debased the coinage of leadership' through 'obfuscation', adding 'It is time that he went.'

Not all Fleet Street saw it quite like that. The *Sunday Times* spoke of 'a vast deal of sanctimonious humbug', and went on to say, 'There is certainly something wrong with a country in which popular newspapers, feeding their readers with what the millions demand, can bid huge sums for the life story of a woman of easy virtue and a man charged with living on immoral earnings.'

Also given an airing was the famous Macaulay quotation, 'We know no spectacle so ridiculous as the British public in one of its periodical fits of morality' – though it was open to question on this occasion whether 'Press' should be substituted for 'public'.

The extent to which Press attacks on Harold Macmillan reflected resentment stemming from the Radcliffe report – as Paul Johnson had predicted – must be a matter for conjecture. Certainly every opportunity was fully exploited. He himself had little doubt. In his diaries he wrote of 'an exultant Press, getting its own back for Vassall. *The Times* was awful – what has since been called a "holier than thou" attitude which was really nauseating. The popular Press has been one mass of the life stories of spies and prostitutes, written no doubt in the office. Day after day the attack developed, chiefly on me – old, incompetent, worn out.' Later, on Press reaction to the Denning report, he wrote that they were 'so disappointed by the lack of scandals in Denning that they all turn on me. It was to be expected. The leading articles are less hysterical than the news pages.'

The Denning report had, like Radcliffe, thoroughly dismissed the rumours and allegations about Ministers. So far as security was concerned, Lord Denning concluded that 'none of the government services was to blame'. This, to an extent, and failing anything else on which to feed, was the end of the matter. Also there were now other matters in the political field on which to focus, with the Party conferences approaching and speculation about the date of the general election and who would lead the Tories into it.

Though in its attacks on Macmillan the Press was no doubt 'getting its own back', it was reflecting also a segment of Tory backbench thinking. When a Party has been in power for a long time there are bound to be backbenchers who are disgruntled with the leadership, either because they have been passed over for Ministerial appointment or because they have been found wanting in a Ministerial appointment and returned to the backbenches. Others will be worried if they feel that the leadership is faltering or becoming unpopular, especially those with marginal seats when a general election is beginning to loom. So, too, within the Party machine, the concern will be less with loyalty to the existing leader than with a cool assessment of who is likely to be the most effective leader in the election lying ahead.

In the summer and early autumn of 1963 political writers would therefore have no difficulty in finding expressions of anxiety about the leadership, both within the Tory ranks in the House and in Smith Square. Whether they themselves were responsible for whipping up some of the speculation is another matter. Each is likely to feed on the other. Then, of course, they would have no lack of encouragement from the Opposition – even in the ordinary flow of events one half of the House is in the business of denigrating the other. In *Punch* Anthony Sampson wrote,

> As soon as Members reassembled after the fateful lie had been admitted the whole House worked itself up into a state of frenzy. Absurd rumours, involving half the Cabinet, were believed, repeated and elaborated. Plots and conspiracies to overthrow the Prime Minister and his colleagues were hatched round every corner. Wild stories and schemes were leaked to the Press who, in turn, built up the crisis and generated still further alarm. Members of Parliament who returned to England in the midst of the furore were astonished to discover that Parliament had apparently lost its head.

Harold Macmillan was similarly recording in his diary, 'The Parliamentary Party was undergoing one of those attacks of hysteria which seize men from time to time.'

Despite it all he went on with the business of government with apparent equanimity, and he had his moments of satisfaction and achievement. The test ban treaty was rightly recognised (except by *The Times*) as an outstanding Macmillan achievement, prompting a letter from President Kennedy in which he said, 'I could not but reflect on the extent to which your steadfastness of commitment and determined perseverance made this treaty possible.' In June the President visited Britain and stayed at the Macmillan home in Sussex, with both sides finding satisfaction in the talks. Yet only a month earlier the *Sunday Pictorial* had devoted its front page and an inside page to a story alleging that the president had 'publicly administered to Mr. Macmillan one of the most monumental snubs in the history of Anglo-American relations', with embellishments by Richard Crossman's writing of dislike, distrust and enmity. In August the Prime Minister paid an official visit to Sweden and Finland, and showed a jauntiness which gave little hint of under-lying stress. At home he made speeches winning warm acclaim, he received hundreds of letters of support, and he finally rallied the Tory backbenchers. When illness struck him down on the eve of the Party conference in October there was every prospect that he would lead the Tories into the next general election.

Few Prime Ministers can have been subjected to such a sustained barrage of Press criticism, much of it amounting to vilification. Yet he survived. The realities eventually assert themselves, not least the political realities. A change in leadership without bringing down a government can take place only if the reigning Prime Minister has lost his will to survive or is too ill to continue. A Press campaign against him is more likely in the long run to unite Party opinion behind him, both in Westminster and in the country, especially if his image, nourished by television, stands well in the constituencies.

And if the Press is unlikely to bring down an individual as Prime Minister (unless he allows his spirit to be eroded), it is still more unlikely to bring down a government holding an overall majority. Only suicide can do that – by the leadership or by its backbenchers. Politics is about power. If you have power you cling to it. When the division bell rings you don't vote for your own extinction, whatever the Press may have been saying and whatever your own grumbles may have been. Even if you abstain, as twenty-seven Tories did in the Profumo vote of confidence, you do it only when you feel sure it won't bring the government down.

At the end of the day, Fleet Street could have had little doubt that its own reputation stood tarnished rather than that of the Prime Minister. Yet the campaign against him would not have reached the extremes it did unless it had been nourished from the Tory back-benches. In Fleet Street, even while it was all happening, voices could be heard calling for new thinking about the ethics of journalism.

In a lecture at Stirling University some seven years later, Alastair Hetherington, editor of *The Guardian*, spoke of the relationship between politicians and the Press. Recalling the findings of the Radcliffe tribunal, he said, 'It's a grim record: a really bad example of the Press going wrong.' One reason, he thought, lay in the intensity of commercial competition between newspapers, so that some tried to cut corners. He went on to say that over the years he believed the standards of newspapers had risen, partly because television gave people a check on what the newspapers were saying and had widened their horizons. 'Politicians are justified in finding fault with the Press from time to time: but, with exceptions, the Press does its job pretty well.'

With that broad conclusion I agree, despite the torrid experiences of 1963: indeed, those torrid experiences may well have contributed to the development of changed attitudes in Fleet Street. Possibly, just possibly, it was all worth while in the long run.

5 Aspects of Summitry

Probably Harold Macmillan made more visits and tours overseas while in office than any other British Prime Minister. Without believing that summitry could replace bread-and-butter diplomacy, he saw great importance in national leaders meeting and knowing each other, especially in a period of acute international tension capable of drifting into nuclear war. These personal contacts fell into four categories – with Commonwealth Prime Ministers, with American Presidents (Eisenhower and Kennedy), with European leaders (principally de Gaulle and Adenauer) and with the Soviet leader, Nikita Khruschev.

He made three Commonwealth tours – in 1958 to India, Pakistan, Ceylon, New Zealand and Australia, in 1960 to Nigeria, Ghana, the Rhodesias, the High Commission Territories and South Africa (the 'wind of change' tour), and in 1962 to Trinidad, Barbados, Antigua and Jamaica. His meetings with Presidents Eisenhower and Kennedy were frequent, often in Washington, but reciprocally in Britain, Bermuda and the Bahamas. Paris and Bonn appeared with some regularity on his visiting list. Rome also had its place, and towards the end of his premiership he visited Finland and Sweden. The dramatic visit to the Soviet Union took place in 1958.

Though the tours were exhausting, No. 10 enjoyed them and developed a notable skill in organising and executing them. The team accompanying the Prime Minister was kept as small as possible, and within that small group – already accustomed to working closely together – the shared demands, experiences and vicissitudes on safari enhanced the sense of camaraderie. From the moment of take-off to the moment of landing the Prime Minister's aircraft became the No. 10 office. As seatbelts were unfastened, lids of dispatch boxes opened and the clatter of typewriters began.

On the more extended tours there would usually be two private secretaries, an archivist, two or three girls from the Garden Rooms, a cypher clerk, and the Prime Minister's personal detective (possibly with the support of a colleague to ensure the security of the dispatch boxes). Sir Norman Brook usually came, bringing his own secretary, Joan Porter. On the first Commonwealth tour and the African tour Lady Dorothy brightened our lives, and with her came her personal maid, Edith Baker. The first task on arrival at any destination would be to set up office in accommodation provided by our hosts, sometimes pleasant, sometimes cramped. My responsibility was to take charge of Press arrangements and to put up briefs and drafts for the Prime Minister.

I hope that the tang of these travels is caught in the diaries, but two of the tours took place before 1960, when the diaries begin – the first Commonwealth tour and the visit to the Soviet Union.

Possibly the colourful success of the first Commonwealth tour in 1958 did more than everything else up to that time to establish Harold Macmillan as a popular public personality.

The tour began in drama. He left London the day after the resignations had been announced of the Chancellor of the Exchequer (Peter Thorneycroft) and two other Treasury Ministers (Nigel Birch and Enoch Powell) on the grounds that their proposals for cuts in public expenditure had not received adequate support from the Cabinet. If the Prime Minister felt bitterness about resignations on what he believed had become a relatively narrow issue – and about the timing of them – he hid it well when he was interviewed at London Airport. His dismissal of them as 'little local difficulties' sent a ripple of amusement through the country, and set the seal on his reputation for unflappability.

Apart from the event itself, the days leading up to it had involved intense strain and overwork for the Prime Minister and all of us at No. 10, so that we set off on this five-week tour at a low physical ebb. These long tours were exhausting in any case – helping to support the Macmillan thesis that the first requisite for a modern Prime Minister is the constitution of an ox. For my part, I fell into total physical disarray within a week of leaving London, and had to spend two days in bed in the President's House in Karachi to recover from what the doctor diagnosed as 'extreme fatigue'.

It had its bright side, however, when the President, Iskander Mirza, came to cheer up the invalid in a *tête-à-tête*. Sitting on the bed with a glass of whisky and chain-smoking, he waxed philosophical about people and events. If only at Suez, he said, the British and French had reached Port Said in forty-eight hours all would have been well. For Macmillan he had warm praise. 'I told my people that when this man says "No" he means it, and when he says "Yes" he means it.' To me he offered doubtful comfort, 'When you are born God writes down when you are to return. Why then worry?'

73

It was during this tour that the Prime Minister rescued me from a serious act of *lèse majestè*. The incident occurred in New Zealand when the Governor-General – Lord Cobham, that great hitter of sixes for Worcestershire – held a full-dress dinner party in honour of the Prime Minister. Unfortunately, I had been told eight instead of seven thirty, and because of heavy pressures had timed my arrival precisely. To my dismay I found that the party had already gone to dinner in the panelled dining room at Government House. What, then, was I to do? Should I silently and ignominiously slip away and go hungry or walk in boldly and brazen it out? The Governor-General was the Queen's representative and, in effect, this was a Buckingham Palace function. Had it been anyone else but Cobham I would probably have fled, but remembering those sixes I gritted my teeth and walked in. All heads turned towards me. A silence descended. Tiaras, white ties and decorations sat frozen. But my faith in the Lytteltons was vindicated. He jumped up at once and came towards me smiling and with outstretched hand. And in the silence the Prime Minister said loudly, 'Mr. Evans will write out one hundred times "I must not be late for dinner."' The party dissolved into laughter and I was saved.

An overseas visit with its own peculiar features was that to the Soviet Union a year later, at the end of February 1959 – the first by any western leader since the end of the war. It represented Harold Macmillan's first essay into East–West summit diplomacy in an attempt to obtain detente rather than confrontation. Mr. Khruschev then firmly held the reins of power in Moscow, and his regime was characterised by what seemed like dangerous impulsiveness. In particular, he was making threatening noises about the Allied presence in West Berlin. The Prime Minister himself proposed the visit by taking up the general invitation outstanding after the visit to Britain in 1956 by Marshal Bulganin and Mr. Khruschev.

He had come to Moscow, he said on arrival, to repay this visit, 'to see something of the people, industry and agriculture of the Soviet Union, and to have talks with the Soviet leadership' in the hope that there could be a better understanding of each other's point of view. He hoped also, he said, that the visit would 'help to alleviate some of the cares that at present bring anxiety to the world'. He had *not* come, he emphasised, to negotiate.

As was to be expected, the visit excited enormous Press interest, particularly in Britain and the United States, and we found ourselves followed by a great caravan of journalists. In general Fleet Street elected to send its diplomatic correspondents, but two or three of the Lobby men also went, and in addition we had a miscellany of writers who were perhaps as much interested in seizing this rare opportunity to view the Soviet scene as in diplomatic reporting. They included Malcolm Muggeridge, representing the *Daily Mirror*, Emrys Hughes M.P., on a *Tribune* ticket, but no doubt hoping also to gather new material for his book about Macmillan, and Cyril Ray (that prince of wine connoisseurs) dispatched by the *Spectator* to renew acquaintance with the Soviet Union after a stint as the *Sunday Times* man in Moscow in the early 1950s. Anthony Sampson was there, as was Randolph Churchill, a conspicuous figure on the airport when we arrived, wearing neither hat nor coat and with a bright yellow pullover as his only concession to cutting winds and scuds of snow. Don Iddon, the *Mail*'s Washington correspondent, came to report for the *Sunday Dispatch*, the *Mail*'s stable companion: he was a man whose work I admired though possibly I was also influenced by the fact that we both had West Midland associations. The Americans were represented mainly by their correspondents in London. This I found pleasing as it meant a group of familiar and friendly faces among many I did not know.

Our own delegation was much larger than usual, as in addition to the Prime Minister's own entourage (including Norman Brook), Selwyn Lloyd came, supported by several of the Foreign Office top brass. Before leaving London we had a thorough briefing about the security problems we must expect to encounter. Everywhere we went, it had to be assumed, we would be within K.G.B. hearing, with all rooms bugged, devices to pick up conversations in the open air, and two-way mirrors not to be dismissed as impossible. To ensure that there was at least one place where the delegation could confer privately the embassy had to fit out one internal room to be designated as safe, with the aid of drapes and other anti-listening devices. If this sounded hyper-cautious, one had only to remember the bug found in the carved eagle above the desk of the American ambassador in Moscow.

The Soviet tour proved fascinating from the moment that the Prime Minister came down the steps of the Comet wearing the white fur hat. 'Oh, that wonderful, wonderful hat,' wrote Tommy Thompson in the *Mail*. 'Tall, white, furry and distinguished, it did more for Anglo-Soviet relations in ten minutes today than diplomatic exchanges do in a month.' The rest of us had been kitted out by Moss Bros. in black or brown fur hats and long fur-collared coats. As we huddled on the tarmac during the welcoming speeches, Norman Brook whispered to me, 'We must look either very silly or very sinister. Probably both.'

The task of looking after Press briefing was shared by Peter

Hope, head of the Foreign Office News Department, and myself. When the Prime Minister left Moscow for Kiev and Leningrad, Peter stayed in Moscow to cope with those correspondents who preferred not to tour. This turned out to be the most critical moment of the visit. After the initial round of talks in Moscow Mr. K. exuded bonhomie to the extent of announcing that he would accompany the Prime Minister and Foreign Secretary to Kiev and Leningrad, though this had not been scheduled. Immediately afterwards, however, he made a very rough speech on a public platform about East–West relations. The Prime Minister took this as a cue at the next session of talks to speak forthrightly but courteously about the Allied view and how firmly it was held, and about the horrors of nuclear war which would leave no one the winner. Mr. K. became very angry (or affected to do so), accused the Prime Minister of threatening the Soviet Union, and decided at the very last moment that he would not after all go to Kiev and Leningrad. The ostensible reason was that he had a bad tooth which needed treatment, but this merely served to underline the snub.

The British spokesmen – Peter Hope in Moscow and I with the Prime Minister in Kiev – had now to explain the British attitude to this snub, which would be assumed to represent the end of meaningful talks (though a final session was scheduled on the return to Moscow), the failure of the mission and a probable exacerbation of East–West relations. I found myself sitting on top of a chest of drawers in my bedroom at the Ukraine Hotel, faced by an array of distinguished journalists no less uncomfortably draped round the room (though Malcolm Muggeridge had ensconced himself in pole position on the bed).

When in difficulty tell the truth and wear a serene countenance. Yes, the Prime Minister had briefly contemplated calling for his Comet and returning to London, but dismissed the idea without more ado. He had come to the Soviet Union, not only to meet its leaders, but also to see something of the country and the people and he intended to carry out the full programme. No, he was not unduly upset by Mr. K.'s decision not to accompany him. After all, it had not been part of the original arrangements and would have been a very unusual courtesy. When Messrs. Bulganin and Khruschev visited Britain they were not accompanied on their provincial tour by the Prime Minister. The talks in Moscow had been valuable, and though it might seem a pity that Mr. K. had made this public speech it had given the Prime Minister the opportunity to talk about the various matters it raised. He had stated the Western position frankly and clearly. That was in no sense a threat. The situation remained that any unilateral interference with the rights of the three Western Powers in Berlin, without provision for alternative arrangements, would create a dangerous situation. The way to solve this problem was by negotiation, as the Prime Minister had repeatedly urged.

Well, the rest is history. Mr. K. had second thoughts, announced that his bad tooth had been filled with the help of an English drill, and sent Mr. Mikoyan and Mr. Gromyko to Leningrad to welcome the Prime Minister and Selwyn Lloyd on their arrival from Kiev. All was sweetness and bonhomie again. Not least, on his return to Moscow, the Prime Minister was able to go ahead with his scheduled television broadcast.

The broadcast proved a notable part of the visit. The *Mail* felt that the journey would have been abundantly justified by this alone. 'Into a ten-minute talk he packed more information about the British people, their achievements, problems and philosophies than the Russians could have heard for many years. It was a master-piece.' The *Yorkshire Post* thought that there was nothing 'so truly astonishing' during the visit. The *Mirror* named the broadcast as one arm of the Macmillan 'Moscow Spring Double'. It was praised also in the American Press. The *New York Herald-Tribune* wrote that with 'direct simplicity and quiet eloquence' Mr. Macmillan had presented 'a view of Western men and minds very different from that which has been ladled out to them by their leaders over the years.'

The *Daily Express* was also very pleased, as might have been expected, since before we left its editor, Ted Pickering, came to see me to say what a wonderful opportunity the broadcast represented and how much he hoped we would not mess it up. Of course not, I told him, I was already working on the draft myself and he had no need to worry! Perhaps that was just why he *was* worrying, since he probably felt that a top journalist from Fleet Street ought to be brought in to do the writing. Fortunate for me that it came out well or my head would have been firmly on the *Express* chopping block. What one could not know for sure, however, was just how many Russians watched the broadcast, but at least it would be some millions in the Moscow area (we were, in fact, assured that it would be seen in other regions as well).

When the visit ended the final communiqué was more satisfactory than had seemed likely. It declared that both sides

endorsed the principle that differences between nations should be resolved by negotiations and not by force. They recognised that, if such negotiations were to proceed, it was important that each side should make a sincere endeavour to understand the point of view of the other. They agreed that the present visit of the British Prime Minister and Foreign Secretary to the Soviet Union had made a valuable contribution towards such an understanding.

The U.K. Press applauded. Said *The Times*, 'The Prime Minister's blend of firmness and politeness was a dominating factor throughout the visit and restored equanimity in the end.' The *Telegraph* thought that 'as a diplomatic performance this could hardly be improved upon. The skill and cool good sense that he has shown in Moscow puts Mr. Macmillan in an enviable position of authority with which to fashion a united policy among the Western allies.'

'Election or not,' said the *News Chronicle*, 'the Prime Minister deserves credit for his handling of a prickly assignment.' The *Chronicle* was reflecting the view of the ill-disposed that the Prime Minister had gone to Moscow simply to boost his chances in the general election which now lay not far ahead. Robin Day, in Moscow for I.T.N., made the mistake at the Prime Minister's formal Press conference of asking, with the cameras rolling, not about the visit, but about the election. 'That is a question from the wrong man in the wrong place,' the Prime Minister told him.

Looked at simply from the point of view of Press arrangements the visit had remarkably few upsets. For the final stage – the journey to Moscow from Leningrad – our hosts provided a special overnight train for both the delegation and the Press. It departed late at night with style and ceremony. 'The station was floodlit,' I noted. 'Martial music echoed from the cavernous roof, and a goose-stepping guard of honour somehow contrived to march along the narrow platform.' The journey was uproarious. For these few hours, most exceptionally, the Press was completely off duty – beyond contact with their offices and not a telephone or telex in sight – and they celebrated accordingly. The official spokesman was taken warmly to their hearts and arrived in Moscow the next morning much the worse for wear.

For other light relief we had ballet, receptions and dinners, the dinners followed by concerts when, over cigars and brandy, we listened to Russian songs. My companion at one such concert was a bluff and bulky Soviet admiral. He quickly established his priorities, 'Song is song, but cognac is cognac.' Then his perception as a music critic. 'He sings but he is no Chaliapin.'

We went three times to the ballet – *Romeo and Juliet* by the

Bolshoi in Moscow, *The Forest Song* in Kiev, and *The Stone Flower* in Leningrad. The last – by Prokofiev – was the most dramatic, representing (said the critics) a sweeping-away of stereotyped forms in Russian ballet. The Prime Minister – no balletomane – had a good word for one pantomimic effect when the demon king made a spectacular entrance, flashing down a wire by pulley instead of shooting up conventionally through a trap door in the stage. 'I liked the Sputnik,' he said.

In macabre contrast some of us were taken to the mausoleum of Lenin and Stalin, with V.I.P. priority over the long queue in Red Square. From the semi-darkness of the gallery one looked down on the two glass coffins containing the embalmed bodies – serenely waxen and unreal. Rose-coloured light fell on the head and upper body of each figure in its blue high-collared jacket with buttoned pockets. A little later, of course, we should have seen only Lenin, the Stalin corpse having been whisked away to mark the ideological demotion of Stalinism.

Though the Soviet visit proved exceptionally dramatic, summit meetings never lacked colour. For the No. 10 spokesman they meant moving into the international Press arena, with microphones and arc lights and conferences more in the nature of public meetings. The first impact could be sharp and disillusioning.

When Harold Macmillan met the American President, which was frequently, one had to confront the full battle array of the White House Press corps. Everywhere the President went the Press corps was sure to go – an indisputable part of the circus, often over a hundred-strong on journeys overseas. Every move, every gesture, every new development, however insignificant, had to be written about, filmed and photographed. They flew in their own aircraft (arranged by the White House), with schedules meticulously planned to ensure that they arrived at precisely the right time in relation to the President's own schedule. In whatever place the President rested his head the address was still 'The White House', though the second line might read 'Birch Grove, England' or 'Lyford Cay, Nassau': and since the Press corps was part of the White House their presence in every location was looked upon as automatic.

Fortunately, when sufficiently frightened, I become articulate. It also did not take long to discover that these great open Press conferences are in part a façade – primarily for the benefit of the American agency men and the American television networks. The serious talking still went on behind the scenes after the conference was over. The British and American correspondents would then separate and meet again immediately, without cameras, with their own national spokesman. The two groups had cross-fertilisation arrangements, however, so that what was said at the national briefings quickly became common knowledge. Other refinements were also possible with inner groups and individuals. All this meant that the big razzamataz conference at the beginning usually concerned itself with bare bones – the reading of a statement or communiqué, if there was one, and then some fairly perfunctory and obvious questioning, so that it tended to be a chore more tiresome than difficult. The hard work followed on more familiar lines.

The spokesman's task on these Anglo-American occasions was also eased because the Prime Minister and the President were meeting as friends and allies and not in confrontation. On only one occasion did a degree of confrontation occur. This was at Nassau in December 1962 when the Prime Minister was determined to obtain an American undertaking to make Polaris missiles available to Britain following cancellation of the Skybolt project. The Americans, especially the State Department, and particularly George Ball, the Under-Secretary, were loath to do this, and a fair amount of gamesmanship went on at the spokesman level before Macmillan eloquence and Kennedy understanding produced a generally satisfactory outcome.

I was fortunate that the presidential Press Secretaries with whom I had to work – Jim Hagerty and Pierre Salinger – were both, in their different way, ready to be friendly and forthcoming. This stemmed in part from professional camaraderie. Hagerty served a Republican President and Salinger a Democrat, but when Kennedy succeeded Eisenhower Hagerty wrote to me to say, 'As a charter member, and about to become an alumnus, of the Self-Protective and Benevolent Association of Press Secretaries, may I ask a particular favour? Pierre Salinger is about to become the latest and newest member of our union. Won't you please treat him gently as you have treated me. He is a good fellow and one that we can truly welcome into our select and harried association.'

The two men achieved their ends by totally different routes. Jim Hagerty, dour, brisk and down-to-earth, was a meticulous organiser. He knew every nut and bolt and personally made sure they were secure. He was also something of a disciplinarian, ready to be rough and tough with his flock so that even the hardiest thought twice about crossing him. It was splendid to be with him in his office, almost next to that of the President, and hear him say grandly to his assistant, 'Let the Pressmen in': and sure enough there they were, waiting at the door to be allowed into the presence. He was extremely close to President Eisenhower, living almost as a member of the family. This closeness to the President, and knowing the President's mind, meant that he was able to act as spokesman without specific directions on every issue – the basis on which, happily, I was also able to work.

Pierre Salinger was as relaxed and casual as Hagerty had been serious and intense. His forebears came from Alsace and his heart seemed to be as much in France as in California and Washington. A Gallic charm helped him to win friends and influence people, and his armoury of talents included notable skill as a pianist. He normally saw the President each morning when they discussed the line to be taken on topics of the day. He thus had less latitude than Hagerty. Whatever the differences in approach he was no less easy to work with and I enjoyed our encounters. He once described himself to me as 'a brash young man from Washington', but brash was almost the last word I would have applied to this sophisticated and cosmopolitan performer.

Because of the large presidential following, meetings with him on British soil involved elaborate logistical arrangements for Press briefings, and the Foreign Office Conferences Department was very good at it.

In Washington, of course, there were no great problems. Usually on arrival there the Prime Minister and his entourage were ferried by helicopter from the airport to the White House lawn, a very convenient and time-saving arrangement. Helicopters were perhaps not taken quite so much for granted then as they now are, and on making the first of these flights in June 1958 I was presented with a card to certify that I had become 'a Genuine U.S. Army Hoverbug' by virtue of 'having remained motionless in space, flown backwards, forward, sideways and vertically in U.S. Army helicopters'. These flights also enabled me to accumulate a pleasant collection of transparencies of Washington as viewed from a moving platform a few hundred feet up.

Not to be outdone, we too mobilised helicopters for presidential visits to Britain. The first occasion was the Eisenhower visit in 1959, when the President stayed at Chequers. Since the Press corps had to be housed and briefed in London a marquee was set up for briefing conferences at the side of Horse Guards Parade. Jim Hagerty and I were then hovered backwards and forwards between Chequers and the marquee via the lawns of the American ambassador's residence in Regent's Park. On President Kennedy's visit in 1962 we again used helicopters, but on this occasion the briefings took place at the Metropole Hotel in Brighton while the President was staying at the Prime Minister's home at Birch Grove House in East Sussex. This journey had, for me, the fine bonus of skimming over my home in Rottingdean with an opportunity to photograph the windmill on Beacon Hill before we flew along the top of the chalk cliffs and Brighton front to land on the lawns at the Hove end.

Summitry, facilitated by the ease and speed of air travel, and abetted by its attendant publicity, especially television coverage, probably contributed to a developing fashion among political writers during the 1960s to suggest that Britain was moving towards an American presidential system of government. Certainly television focuses the limelight sharply. It is true also that television, not only in this way but also as a vivid channel of communication into every home, gives the modern Prime Minister an opportunity to make a personal impact on the mass of the people not available to his predecessors.

No longer have his personality and views to be delivered at second hand under the gloss of other people's comment and interpretation. In theory he can now influence Parliament by going over the heads of Members direct to the people who elect them. But, of course, television supplies him no less with an opportunity to destroy himself if his performance is poor. It has also to be remembered that requirements about the right to reply are placed on the broadcasting organisations so that in practice every Ministerial appearance by a Prime Minister is followed by a reply by the Leader of the Opposition – with the advantage of last word.

Whatever the effect of summitry and television in making a Prime Minister more 'visible', the fact remains that the powers of Prime Ministers are still what they have always been. 'The Office of Prime Minister,' wrote Asquith, 'is what the holder chooses and is able to make of it.' The Prime Minister has to carry with him both the Cabinet and Parliament. The extent to which he does so is largely a question of his own strength of personality and will in relation to the strength of personality and will of his Ministers and of the Opposition leaders. Rosebery put it like this, 'All his colleagues he must convince, some he may have to humour, some even to cajole: a harassing, laborious and ungracious task.' Gladstone, noted Stansfield, 'sought to carry his Cabinet by unconscious steps to his own conclusions.' This is the best kind of chairmanship but it is still chairmanship. The President, on the other hand, to quote from a lecture by Theodore Sorensen, President Kennedy's special counsel, 'may seek advice from the Congress, from the Cabinet or from his personal advisers. He may seek the views of the Press, the parties and the public. But in the final moment of truth there can be only one lonely man – the President of the United States.'

Part Two

1960

Wind of change — Celtic emotions — Despair in Paris — the Lord who rocked the Commons — change of residence — U.N. confrontation — the young President — phase of doubt

As 1960 began Harold Macmillan rode on the crest of the political wave. In the general election in October 1959 the Tories won a landslide victory, giving them an overall majority of a hundred. Looking back on 1959 The Observer wrote, 'For the British people it was a golden year of self-content, in which they exercised the democratic privilege of voting to keep things as they were – only more so.'

The first major event in the Prime Minister's diary for 1960 was a Commonwealth African tour. It began on January 5th, lasted for six weeks and covered nearly 18,000 miles. It followed his visit to Commonwealth countries in Asia and Australasia in 1958.

The journey started in Ghana (independence already achieved) and continued in Nigeria (independence about to be achieved). 'I don't think we always realise the size and importance of Nigeria,' he commented. 'In population it is the biggest country in Africa, with 35 million people'. Within Nigeria the itinerary took him, not only to the Federal capital, Lagos, but also to the regional capitals at Ibadan, Enugu and Zaria.

From Nigeria he went to central Africa to visit the three countries – Southern Rhodesia, Northern Rhodesia and Nyasaland – then comprising the Federation of Rhodesia and Nyasaland. Continuing south, he went to the three British High Commission Territories (Bechuanaland, Swaziland and Basutoland). Finally, in South Africa, he stayed first at Pretoria and then Cape Town. It was in Cape Town that he made his famous 'wind of change' speech to the South African Parliament.

The journey home began by sea in the Capetown Castle as far as

Las Palmas, where an aircraft was waiting for the last stage to London. This was the only occasion during his overseas tours that he travelled by sea – providing not only an opportunity for much needed recuperation but also for some 'quiet, calm deliberation' about the future.

Lady Dorothy accompanied the Prime Minister. The No. 10 staff was represented by Tim Bligh (Principal Private Secretary), John Wyndham (Private Secretary) and myself, together with four of the young ladies (Jane Parsons, Ann Barker, June Baxter and Pauline Cheshire) and the Prime Minister's personal detective, Inspector Harwood. Also in the entourage were Sir Norman Brook, Secretary of the Cabinet, bringing his secretary (Joan Porter), David Hunt, an Under-Secretary at the Commonwealth Relations Office (later to be a High Commissioner and an ambassador and, after retirement, Master Mind of Britain 1977), and James Robertson, an Assistant Secretary from the Colonial Office (with the bonus of being a son of the then Governor-General of Nigeria).

A sizeable Press party came on the tour, though not all stayed the full course. They included (in no significant order) René MacColl (Express), Stephen Barber (News Chronicle), James Bishop (The Times), William Grieg (Mirror), Stanley Bonnett (Mail), Peregrine Worsthorne (Sunday Telegraph), Anthony Sampson (Observer), Fraser Wighton (Reuters), Roland Fox (B.B.C.) and Robert Manning (Time and Life) – plus, unusually and notably, a female of the species, Anne Sharpley (Evening Standard).

For me the tour meant covering much ground that I knew from my West African and Colonial Office days. For four years from 1942 I was posted to Ghana (then the Gold Coast) as a member of the staff of the Resident Minister. Our headquarters were at Achimota College, a few miles outside Accra and a show place of African secondary education. It was there in 1945 that I married Elizabeth Jaffray, a 'bonny' blonde from Aberdeen via the Colonial Office, the ceremony being performed by the Principal of Achimota College, the Rev. R. W. Stopford, later to be Bishop of London.

January 6, Wednesday   *Over Ghana, 0730*

None of us seems to have had a good night and there is a kind of grumpy silence. I shaved at 3.30 which put me a long way ahead of the queue for the two loos (the two aft are for the use of the P.M. and Lady D.). Now Sir Norman Brook, in dressing gown, and David Hunt, looking dishevelled, are waiting. 'And they call this the Whispering Giant,' complains John Wyndham.

The bearded captain has just been along. We are ahead of schedule by about half an hour, he reports. To ensure arrival on the dot he will circle over Accra.

Even at this height the harmattan is evident in curling pages.

Breakfast is arriving. I have three aspirins as the final course.

In other respects I feel well organised. The Accra arrival programme and the top copy of his arrival speech await the great man's summons.

Accra, 1600

We duly flew in circles until 8.30. The ceremonies went smoothly – with a spectacular scarlet-uniformed guard of honour – and the P.M. said his piece as drafted.

I had talked to him while he had breakfast on the aircraft, telling him the order of battle and giving him the top copy of the speech. He was amiable and relaxed and said he had slept well. Ghana and Nigeria, he thought, involved no complications, but in Central Africa Welensky was being difficult.

The temperature was 72°F when we landed, and there was (and still is) a harmattan haze.

While waiting for the convoy of V.I.P. cars to move away, one of the chauffeurs came hurrying to greet me – a joyous reunion with the placid, open-faced Obeng, looking not a day older than when he was my driver fifteen years ago.

We rode to the Governor-General's Lodge – a new building since my day – in gaudy, high-finned American cars. On arrival at 9.15 a.m. we were greeted with champagne! 'The rigours of the tropics', murmured the P.M. *sotto voce.*

Lady Listowel – very, very pregnant – came in a little late.

Peter Snelling is the U.K. High Commissioner, and Brook, Hunt and I are staying with him in the splendid new house the Ministry of Works have built off Cantonments Road. He is cheerful, chatty and relaxed. The house is air-conditioned but in my bedroom it was difficult to detect.

James Moxon is now Ghana's information king, as blonde, pink and massive as ever, but now also a tribal chief. He has been here for nineteen years and talks of staying for another nineteen. He and I should have no difficulty in deciding lines of spokesmanship. I sense, alas, that Ghana is potentially a Ruritania. There is not really anything to talk to them about and it will be difficult to make the talks spread out over two sessions on the evidence of the topics suggested by Kwame Nkrumah.

Accra, 2300

The charm of Nkrumah, but you have to catch him in the mood.

'Why are you getting so thin?' he asks Jimmy Moxon, patting his vast paunch. 'Worry,' Jimmy explains and they both laugh.

'An utter failure to communicate,' reports Snelling after the first evening meeting at Flagstaff House, though it was amiable enough. The two dogs began to bark, the crown bird to croak, Mr. Baako to walk about, and Dr. Nkrumah to consult Mr. Adu just as the P.M. was getting worked up to his peroration about trusting us in East and Central Africa.

I withdraw criticism of the air-conditioning. The bedroom is cool enough to warrant some thought about a second blanket, but I am too exhausted to do anything about it.

January 9, Saturday   *Accra*

A grand motor cavalcade to Achimota (and afterwards the University College) – for me a sentimental journey. There are some new buildings in the parkland, but those occupied by the Swinton circus are still there, and the campus is still dominated by the main block with its high clock tower.

While waiting for the cavalcade to set off I talk to Nkrumah about whether the car should be open or not, and then tell him of my Achimota wedding fifteen years ago which delights him hugely.

The drive makes it clear why people said I would be vastly surprised by the extent of re-planning and new building in Accra. Station Road, now Kwame Nkrumah Road, is blossoming into the main shopping street, with handsome buildings on both sides.

The crowds are cheerful and friendly but not particularly noisy, except for the children who shout 'Bye-bye' or 'Hello' or 'Freedom'.

The P.M. sits hatless on the hood of the car with Nkrumah, and one wonders how wise this is when he was feeling so pallid yesterday. However, he marches rapidly round Achimota, delivers a fine impromptu oration to the school from the steps of the administrative building, and is in tremendously ebullient form at the University College.

He and Nkrumah think it uproariously funny when the photographers, rushing to the top of the tower to await them, jam the lift and are marooned at the top. The P.M. says he supposes it was Jimmy Moxon's weight.

I had seen him at the Governor-General's Lodge just before we left and he was then very relaxed, co-operative about the text of his speech tonight, and professing to feeling perfectly well. Yesterday on the Tema/Volta trip he had us worried because he had to make three unscheduled stops. The U.K. correspondents fussed about his pallor and told each other that he had Accra tummy. I did my best to remind them that without exception this kind of thing was said at various points during all his tours, but a number of them ran it hard all the same.

The Tema harbour project is on a grander scale than I had expected. From Tema we drove north past the Krobo mountains (with Jimmy Moxon telling us of the old custom of keeping the population in check by throwing a selection of virgins down the cliff face each year), then through the Shai Hills (where the stone for the harbour works is quarried), across the Adomi bridge (a spectacular steel arch) and so to Akosombo, where the Kaiser Company recommend building the Volta dam.

At the dam site we had lunch in a chalet overhanging the river (catering by the Ambassador Hotel). Adu had two transistor sets with him (one Austrian, one Japanese), plus a Russian camera, and was twitted by his colleagues.

During lunch we got the B.B.C. news which does the right thing by announcing that Mr. Macmillan is lunching at the dam site and the wrong thing by saying that he was the guest at a reception last night by the Governor-General (it was Nkrumah's 'do'). 'There you are,' say the Ghanaians triumphantly, 'now you know what we mean about the B.B.C.'

January 10, Sunday   *Accra, 2300*

Dinner parties on successive nights at the State House. Last night's was the formal one, when the two Prime Ministers made sober and careful speeches (punctuated by cries of 'That's right' and 'Exactly'). Tonight's was Dr. Nkrumah's farewell dinner party when he presented a Kente cloth to the Prime Minister and another cloth, plus bangle and ivory box, to Lady D.

Helped by Mr. Gbedemah, the P.M. attired himself in his cloth and then announced that he regretted to see that only three other gentlemen present were properly dressed. He also promised to send Dr. Nkrumah a kilt, sporran and dirk.

Ghana State House occasions are apparently notorious for (a) last-minute reversal of acceptances and (b) plain unnotified non-appearance. At least twenty people did not turn up at the formal dinner. The rest of the guests were moved to the absent places so that, to inspire them, the speakers had a forest of unfolded napkins at the far end of the tables.

This morning's Press conference was unexpectedly placid, with few needling questions. He responded with a splendidly urbane and persuasive performance.

Beforehand, however, there had been an embarrassing display of irritation when we met in his room to discuss the briefing, though the irritation was directed – unfairly – at Tim Bligh rather than myself. Again, on the way along the colonnade to the conference, there was another little outburst, but he quickly mastered it. After lunch, at the High Commissioner's house, came the customary apology, this time without ambiguity.

For the conference I used our tape recorder for the first time and it worked well.

We have casualties in varying degree. Lady D. has had toothache ('One of my last three teeth, on which everything else hangs'), June Baxter knocked herself out when she slipped on the side of the hotel swimming pool and had to be taken to hospital, and Ann Barker has tummy palaver.

This afternoon I escaped to the beach with the Carr-Greggs, who have been very kind throughout the visit. Labadi is now a long line of beach huts, but the surf was as magnificent as ever and I stayed in far too long (expunging memories of the occasion when I was rescued at the last gasp by three young Africans). Roland Fox and Ann Sharpley also appeared.

January 15, Friday   *Ibadan, Nigeria*
As we sit in the Heron waiting to take off the P.M. says 'Rather a pleasant place,' and Lady D. replies, 'Very nice indeed – so friendly.'

The dinner given by the Premier of the Western Region produced a very friendly speech by himself, leading to a plea that we should be nice to our friends, which stimulated the P.M. to cast aside his text, a dull one, and make a very good extempore reply.

I sat between two African ladies, less shy than African ladies often are, especially the large buxom wife of the King of Owo. Her main interest was in families. She has four children, of whom one daughter is in England. She herself has been to England twice. I was cross-examined about my own family, with a direct question about why my wife could not have more children. On the other side was a charming African girl, displaying a good deal of shapely bosom behind a provocative fringe of white lace. Her husband is a Minister and she complained of his frequent absence from home.

Earlier we had the 'demonstration' by students at Ibadan University. The U.K. Press contingent said they had written it up as a good-humoured students' rag, but I think it could easily have tipped over into something unpleasant. Some of the placards were hardly good-humoured – 'MacButcher Go Home' and 'MacNato, we who are about to be atomised salute thee.'

The Governor (Rankine) had asked me beforehand whether the P.M. might wish to omit the University visit, to which there could be only a very firm 'No'. The P.M. did precisely the right thing by treating the chanting and shouting as a welcoming ovation.

Mr. Eke, Chief Information Officer of the Western Region, gave a lunch for the Press at Green Springs Hotel, alongside a handsome swimming pool. At the end of a welcoming speech he half admonished the U.K. correspondents to be more responsible, but they did not seem to take offence. I had to reply. Sitting next to me, Ann Sharpley gave me a good opening line – 'My wife and I are indeed grateful . . .'

Two things are mildly disagreeable – the officious red-haired A.D.C. and the excessive security precautions. A.D.C.s are either charming and helpful or pompous and bureaucratic.

I stayed at Ibadan with the Barry Smallmans – three small children (Mark, Joyce, Robin). The lights failed and I had to pack at 6.15 a.m. by the light of an electric torch. Lack of power also meant an uncooked breakfast. They are cheerfully godly. Joyce said grace at breakfast.

As to Lagos, the following are a miscellany of memories.

Staying with the Gardner-Browns, plus June and Pauline, and playing hell with their meal arrangements because of our unpredictable and varied comings and goings, but they were friendly and understanding. An air-conditioned bedroom – to the point of chilliness. Sam, the head boy, remembered me from the Gambia where he was the Colonial Secretary's head boy.

Friendliness of Governor-General Sir James Robertson, whom the P.M. likes. But Gardner-Brown doubts if in Abubakar's[1] interest it would be wise for Robertson to continue after independence on October 1st.

The astonishing memory of the great 'Zik'[2], very effusive when I accosted him at the Governor-General's dinner party, the most relaxed formal party between British and Africans that I have attended.

A flowing Press conference, this time with no off-stage irritation. Also a good off-the-record meeting with the touring party who

[1] Prime Minister of the Federation of Nigeria.
[2] Dr. Nnamdi Azikiwe succeeded Sir James Robertson as Governor-General and was first President of the Federal Republic of Nigeria 1963–66.

seem in reasonably good heart. They are having no lack of stories – somewhat to their surprise. Abubakar gave them a conference, as Nkrumah had done, and was perhaps even better. He speaks in slow and measured terms, but without hesitation. Clearly he is very nimble-minded – and thoroughly briefed.

Percy Roberts gave a Press drinks party at the Mainland Hotel, partly to enable me to meet the Lagos Press. They were cheerful and uninhibited. Afterwards Bill Grieg gave Percy and me dinner at the hotel. The *Daily Times* is still far ahead in circulation, says Percy. The *Pilot* and *Service* don't seem much better than they were fifteen years ago: apparently they don't try very hard.

Bill reveals that Gaitskell had it in mind to make Leslie Hunter the No. 10 P.R. adviser had he won the election. That was scotched by *The Road to Brighton*, however, and it was probable that he would have asked me to stay on.

We had a short launch trip from Apapa after inspecting housing estates and industrial developments. 'Good to feel a deck under your feet again,' declared Tim, and so it was.

I contrived to get Ann Sharpley a passage in the Britannia from Accra to Lagos. All the other Press people had gone in the morning and she would have been unable to get to the P.M.'s informal meeting with the touring party. The skipper said he had one 'legal' seat to spare, and Brook made no difficulties, given my assurance that we were not setting a dangerous precedent.

January 16, Saturday   *Enugu–Kaduna*
8.45 a.m. and airborne in the Heron again, having just left Enugu for Kaduna. It was a good day in Enugu, perhaps for me particularly because of the opportunity to see the Stapledons[3] again. They went out of their way to be nice. Amidst their many other preoccupations this was no small thing.

Government House is pleasantly situated on the edge of a mild escarpment which gives it lovely views. I was invited to the small official dinner party. Afterwards, *en famille*, Sue took her shoes off and we had a last-drink gossip. Their great 'Bananas' secret – that Robert is to be Governor of the Bahamas – was imparted with due pledges of secrecy.

During the evening I talked mostly to the Chief Justice and his wife, whose three boys are being educated in England (two at Marlborough and one at a prep school) and also to the Premier

---

[3] Sir Robert Stapledon, then Governor of the Eastern Region of Nigeria, had been a friend and colleague in the Swinton 'circus' during the war.

(Mr. Okpare, once a wild boy with a chip on his shoulder but now plump, pleasant and earnest). We all attended a very good lunch at his house where I sat between two Ministers with an easy flow of conversation – chiefly on agriculture (one is the present Minister and the other had been) and on the Eastern Region's economy generally.

I also found a reader of *Men in the Tropics*[4] – Sykes, ex-I.C.S., who runs the Civil Service Commission (I think).

In the afternoon there was a display of dancing at the stadium. The P.M. thought it resembled Elizabethan revels. A very big crowd had turned out with the aid of a little judicious pressure on the schools.

David Hunt and I stayed with Greatorex, the U.K. I.O., an ex-Foreign Service Arabist, with a Greek-Austrian wife. They have a good house (plus a large mastiff, Trixie). He is assured and quick off the mark (not least as a car driver).

P.M. last night talked to me about the difficulties there are likely to be in Salisbury with Welensky, said to be a sick man after an operation. P.M. also said he has written 'rather a good letter' to the Archbishop of Canterbury about his comment on the 'dreadful "never-had-it-so-good"' slogan. He had sent it via Rab and didn't mind if it was published in *The Times*.

The P.M. is beginning to get his places and faces mixed up. At Enugu, with his hand on Premier Okpare's shoulder, he said to the surrounding group, 'He gave us a fine dinner last night and made a wonderful speech.' But alas, last night the place was Ibadan and the speaker Premier Akintola. He realised later what he had done and was laughing about it.

January 18, Monday   *Lagos–Salisbury*

We remained on schedule throughout Nigeria and are now back in the Britannia – 2540 miles in eight and a half hours to Salisbury, watches going forward one hour. The Heron flight from Kaduna gave us a useful hour and a half's work and now we have this further period for uninterrupted work. I begin to feel that I am on top of things again.

My host in Kaduna was John Reynolds, an administrative officer filling in the last six months of his service (before taking lump sum compensation) as head of the Regional Information Services – rather taciturn on first acquaintance, perhaps because of un-

---

[4] *Men in the Tropics*, compiled and edited by Harold Evans (Hodge, 1949).

certainties about exactly how to handle an affair of this kind. They had decided to treat me as an addition to the Press party rather than as a member of the entourage. This was perhaps no bad thing since it gave me Saturday evening with the boys.

At dinner at the rest house Steve Barber and René MacColl were abominably rude to one of Reynold's friends, but he largely brought it on himself by brashness and false bonhomie. Steve's line was (a) how helpful it had been for inferior people from Glossop to be able to earn more than they could at home at the expense of someone other than the British taxpayer, and (b) there would be less complaint against them if they had exploited the natives more efficiently on behalf of British trade. True to form he apologised to the wretched man afterwards and bought him a drink. He models his behaviour on Randolph Churchill.

René MacColl again succeeded in getting a single room at the hotel. He willingly retails the line of his colleagues that he does it because he has built-up shoes and doesn't want them to know that he is not really a tall man.

He and Stanley Bonnett are reputedly the wild men of the party. Peregrine Worsthorne seems to be inflating small points of criticism. Fraser Wighton, Roland Fox, Bill Grieg and John Spicer (Argus Newspapers) are equable and balanced. And Ronnie Read, of course, is a cheerful area of stability and common sense. Anthony Sampson takes cracks at me from time to time on grounds of uncommunicativeness and censorship.

Staying with Reynolds was getting closer to real Colonial Service life – a single-room chalet with concrete floor. The boys coped well with my laundry and there again I do not have the problems I had expected.

The Zaria excursion was a good interlude, with a tour of the Emir's palace followed by a *jahi*, the charge of tribal horsemen.

The Emir formally received the P.M. in the small, dimly lit council chamber, lined with settees. The Ministers and the Chief Justice came in one by one, each dropping on his knees before the Emir and prostrating himself. You could sense the P.M. wondering whether this would be a good way to start a Cabinet meeting.

The aircraft skipper has just given me a conducted tour of the cockpit. What an excellent guide, philosopher and friend is radar. He flew in West Africa during the war, recalling Sir Bernard Bourdillon and General Sir George Giffard. Britannias, he says, are likely to remain in service until about 1964–5 – probably the last of the easy-to-fly aircraft since with jets there is little margin for error.

Lunch is lighthearted. Norman Brook professes to be unable to remember either names or places. He can't remember whether it is Kaduna, Kanadu or Kardomah. Hunt recalls the army officer of whom the recommendation was made, 'We should avoid breeding from this officer.' Lady D. thought it was a lot of hooey about sleeping under a mosquito net – but now pays the penalty with her arms a mass of swollen bites.

Though the 'wind of change' speech in South Africa made the biggest headlines, the most difficult part of the tour came with the visit to the Federation of Rhodesia and Nyasaland. The future of the Federation – formed in 1953 – was a matter of heated controversy and clashing personalities. Power in Southern Rhodesia, a self-governing colony since 1923, lay with the small white population. Northern Rhodesia and Nyasaland were both colonial territories, heading towards self-government under black leadership. Sir Roy Welensky, Prime Minister of the Federation, and the white leaders in Southern Rhodesia were determined not to be led into a situation which put dominant political power into the hands of the black majority. The black leaders in Northern Rhodesia (notably Kenneth Kaunda) and Nyasaland (notably Dr. Hastings Banda) were equally determined that their countries should achieve self-government on 'one man, one vote' principles, and Dr. Banda was at that time under detention. British policy – persuaded that the economic advantages of federation were overwhelming – sought to achieve a multi-racial form of federal government. It had been agreed towards the end of 1959 to set up a Royal Commission under Lord Monckton to advise on how this might best be done, but already, even before the Commission had begun to work, there was controversy about its terms of reference, with Sir Roy Welensky vehemently opposed to any suggestion that secession of Northern Rhodesia and Nyasaland from the Federation should be among the options examined.

This was the situation when the Prime Minister arrived in Salisbury late on January 18th. Two days of meetings and functions lay ahead before he left for Lusaka early on the 21st. The central engagement was an address to the Rhodesia National Affairs Association. This was a critical occasion since every word would be weighed by the contending segments of opinion. Moreover, he had been reported as saying at his Press conference in Nigeria that the people of Northern Rhodesia 'will be given an opportunity to decide whether the Federation will be beneficial to them.' White politicians in Southern Rhodesia saw this as allowing the two northern territories to secede and were incensed. In his Salisbury speech he said that he had been 'misunderstood or misreported', and the point he was making was that the Federation could go forward to full independence only when Northern Rhodesia and Nyasaland had achieved fully responsible government and agreed that they could dispense with British protection. In claiming that he had been misunderstood or misreported, the Prime Minister said that he could quote the precise words he had used in Lagos, 'since having some little experience I now go about these conferences with a tape-recording machine.'

January 21, Thursday   *Salisbury–Lusaka*

Ten minutes before landing at Lusaka after a moderately bumpy flight which John Wyndham didn't like. He has had dysentery almost from the moment of setting foot in Africa.

Rhodesians are now chewing on the Tuesday 'keynote' speech. They didn't seem to see all its implications at the time of delivery. Now there are signs of pessimism. 'Well, you're over the hump,' was Anthony Sampson's comment last night. The London playback is in general excellent. René MacColl now likes Mac in a big way.

But we had a critical day with them all on Tuesday after the speech. They resented the Prime Minister's reference to being 'misinterpreted' at the Lagos Press conference and to the necessity to travel with a tape recorder. They accused him of quoting himself out of context and three or four of them waylaid me as we left the hall, 'insisting' that the whole of the transcript should be made available to them. But the P.M. agreed to have another off the record talk with them at Government House and did it beautifully. Also, as an act of grace and not on 'insistence', I had copies of the transcript made for them. The tape had failed in places in the second answer so that it was incomplete, but at least they showed no disposition to suggest that I was fiddling. Indeed, I was warmly grasped by the hand by Stanley Bonnett.

Anthony Sampson was probably right. This Salisbury Tuesday was the Kiev Thursday of the Soviet trip.

Yesterday, in his speech at the Salisbury civic luncheon, the P.M. again interpolated a complaining piece about the problems of doing international business with every word weighed by the Press and every expression on his face recorded. Steve Barber was a little gloomy about it afterwards. At last night's reception the P.M. had a quick word with me on much the same theme and, in particular, how he thought it unreasonable that if he looked in the least tired – and after all he was sixty-five (he seems to have forgotten that it is his sixty-sixth birthday next month) – it was blazoned all over the world in the next day's newspapers.

However, the local Press don't seem to have taken offence since, under the inspiration of John Appleby (B.B.C.), they presented him with a Rhodesian slouch hat, with leopardskin hat band, when we arrived in Lusaka. Though I'd warned him, he at first thought he was being approached for an interview, but then accepted it with friendly words and gladdened the photographers' hearts by putting it on.

At our second civic lunch in succession (with two more to follow) the Mayor of Lusaka made a speech with some truculence in it, but it was turned aside blandly and with good grace.

'You don't get someone to change his mind by making public protestations. The way to do it is by private talks and discussions,' the P.M. tells me.

The white Rhodesians are generally on the offensive-defensive. Most of them preach to you their achievements in building up Rhodesia and Britain's duty to stand by them and not to acquiesce in their being 'swamped by the Blacks'.

Evelyn Hone is governor here which establishes me in Government House, one of the better Government Houses and improved since I was here in 1953 by the addition of a delightful swimming pool. I had a quick dip at 4.30 and the water was refreshingly cool.

January 23, Saturday   *Kariba–Livingstone*
En route (Dakota) from Kariba to Livingstone (civic lunch) and thence by car to Victoria Falls ('quiet weekend'?).

Yesterday, Copper Belt day, gave us (a) the Ndola demonstration outside the Savoy hotel, (b) the gelignite incident and (c) Lady Dorothy's gashed leg.

As to (c), she came into the aircraft dripping blood over the carpet and swearing hard (with apologies). Cause of the trouble – the aircraft steps. From the aircraft we radioed for a doctor, and at Broken Hill the small, chubby, cheerful Dr. Dunn was waiting. I teamed up with him and went to the hospital (instead of going to the civic tea party) to ensure that the Press got the facts right about the gashed leg. While the stitching was done the green-uniformed matron gave Mrs. Metcalfe and me a cup of tea and told us all about her career and about the Combined Hospital.

News of the gelignite came from Bill Harwood when we stopped for tea and biscuits at the Kitwe Club. By evening the hounds were on the scent. They came to Government House for me in two batches – first Bishop, Worsthorne and Fraser Wighton, and then René MacColl and the S.A.P.A. man – so that I was twice fetched out of a Government House banquet (band playing on the terrace). In due course the sensible thing was done and the police, who had discovered the gelignite, issued a clear factual statement.

January 25, Monday   *Salisbury*

The Livingstone weekend, or at any rate the Livingstone Sunday, was an agreeable interlude.

On Saturday it looked unpromising. The entourage received small-fry treatment at the airport, we had to attend a fourth successive civic lunch and listen to Mayor Olds making an aggressive speech, and then when we arrived at the Victoria Falls Hotel no one seemed in the least interested in making it possible for us to go and look at the Falls.

On Sunday, however, my old friend from Colonial Office days, Martyn Morris, turned up and took me on a privately conducted tour of the Falls, which gave me an ideal opportunity for photographs, especially with the rainbows exceptionally clear after yesterday's rain (we had a difficult landing in a forty m.p.h. crosswind after bumping through a thunderstorm).

This meant missing morning church and the P.M. looking at the Eastern Cataract, and that in turn meant missing the sad incident when the P.M. rounded on Ronnie Read, of all people, because of the hordes of photographers (mostly amateurs anyhow).

For the excursion in the afternoon to the Rain Forest, and then on the launch, we appealed to the Press to lay off completely, and this they did. There were also some good unobtrusive police arrangements which made it possible to escape the public. At first the P.M. was grumpy, but when he found that we had, in fact, escaped the Press and public he became genial and relaxed, and I was singled out for a gossip over a picnic tea on Kandahar Island.

'Proof of Darwinism,' he commented when I took a photograph of John Wyndham and a monkey silently contemplating each other.

The Zambesi could have been the Thames at Hampton Court except for the hippos lazily watching us from eyes just above the water. 'It seems an awfully nice life,' he said enviously.

From the morning outing to the Falls I had acquired a fiery suntan which worried Lady D. She is as cheerful and zestful as ever despite the gashed leg (there was a wheel chair for her in the Rain Forest).

On getting back we had a meeting in the P.M.'s drawing room to prepare for the Nyasaland–Banda visit.

Footnotes:

Baboons making a nuisance of themselves in the hotel grounds (one discovered wearing a placard: 'One Man: One Vote').

'I knew there must be a catch in it. The main railway line goes through my bedroom' (P.M. on arrival at the hotel).

On the parochialism of the Mayors, 'But have you ever electioneered in Britain?'

The P.M. says that he doesn't yet see the answer to the Central African problem. There is always a stage in the development of a new country when the people who are really building it – the Ronnie Prains – have no time for politics. Even in the U.S., except for Teddy Roosevelt, there was no leader from these groups until F.D.R. The trouble is that here, in central Africa, there is no time.

Following Lusaka and the Copper Belt came Kariba, Livingstone and Zomba, capital of Nyasaland. The Prime Minister then returned to Salisbury and left there by air for Francistown (Bechuanaland) en route to Johannesburg and (by road) Pretoria. Five nights were spent based in Pretoria, and during this period visits were paid, by road or air, to various points of interest, including Durban, the West Driefontein gold mine and the Bantu University near Petersburg.

January 28, Thursday   *Pretoria*

It is 0755 and David Hunt and I sit in John Maud's[5] house waiting for the car which should have arrived at 0730 to take us to Johannesburg. Strange that the Union Government, which so despise the capability of the African, should be less efficient in its arrangements than either Ghana or Nigeria. The U.K. High Commission people say that this inefficiency and dilatoriness is characteristic.

The Mauds, our hosts, are tremendous extroverts. He is tall, slim, white-haired, with long, narrow face, bounding with energy, enormously voluble, lavish with effusive gestures, and supremely elegant (today, for Johannesburg, a blue pin-striped flannel suit, brown suede shoes, brown snap-brim and rolled umbrella: yesterday, pearl-grey suit with lapelled waistcoat and Old Etonian tie). Lady Maud a pianist, a diarist, and also lavish with effusive gestures. The long-legged Caroline, a young actress taking a five-week holiday in South Africa before rejoining the Pitlochry Festival Company, exactly like her parents in her bouncing zest without obvious affectation.

[5] U.K. High Commissioner in South Africa. Later Lord Maud.

Add the erudite David Hunt (though he can be caught out in a bluff) and it is all fizz, crackle and pop. But Evans, alas, is feeling low with fatigue and a bursting head cold and cannot fully enjoy it. James, the butler and general factotum, produces large red pills and I take twelve hours in bed and feel moderately repaired. We were all at low ebb in Salisbury – combination of fatigue, nervous strain and reflection of the Prime Ministerial mood.

The P.M. and Lady D. are staying at Libertas, the V.I.P. guest house, situated in splendour, with a cool and grassy terrace looking across the valley – but the furnishings are oppressive.

Later. The day took us into a gold mine and then, in the heat of the afternoon, to a Bantu re-housing area and hospital, ending at the Mayor of Johannesburg's garden party where the P.M., who should have been exhausted, volunteered to shake hands with every guest.

Eric Louw, who is officially representing the Union Government, hates the enthusiastic reception the P.M. is getting. He tells the P.M. that the warmth of the reception is not what it seems and draws attention to 'sullen' Africans. There was, in fact, a tumultuous African welcome in Meadowland though much of it was from marshalled schoolchildren. A few people held placards along one short street. One said, 'Apartheid must fail. Even Mac can't save it,' which seemed a bit hard on Mac.

January 29, Friday *Pretoria*

Five minutes with the P.M. on the grassy terrace of Libertas. He expounds his thesis about the foolishness of elevating segregation into a doctrine. If they didn't make an ideology of it they would almost certainly succeed in getting the results they seek with a minimum of concession. Economic differences between black and white would alone be sufficient to achieve practical separation. Of course, they would have to accept the really talented African (I wonder about this: how could the demand for political rights by the talented African be met).

Afterwards I sit at the feet – literally at the feet – of Lady Dorothy, she giving me the cushion from over her gashed leg (put there to keep a poultice warm). She positively refuses to admit to any pain or discomfort from her leg though she has at last accepted the doctor's advice about resting it.

The Mauds were delighted with their dinner party for the P.M., deciding that everything was precisely right, including the food and wine produced under the urbane direction of James.

I had a heart-to-heart at dinner with the pleasant and unassuming

little Mrs. Louw who told me all about her husband's high
principles – to serve and only to serve. He believes that in order to
serve with complete disinterestedness you must have private means
(his means came from success as a lawyer). For this reason he had
discouraged his eldest son from entering politics, though had he
done so he would probably have been a junior Minister by now.

January 30, Saturday   *En route to Durban*
'That's Swaziland that was,' as we rush in and out along the red
dust roads – yet another country on which No. 10 can now regard
itself as an authority. I felt some doubts about the almost con-
temptuous shortness of this particular visit, especially since the
P.M. for once made an inadequate speech.
Regiments of Swazi warriors stamped and pranced behind their
shields, and the Paramount Chief wore top hat and frock coat. He
recalled his visit to London for the Coronation, and talked in good
Macmillan vein about the value of visits for keeping people out of
mischief.
Now we are flying to Durban. The friendly Captain Smitt, who
travels with us as security officer, announces that we are over his
home division. 'Just look how well behaved they are down there,'
says John.
At Durban – sunshine, beaches, the front at Brighton (but no
pebbles), Union Jacks, children sitting on car bonnets, bathers,
riders and tennis players among the crowds lining the route in the
muggy heat.
'Pity you had to come on a Saturday,' says the Mayor. 'Otherwise
there would have been a really big crowd.' The Indian population
was much in evidence, but not many Africans. Some had home-
made placards, e.g. 'We've never had it so bad.'
Eric Louw let himself get rattled again. 'Why are we coming this
long way round?' At the airport the crowd were calling to him,
'Poor old Eric.'

January 31, Sunday   *Pretoria*
A free day, ending with an entourage dinner party at Libertas.
The P.M. is in his gayest mood. He even gets up from the table to
give a personal demonstration of a Morris dance in evidence that
the English also have tribal dances.
He had not failed to notice the sock suspenders worn by the
dancing warriors in the Northern Transvaal – nor the stiletto heels
of the school choir mistress at Meadowland.
On the national anthem, he claims to be tone deaf, and recalls an

occasion when, on springing to attention, he found that it was only 'Oranges and Lemons'.

Twice during the evening he rumbles to me about not staying in politics much longer.

Reminiscences of Oliver Lyttelton. Jack Johnson quotes the three Lyttelton precepts for politicians – flattery as the infantry of negotiation, 'Remember it was the geese who saved the Capitol', and 'If the others were as clever as we are where would we be?'

Jack also recalls the geese precept being told to Winston who professed not to understand. 'Geese – plural of goose,' explained Oliver Lyttelton. 'Oh, it's a joke, is it?' growled Winston.

The P.M. ranged widely. Effect of the war in accelerating black nationalism. Foolishness of the N.A.T.S. in elevating their policy into a doctrine. The Durban welcome to be seen as the first round in the battle of the plebiscite. He must buy some books in Cape Town since the ship's library will certainly have only Rider Haggard.

February 1, Monday   *En route to Cape Town*

In the Viscount from Bloemfontein to Cape Town. Mr. Louw is with us, sans collar, sans tie, and very sad face because we have to fly above cloud without seeing the Garden Route – 'The most spectacular approach to any great city,' he says. Sir John Maud is in braces. He produces a clean collar and pulls a face at me in triumph, having boasted of foresight in bringing a clothes brush.

Basutoland gave me two personal reunions, beginning with Geoffrey Chaplin, who is now Resident Commissioner. He looks weary and I am told he has been ill. I had not realised that he is a cousin of Charles Chaplin. It was a most efficiently organised show (except that the dais lacked a protective canopy), and to him must go the credit. The second reunion was with Bill Gillett, who has acquired a comely and attractive wife. At the airport ceremony I sat between Lord and Lady Fraser: they apparently spend the first three months of the year in Basutoland.

We had a bumpy Dakota ride to Bloemfontein to join the Viscount, but the girls had four and a half hours of it in a direct flight from Pretoria. At Bloemfontein there was the thinnest welcome of the tour.

In Cape Town, where we had four nights, the programme was so full that I had no time for recording. The Prime Minister and Lady Dorothy stayed at Groote Schuur, an official residence in Dutch colonial style in a magnificent setting above Cape Town. The main event was the address to both Houses of Parliament – the 'wind of change' speech. It was made in the dining room of the Houses of Parliament (previously the chamber of the old Cape Colony Parliament), and I watched and listened from the gallery. Anthony Sampson wrote in his biography of Harold Macmillan, 'It was a speech of masterly construction and phrasing, beautifully spoken, combining a sweep of history with unambiguous political points. It was probably the finest of Macmillan's career.' Perhaps because of the perfection of the oratory the Members of Parliament did not seem to see immediately its significance as a statement of British attitudes at odds with those of the South African Government. When the playback came from London, however – the speech was widely acclaimed there – the message emerged loud and clear. Even so the South Africans in Cape Town showed no public signs of being disenchanted with their guest, and turned out in large numbers to line the streets when he drove to the harbour to board the Capetown Castle, and it was an emotional leavetaking.

February 11, Thursday　　　　　　　　　　*Capetown Castle, at sea*

Shipboard life intensifies personalities. Hunt and Robertson are left in Cape Town – James with a catch in his throat. The girls think he was 'rather sweet', though he plagued them in the middle of busy evenings with dictation of the record.

The girls have constituted themselves into my harem and I am cast for the role of the Emir of Zaria. We even had an 'Emir of Zaria Surprise' on the menu one evening by arrangement with the chef – an ice pudding made for the table, very rich and filling. Half way through a large portion I had to demand a rest which caused Joan, who blossoms delightfully under the influence of a little gin, to comment, 'Well, of course, the Emir does need a rest in the middle of his labours.'

The Prime Minister has so far accepted with equanimity the indolence of life on board. He works, of course, but in the afternoon he lounges happily enough on the boat deck, and last night (his birthday) he put in an hour and a half at a cowboy film, *The Big Country*. Afterwards I suggested to him that it was a better way of handling affairs than politics – simple and decisive – to which he retorted, 'But it takes an awfully long time.' He seemed genuinely pleased by our box of cigars and by the ship's birthday cake. He was also sent a large and ornate card of the Changing of the Guard by Joe, the masseur, for whom one of life's great moments came when the P.M. appeared in the gym for a massage. When I said to him afterwards, 'The P.M. thoroughly enjoyed the massage,' he sprang to attention, clasped me warmly by the hand and said, 'God bless you, sir.'

Venturing on to the sun deck during boat drill yesterday the P.M. could not bring himself entirely to plunge into small talk – though he admired my Delhi sports shirt – and wandered into a discourse about the three current problems: Welensky's tantrums, the threatened railway strike and Cyprus. On all three he tended to be philosophical saying that, of course, when you come to the end of the year and looked back it all seemed pretty trivial.

Welensky, he thinks, is not the man with real power: that is Whitehead (manoeuvring to jettison the reserve powers).

On the railway strike, it seems incredible that the N.U.R. should elect to have a strike now when they are promised a pay increase in a month's time: what advantage is there in striking for an immediate increase since you would then not only have failed to get it but union funds would have lost a month's issue of strike pay – 'but, of course, its all bluff and counter-bluff.'

As to Cyprus, the issue has so narrowed down that he can't think the Cypriots would be willing to expose themselves to having 'that man' (Grivas) back again for so small a sacrifice.

There has undoubtedly been a mellowing since the triumph of the Cape Town speech and the relaxation of tension and he finally got round to an apology to Tim about the Accra incident.

Lady Dorothy is engagingly her cheerful self, though she was again in the wars – this time with more tummy trouble – during the first day or two of the voyage. She enjoys the boat deck and a gossip. Harold, she says, simply won't use new things when she buys them for him. For example, she bought him a new toilet case to bring on the tour but he said it was much too good to use and put it away. Nor will he have anything that is in anyway different from what he has always had. She took a lively interest in boat drill yesterday, being much struck by the piratical appearance of the crew.

Norman Brook relaxes easily and plays happily enough at whatever is going, whether cinema or swimming or deck tennis or dancing. He wears informal shirts, blue or red, bought with Joan's help at Stuttafords in Cape Town. His dancing style, which is enveloping, causes difficulties for the girls and they can hardly avoid implanting lipstick on the lapels of his white dinner jacket about which he then complains.

Funniest incident of the tour, thinks Brook, was John Wyndham going to sleep in one bed in Government House, Zomba, and waking up in another without being able to explain how it happened.

1960

February 15, Monday *Las Palmas–London*
February 15, Monday   *Las Palmas–London*

In the Britannia, on the home straight, the P.M. continues in top-of-the-world form.

I sit with him, Tim and John at lunch. He has taken off his tie and is wearing a brown cardigan, unbuttoned. He chuckles at the thought of the world seeing his African tour as a move of profound and statesmanlike wisdom, whereas (he says) it was just to get away from London in the middle of winter.

Earlier, on the bridge of the *Capetown Castle*, while we watched the saluting Shackletons from Gibraltar, he talked to me about central Africa. What we had now to do was to soothe the alarm of the Rhodesian settlers and avoid a Boston tea party: he is well aware that his visit could result in the break-up of the Federation. And he now feels that Banda can't be released until there is confidence in the ability of the Nyasaland administration to handle the security situation.

For the rest, an exchange of anecdotes between the P.M. and John about the aristocracy – including the spluttering duke at dinner, 'Edie, I think that's a bit of my lobster' (scraping it off her bare arm).

The affairs of the Central African territories continued to take up a considerable amount of Ministerial time after the Prime Minister's return from Africa, and indeed did so throughout his administration. Not least they provoked clashes of view between the Colonial Secretary (Iain Macleod) and the Commonwealth Relations Secretary (first Lord Home and then Duncan Sandys), and Iain Macleod determined that Northern Rhodesia and Nyasaland – both the responsibility of the Colonial Office – should follow the established route to democratic self-government. They did not, however, excite a comparable amount of public interest. The fact was that given the political and racial issues involved, the Federation had no chance of survival in the long term. With hindsight it can be contended that it should never have been brought into being, but this was a period when colonial policy seemed to see in federal arrangements a panacea for the economic weakness of individual territories. There was hardly an area of the colonial empire where some form of federation was not attempted, but in few instances did economic desirability withstand the blast of political reality.

However, the return to London saw many other topics coming into the foreground at No. 10.

February 27, Saturday   *Rottingdean*

A week in which secrets were kept – Princess Margaret's engagement to Antony Armstrong-Jones, Iain Macleod's rumblings about resignation, and re-thinking about missiles.

The Margaret secret stood until the chosen moment – yesterday evening – which was astonishing given that all the Cabinet knew (plus myself!). There was the constitutional angle to be taken care of as a piece of No. 10 spokesmanship. After a Bligh/Sir Charles Cunningham[6]/Sir George Coldstream[7] meeting in the waiting room at No. 10, I produced a list of supplementary questions to which Cunningham provided the answers. Thus armed, I saw Richard Colville[8] at the Palace on Thursday morning with Griffin, the Queen Mother's Press Secretary. In his room Richard now has an enormous mural of the Armstrong-Jones silhouette photograph of Charles and Anne with the globe.

He proposed to see the two agency court correspondents at 2.30 yesterday, so that it was simply a matter of arranging for them to come on to me for the constitutional aspects. They would thus have the complete story on the tapes without the need for last-minute scrambling by Lobby correspondents and leader writers. And so it went. I had not met Mr. Gomer Jones and Mr. Louis Nicholls before. They looked and behaved exactly like court correspondents should, even to the black ties of mourning for Lady Mountbatten. Subsequently we had only a few calls from Lobby men to ensure that no angle was being missed, and in the end I was able to catch the 8 o'clock train to Brighton instead of having to stay the night in London as I had expected.

The Macleod business hasn't emerged at all, though the Cabinet pricked up its ears when he spoke of having to consider the implications of the decision about Banda. However, only a few knew that he did follow it up with talk of resignation. Rab, probably scenting the removal of a rival, spoke somewhat freely of 'quite a number of us feeling fed up,' but in the end a formula was found (and, astonishingly, sold to Welensky by Alec Home) which Macleod felt would save his face sufficiently. Given his reputation for cold calculation and for looking more moves ahead than anybody else, it was a strange episode. Charles Hill simply refused to believe that he *would* resign, and Tim Bligh concluded that he was being emotionally Celtic.

[6] Permanent Under-Secretary, Home Office.
[7] Permanent Secretary, Lord Chamberlain's department.
[8] Press Secretary to the Queen.

The Press also failed to see coherently the signs which point to major Government re-thinking on missiles – whether to abandon the British Blue Streak and put the American Skybolt in its place. I thought it was well to suggest to the Prime Minister that he should warn Sandys and Watkinson about the dangers of being lobbied during this phase of discussion.

My note of this meeting says:

> I seek and get an audience at the House. It is a great act and highly mobile. He starts orthodoxly in his chair at the long table, then suddenly gets up, which I take to mean dismissal, but no, it is just to go to the windowsill overlooking Palace Yard and to sit there with his feet on a chair. One wonders how hot the radiator is. Again there is a sudden move, seemingly of dismissal, but after moving about the bottles and glasses on the tray of drinks, he throws himself into the leather chair in the recess by the door. And all the time, the alert birdlike look. 'Well, Harold, I think you ought to know . . .'
>
> And what do I learn? (a) The American administration is virtually non-existent, the pre-election rot having set in un-expectedly early. Eisenhower will not decide anything and has rushed off on another tour. (b) We are not going to fill the vacuum and make ourselves the whipping boys for the French and Germans. The Summit committees are getting nowhere. It will all have to be done in the last three days: in the meantime H. Macmillan stays mum. (c) There is also a marking time on nuclear tests: the Russians are probably saving it up for the summit. (d) There is plenty to be going on with at home: he has written a very good paper on railways and 'they' have accepted it. (d) There is no row over missiles. The preliminary work is done and Wednesday's Defence Committee will have to decide: but he makes a note about warning Sandys and Watkinson.

I had my first close-up of Ernest Marples[9] during the week when I deputised for Charles Hill at one of the Ministerial briefings for the American correspondents. It is easy to see why he impresses people despite his flashiness. He bubbles with enthusiasm, shuffling about in his chair, pulling out pieces of card from his wallet pocket to sketch something or make a note, while at the same time leaving no doubt that he has thoroughly mastered his brief. He can also be disarmingly candid, for example in speaking of the loneliness of the

[9] Minister of Transport.

dispatch box, especially when the ranks behind are ominously quiet. Among other things, he expresses himself keen to introduce the breathalyser into this country from the States, where it has apparently been particularly successful in Detroit in cutting down accidents. He also said that the possibility could not be dismissed of the railways finding a new lease of life from development of the hovercraft principle which would remove the basic limitation to development of rail travel – the wheel-to-rail friction. He spoke of his vineyard in France and of enjoying alcohol, but if he had a drink his wife always drove.

At the Prime Minister's after-dinner reception for the President of Peru on Wednesday night I talked to the Carringtons (she in particular, as charming and vivacious as ever), Lady Rhys Williams (incredibly voluble, telling me at length of the obtuseness of the Air Ministry in turning down her idea of a chloroform pill beneath the lapel to be used by aircrew shot down in flames), the Carleton Greenes (she spending two hours away from the hospital where she is staying with a small son having his tonsils out), the Tony Barbers and H. V. Hodson,[10] who said that under the Thomson regime he is enjoying more freedom of action than ever before.

The Ambassador of San Salvador collapsed, as had Sir E. Crowe at the last reception but one, and the new arrangement for calling doctors was applied with part success (the second doctor on the list took rather a long time to come). This meant that I did not get away until very late.

March 11, Friday   *Artillery Mansions*

11 p.m. Coming down to the car with Prime Minister after the Parliamentary Press Gallery annual dinner at the house, he is relaxed and pleased because his speech has gone well. With so much to do he could not manage, he says, if we didn't help him with the texts, and he is very grateful because he then has something to develop (the piece I had done on the Commonwealth he made sound wise and profound). He then says that he is pleased I am going with the Chancellor of the Duchy to South America because he wants him kept happy. The Chancellor has done a wonderful job and he wants him to carry on, so please will I do this for him?

As usual, the dinner was an occasion for meeting old friends. They included David Willis and Norman Cursley. David quoted one of his boys watching television news during the P.M.'s African tour. 'Daddy, who is that man with Mr. Evans?'

---

[10] Editor, *Sunday Times*, 1950–61.

René MacColl took me to lunch at the Savoy Grill today with his foreign editor, Terence Lancaster, who has been in the job for only six months. René recently returned from giving evidence at the Blantyre enquiry into allegations of excessive police violence during demonstrations there. With that fabulous charm he appears to have made an impact on judge, court and hostile European spectators alike, yet without conceding very much about exaggeration in Press reporting. After the tour he wrote me a flattering little note about help he had received. In the annual national book sale – what a disappointing affair it is – the only book I could find that appealed to me was his work on Casement. He is now off to the States for the election primaries. He will cover the election itself and speculates about a Catholic President for the first time (revealing that he is himself a lapsed Catholic).

I had a show of transparencies taken during the African tour on Tuesday evening. It went well, stimulated by a Capetown Bomb-shell for which Esme – how wonderful she is at this kind of thing – had obtained a recipe from Mr. Pettifer (bottle of gin, half a bottle of dry vermouth, half a bottle of sweet, and half a bottle of orange juice). Afterwards four of the girls had supper with me at the Corner House: with music from W. Ben Evans it was almost like being back on the *Capetown Castle*.

Railways have occupied a lot of attention during the last fort-night, and they were at the centre of Rab's Thursday Lobby meetings. He went out of his way to be nice: 'You have given me an excellent brief – as you always do.'

March 26, Saturday   *Rottingdean*

The tension has gone out of politics and government at the moment, with the Conservatives at the beginning of a term of office with a large majority. In any case, the public relations work is now so thoroughly organised that it is simply a matter of pressing buttons. The P.M. no longer feels any compulsions in his Press relations and has largely lost interest, though so far as I am concerned he is kindness and friendliness itself. On the *Capetown Castle* I had asked Brook about my future and we met for a talk on Tuesday. We got nowhere, however: I must soldier on.

After that we gossiped. Is the P.M. becoming too godlike? The last P.M. was ruined by failure. It would be ironical if this one was ruined by success. In the early days he did not interfere with his colleagues – that was one of his strong points – but now he inter-feres a good deal. 'He is doing very well, of course, but he's not a Churchill – yet.' Will he really retire in two or three years time? Or will the allurements of power prove too strong? Last week he spoke of going on until he was eighty (I had not taken it seriously). Except, of course, that he tends eventually to say indiscreetly in public what he has been saying discreetly in private, e.g. the British as the Greeks in the Roman Empire of the Americans.

I suggested to Brook that he should take an opportunity of warning the P.M. about this. As things turn out, however, I got my own opportunity when he summoned me for a gossip after seeing the Nepalese (how well he does it, producing out of the hat bits of erudite knowledge about Nepal which pleases his visitors). He wanted to talk to me about how the cards should be played after the Sharpeville shootings in South Africa. The Government did not handle it well on the Front Bench and the initiative has passed to the Opposition. He agrees that it would be well for him to take an early opportunity to say something on the theory of Commonwealth, not least on how to influence one's friends. He has no intention of being a Lord North, though Gaitskell might like to play the role.

Don Cook returned this week from his long vacation in the States, and we had lunch at the Garrick. He seems genuinely glad to be back. I suppose he had intended to pump me, but he did most of the talking. Herter, he says, does not expect to continue as Secretary of State, whatever the next administration. It would be a mistake to assume paralysis in the outgoing administration (on the contrary, electioneering might tempt them to rash deeds). American thinking believes that there must be a marking time on the international scene until after the German elections in 1961.

General de Gaulle paid a State visit to London in April 1960, staying at Buckingham Palace.

April 11, Monday   *Artillery Mansions*
Encounter with P.M. by the tape machine while he is waiting, in tails, to leave for the state banquet at Buck House for de Gaulle. He is well content with reactions to the Budget, he tells me. What he had feared was an assumption that we had gone into reverse in our economic policy, with a consequent loss of confidence and the creation of the very crisis we were trying to avoid (with an oblique reference to his arguments with the Chancellor – 'You know the trouble we have had'). As it is, the critics are making a good deal of noise about things that don't really matter, and we hold the situation until we see what the autumn brings in. That leads him to

112

the old theme of the precarious balance of our economy. £100 million – two per cent – can make all the difference either way. It is a miracle that 50 million people should be able to enjoy the second highest standard of living in the world when they lived on a small group of islands virtually without natural resources – and yet they take it as no more than their due. On de Gaulle, with whom he had just talked *à deux*, 'He is in a very good humour. He teased me about Washington, which was all to the good' (some quotations in French which I had to pretend to understand but didn't). De Gaulle says that he does not understand all the fuss over the ending of the Common Market/EFTA negotiations. Is it simply a matter of money? That has no significance. Which brings the P.M. back to the British economy compared with the French, and how wonderful it must be to be able to feed yourselves. By this time we have walked the length of the corridor to the front door, but he is so immersed that having gone outside he comes back to make a new point.

The de Gaulle visit was an unexpected success. One reaction, however, is that it cuts the P.M. down to size, and makes the fuss about the Common Market all rather over-done. Even the *Sunday Times* got round yesterday to saying something of the sort.

In foreign affairs during his first three years as Premier Harold Macmillan had concentrated on trying to reduce the dangers of a nuclear confrontation between East and West, with Berlin seen as the potential flashpoint. To this end he worked steadily and persistently in order to create conditions in which discussion and detente could take place. In particular, he thought that summit meetings should take place from time to time between Soviet and Western leaders, provided the ground had been well laid at Foreign Ministers' level. By 1960 enough progress had been made in discussions on armaments, nuclear tests and Berlin for agreement to be reached that a summit meeting – Khruschev, Macmillan, de Gaulle and Eisenhower – should be held in Paris in May. As the great men gathered, alas, an American spy plane was shot down over Russia and its pilot captured. Whether the Americans should have suspended such flights with summit talks in the offing can be argued. Equally it can be argued that the Russians found the incident a suitable pretext to call off a meeting to which their 'hawks' were opposed. Failing to obtain the abject apology from President Eisenhower for which he called, Mr. Khruschev refused to let the talks proceed. For the moment it seemed that almost anything could happen. The drama stopped at words, fortunately, but for Harold Macmillan it was a moment of despair. This was his first serious setback since becoming Prime Minister, and it now seemed that one of his main policy objectives had been reduced to ruins.

On the evening of the day that the summit collapsed the inner group of the British delegation dined as guests of the British ambassador, Sir Gladwyn Jebb, at the official residence – Prime Minister, Foreign Secretary (Selwyn Lloyd) and eight or nine officials.

May 19, Thursday   *Paris*

Despair had to be swept under the carpet, so it was teasing all round.

'I rang the Chief Whip and asked him if I should resign now my policy is in ruins around me,' said the Prime Minister. 'He told me to hang on. But we ought to find a scapegoat. Perhaps we should make Selwyn resign.'

For his part, Selwyn took some swipes at government by private secretary – especially No. 10 private secretary, addressing Freddie Bishop as 'Sir Horace'.

Of his own private secretaries, he said they were impossibly insolent and quite out of control: nor could one banish them to remote capitals because there could be no confidence that they would be satisfactory representatives: and anyhow what was the good of sending them away when others exactly the same would succeed them.

I duly came in for a crack. Dwelling on the phenomenon of Hagerty, the P.M. said that fortunately this was something from which we were saved by parliamentary questions: 'Harold rarely has to say anything at all.'

Gladwyn Jebb got teased about the Channel Tunnel.

At one point we drifted to the family history of the Leconfields and the P.M. speculated on the desirability of making John Wyndham Lord Egremont.

Memoirs also got discussed. Gladwyn Jebb said that he would not write his 'unless I become hard up.' The P.M. said he kept a diary 'on and off . . . But writing is a difficult art.'

May 22, Sunday   *Rottingdean*

We returned to London on Thursday evening, after five days in Paris instead of the expected ten or twelve. Now the great post mortem goes. The Prime Minister simply poses the question – was it an episode based on K.'s anger and disillusionment with Ike, or is it a calculated change in Soviet policy from detente to cold war? Those who put their money on a calculated change point to changes in the Soviet hierarchy, Malinovsky at K.'s elbow, the demotion of Mikoyan, and K.'s own alleged uncertainty of manner, particularly as observed in his attitude to Malinovsky and Gromyko. Indeed after the first meeting with K. on Saturday at the Residence the P.M. commented on the fact that K. seemed to be keeping a wary eye on the other two for indications of approval and support whereas in Moscow fifteen months ago he treated all those around him as complete subordinates. In some balance against that is K.'s readiness to make a public joke about Malinovsky's presence in Malinovsky's presence – his remark to the Prime Minister coming up the Residence stairs at the farewell meeting, 'You see the Field Marshal has come with me. He thinks you are such an astute diplomat that unless he comes with me you will twist me round your little finger.'

Then there is K.'s vitriolic performance at his Press conference which shattered the British diplomatic correspondents, especially the older ones such as Trilby Ewer, who remember Hitler. Yet there again K. in no way committed himself to departing from negotiation and co-existence. Also to the optimistic view must be counted the tone and content of his speech last night in East Berlin, the assurances given by both K. and Gromyko in the private conversations, the affability of Soviet officials and correspondents and the apparent wish to push the nuclear tests conference to agreement.

On the whole, sticking my neck out, I take the view that the basic explanation lies in the deep sense of personal affront felt by K. in his relationship with Ike: here was a man in whom he had expressed public confidence 'letting him down' in a way likely to cast doubts on his judgment with the Soviet hierarchy and people. He simply can't do business again with Ike – hence the six to eight months' formula.

Shortly after the Paris summit collapsed I embarked on a long tour of South American countries with Dr. Charles Hill in his capacity as co-ordinator of the official information services, and my No. 10 notes do not resume until the end of July. A major ministerial re-shuffle was then about to take place, with Lord Home – at that time Commonwealth Relations Secretary and a relatively background figure – succeeding Selwyn Lloyd as Foreign Secretary. The changes stemmed from the resignation of Derick Heathcoat Amory as Chancellor of the Exchequer and this vacancy was to be taken up by Selwyn Lloyd. For the Foreign Secretary to be in Lords was bound to draw the wrath of many in Commons, quite apart from any questions about the suitability of Lord Home for the appointment. The Prime Minister was entirely convinced that he was backing the right man, however, and that the arrangement would work perfectly well given the supporting appointment of Edward Heath, in the office of Lord Privy Seal, as Foreign Office spokesman in Commons. In this new role Mr. Heath also took special responsibility for European affairs. These appointments were announced on July 27, but the possibility of the Home appointment had become known a week ahead. It caused great excitement in the Press.

Francis Boyd, political correspondent of The Guardian, set the ball rolling. Others quickly followed and among the weekend papers the Sunday Express gave the story banner headlines over a report by Wilfred Sendall that 'a tremendous political storm is about to break.' Monday's papers then let themselves go. 'MacWonder: Major Blunders' said the Mirror headline. A leader in the News Chronicle said that if the appointment was made the Prime Minister would have been 'too clever by half'. The Mail thought that to give the job to a peer 'would be, to say the least, unusual.' The Guardian was cautious: for the Foreign Secretary to be in Commons was 'a matter of convenience not dogma' but the onus would be on Mr. Macmillan to show that Lord Home was especially well-fitted to be the Foreign Secretary – and he would have great difficulty in doing this. In the Evening Standard, George Hutchinson wrote that, 'A group of influential Tory M.P.s – among them leading members of the back-bench Foreign Affairs Committee – propose to serve notice on Mr. Macmillan that they are utterly opposed to the appointment of Lord Home as Foreign Secretary.' The Daily Telegraph declared itself against a Foreign Secretary in the Lords. 'Tories in Rebellion' said an Express headline. The Mirror published a front page containing little more than the words 'No! No!! No!!!'

By the time the announcement was made on July 27th there was a sense of anticlimax. The Times declared that the new arrangements – including the removal of Selwyn Lloyd to the Exchequer 'where he will have much to learn' – were those of the Prime Minister's personal choosing against the weight of much political opinion: 'He will bear a more than ordinary personal responsibility for its success.' The Mail said, 'Give him a chance,' adding that the whole affair had been 'surrounded by a false excitement induced by clever advance publicity' (but Francis Boyd denied that Lord Home's name had been leaked to him from an official source). The Mirror thought it was all in aid of old Etonians. In Commons the Opposition moved a vote of no confidence and were heavily defeated, with no Tory abstentions, while in Lords Labour peers joined in praise of the new Foreign Secretary. In the Mail the following day a National Opinion Poll showed seventy-two per cent declaring themselves 'satisfied' with Mr. Macmillan as Prime Minister. But the last word went to Lady Home: of her husband she said, 'As far as I am concerned he is able enough for any post in the Government, even Prime Minister.'

July 24, Sunday   *Rottingdean*

We are now entering the last week of the session, with the long-heralded announcement of Ministerial changes in the offing. There is the customary weariness of July, with tempers a little ragged.

An uproar seems likely with the Home announcement, though Wilfred Sendall may have overstated it in the *Sunday Express* today. Also today there has been the unexpected conversational gambit provided by the Hayter[11] article in *The Observer* arguing that the Foreign Secretary should always be in Lords. Alec Home rang just after lunch (wrecking my Sunday siesta), asking to be 'rescued' following an invasion by the *Daily Herald*.

The Sunday calls chore at home is becoming more and more of a burden. No longer is there general observance of the time band, and today the calls began before lunch.

Following a defence spokesman nonsense on the R.B.47 incident, we had a long, desultory and in parts amusing post mortem in the Cabinet room, with the P.M., Watkinson, Charles Hill, Brook and Playfair. 'What a peculiar way of spending a Friday morning,' says the P.M., who goes on to argue that four days a week is enough for work. On leaks, he comments that every barrel leaks at the top. But he is impatient about official spokesmen, arguing that 'no comment' is enough between revelations in Parliament by Ministers – 'after all we politicians are trained in the art of evasion.' However, there is lip service to the thanklessness of the spokesman's job. Playfair crystallises the Establishment attitude in describing the spokesman concerned as a nice man, upright and decent, but not very clever or intelligent. 'If he were clever and intelligent he would not be doing this job.'

July 30, Saturday   *Rottingdean*

We meet as he is coming out of the Cabinet room and he says, 'Come and talk to me, Harold. We'll go into the garden.' I ask him if Press reaction to the Cabinet changes worries him. He is

---

[11] Sir William Hayter, Deputy Under-Secretary of State. Foreign Office, 1957–58. Ambassador to U.S.S.R. 1953–57.

astonished – or professes to be astonished – that I should think it
possible: it's just a nine-day wonder. What *is* worrying him, he says,
is August 1914. And I hear again how we drifted into the 1914 war,
the second war probably being unavoidable because it was planned
by a wicked man. Now, he thinks, we are in danger of drifting again
and of finding ourselves at war by miscalculation or misunderstand-
ing. He has said this in his letter to Mr. K. ('I wrote it,' he said, 'to
get back the initiative for our country and for myself, which I think
it did!') The danger is that Mr. K. may try to force the Berlin issue
at the height of the American election – and what would we do
about that? 'Then, of course, the country is going bust – or so they
say.' And he goes on to express scepticism about the prognosti-
cations of the experts. Borrowing short and lending long is no doubt
risky, but you had to take risks if you were to get anywhere. 'If my
grandfather hadn't taken risks I should still be on Arran. We started
the business on borrowed money. We never took anything out and
when we sold the business in America – except for thirty per cent –
we got a million and three-quarters for it. Well, that is what this
country must do. From time to time we are able to collect a high
return and we must always remember that.'

Then he drifts to the Cabinet changes (which is really what he is
thinking about). He had to hold the balance. Some of the younger
ones were not ready yet. It was a loyal Cabinet with a good spirit.
Selwyn could not have been expected to carry on as Foreign
Secretary indefinitely. 'Ernie Bevin and I were good friends. We
watched him die on his feet. He had reached the point when if you
asked him to have a drink he said, "Well, all right, but it will kill
me!"'

But there I had to leave as the German ambassador came across
the lawn from the garden gate.

*In August No. 10 was vacated to enable rebuilding to proceed, and
the Prime Minister and his office moved to Admiralty House in the
opposite corner of Horse Guards Parade (though its front door gave
access to Whitehall). Here he was to stay for three years. Admiralty
House had many of the attributes of No. 10 and to an extent was
more spacious and 'grander' (though lacking a garden except for a
narrow strip of lawn at the back).*

September 4, Sunday   *Rottingdean*
Three quietish weeks, with leisure to settle down at Admiralty
House.

The Olympic Games ('Flop, Flop, Flop,' says the *Mirror* headline
– except for the swimmers); Congo uproar; another salary rise for

the Civil Service (we've never had it so good); and, within the last few days, the announcement that Mr. K. intends to lead the Soviet delegation to the U.N. in the autumn (this caused the only flurry of the recess when Philip de Z. and I recruited the P.M.'s support in Scotland against a Foreign Office proposal to issue an immediate statement).

Mr. Cousins is emerging as a Labour Party king-maker, with a strong dash of Communism. The Labour Party has now lost, not only Bevan, but also Morgan Phillips (a stroke in Scotland), and with Cousins leading a left-wing revolt against the leadership on defence and nationalisation the Party conference could be more than usually interesting.

Three Lobby chums gave me lunch – Harry Boyne at the Theatre Arts, Bob Carvel at the Caledonian (like Dad) and Lawrence Thompson at Rules (also like Dad).

Harry Boyne admires Coote[12] and quotes his leader, on Salisbury's resignation, written in twenty-five minutes, which he believes had a decisive effect on Tory Party thinking.

Bob Carvel reported that the *Herald* had been negotiating with him about becoming their Lobby man under the new regime, but he has decided against it, partly because it would prejudice his television opportunities. In talking about the background of the Caledonian Club he said that in the past, at any rate, it had been High Tory, to the extent that his father was reprimanded by the committee for taking Stafford Cripps there when Cripps was Chancellor. As between Tories and Gaitskell Labour he thinks it is only a change of management.

Lawrence Thompson confesses to disappointment with the Lobby job and disappointment in many of his Lobby colleagues, though he praises David Wood and Francis Boyd. He admits that he can offer no serious criticism of the Government, or suggest anything that it ought to be doing that it is not doing, but he suspects that defence policy is in a genuine muddle and has doubts about economic policy (with more expertise he thinks he would be able to detect serious flaws). He is a dedicated European and dismisses counter-arguments.

I sought an audience with Norman Brook to raise points about Cabinet committee organisation on the information side. He wishes the P.M. would take a real holiday and sees no reason for not doing so. Had I come by car, or had I preferred to walk, he asks. What is the significance of that? He had lunched with Winston at Chartwell the day before and found him remarkably buoyant.

[12] Sir Colin Coote, managing editor, *Daily Telegraph*, 1950–64.

September 18, Sunday   *Rottingdean*

The P.M. came back from Scotland on Wednesday and is now immersed in all the pother of whether or not to go to the U.N. – thought it does not seem to be fussing him unduly. I rang him early on Friday morning, when he had no engagements, and said I'd like to have a gossip. He was in bed. This was my first visit to the Admiralty House bedroom – pleasant enough, with windows over-looking Horse Guards. He was sitting up, wearing a brown cardigan (darned at the elbows), with the morning newspapers scattered over the bed.

We talked first about a memo I had sent him about meetings with the Press during the next few months. Then looked at coal prices (not worried about the wail of anguish and anger from the industry – they'd hate it if Government put up a subsidy: I doubt if it was as simple as that though broadly I don't disagree). So to rents ('It will blow over') and defence. Then we get down to the real topic.

I start provocatively by saying that I assume he will go and he bridles a little but then looks at me and a twinkle comes into his eye. 'That's not at all to be assumed,' he says. The most important thing for us at the moment is a solution to the E.E.C./E.F.T.A. problem. We are now in a better posture with them and must take their attitudes into account: already de Gaulle has sent a message to say that he hopes the Prime Minister will *not* go. It is true that one might win Adenauer's support since Germany is not a member of the U.N. and if K. raises Berlin he might be glad to have a strong voice to put the counter-arguments (though the P.M. is at some pains to emphasise that Alec Home is an absolutely first-rate speaker on the great occasions). Then there is the question of whether a speech in the vein of his last letter to Khruschev ('I really do not understand what you are up to') is enough – it would have to be backed by something more positive and constructive. I argue the importance of not letting K. get away with it with the uncommitted, especially with the newly joined uncommitted, and he accepts this, as also the danger of the Communists appearing to take the U.N. seriously and the West not (though here we are being helped by the Soviet attitude on the Congo). As to the U.N., there is always the possibility (as Dulles sometimes speculates) that the U.S. would get fed up and pull out, in which case the whole thing would probably fold since it was kept going by American money. Those are some of the pros and cons and he will not make up his mind until he has heard from the Commonwealth Prime Ministers, and from Alec Home after the latter has had discussions in New York and

120

Washington. As to timing, if he went it would probably be the week beginning the 26th and he would probably have to spend a week there which would spoil his proposed defence weekend at Chequers – a bore when they had all been working so hard with this weekend as the intended climax.

On defence, I had earlier seen Harold Watkinson[13] with Charles Hill. We have been trying to infiltrate into defence public relations (with some encouragement from the P.M.) and I had done a basic paper plus questions. Watkinson is a man of many merits, but apt to be prickly if he thinks criticism is implied. Charles Hill concluded that we would not get anywhere but I am not so sure.

September 30, Friday   *Rottingdean*

A week's leave at home, having been omitted at the last moment from the entourage travelling to New York – victim of a Foreign Office ploy aimed at Freddie Bishop. After names of the party had been telegraphed to New York, a long cable came from Home which included a comment that the Prime Minister's party seemed rather large and might excite suspicion that we were aiming at a summit. This is so off line that other causes must be sought. It can only stem from the perpetual resentment of the Foreign Office against others than themselves having the ear of the Prime Minister on international occasions. If the Prime Minister *must* interfere in foreign affairs then they will see to it, if they can, that he is in their hands and theirs alone. One recalls Selwyn in Paris on Freddie as 'Sir Horace'. The Prime Minister was determined that Freddie should go but felt that he had to make a gesture to keep new boy Home happy and so there had to be a victim and Evans was the man. It saddens me, not only because at the U.N. I should have been operating on familiar ground, but also because I think the P.M. should keep his personal team intact. The Foreign Office are single-minded in pursuit of their own objectives, and have scant regard for the nuances of the Prime Minister's personal and political position at home. Then again I am deprived of an important piece of inside experience which can only lessen my ability to talk with knowledge and confidence. The continuity is broken. If the Prime Minister cannot see all this – or, seeing it, not consider it important – then has not the time come for me to try and depart?

Before he left the Prime Minister acquiesced in my contrivings to feed in Oliver Woods, who has now left the colonial pastures of *The*

13 Minister of Defence, 1959–62.

Times for wider editorial responsibilities. It went well and Oliver was delighted.

On the international scene the P.M.'s line was, 'You can't help liking the old rascal, K. He is the old Russia – unlike the thin-lipped people around him (looking at me). Of course there is nothing to be done for the time being. There can be no reconciliation between K. and Eisenhower. So, I think I shall say to him, "Well, you said after Paris you meant to let the dust settle. You haven't exactly done that, but no matter. What we have got to do now is to decide how to play the hand next February or March when the new president is in office. For the time being, of course, we have to go on with play-acting!"'

On Eisenhower: 'A nice man, with vision. He does not really understand or like the people round him – the hard-headed politicians. That is why he likes coming to London. He feels he can talk just as he likes when he comes here – that we don't want anything from him.' Then a memory of the dinner that Ike had for his wartime comrades during his London visit last year. 'I said I would go only if I did so as the Minister Resident in North Africa and not as Prime Minister. I sat at the far end of the table next to a nice American general named Goodpaster. Ike called down the table to me, "Hey, Harold, did you ever see so many generals in one room before?" My answer was, "I don't know about that, but certainly I've never seen so many authors in one room before."'

On the Monckton Commission report: the importance of trying to get it into perspective. All the controversial bits will leak and all the pieces that people will get angry about. What Monckton really says is that it is vital to keep the Federation together, but to do that a lot of concessions will have to be made. (I had an opportunity to take this line when James Margach rang me to report a massive leak from Salisbury on which both the *Sunday Times* and *The Observer* intended to lead. This leak I reported to the Prime Minister at Chequers where Sandys had gone direct from the aircraft on his return from central Africa.)

The Prime Minister scored a considerable personal success with his speech to the General Assembly of the United Nations, aided by his parliamentary style and by his good-humoured skill in handling interruptions from Mr. Khruschev, who was at one time banging his desk with his shoe.

October 8, Saturday   *Rottingdean*
P.M. arrived back from New York on Thursday. I had sent telegrams about meeting television and the Press on arrival and he

had agreed, provided he could see the questions to be asked by the television interviewers. This I duly organised. The aircraft had stopped at Bermuda and the Azores so that the flight had been less tiring than it often is and he was relaxed and amiable. I had prepared briefs, particularly on defence and on points arising from the Labour Party conference. It went more smoothly and with less irritation than most airport occasions, and his opening statement dominated the television evening bulletins.

He returned with the limp which the Press had already noticed in New York and he was asked about it. Patting his left thigh, he said it was a legacy of the war wound he received in 1916 – it gave him pain if he became tired. In fact, he had to have treatment on both Friday and Saturday mornings at St. Thomas's Hospital.

On Friday I had a brief encounter with Lady Dorothy who has been in the news by reason of getting a ticket from one of the new traffic wardens. She looked tired and wearily enduring. Oh, how she hated London, was (cheerfully) her theme. I suggested that she would at any rate be escaping to Scarborough next week, at which she threw up her hands and exclaimed, 'With all those Conservatives!' She asked how Harold had got on in New York: how does one answer questions like that?

October 23, Sunday   *Rottingdean*

The P.M. needs increasingly to rest his leg. Tim Bligh reports that on returning from the Tuesday audience last week he was whimsical about it in the lift, but then stamped round the drawing room, swearing and saying he did not know what he was going to do about it. He went on to say that he had told the Queen that he might have to resign (apparently she did not react with the consternation he had expected). To Tim he said he thought 'We'd really better start thinking about the succession.' Yet after calling off attendance at the Covent Garden gala performance for the King and Queen of Nepal he travelled overnight to Scotland for a shooting party with the Homes (providing a comical picture in the *Mail* showing him sitting on a shooting stick, knees together like a modest Victorian maiden).

During the week I arranged for him to see Don Cook, who is leaving London to become chief European correspondent of the *Herald-Tribune*, based in Paris. Sign of London's declining importance? The encounter took place in the inner drawing room at Admiralty House – and what a lovely room it is. High-ceilinged and vast, yet so perfectly proportioned that, as the P.M. said, one can sit in it alone and not feel overwhelmed. The fireplace is superb. On the table, beside the fireplace, Lady D. had put a vase of pink roses which, against the background of white marble, was a touch of perfection.

The week also saw the drama of the extinction of the *News Chronicle* and the *Star* – sordid and undignified because of the secrecy and deception that went with it. With the *Mail* absorbing the *Chronicle*, Tommy Thompson came to see me to try to extract a message from the P.M. I drafted one but on balance thought it should not be sent and he agreed. How right this was has since become apparent. His own reaction was that the collapse was inevitable given excessively high wages and restrictive practices. When I took the draft to him he was in the study, sitting in an armchair with only a table lamp to light the pages of his book. This is genuine Macmillan. One might have expected a certain feverishness in catching up on accumulated jobs, not least preparation for the Party conference at Scarborough and the defence talks at Chequers.

Fleet Street has since been having a great (and angry) post mortem. One thinks chiefly in personal terms, however, and I wrote to David Willis, Lawrence Thompson and Bob Carvell. From David there has so far been no reply, but Lawrence and Bob say, in effect, that for them the future is not necessarily grim. Lawrence has refused a transfer to the *Mail*. Bob has joined the *Evening Standard*: who adjusts to whom?

Lately I have not been seeing much of Charles Hill, but we had an opportunity for a gossip when he addressed the Royal Commonwealth Society. We noted that the political writers are chiefly interested at the moment in Labour Party dissensions as Wilson steps into the arena to challenge Gaitskell for the leadership. He thinks one must begin by recognising that the leadership is decided by the Labour Party Members in the House and that their main preoccupation is to stay as Members: they will therefore be intent on getting the sentiment of their constituencies which is likely to be pro-Gaitskell. This is also true of most of the trade union Members since they do not necessarily depend financially on their unions and the House of Commons always casts its spell over them and commands their first loyalty. On the Tory Party succession, he thinks that at the moment Rab is out alone, notwithstanding the Macleod achievement at the Party conference (backbenchers don't attend the conference). He himself would canvass for Rab because he thinks the succession is due to him, though he does not think he would get an appointment in a Rab administration.

Neil Cairncross has a good anecdote about Rab whom he accompanied on a visit to a police college in the north of England. Knowing that the board considered that the dormitories were too small and proposed to lobby the great man for funds, Neil gave him due warning. As expected, the chairman got Rab into a corner and spoke at great length about the dormitories. Forewarned, Rab's only reaction was to say thoughtfully, 'I think I shall wear my hat.' Another harangue followed and Rab then said, 'You see, I shall be able to raise it when they salute me at the parade.'

October 30, Sunday   *Rottingdean*
The P.M. agreed to have a valedictory talk with Robert Manning who is returning to the States after his stint in London for *Time/Life*, Bob seemed somewhat muffled, and the thick lenses of his spectacles added to the feeling that though there is a shy and sensitive creature lurking in the undergrowth you never really get a full view of it. The P.M. tried to put him at his ease by showing him that magnificent view of St. Paul's that you get so unexpectedly from Admiralty House when looking along Whitehall Place.

The P.M. would not be drawn – obviously – on topics like Nixon and Kennedy, but waxed philosophical instead. The uncertainties of our day arose partly because great empires had faded or been destroyed – the Turkish, the Austro-Hungarian, the British. That might or might not be a good thing, but if you destroyed great systems of government and administration and put nothing in their place then, inevitably, you had chaos. After the collapse of the Roman Empire came 500 years of the Dark Ages. It was all very well to pull things down – and the Americans had helped to pull down the British Empire – but it was as well to know what you intended to put in their place. In Russia they had substituted an idea – Communism. It was no doubt a bad idea but it served its purpose. What was the West going to do? Return to Christianity? For our part, in our small way, we had the opportunity to experiment with the Commonwealth as a system of partnership between people of different race, background and tradition. So to Britain and Europe. He was not afraid of confederation and de Gaulle would have nothing closer than that. Politically the difficulties were not insuperable, and given the political will the technical problems would be overcome. Then back to the thought about Atlantic union. On the problem of organising financial aid for the Third World – one had to be selective. In the east, India was all-important: if India went Communist so would all the rest.

Finally, what really worried him was the possibility of an economic slump.

The Prime Minister has inhibitions about having Admiralty House on this year's Christmas card (abusing the hospitality of someone unspecified) and decided he would like a photograph of himself and Lady Dorothy with the scaffolded No. 10 in the background. I thought that this might be poor symbolism, and so did Lady D., but we clambered about on the site and suddenly, as we were leaving, I saw precisely the right background, so that has now to be organised.

Lady D. always sees him as husband rather than great man and talked doubtfully about the wisdom of chatting, as he had done at Scarborough, about resigning. On the family element in that day's minor Ministerial changes, she said that it had been hard lines on Maurice to be the son of the P.M.

The Press inevitably made something of the Devonshire[14] appointment, but it could have been worse.

This week, for the second in succession, the American group – or, at any rate, the aggressive Graham Hovey, who has a bee in his bonnet about summitry – harassed me about the P.M.'s alleged addiction to summitry at any price, with some emphasis on the implication that he was two-faced in talking about it to his allies – this being based on a reported statement by Khruschev that he had taken the precaution of tape recording his talks in New York with the P.M. I became tough and rounded on him (and them) for falling for elementary suspicion-sowing tactics of this kind. Soundings afterwards with Drew Middleton and Dick Wald suggested that no bones had been broken: they felt I had been a bit sharp but that Graham had asked for it.

Leonard Miall gave me a pleasant visit to the Television Centre on Friday, centred on an excellent lunch in one of the private dining rooms. With him was John Grist, producer of their political programmes (television). I talked about the burden of responsibility that fell on them in shaping discussion on critical subjects, quoting as an example a discussion this week about facilities for American Polaris submarines in Scotland: dominated by Paul Johnson, it must surely have spread alarm and despondency in the general public and given encouragement to the unilateralists.

Roy Lewis also gave me lunch (at the Saville). He is going to Washington to represent the *Economist*. I tried to get him to define

[14] Duke of Devonshire, the Prime Minister's nephew by marriage, appointed Parliamentary Under-Secretary for Commonwealth Relations October 1960.

failings in the Government, but did not get anything to bite on. That is always the trouble. Though one gets allusions to problems (the P.M. would call many of them 'situations') they are rarely coupled with constructive criticism of policy.

I thought Ernest Marples put up a deplorable performance in the House on railways in Wednesday's debate, but perhaps the good sense is being held back for the White Paper which is to cover the Stedeford report. Marples is disliked in many quarters, chiefly on the grounds that he is too 'slick'. There is some danger that the lash will fall on the P.M. for keeping him in an office as important as this at this time.

The week saw Randolph Churchill winning his action for slander against Gerald Nabarro, and conflict developing in the Labour Party about the leadership. With Gaitskell fighting Wilson and Churchill fighting Nabarro life is just too easy for the Government.

November 6, Sunday   *Rottingdean*

A week of no great excitements but plenty of interesting encounters.

Michael King and Sidney Jacobsen of the *Daily Mirror* took me to lunch; James Holburn, editor of the *Glasgow Herald*, came in for a talk; we had the Lobby for drinks at Admiralty House for the first time; Charles Hill had our old friend the Lord Mayor of Lima at his office for a sherry; and there was the commotion of the first week of the new session, with the Queen's Speech and a spate of Bills.

Michael King, with that odd mixture of aloofness and friendliness, praised Ormsby-Gore (though not thinking him a major figure) and Ted Heath; noted differences in emphasis between Macmillan and Home; and said it was a mistake for me not to go on the great international jamborees.

James Holburn could think of no serious criticisms to make of the Government; showed scorn for those who despised washing-machines and other symbols of the affluent society; and said that there would be no serious objection to the Polaris base in the Clyde (it did, in fact, cause me some hard talking, because the State Department lapsed into insensitive chatter).

With John F. Kennedy elected President of the United States there was a spate of speculation about what this would signify in international affairs and in Anglo-American relations.

November 12, Saturday   *Rottingdean*

The P.M. is feeling his age, chiefly in reaction to the Kennedy victory in the American presidential election. I found him brooding in the Cabinet room on Wednesday morning over the *Mail* cartoon showing the young and eager Kennedy and Nixon hauling the bath-chairs of Macmillan, de Gaulle and Adenauer 'into the twentieth century'. He had torn it out of the paper. 'I don't think it's quite fair,' he said, and then, as an afterthought, 'They don't even seem to know which century we're in.'

With me he continues to be patient and friendly. I drew his attention to the Drew Middleton article in the *New York Times* on Britain going neutralist, with the Government doing nothing to stem the tide. (Personally I think it is nonsense, but Dick Wald, who took me to dinner with his wife at the White Tower before the eve-of-election American party, said that it was generally believed by the American correspondents and, indeed, by the foreign correspondents as a whole.) The P.M. volunteered to see the group next week and that will be most timely. On Thursday, after the previous week's fracas, they were very earnest and all was sweet-ness and light.

The presidential election party at the Savoy had too many people and too few places to sit. The prospect of standing for seven hours was too much, and I took flight at 1.30 when, on the evidence of the Connecticut and Bridgmont results, the wise boys were already prepared to say that Kennedy would win.

November 20, Sunday   *Rottingdean*

A Macmillan tour de force at the luncheon of the Newspaper Circulation Executives on Friday (in the presence of all, but positively all, Fleet Street top brass). I came in for an emotional compliment when we arrived back at Admiralty House, but it was essentially, as always, his own doing, plus a notable contribution by John Wyndham on political vituperation. However, I had put it together and got right the two serious themes – affluence and greatness – so let me gather rosebuds while I may. Harmon Grisewood on my left said he had not heard the P.M. in better form. On my right I had Oakley Dalgleish, the Canadian newspaper magnate, with black patch over left eye. But with all the strength and greatness of Fleet Street there they could not produce anyone capable of taking a note so that later on Friday I spent much time on the phone trying to get some fuller version available for those (especially *The Observer* and the *News of the World*) whose bosses had returned to their offices saying a full text should be obtained. Today's *News of the World* describes it as 'brilliant and witty'.

En route in the car we talked about the insoluble economic

problems of Northern Ireland (Brookeborough had been at Admiralty House immediately before lunch), and the spanner the P.M. had thrown into the Covent Garden Bill (espousal of the idea of building it over Kings Cross).

His meeting with the American group also went well – once he had got going. Despite a reading of the riot act by Drew Middleton on secrecy the next day brought a call from a reluctant Bob Carvell to say, 'The *Evening Standard* understands that the Prime Minister saw a group of American correspondents privately last night and said he was in favour of Atlantic Union. Is this true?' With Bob it was possible to talk frankly and we left it that if the *Standard* really wished to pursue the matter he would put the question to me formally tomorrow. When he did ring it was to say that he did not wish to put the question, and he felt it was ninety-five per cent certain that the *Standard* would not run a story.

But here it is again – the impossibility of saying anything to the American group without having it immediately blabbed all round Fleet Street (and garbled in the telling). I spoke to a sad Drew Middleton who thought that the group might have to be disbanded and reconstituted on a smaller scale a little later on. ('There are only four or five who matter anyway!')

While they were at Admiralty House the P.M. took them through the inner drawing room and the dining room (table laid for two), and they, like others, seemed to feel that going back to No. 10 would not be easy. Afterwards the P.M., Philip and I gossiped over a final drink and he came to the top of the stairs to see me off.

At the beginning of the week I was summoned to the Norman Brook presence to talk about arrangements for the Central African review conference, and afterwards he went on chatting in the nice way he does – about the Prime Minister and retirement and about his own plans. He didn't feel, he said, that he would be able to carry on for more than another couple of years without having a physical and mental breakdown. I expressed astonishment – a seemingly less harassed and fitter man it is difficult to imagine – and he then said that might seem to be so but, in fact, he was doing the rounds of Harley Street.

I was dismayed during the week to find that the recommendation Charles Hill and I had put in for a C.B.E. for Staccy to mark his twenty-five years in the Lobby had not got through the selection committee. I waxed vastly indignant and Tim Bligh responded nobly but with a choice of an 'O' now or a 'C' probably in the Birthday Honours. I opted for the 'C' later.

November 27, Sunday   *Rottingdean*

Sheila Minto passed her driving test at last and the temperature of Admiralty House should be reduced.

For me a disillusioning week, first with the *Standard* feeding their garbled account of the P.M.'s talk with the Americans into the Lambton column. Today the *Sunday Express* and the *Dispatch* are happy to base their main editorial page feature on this same garbled account – and this despite the fact that in Rome the P.M. had denied its accuracy and developed the theme just as he had developed it with the Americans. Another repercussion is a wail of anguish from the American agencies, in the persons of Gavshon and Thaler, who also alleged that some of the Americans had written it up with undisguised attribution. Then, of course, to keep the pot boiling, several of them rang John Russell[15] to invite a Foreign Office interpretation.

Next, despite recent reassurances from the Lobby about observing the rules about final revises, there were two flagrant breaches on the police pay report.

Finally we had *The Times* messing up the information given to the Lobby about the Prime Minister's weekend arrangements. When I protested they put it right the next day with a bland lie, 'The Prime Minister has slightly changed his arrangements for the weekend.'

However, there was the pleasantness of being James Margach's guest at a Guinea Club lunch. Their guest of honour was the Lord Chancellor, Lord Kilmuir, attired in knee breeches ready for the Woolsack, and very good he was, too, though Guy Eden matched him. A politician, he said, must be perceptive but also ruthless – a good dispenser as well as a good picker: he must respect Parliament as an institution, and immediately recognise and applaud a great parliamentary performance, even at his own expense. Finally, a sigh about his own fame – as Rex Harrison's brother-in-law!

December 11, Sunday   *Rottingdean*

A rash of Press attacks on the Prime Minister, including Cassandra in the *Mirror* and Paul Johnson in the *New Statesman*. Probably they don't matter very much because they are plainly journalistic fireworks, and do not contain criticism of substance. But there is certainly a phase of doubt. At the Lobby annual lunch I sat next to Lord Mancroft who summed it up in recording the comment of his Norfolk farmers on the Devonshire appointment –

[15] Head of News Department, Foreign Office.

'Mac went a bit far that time': it would be all right, however, as long as Mac continued to deliver the goods.

As Lobby chairman, Barney Keelan put on a scintillating performance. He gave himself a good start with, 'Lord Chancellor, Your Grace, My Lords, Mr. Wedgwood Benn, ladies and gentlemen'. Later we had the art of interpolation. 'Within these four . . . rococo . . . walls.' 'With circles under our eyes . . . well informed, of course.'

Mancroft said that he missed the camaraderie of politics. Isaac Wolfson considered that if he hired you he hired you for the whole time. For twenty-five years nobody had said 'Poppycock' to him, and it was a new experience for him. It was all business and nothing but business.

On the Atlantic union row I had words with Drew Middleton about his follow-up piece on the parliamentary questions. I thought it deplorable, and the *Standard* exploited it, of course. He turned up at Thursday's meeting but broke it up before it really got going. Probably it springs from resentment about criticism of his 'Britain going neutralist' articles. 'He gets it all at the Garrick,' was Bill Stoneham's comment. John Russell helped to keep the ball rolling with some gratuitous spokesmanship in Rome which got picked up in the House: at least it enabled me to point the moral.

The P.M. gave a strange party at Admiralty House on Thursday evening for private secretaries and other civil servants who had served in his immediate entourage during the last twenty years, with John Wyndham the only notable absentee (performing his duties at Lewes Assizes as High Sheriff). Those invited included Makins, Reilly and Kirkpatrick (all his Foreign Office boys have ended at the top), Bridges and Brook as Cabinet Secretaries, Parliamentary Private Secretaries from Bevins to Barber, and Peter Brown to represent public relations in Housing days. Those days the P.M. described as the most exciting of his career. 'Then the dear old Treasury, the Balliol of Whitehall. I never quite understood what it was all about.' I asked Roger Makins if in 1942 he saw Macmillan as a future Prime Minister, to which he replied, 'Foreign Secretary certainly. He showed immense talent for diplomacy.' Alcohol flowed freely, including champagne, and it developed into an uninhibited wagging of tongues. To me the P.M. talked about all the trouble 'your Americans' had caused him, though he treated it philosophically. I asked why he had dealt so gently with Lambton's unpleasantness, to which he answered, 'Oh, you don't knock down one of your own people.' Lady D. said she had been interested to read in Cassandra how many relatives she was supposed to have:

some of them she had not heard of before and she had gone through the list (producing a pencilled note from a pocket book). She let me have it and in the fullness of time it should help to stop some of the nonsense.

Footnote:

When the P.M. speaks informally he tends to do a kind of soft-shoe shuffle – a sliding step forward, then back, then rapidly with the other foot. Slow, slow, quick, quick, slow. He is skilled in introducing sentiment which imposes silence on the audience – to the extent that you suddenly become aware of the loud tick of the grandfather clock.

Christmas begins to be intrusive. The Commonwealth group gave Jimmy Miller and me their annual lunch at the Waldorf. What excellent companions they are. Next week there is the Press Gallery cocktail party, and after that the No. 10 internal party.

I was summoned to a session with Ernest Marples on his White Paper publicity, and found him rather readier to listen than reputation had anticipated. But he didn't offer me coffee from the large flask to which he kept returning.

December 26, Monday   *Rottingdean*

Hugh Greene and Harmon Grisewood gave me lunch at Broadcasting House just before Christmas. Hugh recalled one of the few comments on Suez attributed to Winston (on the authority of Colville): 'I would not have dared – but had I dared I would not have dared to stop.' I paraded my thoughts about the use of Ministers in television magazine programmes and they thought they had better invite me back later on with Baverstock and Peacock. On Winston, I suggested that they should have a poem by Betjeman on the stocks.

1961

New archbishops — Fleet Street tycoons — Rhodesian tangle — exit South Africa — lunch at Key West — Gagarin — Macmillan at bay — knocking at Europe's door — Berlin Wall — Macleod moves up — television romp — de Gaulle at Birch Grove

A message of greetings from Mr. Khruschev heralded the arrival of 1961. 'I remember with satisfaction the useful meetings I have had with you during the past year,' he told the Prime Minister.

Fleet Street, however, was in a carping mood, and the more unfriendly critics spared the Prime Minister no barbs. 'He is a very empty man,' pontificated Malcolm Muggeridge. Arthur Butler reported in Reynolds News, rightly or wrongly, 'Some disgruntled Party members believe that 1961 may be the last full calendar year they will have to put up with the whims and the wiles of the man many now call MacTarnish.' Who the 'many' were he did not specify but they were not enough to give the tag currency. Nor did the Pictorial's 'Harold MacBromide' make any headway in replacing 'Supermac'.

To an extent these rumblings reflected the absence of major political excitements. Perhaps it is a good precept for Prime Ministers to keep events moving. However, as Peregrine Worsthorne noted, a 'fresh season of top billing' lay ahead, 'with the Commonwealth conference as the first act, the West Indian tour as the second, and his meeting with President Kennedy as the spectacular climax'.

In the meantime political headlines made the most of divided opinions on the future of the Central African Federation, the immediate point at issue being the next constitutional advance in Northern Rhodesia. A White Paper containing proposals for this next step was due to be published during the second half of February, and a substantial number of Tory backbenchers clearly felt that Iain Macleod, the Colonial Secretary, was prepared to concede too much

133

to black nationalism and, in so doing, might bring down the Federation. Ninety-six signed a Motion which was regarded as a warning to the Government in general and Macleod in particular. When the White Paper came it involved controversy but no catastrophe, though Lord Salisbury made the headlines with a reference to Mr. Macleod as being 'too clever by half'. 'Bobbety Rides Again,' said a Mail cartoon, with Harold Macmillan and his colleagues cowering beneath the table as the angry marquess appears with his six-shooter blazing.

Fleet Street tycoonery also made the headlines when Roy Thomson and Cecil King wrestled for control of the Odhams publishing empire. They were chiefly concerned with the women's magazines, but political interest focused on the fate of the Daily Herald and The People, both published by Odhams. Cecil King won the battle and gave a guarantee that the Herald would be kept alive for at least seven years. The Prime Minister was put under pressure to intervene but refused to do so, though he announced the setting up of a Royal Commission on the Press.

Archbishops as well as Press tycoons engaged the Prime Minister's attention with the necessity to make recommendations to the Queen following the retirement of Dr. Fisher as Archbishop of Canterbury. The choice fell on Michael Ramsey, then Archbishop of York, so that a new Archbishop of York had also to be found. This was Dr. Donald Coggan, Bishop of Bradford.

January 22, Sunday   *Rottingdean*

The Ramsey and Coggan archbishoprics were well received, though the Press (except the *Financial Times*) had somehow contrived to see Ramsey as well down the field. They began with a tendency to run Robert Stopford hard (Redfern, in the *Express*, mentioned him in his Tuesday morning scoop about the retirement). This worried me because I knew he was not up with the leaders and (remembering that he conducted our wedding ceremony in West Africa) I did not wish to see him embarrassed or hurt. Accordingly I took it on myself to suggest to the Lobby that they should not look in his direction. David Wood and Francis Boyd ran it rather hard, but it had the desired effect though some of the ecclesiastical correspondents remained incredulous, which was silly of them.

Other nice points during the week included treatment of the invitation to Andrew Devonshire to attend the Kennedy inauguration (political connotations seen in an invitation arising from family links), and the Queen's involvement in a tiger hunt at the beginning of her Indian visit.

Arrangements are going ahead for the Prime Minister's West Indian tour, followed by the first meeting with Kennedy in Washington. I shall be making my number with the new White House Press Secretary, Pierre Salinger. There was a nice letter about him from Jim Hagerty, saying not least, 'Won't you please treat him gently as you have treated me.'

On Wednesday I had been invited to lunch at Thomson House by J. M. Coltart, the power behind the throne in the Thomson empire, but since Roy Thomson had returned from Canada the previous day it became *à trois*, with the great man himself as host. He is as plain, uninhibited and friendly in disposition as reports had said. He looks more in this character when he takes off (to wipe them) those thick-lensed spectacles.

Since we touched on some matters of practical significance in the discussions going on about magazine projects I made an official note afterwards which led to action on the Charles Hill front.

For the rest he talked enthusiastically about the *Sunday Times* and about the success they are beginning to have in re-establishing the Kemsley provincial papers as genuine local papers instead of pale reproductions of a Kemsley House master print (he spoke especially of the *Western Morning News*, and said that they now strongly hoped to achieve the same results with the *Sheffield Telegraph*, which had been the weakest of the chain: he and Coltart praised Gordon Linacre whom I mentioned as a colleague at Sheffield in the 'thirties).

We lunched in the panelled dining room high up in Thomson House in the management suite. He and Coltart have adjoining offices with large windows, giving a sense of space and light despite the floor-to-ceiling panelling which most of the Fleet Street bosses see as their appropriate setting. I was last in the building twenty-five years ago – suppliant for a job and in a high state of nervous tension.

January 29, Sunday   *Rottingdean*

Some preoccupation on the part of Roy Thomson might have been forgiven since he was on the eve of massive tycoonery – negotiations for a merger giving him control of Odhams. But now tycoon King has stepped in and it seems that Thomson must be out-manoeuvred, while there is uproar among the politicians, especially on the Left, since the *Herald* seems to be under threat from the *Mirror*.

Rab had become strangely excited on Thursday by the Thomson announcement. It was 'an abuse of capitalism', he thought, and he had involved the Prime Minister heavily. The latter, from Birch Grove on Friday before leaving for Paris, had put Norman Brook and myself into action, but now, of course, with the King intervention, there is a new situation.

The P.M. also became involved in coping with severe Press criticism (led by the *Mirror*) of tiger shooting activities in India by the Royals. He thought it would be unwise to give way completely, since one thing would lead to another, but hoped it would be possible to avoid photography – assuming that the Queen did not elect to go on some other, more maidenly, expedition. Perhaps it will solve itself by the visit to Nepal being called off.

The White House are making heavy weather of the announcement of the Prime Minister's visit, for reasons which are not entirely apparent, and we shall have a tiresome twenty-four hours.

Domestically there was a desperately alarming time last weekend with Annabel struck down by acute pain in her limbs. It involved an all-night vigil, and four visits from Dr. Butcher, but in the end it appears to have been no worse than rheumatic pain, and she now seems perfectly well and full of energy and activity.

February 4, Saturday   *Rottingdean*
This was a twelve-hour-day, twenty-minutes-for-lunch week – but at the end of it what? Some credit for the P.M. for his handling of the Thomson–King–Odhams uproar: the West Indies – Washington announcement finally out in a sensible manner (but only by a last-minute swerve into common sense by the White House); and a so-far-so-good handling of the crisis now brewing on Central Africa.

The Odhams affair and the possibility of Government intervention had been pushed right into the headlines by Rab, but he has now, under guidance from Cunningham, pulled away, which leaves the P.M. with the baby.

We had a characteristic Macmillan performance. He thought into the issues deep and long, sharpening his ideas (and his phrases) on all of us. Brook was set to work to organise official thinking and drafting. He consulted Ministers in various combinations. And then, overnight, while officials laboured on a draft statement, he dictated one of his own and that in essence was what he used.

Inevitably it put the affair into a long perspective – the age of the editors passing into the age of the barons, passing into the age of the financiers and the managers – and debunking the idea that it was a matter of political power. It is to be seen rather as a problem in economics, in particular trade union economics. As usual he is one jump ahead.

Picking up his theme of the decline of the Press barons, I had come across (in *The Baldwin Age*) the precise terms of the challenge which Baldwin successfully made to Rothermere and Beaverbrook when they made the mistake of demanding, in writing, that he should submit ministerial appointments for their approval as the price of their support. But when I produced it for inclusion in the draft it was already there.

In a gossip (over whisky) in the Cabinet room he embroidered the theme of Baldwin's courage in standing as he did. At that time a very real degree of power rested with the Press barons, and 'a politician must deal with power where he finds it'. Another basic rule for politicians came when we discussed the increase in health charges: 'I wouldn't have the milk as well. Never have two lobbies against you at the same time.'

On Central Africa – now at crisis point with a virtual Welensky ultimatum – he spoke of the tug of war with which he has to contend both here and in the Federation. 'Sandys is very strong. He is a great help to me.' Greenfield[1] came to dinner at No. 10 and is now invited to Chequers for Saturday night. Macleod wanted us to muffle this and at first the Prime Minister acquiesced, but it was so unrealistic (Greenfield himself would have seen to that) that I sought an audience and talked him out of it. This was in the study upstairs. He showed a flash of anger – 'They are making it impossible to do business' – but laughed when I said, 'The sooner they all merge and become women's magazines the better.'

I shan't be popular with the colleagues. Rab, too, had shown a slightly weary resentment that I had put back his Lobby meeting briefly in order to handle the announcement of the P.M.'s visit to Washington – or perhaps he was huffy because it turned out that he had not been told of the West Indies–Washington excursion. 'I hadn't been told about it, you know.'

The *Standard* reproduced in Londoner's Diary the canard about a patronising letter allegedly sent to Kennedy by the P.M., resulting in a brusque reply and a huffy Macmillan. Fortunately, I had a chance of dealing with it both with the Lobby and with the American group, and did so with some fervour. It doesn't seem to be running now, especially with surprise being expressed by Washington correspondents, for example the authoritative voice of Henry Brandon in the *Sunday Times* today.

---

[1] J. M. Greenfield, Minister of Law in the Federation.

February 12, Sunday   *Rottingdean*

Friday saw Central Africa come to the boil without boiling over –
though it was not until 8.30 that we were able to stand down. Iain
Macleod had said that if a telegram to Welensky did not go in terms
that accorded basically with his own thinking he would resign. But
somehow it was patched up enough to see us through the weekend,
with a Cabinet on Monday instead of Tuesday (fortunately the
Greek talks on Tuesday make it reasonable to expect a Monday
Cabinet).

Some papers speculated about a Macleod resignation, especially
after he had failed to satisfy the backbenchers on Thursday. It led to
a Motion being put down which was, in effect, a warning shot across
his bows – and those of the P.M.?

Considering that all the evidence is there to be seen, that we have
made little effort to conceal it, and that much of it has been written
up clearly and well (not least by Wilfred Sendall in this week's
Crossbencher) I am surprised that it has not caused more excitement. Surely its implications are seen, not only in terms of U.K.
politics and the future of the Federation, but also for Africa in
general and in international politics? Once again, it seems, one
must recognise a fundamental disinterest in Africa and the
Commonwealth.

The P.M. announced the Royal Commission on the Press on
Thursday: it was generally well received, except by the *Financial
Times*.

Fleet Street continues to take knocks at the P.M., but if knocks
there have to be this is perhaps the best time to have them. Less
easy to stomach was Maurice Macmillan's attack on Government
leadership during the economic debate. However, the P.M. turned
it neatly during questions on Tuesday. Peart introduced the inevitable supplementary about 'a rift in the family', to which came
the retort, 'The Member for Halifax has intelligence and independence. How he acquired these qualities it is not for me to
say.'

February 26, Sunday   *Rottingdean*

A fortnight dominated by Northern Rhodesia, with even more
drama behind the scenes than the headlines suggested.

Iain Macleod was again teetering on the edge of resignation
(though Charles Hill and I doubted if he would when the crunch
came), while Welensky blustered and threatened from Salisbury,
even to the point of suggesting that he might seize the airfields and
declare the Federation independent.

1961

We had two crisis weekends.

After the first we thought we were through it, and the P.M. slumped into extreme tiredness after the tension had apparently broken. At the reception for the Greek Prime Minister and Foreign Minister on Monday night he steered me into the dining room, which was being used as a service room, and we sat and talked for half an hour until Alec Home came to say that Karamanlis wanted to go home. He was desperately tired, greatly relieved and a little mellow, and he simply wanted to find someone to relax with.

It went something like this: 'We've brought it off . . . They have accepted my formula of 3-3-3 (later Macleod was to claim it as his own) . . . It has been absolute hell . . . Duncan has been wonderful. He is so patient and persistent. He will listen for hours. It pays, though it may seem boring. It's no good being too quick. Iain's a bit like that and so was I when I was younger. But you learn to let them talk. Iain's been very good, too. I couldn't afford to lose him. It would mean losing all the forward-looking people. I thought I was going to lose both a Minister and a continent. The Government might have fallen within a week. On Friday afternoon I really thought he was going to resign. It was all quiet and reasonable – a matter of principle. Nothing petty about it . . . I am tired out. But I recover quickly – though I need two days now instead of one. If I can get away to a book for an hour or two it makes all the difference. Two hours reading Jane Austen puts you right. It's having to see so many people I find so wearing – not the problems . . . It's really very hard the way they take people away from me. Tony Phelps is going now. Just because it is Buggins's turn. They even talk of taking Philip away because of his career. He under-stands the way my mind works. I don't have to explain everything to him . . . I mean to make a really big speech in America – at the Massachusetts whatever it is. I can speak better to the British people from overseas. They talk about the old boy, but I will out-do Kennedy. I shall take the theme of interdependence and bring it up to date . . . This awful Press business. They don't understand. They think every man is trying to become Prime Minister. They don't realise people get really interested in their jobs. Look at Henry Brooke. He is absolutely dedicated. My own three happiest years were at Housing.'

Charles Hill also unburdened himself the next day. He is bored and yearns for a department. If he doesn't get something else he will pack up at the end of the year. By then he would have had ten years as a Minister, including five in the Cabinet. But he would like to see it out with Macmillan. If, as now seems likely, there will be a noisier

Commons he thinks he may get more calls to 'bash', as last year in the pensions debate.

Northern Rhodesia then went back to crisis point. The inner group of Ministers, including Kilmuir and Home, spent most of Saturday with the P.M. Then on Sunday morning the P.M. saw Kaunda and Nkumbula. The Press concluded that Macleod had been bulldozed by Macmillan and Sandys under threats from Welensky, but when it came to the White Paper and the statement to the House on Tuesday Macleod handled it with such cool competence (and effrontery) – as he did with the Lobby afterwards – that the Government emerged in a good posture. This was strengthened in the debate on Thursday by a first-class performance by Sandys which took the next day's headlines for his 'rebuke' of Welensky.

I had an opportunity of talking briefly about it with the P.M. when he sought me out at the Phelps farewell party. He suspects megalomania in Welensky and is still alarmed. The problem is to stop people from doing silly things. Doesn't the Press realise, he asks, what an impossible military situation we are in? When you were building an empire you began with a fort on the coast – like the Danish fort at Accra and the Presidencies in India – and you pushed out from there. If anyone gave you a bloody nose you returned to base and got over it before you pushed on again. But if you were pulling out of an empire precisely the opposite happened. We might not even be able to get over-flying rights. I agreed, but said that it was nevertheless not an argument we could use since we should be calling our own bluff.

It was sad saying goodbye to Tony Phelps. He has always been patient and helpful. On occasions such as this the P.M. produces nice touches of humour. 'At the Treasury he will have nothing to do, of course, except to stop other people from doing anything.'

March 12, Sunday *Rottingdean*

Winston Churchill came to see the P.M. briefly before leaving for his West Indian cruise with Onassis. I was by the tape machine when he came shuffling in with the P.M., and the latter called me over to be introduced, saying, 'He looks after me wonderfully.' Winston has become very tiny, his blue eyes are watery and staring, and there is that pitiful little shuffle with stick. He shook hands and there was a smile, but he didn't say anything. It must have puzzled him since he did not know me from Adam or where I fitted in. But there it was – I had shaken hands with Churchill! By courtesy of Macmillan.

140

We have had the Commonwealth Prime Ministers' conference all week and the second week stretches ahead, with the South African issue due to come to a climax.

March 20, Monday   *London*

Looking back on the week that saw South Africa's departure from the Commonwealth.

At the outset it seemed that there would be no difficulty in reaching a formula based on condemnation of apartheid but without opposing continued membership by South Africa after becoming a republic. Certainly talks with individual Prime Ministers beforehand pointed that way. But as discussion developed opinions hardened, and though a formula could still have been found there was general acceptance that it would have been unrealistic.

So Verwoerd elected to go – in dignity. He made a good personal impression, both in the meetings and on the general public, aided by the gentle benevolence of his appearance. At the end, however, before leaving, he could not resist some barbed attacks on the 'Afro–Asian–Canadian' bloc. Yet one cannot help thinking that had he come on previous occasions, and not Louw, there might have been a different story.

Yesterday's Sunday papers had a great inquest on how it happened, each with a different verdict.

What *did* happen? As I saw it, there was first the Prime Minister's compromise draft which came before the conference on Tuesday morning, and on which I had caused guidance to be given. By the end of Tuesday, however, the position had already so hardened that when I was summoned to join the P.M., Iain Macleod, Norman Brook and Tim Bligh in the Prime Minister's room at Lancaster House it had been assumed that a showdown seemed probable and that the question was how it should be handled. It was Iain Macleod's suggestion that Verwoerd might be persuaded to make a statement formally withdrawing from the Commonwealth. The P.M. promptly called for a girl and dictated the kind of statement that Verwoerd might see fit to make. He then sent Tim to enquire what time Verwoerd went to bed at the Dorchester, with the intention of going to see him at the hotel forthwith. While Tim was doing this I intervened. It would be altogether too dramatic, I suggested, and was likely to be misunderstood, not only by the Press, but also by the other delegations. The Prime Minister accepted this without more ado, and the alternative course was adopted of putting back the session next morning from 9 to 9.45 to enable Verwoerd to come to Lancaster House at 8.45 to see the P.M. as originally planned.

What transpired at the meeting between them I don't at the moment know. Certainly Verwoerd did not immediately take this line when the conference resumed, and the discussion was adjourned until the afternoon to provide time for Makarios to be welcomed. In the afternoon session strong, if not angry, words began to be used (raised voices from the music room) and they adjourned at 4.15, ostensibly for tea. But when they resumed rather more than half an hour later Verwoerd produced his withdrawal statement in terms envisaged at our meeting the night before.

It came as a complete shock to the outside world and, indeed, to the South African delegation, for during the morning their spokesman had been making optimistic noises to the Press. The morning Press had almost without exception reported a 10-1 line-up against South Africa (thus emphasising that this was not a racial line-up) based on talking to the delegations and on a form of words I had devised after talking to Duncan Sandys. This, at any rate, formed a clear background for the announcement when it came – a typewritten communiqué with balloons and insertions in Norman Brook's small, neat handwriting, of which Ann Barker made fair copies for me before it was read to the Press at the front door.

Afterwards I joined the P.M., alone in his room, to suggest that either he should talk to the Press himself or discuss with Duncan Sandys on the telephone the line to be taken at the Press conference at 6.15. He chose not to do it himself, and the briefing he suggested to Sandys should be built round the two basic questions – how did it happen and what now? – on which I said it was vital to have a clear line. He then wanted me to stay and talk, but I wanted to get away to the Press conference and I left John Wyndham with him after he had agreed that I should borrow his car to dash to the C.R.O.

He was in an emotional mood. 'I can't help thinking about all those people in Durban. You remember them, Harold. It wasn't me they were cheering. It was the old country – "home" they called it. It is those people I care about.' Then the effect on his own position. 'Don't think I am under any illusion about it' – putting his hand on my arm. 'It is a defeat. Perhaps my first real defeat. You can imagine the things Gaitskell will have to say. I could retire, of course. But I won't. This makes me all the more determined to go on.'

Considering the cruel load on him he showed extraordinary resilience throughout. The night before, when I went in, he was getting himself a whisky and gave me a broad wink, telling me to help myself.

For the rest, there was a sudden summons the following morning from Tim at Lancaster House arising out of an appeal by the Chancellor of the Exchequer for a Verwoerd declaration that South Africa intended to stay in the sterling area – otherwise sterling was likely to crash around our ears. Verwoerd agreed to do this, but on the basis of a Press question. This had accordingly to be prompted with the P.A. man at the door (the stage father type, with leonine grey hair and a rolled umbrella). When I talked to him before going down to the hall, however, Verwoerd decided to scribble out a statement. He then went down and read it to the P.A. chap and three others who happened to be there. So, briefly, I acted as Verwoerd's Press Secretary.

Altogether a week of drama. What happened was probably inevitable (as we had foreseen), but I felt sorry for the South Africans who, for all their implacable obduracy, behaved with politeness and dignity.

The Prime Minister's tour in the West Indies began in Trinidad on March 24th. From the West Indies it was intended that he should go to Washington for his first, crucial meeting with President Kennedy. In the event a note of drama was struck when a message came to Trinidad from the President to ask if the Prime Minister would interrupt his programme in order to fly to Key West, in Florida, for an urgent meeting about the situation in Laos which seemed in imminent danger of falling to the Communists. A SEATO meeting was about to begin in Bangkok and the President felt the U.S. and Britain should present a united front. He was, in fact, under pressure from the Pentagon to make a military intervention, though doubting whether this would be the right action at this time, especially without the support of the principal allies. The British view was that military involvement should be avoided, if at all possible, and that (to quote Harold Macmillan), 'While planning might go ahead, we must make every effort to persuade the Russians to accept the British proposal for a ceasefire and conference.' The President also felt that this was the wiser immediate course, so that the Key West meeting produced an agreed attitude.

Satisfactory as this was in itself, the meeting also established that the new, 'young' President and the 'old' Prime Minister were strongly in rapport. 'We seemed immediately to talk as old friends,' wrote the Prime Minister. In his book, Conversations with Kennedy, Benjamin C. Bradlee also noted that 'the two leaders had hit it off ever since their first meeting . . . Macmillan had instinctively understood the surest way to Kennedy's affection and esteem – by leavening serious, knowledgable discussion with humour and style.'

Later, in their memoirs, two of the President's top aides were to write in similar terms of this relationship. Theodore Sorensen, his Special Counsel, wrote that 'a fondness developed between them which went beyond the necessities of alliance', while the Press Secretary, Pierre Salinger, spoke of 'a superb working relationship'.

The round trip to Key West represented a journey of 3,600 miles in the Prime Minister's Comet, so that it was a longish way to go for lunch. Before we left I had to placate the five correspondents who had come to the West Indies to cover the tour and now wished to get a lift to Key West in the Comet. However, coverage of the Key West meeting was being arranged from Washington (hordes travelled down) and there was no strong reason why the Prime Minister should make a break with precedence and have his privacy for work and relaxation on the aircraft invaded.

On the Key West expedition the Prime Minister had with him only Tim Bligh and myself, with two of those delightful No. 10 girls (Jane Parsons and Susan Hamlin) to undertake the chores of dictation and typing. In his memoirs the Prime Minister commented, 'It is always more important at these international conferences to have good shorthand girls than to have generals and admirals.'

March 26, Sunday   *En route Trinidad–Key West*

In the aircraft I sit in one of the seats opposite the P.M. who is in his stone-coloured cardigan. He makes himself agreeable. Am I not cold sitting by the window? Why don't I move to the inside seat opposite him? He thinks the reporting and comment in the *Trinidad Guardian* are good, and listens understandingly when I tell him about the disgruntled group left behind in Port of Spain: he will have a talk with them tomorrow, he says, which is splendid. He tells me to read through the telegrams – 'It will need very delicate handling. I suppose I shall have to get Cabinet agreement. I remember Winston. You must bind the Cabinet to you.'

Later, after reading through his papers, he is sufficiently relaxed to doze off, hands folded in lap, head resting sideways on the pillow of the seat – looking very much younger as he sleeps. He wakes suddenly and immediately begins to scribble revisions and additions to the notes on 'who, what, when, where, how'. When that is finished he lights a cigar and reads a novel.

'Do you realise that this is like flying to Cyprus for lunch?' says

Tim Bligh. 'Or Moscow,' I suggest. He asks me to re-draft two bits of the West Indian legislature speech.

I then begin to work out the kind of communiqué we shall have to issue at Key West, assuming agreement. It comes out sufficiently well to try it on Tim. He says, 'Yes, why not try it on the P.M.?' Which I do. He reads it, broods a moment, and then says get it typed.

Arriving over Key West (having flown round Cuba) we are kept in the air while Kennedy lands. He is V.I.P. Code I. We are V.I.P. Code II.

En route Key West–Trinidad

Kennedy is physically and mentally at the double.

At the end of the morning's meeting we trooped from the administrative block to the admiral's house behind it, and there took lunch off large wooden platters in the Anglo-Saxon manner.

At that stage there was an air of gloom induced by an inability to see completely eye to eye. The P.M. muttered to me, 'He is pushing me hard but I won't give way.' But over lunch some cheerfulness began to break through, and by firing in our own drafts, dictated to Jane while the bevy of American secretaries sat around the house, a satisfactory formula eventually emerged. The drafts included my own draft of the communiqué prepared on the aircraft. The P.M. suddenly called for it as he and the President sat at the round table where they had eaten. We had momentary panic before Jane located it, but when it was pushed in front of Kennedy he immediately said it was precisely right and that was that.

There was then the absurd business of reading it to Press, radio and television in the admiral's backyard. Questions were not very penetrating, but two of my answers prompted the television people to want them repeated to cameras. The whole thing was done in that alarmingly unprepared way that seems to be the American method (and to some extent our own on these occasions when the principals are preoccupied with things other than spokesmanship: this, I suppose, is where spokesmen earn their money).

I liked the new Hagerty – Pierre Salinger, plump, friendly and relaxed. His approach is altogether more casual, and some correspondents appear to prefer to be tightly organised.

Now, on the five-hour return flight, we can contemplate the results. The P.M.'s first reaction was, 'Well, I don't know. I think it was all right.' He thought Kennedy 'an attractive young man – willing to listen and not to dominate – easier than the last one – he pushes you hard but doesn't get upset when he doesn't get it all his own way – we had a lot of jokes and banter – they tried some fast ones, of course, and they are tough, but they laugh at it.'

March 27, Monday   *Port of Spain*
We got back at 9.30 in darkness, a small crowd clapping at the airport. Our angry journalists were there – now much less angry – and I was able to placate them further by (a) the P.M.'s invitation to drinks and a talk tomorrow, and (b) my own willingness to join them at the Normandie after dinner for a midnight briefing. (Don Iddon is so much less angry that he says, quite seriously, 'But are you sure you're not too tired?')

We dined – P.M., Sir John Richardson,[2] Tim Bligh and myself – on the verandah above the porch of Government House. The P.M. was cheerful and recalled the first American supply ships arriving in North Africa during the war and unloading nothing but dental chairs.

The A.D.C. was efficient in rustling up transport for me despite the lateness of the hour (a Pontiac taxi), and on arrival at the Normandie I found that Willie Richardson had also assembled the *Trinidad Guardian* people, which was sensible of him. It didn't seem difficult to talk and answer questions for half an hour at a table in the deserted restaurant and they seemed to think it was useful: at any rate Douglas Clark came up with an unusually warm expression of thanks: 'It is incomparable.'

They seemed pleased, too, with their gossip today with the Prime Minister though it tended to drag along the bottom at times. Don Iddon thought it was 'terrific'.

The rapport achieved in the unscheduled talks in Key West was reinforced during the scheduled talks in Washington. They included a final session on board the presidential motor launch Honey Fitz, cruising along the Potomac as far as Mount Vernon, the eighteenth-century home of George Washington. 'The Honey Fitz,' reported one correspondent, 'set a spanking pace. Reporters and photographers were left far behind in the launch they had chartered for the occasion.'

The talks were regarded by both sides as highly successful. Michael King reported in the Mirror, 'Mr. Macmillan has achieved his aim in coming here for talks with President Kennedy. The Prime Minister has established a friendly and close working relationship with the new American President. He has thereby confounded forecasts that

[2] The Prime Minister's doctor.

146

he would find this either difficult or impossible.' But, King added, 'Mr. Macmillan will have a less spectacular role to play in the future, particularly in East–West relations.' Given a strong President there could be no doubt, of course, where Western leadership lay: for Britain what mattered was the degree of influence that could be exercised in Washington, and it was in this context that the Kennedy–Macmillan rapport had special significance. Some British reporting took its cue from a report by Marguerite Higgins in the New York Herald-Tribune that the President had, in effect, told the Prime Minister where to get off. The Express gave banner headlines to the report, as relayed by Douglas Clark, but noted official denials on both sides and observed also that Marguerite Higgins was 'known for anti-British views'.

While in the United States the Prime Minister also talked to the Senate Foreign Relations Committee and made a major speech at the centenary celebrations of the Massachusetts Institute of Technology. In this speech he called for still closer co-operation in the West in defence, economic and political relations. 'Today I say that inter-dependence is not enough. We need unity – a wider unity transcending traditional barriers – unity of purpose, of method, of organis-ation.'

Work on the speech went on to the last minute, as it did with all major speeches, and both on the flight to Boston and in the hotel when we arrived additions and amendments in detail continued to be made. With the British correspondents facing a time-difference of five hours and clamouring for advance copies, I hastily prepared an extended summary containing the principal passages and enlisted the aid of the girls in an all-out effort to get copies typed. Necessarily the copies had to be rough and ready. All is grist to the Fleet Street mill. The Times began its report by drawing attention to 'evidence of some last-minute alteration in the text, arising presumably from his talks with President Kennedy'. However, it went on to use most of the text and to describe it as 'a ringing call for greater unity of the free world'.

From the United States the Prime Minister went to Ottawa for talks with the Canadian Prime Minister – the customary procedure on transatlantic forays. He returned to London on April 12th after three gruelling weeks on the road – Trinidad, Key West, Trinidad, Barbados, Antigua, Jamaica, Washington, Boston, Washington, Ottawa.

April 3, Monday   *Kingston, Jamaica*
The girls are having a rough time, slogging away through the day and into the small hours, with meals on trays.

Getting to know John Richardson. He has a deep interest in people and a gentle bedside manner which extracts inner thoughts. He comes from a Sheffield family and lived there until he was ten. His grandfather Roberts made money in coal, and the Roberts have been Sheffield M.P.'s for three generations. In London, as a boy, he lived in Whitehall Court, his father having been killed during the first world war. His grandfather was a church warden at St. Margaret's and there was the agony of Sunday morning services in top hat and Eton suit, but with the consolation of a visit to the zoo in the afternoon. When his grandfather met parliamentary cronies he was told to go and look at the polly parrots. He doesn't smoke (but would still like to, after many years) and uses no oaths. He has become my champion, and I saw him indignant for the first time when, at the foot of the King's House stairs, he told the A.D.C. how disgraceful it was that I should be in a poor hotel, without a phone.

And the Blackburnes? Kenneth[3] is full of 'flu, with a cold and clammy handshake, but as resolute in duty as ever. For them this is the last lap and their minds are largely on retirement.

We had a lively dinner party at King's House – *en famille* apart from Señor da Cunha, travelling through and invited because he was Brazilian representative in the North African days. He and John Wyndham and the P.M. kept their end of the table going on Algerian reminiscences. John recalled the Maison Blanche air crash when, as he says, he was ahead of the P.M. for the first and only time. The P.M. capped this by recalling the French admiral, also a passenger, who immediately after the crash, went round wringing his hands and crying repeatedly: 'J'ai perdu ma casquette.' He, Macmillan, lying on the ground in agony from burns, was moved to exclaim, 'For heavens sake! J'ai perdu half my bloody face.'

The P.M.'s cheerfulness belied the gout condition which he seems to have developed, causing him to limp and shuffle.

Tim, Jane, Eunice and I played hookey on a Good Friday outing to the north coast, with Yvonne, a Jamaican–Chinese girl, as guide and chaperone. Most of the guiding was done, in fact, by our driver, a cheerful black Jamaican who rocks with laughter when we stop at the roadside for coconut milk and he tells us about the calypso which says that it makes the male animal 'as strong as a lion'. We lunched and bathed at the Tower Isle Hotel.

April 6, Thursday   *Washington*

As we cruise along the Potomac on the *Honey Fitz* the Prime Minister says, 'You remember Harold Evans?' and Kennedy

[3] Sir Kenneth Blackburne, Governor-General of Jamaica.

---

replies, 'Oh yes, he wrote the communiqué at Key West before we started. He'd better write another one now.'

In the saloon there is a television set and a painting of the *Independence* in a storm. The stewards look like Filipinos. On the deck the wind is chilly and I borrow Philip's velvet-collared overcoat. Pierre Salinger says he smokes eight to ten cigars a day, but then concludes that he doesn't really keep count.

April 12, Wednesday   *Ottawa–London*

Two hours to go. The aircraft is hot and stuffy. Norman Brook sits opposite in a navy blue cardigan, dictating at length to Joan Porter, which is hard on Joan at 10 p.m. (though, true enough, it is only 4 p.m. Canadian time). I feel lethargic and muzzy, but that is not so much the aircraft as a tour hangover. In Ottawa I felt overtired, with perhaps a touch of gastric 'flu. The Garners[4] were again the most pleasant and relaxed of hosts. Ottawa seemed grey, miserable and wintry. The Canadians are currently enjoying an orgy of self-analysis and self-criticism.

At Goose Bay (a late switch from Gander) I talked briefly with the P.M. 'Everything in your department', he felt, seemed to have gone well. He didn't mind the Press saying he was under pressure from Kennedy. The time he had spent alone with Kennedy had been all right.

Our best take-home anecdote is of Lady Dorothy finding the P.M. wandering in the corridor outside his bedroom at Rideau Hall, wearing shirt and underclothes but no trousers, and asking plaintively, 'Where is the office? I want a young lady.'

As to the Press, Douglas Clark made the most of Maggie Higgins's snide reporting, but otherwise seems to have written in a friendly vein. The Sunday papers had some peculiar stories written by people of whom I have never heard about 'master plans' and Kennedy 'pressurising' the P.M. Then there was the strange business of the P.M. allegedly 'pressurising' Diefenbaker on West Indian immigration. Ralph Harris (Reuters) said nice things when we parted at Ottawa – but then, of course, he's a nice man.

Shortly after the return to London I accompanied Charles Hill on a long tour through middle Europe – Bonn, Berlin, Warsaw, Vienna, Rome – to assess how well (or badly) the voice of Britain was being heard via the official information services, the British Council and the B.B.C.

[4] Sir Saville Garner, British High Commissioner in Canada 1956–61, subsequently Head of the Diplomatic Service and life peer.

In London the Prime Minister was preparing the ground for Britain to apply for membership of the E.E.C. First the Cabinet had to agree in principle, which it did, and consultations were then put in train with Commonwealth governments. These consultations began with visits to Commonwealth capitals by Duncan Sandys, as Commonwealth Relations Secretary, and four other Ministers. Meanwhile, the Conservative backbenchers had to be carried as a prelude to a statement in the House and a debate timed for the week preceding the summer recess. The negotiations for entry, once begun, would clearly take a considerable time, and while they proceeded the case for entry would have to be firmly established in the country. For my own part, given a Commonwealth background, I was a reluctant convert, finally convinced by the political argument for a united Europe (and perhaps disillusioned, too, by evidence that the Commonwealth vision was fading under the impact of the realities of world and local politics).

Other matters coming to the centre of the stage included the threat to Kuwait by Iraq, leading to a call from Kuwait to stave off the immediate threat by a British military presence. This was effectively supplied by an airlift on June 30th and Kuwait survived. Astonishing, after Suez, that Britain could still make military interventions in the Middle East (as early as 1958 paratroopers had been flown into Jordan at King Hussein's request, though that intervention had nearly been brought to grief at the last moment by Israeli reluctance to grant over-flying rights).

In the Press the Government in general, and the Prime Minister in particular, were being given a rough time for alleged indecisiveness on the European issue and complacency in the face of a deteriorating economic position (in fact, the first pay pause was about to be announced, though the Prime Minister saw it more as a 'touch on the brake').

July 16, Sunday   *Rottingdean*

'Now is the winter of our discontent' – but seemingly there is no sun of York to turn it into glorious summer. Almost without exception the political commentators are firing their barbs at the Prime Minister, with Fairlie leading the pack (how that man twists and turns). 'Dithering' is the cry, initially on the Common Market issue, though perhaps the wisdom of long consideration and non-committal begins to be apparent as the difficulties emerge in their full panoply. Kuwait was timely in the sense of showing decisive action, effectively taken. But now, of course, there hangs over us the sharp deterioration in the balance of payments and the warnings that drastic action is to be taken. Also lying ahead is the showdown on Berlin threatened by Khruschev.

Before Thursday's Cabinet David Eccles told me that he felt seriously worried about the state of opinion in the Party: that same evening, however, the P.M. had his end-of-session assignment with the 1922 Committee and the political correspondents agreed that he had calmed those who had begun to doubt his leadership. He is contemplating a broadcast at the end of the month and I have been discussing its status and form with him. A Party political is not practical: a Ministerial is unsatisfactory on nearly all counts: and so we contemplate accepting a B.B.C. invitation which Harmon Grisewood has already offered by phone. By then there should also be something to be said on the Common Market.

When I was talking to him in the Cabinet Room on Thursday after the Gagarin[5] visit he said, 'I am in a dreamy mood at the moment. When I have decided I shall need your help.'

He is himself fully aware of the dangers, of course. In a semi-serious footnote about an engagement in August he wrote, in effect, 'If, of course, the Government is still in power. Do you think it will be?'

What *does* worry some of us is evidence of a slowing down. He seems unable to sustain the same intensity of concentration and effort over prolonged periods. Yet he still rises splendidly to the occasion, and his standard of effort remains far ahead of most of us.

My week included a successful intervention in the arrangements for Gagarin – in getting out a quick announcement on Tuesday evening (hearing of a *Mirror* build-up), in removing the venue from the House to Admiralty House, and in substituting a silver salver for the stock autographed photograph. The arrangements worked well. We made no effort to organise a camera rota for photographers for the courtyard and this proved justified.

Yuri himself? Smallness: the ready smile: a manner confident and assured without bumptiousness. Some descriptions have exaggerated his good looks. He is pleasant-looking rather than good-looking. He was once a foundryman (say the biographical notes) and he did look to me like a nice Black Country steelworker. He came attended by the Ambassador, by Lieut. General Kaminin (hero of the Soviet Union, really his watchdog), the fluent Boris to interpret and A. N. Other.

The P.M. felt at a loss for conversational gambits, apart from the obvious mutual felicitations, but talked about his frolicsome week-

[5] Yuri Gagarin, the first man in space, April 12th, 1961.

end at Khruschev's dacha. Mr. May[6] produced whisky and soda all round. Gagarin sipped his but left most of it. He refused cigarettes. The P.M. took them round the first floor, including his study, where he flung open the window for the view of St. Paul's to be admired. Then, downstairs, he showed them the Cabinet room, whispering to me, 'Is it long enough?' It was, in fact, twenty minutes which I thought *was* enough. And certainly the Press did not carp, though they had been looking for opportunities to do so.

John Gunther sent me an inscribed copy of his latest book *Inside Europe Today*. 'For Harold Evans – The author of much of Chapter 16 herein – Best thanks and in memory of a splendid talk at No. 10.' Chapter 16 is adulatory about the P.M. At this moment some of it has a hollow ring.

The *Mail* continues in anti-Macmillan vein, with renewed demands that he should 'tell the people'. I was moved to write to Bill Hardcastle to say what the hell good is it trying to tell the people in major speeches, as at Bowood, if the Press don't report them. Possibly, just possibly, an occasional protest has some long-term effect. I shall have a chance to reinforce it when I lunch with him and Tommy Thompson next week. In the meantime Tommy has sent me an unpublished public opinion poll on Berlin. It shows forty-five per cent declaring themselves willing to fight over Berlin if necessary. In sending it on to the P.M. I minuted that I thought it a surprisingly high figure, on which he commented, 'So do I.'

Guy Eden was my guest at the Authors Club. As Beaverbrook's political correspondent for twenty years there must surely be a hard streak in him, but so far as I am concerned he has never been anything but pleasant, considerate and helpful. I discovered that he is an enthusiastic and knowledgeable gardener, rejoicing in the acquisition of a new split-level bungalow at Broadstairs. He advocated toughness when Lobby rules are breached, but agreed that the Lobby is hardly as susceptible to disciplines as in the palmy days of his own chairmanship. He deplored the open noticeboard in the Press Gallery, and the French news agency man wandering at will. He is contemplating memoirs. The Beaver, he said, never sent him a rocket and maintained contact with him after he had left the *Express* organisation. One scoop he recalled was the resignation of Oswald Mosley, resulting from a chance encounter with Bevan as he was leaving the House late at night.

[6] Office keeper at No. 10.

July 29, Saturday   *Rottingdean*

'Macmillan at Bay' said the *Mail* headline on the economic debate. Certainly this is the mood at the moment. Selwyn Lloyd's economic measures had the most universally critical Press that I can remember for any government proposals, aggravated by maladroitness in handling the teachers' pay rise. However, I suspect that this very violence in criticism will cause some tendency to swing back into second and more sober thoughts.

The *Mirror* and *Herald* have launched full-scale personal attacks on the P.M., making the most of quotes from the Tory Press, and this may cause a closing of the ranks on the right. Similarly, the crude barrage of noise directed against the P.M. in the debate cannot but close the ranks of the Tory backbenchers – although some rebellion is inevitable on the Common Market statement next week.

Unhappily, the P.M. was off form when he wound up the economic debate on Thursday, and this has added to speculation about overtiredness and the state of his health. Strangely, he seemed to have no sense of a poor performance when I talked to him on Friday morning. He seized avidly on William Barkley's report in the *Express* which, alone, gave him good marks. The others he tended to dismiss as reports written under editorial direction. 'That at least must be said of the Beaver – he lets his reporters write it as they see it.' I think he is widely off beam. In general the writing in the *Express* is as the Beaver wants it. And the reporting in the other papers came nearer to the general impression, and my own, than Barkley's 'great success' for the Prime Minister. From the Gallery it looked sad. 'He's tired and worn out,' Graham Cawthorne said to me. 'You must get him away for a holiday.'

Yet on the three occasions I had sessions with him during the week he did not seem in the least like that. All three arose from the proposed broadcast 'to the people' at the end of next week.

On Monday (July 24th) Charles Hill and I, plus Philip de Zulueta, saw him in the Cabinet room to decide finally whether or not he should broadcast, bearing particularly in mind that with the Common Market debate extended to two days he could not do it before the Friday of August bank holiday weekend. He accepted that it was then or not at all and decided to go ahead. That decided he said to Charles Hill and myself, 'I'm going into the garden. I've really nothing to do. Come and talk to me.'

So off we went to the narrow strip of lawn which the Ministry of Works has constructed under Lady Dorothy's direction between the house and Horse Guards. Master wears his floppy trilby and decides to sit in the deck chair into which he had at first put me. It's not really a very pleasant afternoon – overcast, rain in the air and just a little chilly. However, he seems to think it is all very good and also says how pleasantly and unexpectedly private it is – notwithstanding the rows of overlooking windows, not only of No. 36, but much of the Admiralty! It is a desultory conversation, but the P.M. gets round to reminiscences of his father and two uncles who all died in their eighties within three months of each other.

On the day of his father's funeral Uncle Fred had a stroke and had to be taken to the London Clinic. He lived in a house opposite the Clinic and had packed into it, in the Victorian manner, an overwhelming profusion of bric-à-brac. Nothing could have been in greater contrast to the austerity of the Clinic. When he called there the day after the funeral, Uncle Fred was saying how nice it was of Harold to come though he was a little worried about how he would 'get back' and didn't quite understand how he had managed to get there. However, said Uncle Fred, all the young women were nice to him and they had even let him have some champagne, though it was a little sweet. Altogether he thought it was not at all a bad place. After running on in this way he again began to worry about how Harold would 'get back' – and at last it dawned on Harold that Uncle Fred thought he had died and was now on the other side.

Of the three brothers, said the P.M., he thought his father was probably the cleverest, but he was shy and retiring. It was he who developed the educational side of the business. On developments in publishing he said that Macmillans had just had a very good year. About two-thirds of their output went overseas so that they were good exporters. I asked about the effect of paperbacks and he referred to the Pan titles, 'You see, we keep a pub as well.' I mentioned Gunther's book and its friendly profile. He said that he thought Gunther wrote well. 'One always thinks how jolly good these books are when they are dealing with other people and other countries. But they seem to have got it all wrong when you read about yourself. They ought to have national editions with the appropriate bits left out.'

We also talked about newspapers and the departed days of the politically powerful Press lords. He wondered whether Thomson could be considered in line for a peerage. After all, Northcliffe, Rothermere and Beaverbrook had all been Ministers of the Crown. I say that I've no doubt that Roy Thomson would be only too happy to accept an invitation to join the Macmillan administration!

And so on – a gossip lasting over an hour at a moment when the

Government is said to be in danger of falling and Macmillan a desperately worried man. He goes on himself pretending that there is a serious possibility that a backbenchers' revolt will cause the Government to fall when the House divides next week at the end of the Common Market debate. In fact, the Whips have counted heads and are absolutely confident. But this and his poor showing in the economic debate make it important that he should do well both in the House on the Common Market and in the broadcast.

'That bully, Philip', as the Prime Minister fondly calls him, was at Birch Grove today. He is more than ever dominating (and domineering) in the Private Office. A formidable figure with his combination of charm, arrogance and ruthlessness. Of the charm I saw something on Monday when he, Marie-Lou[7] and I went to the Associated Rediffusion studios at Wembley to be shown round and dine as guests of David Hennessey, Marie-Lou's brother, who has recently become Director of Features, a promotion over several heads. Reputedly an up-and-coming man, heir to the Windlesham title, twenty-nine, unmarried, chairman of the Bow Group, law at Oxford, the family business (brandy), politics, 3000 off a safe Labour majority at a Tottenham seat in 1959. He left brandy (disappointment to father) because he would have had to do a great deal of travelling and wanted time for politics.

He gave us a conscientious tour of the studios (with lucid explanations of the engineering mysteries) before providing dinner in a converted control room overlooking one of the main studios. We had canteen food served in West End manner. We talked long – chiefly about politics and broadcasting – which kept the waiters until 11, when the vacuum cleaners were whining, but they were content – 'It's all right: double time, you know.'

Footnotes:

(1) Charles Hill and I interrogated Selwyn Lloyd on the eve of his statement on the pay pause. We succeeded in concentrating attention on those questions which were, in fact, those the House and the Press fastened on – except the teachers, on which earlier Charles Hill had taken a solitary stand with his Ministerial colleagues (the failure to reveal the exact terms of the offer left the impression, on which the headlines focused, that the teachers were to get nothing at all, instead of £42 million).

(2) Within hours of Thursday's Cabinet the world had news of the decisions on Kenyatta (via the London correspondent of the *East*

[7] Marie-Louise de Zulueta.

African Standard) and on the Common Market (from Rab at Lobby, chatting gaily about Article 237, causing a flurry at the Foreign Office and a telephone call from Rab seeking reassurance that he had not really sold the pass).

(3) Rab is put out by not being brought into the discussion about the P.M.'s broadcast. He has been under pressure from Toby Low[8] to try to move it forward to earlier in the week. 'You needn't worry, Evans. I shan't try to interfere. I hadn't been consulted at all, you know.' Rab is having to steer delicately at the moment when leadership questions are being so freely discussed (Fairlie has now become his advocate). He has been trying to get the P.M. to name him as in charge of the Government when the P.M. goes to Yorkshire in August, but that isn't likely to happen.

(4) The P.M. says he can't now learn scripts word by word.

August 6, Sunday   *Rottingdean*
A dramatic closing week to the session, summed up in an *Evening Standard* headline, 'Premier Bounces Right Back.'

That was after the speech in which he opened the Common Market debate, but the chronological sequence is: Common Market statement (Monday), Common Market speech (Wednesday) and broadcast (Friday).

The statement had an excellent Press, but, alas, the Prime Minister's meeting with the Lobby was a disaster. He had lunched at Bucks (on top of pills), and though he got through the statement effectively, its success, coupled with post-prandial afterglow, had induced a too lighthearted mood by the time he reached the Lobby room. He opened with a vigorous attack on Douglas Clark, took a swipe at the *Mail*, swung the chairman's gavel perilously backwards and forwards, talked about the trenches and how they enabled you to appear calm when you felt terrified, said that he could still do the eighteenth in four and that he was now going away to let off three or four hundred cartridges – on which cue he did, in fact, suddenly get up and go.

Yet in between he had given them much for rumination and at least one item of news – the likelihood of a meeting with de Gaulle. He insisted on my going down to his room and there I had a dissertation on European history – how ironical it was that this small peninsula attached to the land mass of Asia, thinking itself the hub of the universe, should now be utterly dependent on all the

---

[8] Deputy chairman Conservative Party organisation 1959–63. Later Lord Aldington.

people it had driven overseas by persecution, punishment or poverty.

The Lobby, feeling it necessary to defend Douglas Clark but not quite knowing how to do it, eventually drew back from protesting directly to the great man and wrote instead to me, though declaring it was not a formal protest. For elucidation I tackled Spenny Shew who thought I should simply acknowledge the letter and leave it at that. Pretty pusillanimous, I feel. It would have been better to give themselves a feeling of magnanimity by talking, as some did, of the satisfaction of being treated so plainly as members of the Westminster family.

Following the statement came his splendidly authoritative and vigorous speech on Wednesday. It followed only a few hours after a Tokyo report said he had collapsed from a heart attack. I went on the record with, 'Poppycock and balderdash, and anyhow see for yourselves this afternoon.'

In fact, this carrying of comment and speculation to a ridiculous point was probably a factor in bringing people back to a sense of proportion – as had Fell[9] by his passionate personal attack on the P.M. in the House on Monday. At any rate – to extremes as ever – Thursday's Press was universally approving, even panegyrical, with a notable volte-face by the *Mail* in headline, leader and 'Hardly Hansard' (Tommy Thompson declaring this to be the week when Macmillan won the 1963 election).

Finally, the broadcast. The Central Office had rumbled complainingly in the background about both its desirability and its timing (George Christ, for example, unhappy about not being asked to do a draft). Also there had been a fracas with Independent Television. But in the end its timing proved to be exactly right in that it served to exploit success as well as to wrap up the session neatly, logically and triumphantly.

Just how it turned out such an effective piece of broadcasting goodness knows. It could hardly have been a more tiresome, frustrating and worrying process. Everyone was trying to get into the act. Charles Hill and I did one draft. Norman Collins, ostensibly advising on form of presentation, infiltrated into the drafting process and in particular wanted to reverse the sequence of subjects in the Hill-Evans draft – Berlin ('We stand firm'), Common Market, and the economic situation at home ('Earn first and spend afterwards'). The P.M. then dictated a draft based on the original sequence. This draft I tightened up to reduce it to the right length.

[9] Anthony Fell, M.P. (Conservative) for Yarmouth.

Then Freddie Bishop put in a draft independently. When I talked to the P.M. on Monday he was still thinking about the Collins sequence but decided it would be better as originally proposed. On Thursday evening we had a long session in the Cabinet room with Norman Collins among those present. It was a shambles, but at any rate the argument about sequence was resolved by deciding that the P.M. should begin by saying that he intended to deal with three subjects and naming them. Philip de Zulueta was then left to put the bits and pieces together. With the aid of midnight oil he did an excellent job, but the P.M. also did some midnight re-dictating so that by the morning there was a text which read well.

The recording had been arranged for Friday at Admiralty House after lunch – a sandwich lunch for Philip, John Wyndham, Norman Collins and myself for discussion of any final amendments. Since it was a B.B.C. occasion Norman Collins accepted that it would be better for him to take no part in the production. So I had his black Bentley organised at the Horse Guards door and saw him off with protestations about how jolly nice it had been to meet each other.

The P.M. seemed cheerful and relaxed and wanted to plunge in more or less right away as soon as he had donned his grey suit. John Grist and Anthony Craxton, having been told to be ready at 3, had now to start at 2.30. The P.M. did a pretty successful first run. They had not put it on tape, however, so that it was lost (we ought to make sure that the first run *is* regarded as an actual run and not simply a rehearsal). The text had in fact sagged here and there in the middle, and Philip, John Grist and I did some hurried cutting which in the main the P.M. accepted. This took a little time, especially as we decided to have the opening and closing passages complete on the teleprompter. The first actual run was good, but the teleprompter had not really helped and also the P.M. had used the original figure of £300 millions for invisible earnings losses as against the new figure of £200 millions. He had been given three hundred for the debate and it had stuck in his memory: hardly surprising that our finances are in a mess when the Treasury are prepared to vary their estimates by £100 million from one day to the next! So he ran through it again, minus teleprompter, and this time it went sweetly enough, despite some initial hesitations which on the whole we thought more effective than not.

He refused to see it played back, and I took Grist and Craxton for a drink with him in the drawing room. He chatted lightheartedly, among other things about the impossibility of painting Churchill as he is because his face is completely expressionless. He has to be painted in one of his roles. This was true of Garrick also. He is proud of his hands and the rings he wears, especially the Lord Randolph ring.

With the whole operation finished by 5 the B.B.C. were able to get the text out in good time, and this contributed to the excellent Press on Saturday morning, notably in *The Times*, *Telegraph* and *Mail*. Today, Sunday, the *Express* (leader) and *News of the World* (Randolph Churchill) acclaim it also.

So within three days we see a transformation in the Prime Minister's standing. Even Peregrine Worsthorne hails him as a statesman.

With August reputedly a dead month politically, the Prime Minister went to Yorkshire to shoot grouse and to Gleneagles to play golf. But this proved to be the month when Mr. K. stepped up pressure on the Berlin issue by prompting the East Germans to build the Berlin Wall and an international crisis appeared possible. However, in an impromptu Press conference on the eighteenth fairway at Gleneagles the P.M. declared 'Nobody is going to fight about Berlin.' For this airy nonchalance he came under fire from the Press (perhaps because he had added 'I think it is all got up by the Press,' which wasn't very helpful to his Press Secretary in London). But he was right, of course, and the 'crisis' evaporated. The topic now coming to the centre of the No. 10 stage was the planning of a major Cabinet re-shuffle, stemming from the Prime Minister's wish to appoint a younger man as Party chairman. His choice was Iain Macleod, then Colonial Secretary. Such a move, however, required the goodwill and co-operation of R. A. Butler, who was Party chairman, Home Secretary and Leader of the House.

September 7, Thursday   *London*

Just before I went on leave John Wyndham came to talk, *inter alia*, about the choice of an heir apparent and the timing of the succession. He did not, however, produce any new or novel ideas. We simply raked over the known factors, not least the absence of any predominant candidate. As to timing, John seems to have concluded that retirement must be expected within the next year or two.

September 16, Saturday   *Rottingdean*

Planning proceeds on the re-shuffle. Rab has agreed to give up the Party chairmanship. He had lunch at Admiralty House on Tuesday and the P.M. lunched with him at Bucks on Thursday. Iain Macleod is to be chairman and current thinking plays with the idea of making him Chancellor of the Duchy as well. Tim consulted me and I said it would not do to give oversight of the official information services to the Party chairman: but there was the Woolton precedent for making the chairman Chancellor of the Duchy without any specific schedule. As to information, I said it could be split between presentation (which could be attached to any of a number of Ministers but preferably Charles Hill if, as Tim thinks, he now gets a department – Housing is suggested) and overseas organisation and finance, which could be attached with some logic to the Secretary for Technical Co-operation.

I had, in fact, ventilated the possibility of giving information co-ordination to the Secretary for Technical Co-operation (Vosper) and elevating him to the Duchy. This would have the effect of bringing a younger man into the Cabinet. Tim said that this was simply not on – presumably because there is no other way of giving Macleod a Cabinet post (from which I infer that Hailsham stays as Lord President and doesn't get upped to Lord Chancellor which I had considered a possibility).

I told Tim that the reconstruction would be looked at by the Press first and foremost for the light it threw on the succession. His reaction to this was that Macleod's appointment to the Party chairmanship clearly pointed to him as next-but-one P.M., which was the way you had to approach it – and an assumption that Rab must have made in agreeing to give up the chairmanship. But, of course, the assumption that Rab would automatically get the succession if Uncle Harold fell down the stairs tomorrow is not to be made too lightly (Harry Boyne, who lunched with me, thinks that Rab is 'out' in any circumstances). Tim says that the understanding is that the Queen would consult the Lord Chancellor and the Chancellor of the Exchequer. (Selwyn Lloyd – but is not Selwyn to be regarded as a candidate?) Charles Hill must weigh his chances in the re-shuffle as well: by a coincidence he was this week offered a company chairmanship. Ideally he would like to see the P.M. out, so to speak, but to do so as a Minister with a department: but he has told the Chief Whip that he would neither expect nor want to continue as a Minister after the General Election (assuming the Conservatives came back yet again).

I went with Charles Hill to Broadcasting House to hear a play-back of a piece he had done for a programme about Nye Bevan. In fact, they have talked to a large number of people and lifted anecdotes from all these pieces to make up the programme so that there is no single Hill contribution (I think he was a little nervous that he might have been over-generous, but the point did

Through the garden gate.

A Garden Rooms girl is a very special person. Ann Barker, Joyce Cutler, Jane Parsons in Moscow.

No. 10 Private Secretaries: *left to right,* Timothy Bligh, Principal Private Secretary; David Stephens, Secretary for Appointments (*behind*); Philip de Zulueta, Foreign Affairs; also *right,* Martin Redmayne, Chief Whip, at Trooping the Colour, 1961.

Lady Dorothy with Australian friend in Sydney. Also Jane Parsons, *left*, Lady Carrington and Sir Norman Brook.

'Why can't they do that in England?' asks the Prime Minister, as a fervent supporter kisses Dr. Nkrumah's feet.

High wind in Bermuda. An interlude during the meeting with
President Eisenhower in 1957.

We, too, mobilised helicopters. About to board an RAF helicopter
with James Hagerty, President Eisenhower's Press Secretary.

Working with Charles Hill carried the bonus of laughter.

Waiting for cue. The joint television broadcast from No. 10 by
Harold Macmillan and President Eisenhower, 1959.

In Accra, with Robert Manning, *Time* bureau chief in London and
later spokesman for the State Department.

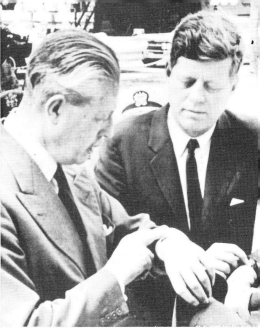

Against the clock. The Prime Minister checks with Harold Evans at Heathrow and with President Kennedy at Key West in 1961.

With Pierre Salinger, President Kennedy's Press Secretary, aboard the President's motor launch, *Honey Fitz*, on the Potomac, 1961.

The Macmillans at home.

not arise). Arthur Christiansen was also there, going through the same hoop, the first time I had met him. Fresh-complexioned, open-faced and cheerful, in a tweed suit, hatless but with umbrella. His memoirs, *Headlines All My Life*, had involved him in criticism for letting Beaverbrook make all the political policy of the *Express*, he said, but Hell, Beaverbrook *was* the proprietor and the era of great political editors had long gone by.

I lunched with Drew Middleton and Cy Sulzberger (fresh from his massive interview with Khruschev) at the Garrick. Drew had rung me dramatically at Broadcasting House to say that I might not know (but ought to) that while I was in Europe he had tried to get Cy into the Prime Minister through Philip de Zulueta but, as he fully realised was inevitable (?), the effort had not succeeded. Sulzberger had also been told this and Drew was clearing the way for me (a) not to dissent and (b) to be prepared to smooth down ruffled feathers. Point (b) didn't prove difficult (Cy doesn't have to bother too much at this moment because of his triumph with K.), and point (a) was unnecessary because no effort had been made since June to get him into the P.M. Finding from Philip de Zulueta, on my return from lunch, that no approach had been made to the P.M. I went in to see him there and then and he agreed at once to see Sulzberger the next morning ('though I am not very good at this kind of thing'): but Sulzberger was already about to take off for Paris and it couldn't actually be done. However, the myth of a down on Sulzberger has been destroyed.

This was the first time I had seen the P.M. since we both returned from leave on Monday. He greeted me warmly. Philip says he is 'in tremendous form'.

Lunch for Harry Boyne. He sees little likelihood of a major re-shuffle because of the 'fixtures' – Lloyd, Home and Butler (at the Home Office anyhow). He was completely wrong, he says, about Alec Home: it had been an appointment he had expected to flop, both because of the Lords–Commons angle and because he had underestimated Home. He thinks Sandys a dark horse for the premiership: if only he had a livelier sense of personal and public relations.

The political commentators have little to write about at the moment and they are getting grumpy and complaining in consequence. (Worsthorne in today's *Sunday Telegraph*, for example: 'Is ignorance bliss? If it is, then the British people should be happier today than they have ever been before, since never have they been so completely in the dark about what, as a nation, they are trying to do.') However, there are the Labour and Tory Party conferences during the next three weeks, and that should keep them hard at it.

September 21, Thursday   *London*

I had arranged this evening for the P.M. to see Anthony Sampson, at the end of a year's work on his book *The Anatomy of Britain*. He saw him in the upstairs study and talked for nearly an hour and a half. His leg was bothering him and he continually had to shift position, but his mind seemed aloof from it.

On Prime Ministerial burdens, he spoke of the new loads that result from summitry (originating, I suggest, in the existence of a Mr. K.), from the aeroplane as a means of transport, from the speed of modern communications and from the demands of modern publicity. It wasn't only the fact that one had to travel oneself, but that almost everyone turned up in London – and the smaller the country they came from the more thoroughly you had to do the honours. The P.M. had to give a dinner and reception, attend the return dinner, attend the Palace dinner and have talks with the visitor – the best part of two or three days full work (or at any rate allocation of time) to virtually no purpose. Then, of course, Parliament was more demanding than it used to be half a century ago when the long recess lasted until February. Ministers went to their country houses, wrote long letters to each other, thought long and hard, and governed the country in that way.

On parliamentary questions, the P.M. said they fell into two categories – those on major policy which could not possibly be dealt with within the scope of a parliamentary answer and were really matters for debate, and those which were designed to lead to harassing supplementaries (this latter category, he thought, were rather fun). In the old days, however, the Prime Minister and other senior Ministers got relatively few questions (Edward Grey had only two or three in a year); points of detail were directed at junior Ministers. Some Ministers had become very seriously overburdened. Cripps and Bevin were killed by overwork and it was the burden he carried at the Foreign Office that really broke Eden's health. 'That was why I moved Selwyn.' That was why also he had double-banked the Foreign Office by giving them two Ministers of Cabinet rank – an arrangement which, he believed, had come to stay. It might also have to be applied to the Treasury. (I wonder if Sampson saw the immediate significance of this?) The appointment of Ministers of State had been intended as a device to take away some of the burden but the House refused to accept them: they became, in effect, additional under-secretaries. Of course, there was a tendency in modern conditions to make work for its own sake – a tendency due in part to 'aids', whether in the form of a dictaphone or a young lady waiting to take dictation.

On changes, the P.M. said that the Press seemed to preoccupy itself with a world that no longer existed. They seemed obsessed by the Establishment though this no longer effectively existed. The news and gossip columns were filled by items about the aristocracy, also no longer significant, and people who did nothing. One very big change, that had gone relatively unnoticed, was the influx into industry and commerce of the type of boy who in the old days would have gone into the Church, the Civil Service and the professions. You often couldn't tell at meetings today which was the civil servant and which the business executive. It was also satisfactory that industry and commerce drew away some of the best of the senior civil servants, not least because it might well have the effect of making the Civil Service more attractive as a career since it could be seen by the ambitious and talented young man as a stepping stone to other things. Anthony Sampson said that scientists seemed very conscious of a gulf between them and the administration – to the extent almost of a persecution complex. The P.M. thought this might right itself since people with science degrees might be expected, by their very numbers and by the high proportion they represented compared with the humanities, to move into the administration and the professions.

September 24, Sunday   *Rottingdean*

'What kind of reaction would there be to Rab as deputy Prime Minister?' asks Tim, on instructions. A pretty dusty one, I suggest. On the premise that the changes will be looked at for the light they throw on the succession it would seem very peculiar indeed. (Tim notes that Eden, named as deputy, did in fact become P.M., which in this instance is probably not the idea at all.) Rab is clearly putting a high price on giving up his Leadership of the House and/or chairmanship of the Party. Quite apart from the undesirability of appearing to fetter the Queen's choice the Party would take very unkindly to anything that might seem to prejudice their own choice. Nor would it be workable. There would be great pressure for spheres of action to be spelt out. Then, of course, one reaction would be to see it as evidence of an ageing Prime Minister.

In the end I gather from Philip Woodfield that the idea is not being pursued, that Rab has agreed to give up Leadership of the House and that Macleod is to get it. That and a decision to double-bank the Treasury, as already at the Foreign Office, seems to be as far as we have got. The intention is to offer Henry Brooke the finance schedule at the Treasury (Cabinet rank) with Selwyn doing the economic planning.

Gaitskell popped up at Chequers out of the blue to talk about foreign affairs and to ask for the recall of Parliament 'immediately' (with his tongue in his cheek and content, in fact, with an arrangement for the House to come back a week earlier). This suits the Government perfectly well and so I found myself with a recall of Parliament announcement.

Considering how momentous are some of the issues there is a strange lull at the moment – Katanga (Indians and Ghanaians slanging us hard), the Secretary-General succession, and of course Berlin. On Berlin a course is set. So, too, on the Common Market. Katanga and the U.N. are largely out of our hands for the moment.

September 28, Thursday   *London*
Seeing off Sir Folliott Sandford, now Registrar of Oxford University ('Hotspur' no longer),[10] I was drawn into conversation in the hall with the P.M., waiting to welcome the Archbishop of Canterbury. He was anxious to tell me about the proposed changes which he thought would be regarded as far-reaching. Henry – good old Henry, or words to that effect – had agreed to take the new post of Chief Secretary at the Treasury. That would need careful presentation. So, he agreed, would the new arrangement with Rab. Giving Iain the chairmanship and Leadership would not please the right wing but that would have to be endured. And he had just heard from Washington that Reggie Maudling was willing to go to Colonies. That was good. Reggie was looked upon as middle of the road. Trade had now to be filled. Perhaps he could bring in a bright young man. On the re-allocation of information, did I think there were any difficulties about overseas co-ordination going to Vosper – had it any 'black' propaganda connotations which might prejudice his work? I said I thought not – it was essentially finance and organisation. What of the home side? Was there much to do? No, I said, it could well go to one of the home Ministers. He would need only to hold a weekly meeting of the chief information officers and to see the Lobby. So, said the P.M., he might give it to one of the less busy Ministers – or if Charles Hill went to Housing he could take it with him. That I said would be excellent in every way – he had been loyal and good and it had certainly long been his hope that he might eventually get a department, perhaps doing the in-

---

[10] Formerly a colleague in the Resident Minister's office in West Africa: he was Lord Swinton's chief of staff.

formation co-ordination as well. As to the Lobby, the P.M. said that Iain Macleod would do the Thursday meeting as Leader of the House – and he thought would do it very well. Rab would *not* go on having his weekly meeting. With a twinkle, he said that Rab would now be in charge of the committee doing the Common Market negotiations, and that ought to allay the apprehensions of the agricultural people.

For the rest, I spoke of the peculiar lull in affairs in London at the moment and of calls for a 'lead'. Perhaps the Brighton speech? But he made a mouth and having since seen the draft I can well understand why. What about Alec's speech to the U.N., he asked; was that not a pretty good lead? Things were going well with the Americans. But, of course, we could not say this. Was it not realised in some of the inner sanctums? I said I thought it was (and indeed when Ian Waller came to see me earlier we had talked on these lines).

October 14, Saturday   *Rottingdean*

The fortnight's chief interest lay in the re-shuffle – drama behind the scenes (with Rab turning pressure on me), announcement (no complications) and Prime Ministerial gratification (to the extent of a manuscript note of thanks).

Rab seemed suddenly to wake up to the implications. He talked to me four times, including three late telephone calls from home. The Prime Minister's idea had been to announce on the Wednesday or Thursday of conference week, but I said that this was leaving it much too late – that there would inevitably be leaks and that, anyhow, there was only one day on which we could catch the Lobby seniors between the Party conferences at Blackpool and Brighton – Monday, the 9th. He accepted this.

On the preceding Thursday, the 5th, the Chief Whip had arranged a meeting with Tim Bligh, myself and George Hutchinson (because of the intended change in the Party leadership). That night Rab rang me from Stanstead, in indignation that Hutchinson should have been told when he, Rab, had told no one at all at the Central Office – not even the vice-chairman – and had not intended to do so until Monday. Now several people had been ringing his wife from the Central Office – 'it was she who alerted me' – to say that they had been upset to hear that he was giving up the chairmanship and it was being talked about. 'Our adjutant' really seemed to have acted without adequate forethought: but we mustn't blame 'the nice young man' (Hutchinson). He felt sure they would not leak it to the Press, at any rate tonight, and he was coming up on an early train to sort it all out at the Central Office. 'I am in a spot. It is a turning point. Giving up two plumes is a big thing. I am doing it with full courage – keeping the Home Office. We have a difficult time ahead – there will probably be trouble this winter and next week at the conference on hanging and punishment.' How did I think the announcement ought to be presented. He agreed that the double-banking idea would be the way to do it. Should the word 'deputising' be worked into the formula he had agreed with the P.M.? Of course, he realised that the title 'deputy' could not be used because it was not constitutional. But his wife did not think the present formula was strong enough – she was the only person he could turn to. Then there were the Lobby arrangements under the new dispensation. He had told the other man he was not prepared to give it up entirely. He could not be cut off altogether. There would have to be a compromise. There could be alternate weeks and he would do the first one. Perhaps the other man could have a bit extra but the basis would have to be alternate weeks. Perhaps we could have another word tomorrow.

On Friday we met in the waiting room at Admiralty House just before lunch at the end of a Ministerial meeting which Rab had attended. It went like this: 'I must say it has been a bit of a blow. One doesn't wish to appear to have been pushed out by the P.M. I have talked to him about this and he says I should talk to you as much as I like. If it goes well the Government will be welded together, but if it goes wrong it may prove something of a strain. I took this somewhat courageous decision in Scotland – that I should stay at the Home Office. I decided that with the campaign against Selwyn Lloyd and with Civil Defence it would not be honourable to give up at this time. The Prime Minister, as you know, does not take this very seriously and I have had to carry it very much by myself. I do hope that you will make it clear that it is a positive decision.'

I suggested that he would have a splendid opportunity to explain it himself when he appeared in his *Panorama* interview on Monday evening immediately after the announcement (an interview arranged as an eve-of-conference talk with the Party chairman). Rab was under the impression that the announcement would be embargoed for Tuesday morning papers. He brightened up when he saw that it would lend itself to his purpose and give him first go. 'I shall say there was this special request from the Prime Minister to which I felt I ought to respond.'

Then on Sunday night he rang me at home to say much the same kind of thing – gratified, I think, to find nothing had leaked in the

Sunday Press. (Astonishing, because on Friday afternoon Jimmy Margach rang me to say, 'Well, I've just got back from Blackpool. My dear wife met me at the station. When I sniffed the air I said to myself, "There is something in the wind, Jimmy. I wonder if the Prime Minister is thinking of having a deputy!"' But for some reason, when I assured him that no announcement would be made during the weekend, he did not press it further. Rab admitted talking to him.)

Rab went on to talk about an article in the *Su:.day Times* of the 'Whither Macmillan?' character. Did I know who had written it? I did because Rees-Mogg had sought information about the Prime Minister's working habits. The conclusion of the article was very helpful, thought Rab, since it expressed the view that everything for the P.M. now hinged on a successful negotiation with the Common Market. That being so, it must be seen how important it was that Rab had been put in charge of the Common Market group of Ministers. Ted Heath had rung him to say how pleased he was.

On Monday Rab took his *Panorama* opportunity perfectly. Robin Day suggested that some people were seeing it as a demotion. Demotion, echoed Rab in wide-eyed astonishment: on the contrary he had been asked to give this special assistance to the Prime Minister and naturally felt he could not refuse.

All the same he had been upset by the *Evening Standard* ('Up Macleod: Down – Butler'), and it was about this that he rang me at 10 o'clock. 'For myself I don't really mind. I have a happy home life – the theatre and that kind of thing. But it is the future of the Party. The *Evening Standard* was absolutely bloody. Do you know where Max Aitken is now? He will have to be told about it. Haley was horrified. He thinks it very bad to put me in this position at the conference. I had dinner at the Carlton. There were some awful Tory M.P.'s there. I shan't go again. Some of them are frightful aren't they? (I say, yes indeed, it is often alarming to look along the backbenches of both Parties). Makes your hair stand on end (chuckle). Boyne and Wood spoke to me. Thank you for suggesting it to them.'

With the Lobby I had been prepared for more than they asked, though I had deluged them with background guidance, of course. I had put this together after talking to Tim and the Chief Whip and a final check with the P.M. on Monday morning. He was delighted that only the Macleod succession to the chairmanship had got into the morning papers and said how right I had been to advise nothing later than Monday for the announcement.

In the upshot the Press treatment delighted him, but mainly I would guess because it showed him again, at the psychological moment, as the man of power and destiny – and because, too, there had been sufficient of the mysterious about it to keep tongues wagging (I had made the point to him that there was something to be said for a little mystery).

In fact, I don't think it started out at all mysteriously. He rightly wanted a new chairman for the Party to give it a sense of re-invigoration and drive in the period leading up to the election. He decided that Macleod was the man. But Macleod would not take only the Party chairmanship. 'It would seem very peculiar if I took only one third of what Rab has been doing.' So the P.M. had to persuade Rab to give up the Leadership as well. Rab wanted to be called deputy Prime Minister, but the P.M. would not wear this and then Rab, somewhat unexpectedly, bought the formula. This then fitted neatly into the double-banking thesis, already working at the Foreign Office (Home and Heath) and now planned for the Treasury (Lloyd plus Brooke). And that was how I presented it.

As for the Prime Minister's note, it ran, 'The Press was good and really seemed to understand the principles which actuated my decisions. It was a successful exercise in public relations and I am grateful.' Alas, it can't really be said that the Press understood the principles which actuated his decision, though they reproduced the double-banking thought and also the thought about re-invigoration of the Party. However, there it is.

The Macleod appointment was well received at the Party conference. It also went sweetly for the Government in other ways and so by the end of the week the P.M. was feeling – after a period of anxiety – that it did not matter a great deal if he failed to make a memorable winding-up speech. He didn't (as Betty reports after going to the rally on a Press ticket with Rona Margach). I, too, had been worried by the apparent need for a resounding declaration of leadership, and had proposed a peroration designed to catch the eye of sub-editors, but though the idea was nominally accepted the peroration didn't turn out that way.

I was able to make an effective intervention on re-allocation of responsibility for co-ordination of the information services. By some alarming aberration the P.M. and Chief Whip had decided to give the home information side to Edward Boyle. Nothing could have been more mistaken than to give it to a junior Minister, a junior Minister who would be bound to have competing loyalties between effective information services and finding the money for them, and a junior Treasury Minister at a time when what the Treasury needs is to be influenced by an external and objective view in the presentation of its policies. So it has gone to Housing and Local Government with Charles Hill. He, of course, is delighted.

I met him on his return from Israel and helped him through a television interview for Wales where there is the customary indignation that the Minister for Welsh Affairs should not be a Welshman. He and Mrs. Hill lunched with us on Friday, the new house fortunately looking at its best in the sunshine of a wonderful October day. In the evening Jimmy and Rona Margach came to dinner (Jimmy had originally invited us to dine at the Grand, but the No. 10 spokesman can't afford to have the slightest whisper of a link with the Party). Then today – again glowing sunshine – Betty lunched with them in Brighton and went to hear the P.M. while Annabel and I looked after each other.

What else? Lunch for Leslie Boas, still information attaché in Caracas and shortly to return there: I put him into touch with Richard Colville about Prince Philip's forthcoming tour.

A pay-off from lunch for Hank Hayward – an article in the *Monitor*, well displayed with an artist's drawing, on the Prime Minister back in London 'looking chipper'.

I had a brief talk with Alec Home on his return from New York and Washington. Rusk, he thinks, is quite a fellow. The hard grind of talking to Gromyko – but given *de facto* recognition he would jump at any Western requirements for a free city. The French are thoroughly difficult, of course, and the danger is that they will egg on the Germans (but I stick my neck out and say that, on the evidence of my tour with Charles Hill, the Germans will prefer to count their blessings). I congratulate him on his willingness to do television interviews and his patience in doing them: in fact, he says, he hates them, especially when you have just stepped off a plane.

I went to Broadcasting House to collect the thinking of Hugh Carleton Greene and Harmon Grisewood on the Prime Minister's speech at the B.B.C.'s twenty-fifth television anniversary. I now have four speeches on the stocks – this one plus the P.M. at the Press Club, one for Charles Hill and one for myself at an N.U.J. weekend conference at Folkestone.

'You know my mind so well,' said the P.M. on one of our encounters – his highest compliment.

November 18, Saturday   *Rottingdean*
A month since I recorded. It included one crucial personal decision. Stored up from the *Capetown Castle*, Norman Brook remembered my declared interest in the information services job at

the Commonwealth Relations Office and produced it as an offer, with Tim as his emissary. It was offered at the salary I am now getting but minus the London housing allowance. In cold light – though it would be escape from the ceaseless wear and tear of No. 10 – it didn't look a very rewarding climax for five years in Downing Street. Charles Hill scoffed at the idea. He didn't think that I could do other than stay the two years until the next election and by then, he thought, I would have collected a knighthood (but what would the mandarins have to say about that?). By then, too, I might leave the Civil Service. This, of course, is his own timing. Betty also came down against it, partly I would say because she could not see me going back happily into a groove, especially a groove that included a daily train journey to London and back. And the Prime Minister? It would have to be subject to his agreement, and my own thinking was conditioned by the assumption, from all he has said to me about people being taken away from him, that he would feel hurt, especially now when, perhaps, he is feeling more than ever lonely. At any rate, I decided to stay and told Tim so the morning after the Lord Mayor's banquet. He then said that coming back from the banquet the P.M. had been talking about me, with particular reference to the success of his B.B.C. television dinner speech. Tim took the opportunity to say that Duncan Sandys was after me and he became indignant – could not possibly let me go, I was more than ever useful to him and if I wanted more money I must be given it. So I'm glad I had already taken the decision.

Of course, it's not all virtue. When I originally spoke to Brook I was in a state of frustration at the end of the African tour. At the moment most things are going my way, but another bad patch will come. Next week the P.M. is at the Press Club and if that also goes well (he will speak off the cuff with an introduction which I have undertaken to write in lighter vein) I shall be feeling well satisfied. His Gallup Poll rating is going up again at a gratifying pace.

The television speech undoubtedly caused widespread and favourable comment. People had not before seen him in such lighthearted vein. Beforehand he had little chance to work on the draft and made only trifling changes, but nevertheless he had been asking how one could speak for twenty minutes 'about nothing'. He simply did not see what an opportunity it represented and when he found what had happened he was taken aback. Almost he had fallen for an attempt by the Chief Whip to get him to call it off (Tim consulted me at 10 the night before) because it was the winding-up of the Debate on the Address. (The Chief Whip had again got round to counting heads gloomily and fearing a Government

170

defeat.) Also there was the extreme worry and preoccupation about the Queen's visit to Ghana. To and from the Grocers Hall in the car he talked almost solely of the Queen. 'What a splendid girl she is.' She had been indignant at the audience just before we left at the idea of having the trip called off. The House of Commons, she thought, should not show lack of moral fibre in this way. She took very seriously her Commonwealth responsibilities, said the P.M., and rightly so for the responsibilities of the U.K. monarchy had so shrunk that if you left it at that you might as well have a film star.

November 25, Saturday   *Rottingdean*
I had a bad morning and afternoon on Wednesday – too much to do too quickly, on top of headache, plus worry about the P.M. going to the Press Club at night and how he would perform. I had done what I thought to be a good, lighthearted passage but the bulk was to be off the cuff. He was being harried from several directions and at the end of the morning, when there was the chance of a quick word in the Cabinet room, he said – though without real complaint in his voice – 'Why do you make me do these things?' This is an old one, of course, and so I simply say, 'Well, they always seem a bore beforehand but we're usually glad about them afterwards' – and we get on with it without more ado. I make a note of how he thinks he might develop the substance and put it into note form. And once again it's all right on the night. More than all right, because not only did he do it extremely well and get an enthusiastic reception which will ripple through Fleet Street, but also he thoroughly enjoyed the community singing and the turns (including Bruce Forsyth) and stayed right to the end.

We had the opportunity to throw in a bit of drama by causing Philip Woodfield to come to the Club post haste from No. 10 with a draft letter to spike Gaitskell's guns on the Grantley Adams allegations. I had the concert held up so that the P.M. could come out to the bar to approve the draft so that I was then (9.45) able to telephone the faithful Jim to release it. We thus ensured that the P.M. had the last word in the morning papers. He immensely enjoyed doing Gaiters down when Gaiters had tried on some smart-alecry, and on the way back kept saying what a splendid team he had. This is a fairly constant theme at the moment.

The next day, when I was waiting for Macleod behind the Speaker's Chair, he came along with Knox Cunningham in the highest of spirits (having done well in exchanges on the floor of the House), took me by the elbow and swept me along into his room. There he put his feet on the edge of the table and tilted back the chair – always an indication of good spirits. Once again he says how good we all are, and once again I enlarge on the advantages of a small compact staff which talks and acts instead of exchanging minutes. He then talked about how we should handle the Press for the de Gaulle visit at the weekend which gives me an opportunity to get in some of my points. He laughs at the troubles of his 'poor wife' who was asked to put the General's blood plasma in the fridge with her sausages. But I have to go off to Macleod's Lobby before we get very far.

It is tough going at the moment, with Selwyn making a mess of his pay pause and Rab of the immigration bill.

It had been arranged for President de Gaulle to come to England for talks with the Prime Minister towards the end of November, but to demonstrate that this was a private visit he and Madame de Gaulle stayed as house guests at Birch Grove (as a Head of State the General usually saw the Prime Minister on French soil). The main topic for discussion was Berlin, with the General, as intransigent as ever in dealing with the Anglo-Saxons, totally opposed to any attempt to negotiate with the Russians – though the Anglo-Saxons would be expected to pull the chestnuts out of the fire if the absence of negotiation led to an explosive situation. On the British application to join the E.E.C. he produced his usual battery of doubts and reservations. The talks therefore achieved little beyond re-affirming the inflexibility of the General's attitudes. On the personal level, however, all was pleasant enough, as could be expected from the good relationship established between the two men from the war years.

November 25, Saturday   *At Birch Grove*
'She's a very difficult woman to entertain. She has a thing about people,' says Lady D. 'Won't go to the Hunt, nor the cripples craft school, nor even (nearing desperation now) the Pavilion at Brighton.'

So we pore over a road map on the windowsill in the study and pick out a route for a drive in the autumn sunshine to Beachy Head via Alfriston. But I can't go with them because I have been told to man the study (and telephone) while the talks go on in the library (whence I have been commissioned by Lady D. to carry logs from the long sitting room).

They were still at breakfast when I arrived. The nice butler from Government Hospitality brought me a cup of coffee, but it became an embarrassment when the P.M. appeared and wanted to talk about the excitement in the morning papers, led by the

Express, alleging a leak by the French to the Americans of the text of Ted Heath's statement to the Council of Ministers of the Six in October. The *Express* – pro-Commonwealth, pro-Canada, and anti-Common Market – says in effect that here is the British Government negotiating behind the backs of its Commonwealth partners and look at the kind of people they are negotiating with anyhow. We agree that the answer is to let the Commonwealth governments have the full text and to issue a Press release saying that this is being done and explaining protocol. But the Press release must come from the Foreign Office and not Admiralty House, I argue, which is accepted, though it was planned the other way.

So here I am in the study with the General's A.D.C., Capitaine de Corvette Frohic, a dark, burly young man in uniform who has taken masochistic refuge in a book about Wellington.

I encountered the President at close quarters in the lobby and decided to click my heels and bow. He looked aloof and puzzled, began to say something and then didn't feel equal to it. This aloof, preoccupied, slightly puzzled look seems permanent. Never a smile to be seen. He has very big feet and their size is accentuated by yellowish-brown shoes and his hitched-up trousers.

The camera facility went well – how lucky we were with the sunshine. When the group photograph had been taken several of the rota wanted to take distant views of the house, to which I agreed. One chap, in a kind of frenzy, tried to jump across the deep ditch, almost a moat, from the terrace and sprawled without dignity but unhurt. First one, then two others not to be outdone, went running still farther across the meadow to get a view of the house with a policeman by a tree in the foreground. All the same, it was over and done with in ten minutes and we are all satisfied for various reasons.

But, reports Philip, Old Ramrod is not bending an inch. He won't budge at all on Berlin. We may have to end up with a public row. Then the P.M. takes a break to think up an answer to the General's line of mystique about danger to the European personality if we go into the Six with our tremendous 'escort' and are then followed by the Americans. What he says I don't know, though it can hardly be anything but, 'We are sure you exaggerate, but anyhow there it is.'

At the end of the morning I drove back to London to link up with action on the Press release about the leak.

At Admiralty House

Almost immediately after I arrive Ted Heath is on the phone from the Foreign Office. Will I please join his drafting party about the alleged leak, but I say in effect, 'For heavens sake, can't I eat?' So he reads the draft as it stands which I think is good and say so, also emphasising that the Prime Minister wishes it to issue from the Foreign Office and not Admiralty House.

Then I take twenty minutes to eat at Lyons before joining the party at the Foreign Office (Norman Brook also appears, in his Saturday tweeds, for half an hour). They make terribly heavy weather of drafting niceties while I urge rapid action because of the Sunday papers. The minutes tick away towards 4, with two calls to Washington and one from Birch Grove (when I talk to Philip and he is able to bring in the P.M. again), while the intractable Duncan Sandys is shooting at Broadlands and can't be got at so that eventually it is agreed that he must be forgotten. Ted Heath is calm, good-humoured and friendly ('Like old times isn't it?') but apt to get enmeshed in the small print. Still, by 4.15 it is through.

The explanation given in the Press release was generally accepted as reasonable by Fleet Street (Express excepted), and when the matter came to the House a similar view emerged. 'Leak ends in farce,' said The Guardian, and 'Leak Row Fizzles Out,' the Mail.

November 26, Sunday   *Admiralty House*

Gatwick in the fog but the General shrugs, takes the salute, inspects the guard with hand half-raised in an imperial gesture, and goes directly into the aircraft. Within minutes it has been enfolded in the fog. In the make-do V.I.P. lounge the P.M. then talks to John Russell and myself about guidance, with the help of black coffee and brandy (John looking, as Philip says, like a reporter from *The People*).

On the way back to Birch Grove in the car Philip is able to fill in the details for me. Home, he said, did most of the talking during the Saturday afternoon session but the General simply stuck in his toes. The P.M. covered his face with his hands and appeared to go to sleep (Philip thinks he really did) but came to life in time to explode, 'Oh well, let's have a war then.' Later, at tea, the General quietly ribbed him by talking of his calm soul and his not being the kind of man who went into tantrums.

Philip and I also exchange notes on the mess into which the Government has manoeuvred itself, not least the economic mess. What then to do with Selwyn Lloyd? Make him Lord Chancellor,

174

says Philip. But who then would be Chancellor of the Exchequer? Duncan Sandys? It ought to be Macleod, of course.

At Birchers the P.M. looks to see if I am in the car and says, 'Is there anything for Harold?' We stand in the drive for a few minutes, talking chiefly about tomorrow's Sheffield speech and he says, 'Come and have a look at it.' So I'm given a copy and go into the study while the P.M. changes. I've not much to offer except the fairly obvious things about the distinction that is being seen between restraint and pause. He says he is worried by the lack of understanding shown by the Press. How can I say, 'Well, if you have a Chancellor who can't explain things what can you expect?'

We agree that the immigration bill is also in a mess. 'I'm afraid Rab hasn't done it very well, has he?'

Then back to de Gaulle. He is like Churchill, says the P.M. He won't give any ground or concede any points in discussion. But a little later you may find that he is producing your ideas as his own. And that's about all we can hope for on this occasion. But the personal feeling is good – and he shows me the inscription the General has written in French in the P.M.'s copy of the de Gaulle memoirs.

So I take my leave – but the P.M. says, 'Have you got a pen with you? I want you to sign our book. We want to have all the people who have been here.' So I walk along the hall and sign, and Lady Dorothy says, 'Thank you for everything you've done,' and that's the end of the de Gaulle weekend – except, of course, for answering the telephone at Admiralty House until teatime (after which it is Cecil Madden and *What's My Line?*).

Earlier, at Gatwick, before the Birch Grove procession arrived, I found myself drinking brandy-laced coffee with Lord Munster who, as ever, immediately began peeling off stories – the careful drunken driver, the nun on a penny farthing and the monosyllabic Prince Henry.

November 27, Monday   *London*

The P.M. gets in from Birch Grove just before 11.30 and I am summoned to the Cabinet room where he is going over the ground with Tim. The Press is all right on de Gaulle, he thinks, and he again recalls the Churchill similarity and hopes it may turn out that way. But what are we to do about Press hostility to the Government? He notes this morning's *Mail* poll which shows his own stock rising. 'That's Harold's speech, of course,' he says to Tim. 'I'm all right personally, but it's the Government they are getting at.' I mention all the things we have already agreed to do, including editors' lunches, and he decides to add Haley ('What's his name, Casey, *The Times* man') and Oliver Poole.

But, of course, it's no good thinking the Press is simply being bloody-minded. There *has* been muddle and confusion.

December 2, Saturday   *Rottingdean*

As a bonus contribution to our new campaign with the Press I fed in James Holburn – the hard-boiled, critical and taciturn James Holburn from Glasgow. He received the full treatment for fifty minutes in the P.M.'s room at the House and emerged a little dazed.

The P.M. was at his most relaxed – feet on the edge of the table and chair tipped back perilously. He got on to the virtue of work. In the 'thirties all we thought about was leisure for the workers – with vision of spare time spent in adult education and afternoons reading Plato – but the workers wanted fewer working hours only to earn overtime rates. They wanted, not leisure, but more money. Then there was the problem of flats without gardens. The wife didn't want her husband cluttering up the place and he had no garden to work in. 'I am a lazy man, but it happens to me when I run out of telegrams and papers to read. I feel lost.' Then a look at how Scotland is getting on – with every indication of knowing all about it. So to a dissertation on economic policy, with monetary management seen as the key. Hence the importance of this year's budget surplus which means that you don't have to sell three months bills at high quotation, which is inflationary both because of the money you are spending and because you are borrowing more paper money. We are always on the edge. It is the volume of debt that makes the situation so difficult to handle.

1962

Fifth anniversary — backbench rumbles — Orpington bombshell — North American journey — 'new approach' — Cabinet 'massacre' — Commonwealth confrontation — Europe or bust — Cuba crisis — Vassall — from Nassau with Polaris

Though 1962 was to be a year of high political drama it began quietly enough.

In January Harold Macmillan celebrated his fifth anniversary as Prime Minister. The Sunday Pictorial rendered a predictable verdict, 'The Five-Year Folly of Mr. Macmillan'. Others made less malevolent assessments. The Mail thought that he had the ability 'to watch and wait and seize the flying opportunity'. The Express gave prominent space for Lord Altrincham (later John Grigg) to declare that outward appearances should not deceive – 'in fact, he is yet another radical adventurer from the Celtic fringe . . . but thoroughly modern-minded.' The Guardian had a long leader. Mr. Macmillan, they thought, was 'a consummate political artist', with a sense of history. The central issue of the day was coming to terms with the Common Market. This he had done and 'the wonder is that he has had the courage to move so fast.' But, said The Guardian, there was one 'real failure' – 'his refusal to hold out any ideal to his country'. Material prosperity was 'not enough', though admittedly it had meant 'a great increase in happiness and human dignity'. (That a Prime Minister should be expected to produce more than a great increase in happiness and human dignity is an interesting commentary on the moral climate of the day.)

James Margach and the Sunday Times sought the great man's own views in a set of questions agreed in discussion. This interview was published on January 14th and was followed on January 24th by a television 'talk to the Nation'. Both interview and broadcast took up a good deal of my thought during the early weeks of the year.

Though a 'Party political' label was tagged to the broadcast – with the advantage of simultaneous transmission by the B.B.C. and I.T.V. – it was intended rather to be a Prime Ministerial fireside chat, without any attempt to score Party political points. Given the disposition of many viewers to switch off any Party political broad-cast the moment it began, I felt that we ought to devise an opening sequence likely to hold immediate attention because of its novelty. This led to the idea of using two cameras, so that one could show the setting with the Prime Minister at his desk in the study confronted by cameras, lights, cables and technicians. He could then open with a joking reference to the ordeals of being a Prime Minister in the 1960s – captive in 'a kind of twentieth-century torture chamber'.

The Prime Minister had many other matters calling for his attention, of course, not least the continuing tug of war between the Commonwealth Relations Office and the Colonial Office over the future of the Central African Federation. The Sandys–Macleod confrontation had now become a Sandys–Maudling confrontation. In his memoirs Harold Macmillan was to write of the concluding years of his premiership being 'haunted, not to say poisoned' by the tensions arising from the Rhodesian situation.

January 14, Sunday   *Rottingdean*

The *Sunday Times* interview was published today and we are now coming up to the broadcast.

The P.M. is in remarkably zestful form considering that affairs are so troublesome – pay pause querulousness, uncertainty about a restraint policy, and Maudling rumbles about resignation on Northern Rhodesia (with Perth probably to follow, and if Perth then Macleod – or so he says).

When I went to see him on the 10th (fifth anniversary) – though it was the end of a heavy day – he was in high good humour. 'I have been stopping a resignation. Wouldn't have gone well with this interview would it? The trouble is that these young men don't have any background. They have brilliant minds but they don't have any experience in dealing practically with situations. They don't recognise situations. They think they are problems which can be disposed of by the process of logic and reasoning. We have thought up a new scheme which will keep him busy. Play it long. That is the answer.'

He came back again to the success of 'your' television speech at the B.B.C. anniversary dinner – 'It is still echoing round the world.'

The *Sunday Times* gave the interview great prominence on the centre pages, but there was a hiccup when they tried to do some extensive cutting in order to fit it all in on the leader page. My suspicions were aroused when Murphy proved elusive on the phone and had me put on to Dow, who eventually confessed that he wasn't handling it. Fortunately, I managed to track down Jimmy Margach and sorted out with him what was tolerable from the Prime Minister's point of view. In the end Murphy thrust it at him and said in effect, 'Oh well, you get on with it.' The result could not have been better.

But Fleet Street gossip characteristically fastens on the last two answers which I had written myself simply to round off the article (Gladstone, Disraeli and Churchill as respectable precedents in age for 'a stripling of not quite sixty-eight').

The broadcast I drafted as an extension in simple terms of the interview, leading up to the economic situation. There I found myself inescapably with higher productivity as the key – and with individual effort at the heart of it all. 'Just that little extra effort from everybody,' is how the P.M. has decided to express it.

Tony Barber is now to assist Charles Hill on information co-ordination (they'd thought of Vosper but I suggested either Barber or Woodhouse). We have also extracted pay pause publicity from the Treasury, but goodness knows what progress can be made when there is no policy and Selwyn Lloyd is so maladroit.

At the second time of asking I managed to get down to St. Dunstan's at Catford to talk to two hundred sixth formers about Prime Ministers. It looked like one of those chores one undertakes from unwillingness to upset a friend, but it went well and I came away encouraged both by the boys – bright, confident, intelligent – and by the masters who put on an excellent dinner afterwards with stimulating argument.

January 28, Sunday   *Rottingdean*
Was the broadcast a success? Inevitably the Press was more concerned with impressions than with quotes, but David Wood wrote approvingly in *The Times*. The *Telegraph* said he looked twenty years younger (though thinking the opening two-camera gimmick was too 'mannered'). The *Mirror* launched an editorial attack, headed 'Waffle', because there had allegedly been no direct reference to the Common Market, and followed it up the next day with an unhibited Cassandra onslaught: they must have thought vigorous action was necessary to lessen its impact. The *Herald* put a box on the front page to draw attention to the Prime Minister's quote from their December 23rd leader. The Sunday papers today – to the extent that they refer to it – are critical about its

alleged lack of content (can't they read?). Worsthorne in particular complains that there was no stirring call to arms, but an *Observer* leader says that the intention may well have been to put across a reassuring personal image on the grounds that this is *not* the moment for stirring calls to action: and that if this was the intention it probably succeeded.

In the P.M.'s own circle – Lady D., John, Tim – it was felt that he had done particularly well, and so too did Charles Hill and George Hutchinson. This brought me some compliments since,' though labelled Party political, it had really been my contrivance. 'Still reeling from your triumph?' asked John the next day.

I had not intended to get involved on the day, but George Hutchinson was leaving it all to the B.B.C. and John Grist, and Lady D. rang me in distress to say that they were rigging up an extraordinary lectern on a wooden platform and could I not do something about it. The trouble was that someone had told them he would want to stand while speaking. My idea was that he should do it, as in August, from his small study table. Maurice Macmillan was also hovering around, not saying anything to me, but he had suggested to John Grist that when the text had been spoken and canned his father should be induced to do a completely *ad lib* piece.

To cut through the confusion I went up to the P.M.'s bedroom – he stayed in bed all morning – and he agreed without hesitation that he should sit at the table in the study. With that settled it remained only to straighten them out about the two-camera introductory gimmick. So at 4 the P.M. simply walked in, after being dusted over by Toni, the make-up girl, and got on with it.

Lady D., George Hutchinson, his henchman (taking a transcript), and I watched on a monitor in the inner drawing room. Just before he started Lady D. noticed that his double-breasted jacket was pulling at the buttons, and I rushed out and made signs to him which he at first interpreted as meaning that his flies were open! He then undid the jacket button which revealed him as waistcoatless and this, I think contributed to the image of informality and youthful indifference to clothes and weather.

He did the first take remarkably well and there was agreement that this would do. The second began slowly but worked up to a climax when he abandoned the text without abandoning the argument. I thought this was better, both because of the climax and because it would make a better text. He did a third and some thought this even better, but my own choice was for the second. This was confirmed when the P.M., breaking precedent, decided to see the introduction played back and then sat through the whole thing on the settee. 'Was that the second?' he asked. 'That will do.'

He then became very cheerful and jaunty – 'At least it can't do any active harm' – and stayed talking to the B.B.C. team over Mr. May's whiskies, and ending up with a cosy chat with George Hutchinson. At one time we thought a reference would have to be inserted to the first U.S. astronaut on the moon – 'the man in the moon,' to quote the P.M. – but the attempt to put them into orbit had been postponed until the weekend (and is now postponed again).

Perhaps the overall conclusion must be that the broadcast brought very much the established reactions – with 'insufficiently forceful', 'too unsure', and 'too general' as criticisms, and 'calm and gentleman-like', 'calm and clever leader' and 'a sensible gentleman' as praise (as reported in *Television and the Political Image* after the 1959 election). I don't think that in terms of the ordinary television viewer the broadcast could be said to lack content – it was a clear, well-argued statement of the background to our problems and the involvement of the individual: it was not written for Fleet Street and the Worsthornes of this world.

Simply on viewing numbers it was, as *The Observer* noted, 'an easy winner over all other programmes during the week'.

Whatever the impact of the broadcast there were those in the Party who wished to see changes at the top. The cat was put among the pigeons when Sir Harry Legge-Bourke, a member of the executive of the 1922 Committee, said in a public speech, 'I do not believe it is fair to expect those who have borne heavy burdens so courageously for so long to go on until they either break down or bemuse the public mind.'

February 3, Saturday   *Rottingdean*

Mac on the way out? This has crystallised as the current talking point following yesterday's speech by Legge-Bourke – but the *Express* opinion poll shows both the P.M. and the Government making a small advance. Charles Hill reports one colleague as thinking the P.M. made a deplorable impression at Thursday's 1922 Committee – limp, weary, old and cosy. In the House on Tuesday, however, he scored points, not least for his retort to the supplementary 'How local is local?' – 'Well, I know my own "local".'

Criticism is focusing on the handling of the pay pause. Yesterday's White Paper explaining the approach to the interim phase, has not had a good Press. One despairs, both because of the failure to produce any precision which will make effective presentation possible, and because of the woodenness and stubbornness of Selwyn Lloyd. Everything is pulled out of the hat at the last moment without an opportunity to advise on presentation or prepare it. And his own personal contribution is inarticulate and unimaginative. Should Charles Hill have asserted himself at an earlier stage? And would it have made any difference? He does not accept that this is anything but a trough.

It is true, of course, that with some successes the winter discontent might quickly disappear. But where are successes likely? The railway strike position looks less ominous momentarily, the Tube men are split about another Monday strike, and the postmen have stopped working to rule (not that it made much impact anyhow), but all this is negative. In the international field the day of spectacular Britain initiatives has gone: Kennedy can be persuaded to take those initiatives we think are sensible, but *he* must do them. The Common Market lies ahead – but there are months of negotiation before the issue comes to a point of decision, and in the meantime there is uncertainty.

Then Central Africa. With Maudling's return from the West Indies at the beginning of the week we have had another series of clashes between him and Sandys. But the Cabinet agreed on a formula on Thursday – without many of them knowing what was going on behind the scenes. This enabled Sandys at a briefing with the Commonwealth Writers yesterday to stick within the strict limits of accuracy in saying that there had been no clash within the Cabinet.

Maudling arrived back from the West Indies apparently in a more relaxed mood, and Tim ascribed this to a shrewd move by the Chief Whip who wrote to the Governor-General, Lord Hailes (last Chief Whip but one) to suggest that *he* should suggest to Reggie that a resignation would get him nowhere since Perth would also go and then Macleod – in which case a Maudling gesture would become a lesser issue. The Duke not the Chamberlain would take the headlines. So Reggie returned simulating calm – but by Wednesday he had become very angry again.

This kind of background doesn't make for confidence when on the surface affairs are also in a state of unease and uncertainty.

The week also saw a clash beneath the surface between Heath and Rab. Resuming his Lobby meetings on Wednesday Rab talked about everything under the sun, including the Common Market, and the interpretation appearing in *The Times* and *The Guardian* had Ted Heath hopping mad. He opened the Thursday Cabinet by deploring these stories, which he said presented a pessimistic view precisely at the moment when he didn't want a pessimistic view. Rab said not a word, but buttonholed me after Cabinet to explain that he felt justified in doing so because he did not recognise what *The Times* and *The Guardian* wrote as an accurate representation of what he had said, and anyhow there was the understanding about Lobby meetings: so he assumed that I, too, would say nothing. Heath knew the origin, of course, but not many of his colleagues did. The Foreign Office went into action with a 'corrective' exercise. Result: *The Times* diplomatic correspondent wrote exactly what the political correspondent had written – only in more detailed and categoric terms. But here again is lack of rapport between colleagues.

I lunched at the Boulogne on Wednesday with Douglas Clark, who has been restored to Foreign Office grace, but he pines to give up the job and go, he says, to the Sunday paper. The job he would really like is Robert Pitman's – in charge of features. The shake-up in the *Express*, he says, is not likely to see Robert Edwards confirmed as editor. (The next day comes the news that Roger Wood gets it, with Derek Marks as deputy.) He is frank in his criticism of deterioration in Lobby reporting as a result of excessive sensitivity in news rooms about what the chief rivals are saying.

On Thursday I talked to about fifty members of the Press and public relations branch of the N.U.J. about the public relations job at No. 10. They were responsive and asked good questions.

February 4, Sunday   *Rottingdean*
The Sunday commentators inevitably take their cue from the Legge-Bourke speech and spread themselves in analysing where the P.M. stands with the Party. Peregrine Worsthorne says that the P.M.'s performance at the University Conservative Association's meeting at Oxford was lamentable. Yet he, with the others, concludes that there is no immediate threat to his position – if only because there is no crown prince.

What, in fact, is there in it? Something certainly. He is to an extent a prisoner of circumstances. So much hinges on the Common Market. He can no longer take international initiatives. On Central Africa there can be no decision that does not bring down a storm. His great nuclear and disarmament plan will end with the White House seal on it.

Perhaps because of this very frustration he seems obsessed by 'gimmick' answers, knowing there can be no solutions. On Northern Rhodesia he has spun a web of electoral and arithmetical balances rather than (seemingly) looking for the right answers. He expresses little with precision: all is safely generalised. It is against this lack of precision that some of the revolt is stirring – yet, goodness knows, what *can* be said precisely? Then he does have moments when he is visibly weary and depressed.

Tomorrow in the House he winds up the U.N. debate. How much depends on that? He could rout his critics with a really lively performance at this moment. If then the luck begins to turn, and there are some successes to chalk up, the position could look totally different by the summer.

February 11, Sunday   *Rottingdean*

And what actually happened? Simply this – having been invited to look into the abyss of 'who else?' by Sir Harry one and all took fright and the murmurings are quelled. So now the Sunday columnists are seeking to say that it is simply because the Prime Minister is over-loaded (Worsthorne) or that he has no alternative as leader of the Tories but to mask his liberal policies while he leads them on (*Observer* leader).

His Commons U.N. speech was probably *not* critical, since by then the ranks had closed and it needed only competence. That he gave them. Henry Fairlie, ever unpredictable, thought he gave them more than that – 'Macmillan at his brilliant best'. On Thursday came the nuclear tests/disarmament statement which he did very well. Then at last a Cabinet Minister had something to say in his support – Watkinson. But no other?

There came a moment when I, too, came under fire – a letter to *The Times* from Sir Thomas More saying that what the Government needed was a first-class public relations officer; but here again it was a solitary runner which quickly disappeared from the course under ridicule from Stonham, Cassandra and others. On the morning it was published, Tuesday, about a quarter of an hour before Cabinet, I had a telephone call from the P.M. He said nothing at all about the More letter, but took as his cue the editors' lunches and then chatted about this and that, including his idea of taking a genuine holiday in April 'without telephones and boxes', i.e. handing over to Rab. But it was, of course, a gesture of confidence. Let me not forget that.

The nuclear statement may get recognised for what it is – a Macmillan initiative, and it *ought* to help that Albany in the *Sunday Telegraph* stumbled across the existence of a private line between the White House and Admiralty House.

On Thursday evening (end of a very long day) I joined a

Raphael[1] drinks party in his flat at Greycoat Gardens and found among the guests Worsthorne, Shonfield and Boyd (*Economist*). All, in varying degree, had critical things to say of the P.M. and professed depression about the likely inability of the Opposition to unseat either him or the Tories. Shonfield said that he had created an American-type Cabinet. Worsthorne (striped shirt and bow tie as ever) was preoccupied with the machinery of government and wanted to make Rab economic overlord. I said (a) I couldn't see how a P.M. could fail to keep close contact with both foreign and economic policy, and (b) you couldn't interpose a Minister between the Prime Minister and the Chancellor of the Exchequer. He was really mulling over his weekend piece in which this line was duly developed. As for Andrew Boyd, the P.M.'s U.N. speech on Monday was 'appalling' (but what of Henry Fairlie's 'brilliant best'?).

During the week Philip de Zulueta had similar chatter from Rees-Mogg. And Rab? The Chief Whip, too, is wondering how to make him happy again. Should he perhaps add co-ordination of the information services to his schedule? But no, says Martin, I'd better dismiss that from my mind. This arose from an exchange of notes about Iain Macleod and an unexpected small explosion – 'He's impossibly arrogant' – in reference to Macleod's aloofness. A story going the rounds says that John Morrison, chairman of the 1922 Committee, said to him recently, 'Do you know, Iain, you have spoken to me only twice since you became chairman of the Party – once on the front at Brighton, and the second time I approached you.'

February 17, Saturday   *Rottingdean*

Triumph with the railway unions. So it was acclaimed by the Press though its histrionic undertones did not go unnoticed. Cassandra, indeed, was turned on to do a hatchet job. That's the third time recently the *Mirror* has turned all its guns on a Prime Ministerial performance. They have obviously decided on a systematic tarnishing of the image. How clever is that? As political tactics fairly obvious, but it stands a strong chance of being counter-productive given that the *Mirror* readership has means for checking for itself – notably the broadcast, not to mention reporting in the other populars, especially the *Express*, now running an uninhibited pro-Macmillan line (except, of course, for the Common Market). Should the Conservative Central Office take action to counter the *Mirror* campaign? I talked to George Hutchinson and put in a

[1] Chaim Raphael, Head of Information Division, Treasury, 1959–68.

weekend note to the P.M. Let's see what effect the air of Chequers has.

What really matters is the railway settlement. It could be crucial for the whole restraint policy – and this is seen, of course. But there may still be unofficial action on a major scale. It could also be a turning point in this difficult phase of whispering anti-Macmillanism.

I talked briefly to the great man about the railways. The union leaders were on a difficult wicket, of course; they could not really afford a strike; he had to help them out of the impasse; and 'after all, we are all in this together . . . but how tired I am.'

After the talks themselves I was summoned to the Cabinet room to talk to the P.M., Selwyn Lloyd and John Hare[2] about guidance. It was the dilemma of making it clear that nothing had been given away (to placate Nabarro and company) and yet letting the union leaders get away with such roseate hues as they needed for their own purposes. ('We *don't* want a strike.')

For my part I had a poorish week, perhaps because of the irritant of having to prepare a draft for the dinner the American correspondents are giving for the Prime Minister. It has one good lighthearted passage – if it survives. *Time* had me in a state of indignation with a biased piece on the anti-Macmillan theme: but Robert Elson assured me that he and Otto Fuerbenger were both distressed about it and that it had been given this angling in a New York re-write.

My lunches during the week included Joe Fromm (at the Connaught), possibly the shrewdest of all the Americans, and Dick Wald (at a new fish restaurant, Henri's, in Maiden Lane), certainly one of the nicest. After three years in London Wald contemplates a Bonn posting and welcomes it, rightly, as a young man who has almost decided to settle for being a foreign correspondent. London is a splendid place to live, better than New York; he could be happy to live here but not as a transient; feeling he is a transient he has had enough; and, anyhow, for an American London is too easy and pleasant a beat. On Macmillan he wonders whether there is not a progressive loss of confidence as each critical situation is allowed to become solved without any *show* of vigour and leadership: that they *are* settled, that the method may well be the best way of settling them, he accepts, but there remains a seeming lack of firmness of direction.

Another lunch was the second in the P.M.'s new series for editors, this week's editor being the *Telegraph*'s Donald McLachlan.

[2] Minister of Labour 1960–63. Later Viscount Birkenham.

Henry Brooke filled the fourth corner. McLachlan advocated a Royal Commission to advise on 'whither trade unionism', and cited the victimisation of two Jaguar workers who refused to come out in the recent one-day stoppage by the engineering unions as an example of the undemocratic processes that are becoming increasingly evident.

Seeing more of Henry Brooke I begin to wonder whether he might be the man to slip between the more obvious contenders for the throne: on closer acquaintance he is much more human, much less dour and much less metallic than opinion believes.

I went to see Norman Brook about the pressure on Lord Snowdon to join the N.U.J. (getting information for him about the Thomson House chapel). He was agreeable as always on these *à deux* encounters and very open. Like the Chief Whip he got round to the question of whether some change was necessary in the Ministerial information arrangements. I had to agree that Charles Hill was finding departmental pressures unexpectedly heavy. Charles confirmed this when I saw him later, but said that he would not like a change to be made while presentation was under fire. Brook felt it was a pity that the Prime Minister had filled up so definitely the schedules of the non-portfolio Ministers, one of whom should certainly do information: and again, as with Redmayne, he contemplated the possibility of Rab doing it – if only he could be persuaded that it wasn't vital to have the anchorage of a great department: if Rab would take the job without portfolio he might then become deputy Prime Minister in fact.

February 25, Sunday   *Rottingdean*

American week. First, the dinner at the Savoy with the Association of American Correspondents. Bob Elson and I agreed that it would be best to keep it as informal as possible. Some of his members no doubt didn't agree, but it proved highly successful in the sense that afterwards they were all commenting on how relaxed and cheerful the P.M. had been. He had taken my draft as it stood, led in with Glenn, the space-orbit man, got them laughing with the Press passages, and then put his hands behind his back and talked in his broadest philosophical vein about Communism and the West. After that he spent ten minutes or so at each of the four other tables. On Glenn he was able to report that at his weekly audience with the Queen the previous evening they had spent part of the time listening on a transistor set, to the neglect of State business. Inevitably, several rang the next morning to seek guidance on how they might break through the off-the-record arrangement and use the story.

One of the topics of conversation was the closeness of London and Washington on all major issues – you couldn't put a razor edge between them, Joe Harsch wrote the other day in the *Monitor* – with the by-product that life became dull for the American correspondents in London.

It was timely, then, that on Friday we found ourselves fussed by Washington going ahead in its reaction and reply to Mr. Khruschev's latest letter without consultation. The P.M. told Ormsby-Gore to make various points to Kennedy orally (to avoid a formal approach), but Kennedy was in Florida and a communication had to go from the embassy. So on Saturday, after Michael Hilton had collected a headline in the *Telegraph* for a non-existent Macmillan-Kennedy telephone call, we had reports from Washington of a Macmillan letter to Kennedy. Nearly all Saturday I spent on the telephone trying to get it sorted out – all this virtually without guidance except for an exchange of views and information with Philip Woodfield. Apart from the B.B.C. that evening it came out satisfactorily.

Mixed up in it all were 'words' with John Russell at the Foreign Office. No. 10 and News Department are not in harmony at the moment. I must brush up my anti-F.O. brief: if they wish to fight I'd better be armed: trouble is that I am so lazy and can't bother to remember points of grievance and criticism.

But back to American week. On Friday I had lunch with Bill Clark at the embassy and was taken round the marble halls. I didn't learn a great deal except that a Salinger–Murrow hostility apparently exists.

A domestic political sensation now erupted into the headlines with the loss by the Tories in a by-election of their traditionally safe seat at Orpington. The Tory majority at the general election had been nearly 15,000: now the Liberals had won with nearly 8000, with an insignificant Labour vote. 'The staggering blow of Orpington,' wrote Harold Macmillan in his memoirs.

March 18, Sunday   *Rottingdean*
The week of Orpington which I welcome as the lancing of a boil – assuming it *has* been lanced.

The great inquest now goes on, including criticism of presentation, though most of the political commentators do not put it high among the factors. Nor did Charles Hill have a particularly difficult task in coping with a critical resolution at the Central Council meeting at the end of the week. On the other hand, Hailsham has talked cryptically about trying to lead from behind and criticised the speech-writing efforts of the Civil Service and the Central Office.

Is a new Macmillan speaking style desirable – assuming it could be devised? The one speech with which I was concerned this week – to the Parliamentary Press Gallery Luncheon Club on Wednesday – had a very good reception, both at the time and in the Press itself (as measured by quotation). Nevertheless, this is a good moment to review our public relations work at No. 10, since J. W. Miller is being snatched away for the new Central African Office under Rab, and John Groves joins me from the Treasury.

The announcement that Rab was to take on responsibility for Central Africa drew Opposition scorn and derision in the House, with an intensity that surprised most of us. 'That didn't go too well, did it Harold?' the P.M. said as he was leaving the House. I agreed and said that in part it might stem from a superficial hearing of the sentence about 'certain quarters', though I believed that the Press were likely to see the sense and logic behind it. Which by and large is what they did, thanks largely to a very good briefing for the Commonwealth writers by Rab himself.

The Lobby did not show very great interest and Macleod was not required (and did not choose) to elaborate it when he had his Thursday meeting with them. The Sundays, too, showed little disposition to criticise: *The Observer*, indeed, is enthusiastic, and Anthony Sampson (to whom I talked at some length on Friday) writes it up well in the Pendennis column.

The P.M. rang me from Liverpool on Friday morning (he had gone up overnight) to say that he was pleased with Press reaction, in particular *The Times*, and also, I think, to make sure that I wasn't feeling upset in the aftermath of Orpington.

Earlier – on Tuesday morning – I had gone up to his bedroom to talk about the Press Gallery speech, and he went on to talk about what is his real preoccupation at the moment – nuclear tests. He is determined to get an agreement if he can; or, if it is not possible, to pin the responsibility beyond doubt on Soviet unreasonableness.

'I'm afraid I shall have to have a row with Kennedy . . . We shall have to talk to Khruschev before any tests . . . It is the last chance . . . I may have to go to Moscow in the next week or ten days . . . Certainly we can't have these new American tests before everything possible has been done . . . They could be put off for a few weeks . . . Fancy having them in Easter week, anyhow. Maundy Thursday. What a day to choose. I shall say so to him. He must see that . . . Eisenhower did not bother so much about the politicians. He did what he thought was right and what the people round him agreed was right. He had been a soldier and never had anything to do with Congress. But Kennedy came up through Congress and he is much more conscious of political pressures. Of course, it is true that he cannot get a treaty through unless the Senate agrees.'

But a Moscow trip is not really a serious possibility, though Kennedy has said he does not mind a Macmillan–Khruschev summit.

Looking back further – to the lunch for C. D. Hamilton (with David Eccles and myself) – the P.M. expressed a view which surprised me: that elections are usually won on foreign policy.

March 25, Sunday   *Rottingdean*

Departure of J. W. Miller and the incoming of John Groves. I think he will fit in well. It was a quiet baptism – an unusually placid week. Judging from comment round the office Jimmy had won some very real affection – and this is pleasing because the last thing he would claim are Establishment qualifications.

April 1, Sunday   *Rottingdean*

We are going through the post-Orpington period, with interest now focusing on repercussions in the Stockton by-election next week. Since the P.M. is spending Monday at Stockton his own prestige is to some degree committed. Some say this is a false move when the pundits and pollsters forecast the Tory at the bottom of the poll: others (including Mark Arnold-Foster in *The Observer* today), while accepting this as a possibility, yet argue the value of H. Macmillan being seen to be doing something, not least something that shows courage in accepting hazards.

When I talked to him on Friday he was tending to take this line himself. He was also professing optimism – that signs are accumulating of a turn for the better and that this will percolate to the populace at the customary interval of three to six months. But he feels that he must try to break through the Press and television barrier and wonders whether the open Press conference might be the answer, though he recognises the dangers and disadvantages. I am required to think it out.

April 16, Monday   *Rottingdean*

Night before I return to the office after a five-day break. Easter weekend is coming up and then we go to New York, Washington, Ottawa and Toronto.

Most of the five days I have spent worrying about Annabel's

persistent high temperature (though she is cheerful and active), and re-making the rockeries with York stone (heavy to lug about) in some thoroughly un-springlike weather. Annabel's lack of robustness has me thoroughly on edge. Dr. Butcher advocates a spell under observation at the Great Ormond Street Hospital and this will have to be faced.

I have done little preparation for the North American trip until this evening. The two big speeches are going forward on the de Zulueta–Foreign Office network, but I must see if there are embellishments I can suggest.

The Government continues to slump in opinion polls, though the Prime Minister gained kudos for his Stockton visit which just got the Tory into second place. The Budget (tax on sweets, promise of Schedule A abolition) won't help them very much. The line is 'boredom but we have eighteen months to get things right'.

May 5, Saturday   *Rottingdean*
Look back on the New York–Washington–Ottawa–Toronto visit, April 25–May 3

We took a very small party – P.M., Norman Brook, Philip de Zulueta and myself, plus four girls (Eunice Groves as archivist, Ann Barker and Bridget Earp from Admiralty House, Joan Porter from Norman Brook's office), three Special Branch men (Harwood, Morris and Ravenhill) because of the complications of dispatch boxes at hotels, and Mr. Beecroft (who extended his valeting service to me). It was Bridget's first trip overseas. Poor girl, in Washington she went down with suspected glandular fever and had to stay there which left a heavy load for the imperturbable and cheerful Ann and Joan.

We all felt it was an advantage to have such a small group – a No. 10 group without Foreign Office complications (Shuckburgh joined us at Washington for the talks with the President, and Arnold France, of the Treasury, for the Ottawa leg). It meant a concentration of responsibility which made for quicker and tighter teamwork. It meant also, of course, a heavy burden of work, and on our return early on Thursday (having virtually lost a night's sleep) most of us had lapsed into exhaustion.

From my point of view the smallness of the party was entirely to the good. It brought me into the White House talks and into the speech-writing work more intimately than otherwise would have been likely: also it kept me in close proximity to the Prime Minister (only in Washington was I physically separated from the others). I was invited to all the major social and semi-social occasions, e.g. the ambassador's dinner in Washington when the President, Vice-President, Rusk and Macnamara were all there and I had a brief opportunity to talk to the President alone. He particularly wanted to know if the Bonn leak by the Germans had been deliberate. Norman Brook and I celebrated our birthdays on the same day (Sunday 29th) partly in Washington, partly in Ottawa. The rest of the party, including the P.M., joined in sending us cards and we shared a toast from the Rideau Hall staff in Ottawa (a delightfully friendly group of people headed by Esmond Butler as Private Secretary and Madame Berger as Lady-in-waiting). The Governor-General, Major-General Vanier, is a splendid old soldier, one-legged from the first war, upright in bearing and character, a man of great yet simple dignity, who can unbend without losing authority.

Sunday night at Rideau Hall is the occasion for an informal buffet supper which gave us a relaxed introduction to Ottawa after the strident excitements of Washington and New York. Sitting next to the Governor-General at dinner, I heard that Canadians are in danger of going soft from central heating, cars and lack of exercise. He believes that youth needs some measure of discipline, which is the virtue of national service.

Madame Vanier is almost overpoweringly vivacious. She delights in the eccentricities of her children – an abstract painter, a Trappist monk, a commando and a doctor (the only girl) who has just acquired an assignment in Nigeria. I heard also of an association with Rottingdean from the early 1930s.

Philip de Zulueta is an old friend of the Vaniers, having been at school with one of the sons: Madame Vanier remembers him as a boy in bed with measles.

Government House has extensive greenhouses in which, it is claimed, one can see simultaneously in bloom English flowers of all seasons. One of the gardeners told me that he was a Londoner who came to Canada at the time of the depression after the first world war and had not been back since.

Philip was at his best on this expedition, stimulated by the fact that this was indisputably *his* show – not another private secretary remotely in sight. Only once was his amiable imperturbability breached – the second evening at Ottawa when, on top of the Diefenbaker talks, there was the Toronto speech to be re-jigged, partly because of the Canadian general election and partly because none of us was very happy about it anyhow. But he responded instantly to ribbing about losing his cool and the girls thanked me next day for restoring him to calm and good temper.

And the Prime Minister? He stood up to it extraordinarily well, stimulated no doubt by the ovations he received from the news-paper publishers in both New York and Washington and at the White House correspondents' dinner: and more particularly, per-haps, by the more-than-strictly-necessary friendliness of the Presi-dent (a colourful airport ceremony, including a warmly-phrased speech of welcome: the special relationship atmosphere of the talks: the turn-out for the Ambassador's dinner party – virtually the whole of the top American hierarchy: the enthusiastic re-ception, led by the President, at the White House correspondents' dinner).

The New York speech we had considered a good one and likely to be well received, but the magnitude of the ovation at its end was said to be something quite out of the usual. Robin Day, seeking comment afterwards for *Panorama*, could extract nothing critical, though the British Press (reporting the text and not the occasion) showed no enthusiasm: indeed the *Mirror* and *The Guardian* were critical. Both also made something of the fact that, trying to be helpful as ever, we had arranged a London release. You simply can't win with the Press – try to help them and they will turn it against you, but if you don't help they will be querulous.

The Toronto speech had worried us, but I recalled the political vituperation passage which went down so well with the circulation executives in 1960 and we cabled for that: then the P.M., Philip and I had a final crack at it in his bedroom on the morning of the day and made it at least coherent and balanced. ('Thank you for going to so much trouble, old chap.') In the event, it got off to a flying start with the vituperation passage, and getting excited the P.M. put it across brilliantly. So another standing ovation.

Afterwards we had a happy and animated Prime Minister, hopping from one foot to the other. 'Do you write all your own speeches?' someone asked. 'Oh yes, though *they* help me, of course – with the figures and that kind of thing.'

. But none of the colour and excitement got reflected in the British Press, in part because of the time difference. To report at all they had to report in advance – assuming, of course, that you can't possibly report twenty-four hours later. So the ovations went unrecorded in Britain.

On the basis of advance material, the British Press reported a Macmillan impersonation by Peter Sellers as the highlight of the White House correspondents' dinner: but he did not do a Macmillan impersonation and he came close to flopping, partly from the misfortune of having to follow Elliot Read's masterpiece on a Kennedy Press conference (but the President had the last word with a remarkably cold-blooded and cynical parody of his own steel prices conference).

However, *Panorama* attempted a general assessment of the visit – with good effect, we are told. Just as well that I pushed the P.M. into an interview with Robin Day at the end of the back-grounder for the British correspondents at the embassy on Sunday morning (there was a note of thanks from Paul Fox on my return).

What else? We pleased the U.K. Delegation at the U.N. by giving a boost to the U.N. in the New York speech and by letting it be known that the P.M. had told U Thant that we hoped he would stand for election as Secretary-General and that the British would support his candidature. I did this at an on-the-record Press conference with the U.N. correspondents after we had lunched with U Thant. It went well, though I always have doubts about the wisdom of tackling other people's subjects on their own ground. Haydon wrote to say that it had been extremely useful. Alan Campbell said this to Philip also, and the sceptical Pat Dean thanked me at the airport as we left.

I twice had opportunities for gossips with the great man as he relaxed in bed. We debated the fanatical gleam in the eyes of the West Point Glee Club. I sat within two yards of them on the stage at the Waldorf-Astoria and was struck both by the gleam and by the close-cropped bullet-shaped heads and pale sallow complexions. It was a quality in Americans that frightened him, said the P.M. Its other and attractive aspect was enthusiasm – the zest with which things were done. That brought us to the British *lack* of zest, and so to the British Press and its querulousness. 'Its a sign of decadence, I'm afraid.'

I said that I thought that Ministers must try to meet the current critical unrest by vigour in their speeches. They must demonstrate vigour, and not hesitate to get rough and lash about. 'Like Hailsham, you mean?'

The White House correspondents' dinner gave us a splendidly relaxed and entertaining evening, again characterised by naive but infectious enthusiasm. Spokesmen rank differently here. First Pierre Salinger and then I were called upon to take a bow, theatrically pinpointed in a shaft of limelight in the semi-darkness, followed by Jim Hagerty in the body of the hall.

The Salinger approach again seemed alarmingly casual. Is it really so? One briefing he certainly did not do well. But he was quick enough when, he, Bundy, Philip and I repaired to the map room in the White House basement to draft the communiqué. And he is splendidly 'easy'.

Prior to the talks he and I had a breakfast conference in the White House staff canteen (a panelled room in the basement). I proposed that we should do our damnedest to get into the talks, get the principles of the communiqué agreed and then try to write it ourselves – 'bulldoze until someone stops you' should be our approach. 'There speaks a true member of the fraternity,' was Pierre's reaction – and for the most part we succeeded. We had both been alarmed by the first drafts produced from the two sides. At the State Department working lunch to produce a draft Pierre sent a note across the table, 'We shall need a bomb shelter if this is used.'

May 14, Monday   *London*
Since I was lunching today with Oliver Woods of *The Times* I sought and obtained an audience with the Prime Minister to see if there were any themes he would like me to develop. It resulted in a long gossip.

He started by noting that the newspaper industry was giving a ten per cent increase to the printers though carefully suppressing publicity about it. Obviously it had nothing to do with the merits of the case and had been conceded simply because they were afraid of a stoppage. Repercussions were likely in the book publishing industry and more and more firms might have to do their printing overseas. In all the criticisms of an incomes restraint policy nobody seemed to ask what would happen if we abandoned such a policy. What did people think would happen? Perhaps there was some hope in the fact that the National Economic Development Council was examining with the unions the possibilities of an annual productivity growth of four per cent. It must surely become apparent from these discussions – though we don't want to underline the point for fear of frightening the unions away – that if four per cent was the most optimistic figure for expansion then it was unrealistic to think in terms of income and wages increases above four per cent. If we paid ourselves eight per cent where would the other four per cent come from? It could only be from the international value of the £ – though it was true that this would depend also on what other countries were doing. If all went in for mildly inflationary policies the effect of U.K. inflation on the value of the £ would be correspondingly lessened, though we should have all the disagreeable domestic effects. If all countries lapsed from virtue a kind of equilibrium might be established. In that case the pay pause policy would have put us a year ahead. It would be nice to know what alternative policy *The Times* and other critics would suggest, or indeed what was Labour policy and Liberal policy.

We then talked about the current trends in by-elections and local elections. The P.M. thought it represented a conjunction of a spiritual vacuum and a vague feeling in the middle classes that all they had striven for was turning to Dead Sea fruit. They were becoming aware that power was passing to organised labour, and that the period since 1832, in which the middle classes had dominated government and politics, was disappearing. Even their material wealth was not bringing them the rewards for which they had hoped. Many middle-class families now had two cars, but what good were two cars when driving had become such a hazard? Then there was the discomfort, frustrations and irritations of the London commuters. The whole of south-east England was becoming an uncomfortable place in which to live. But what were the remedies?

On prospects for the Common Market negotiations, the P.M. felt that possibly the problems of incorporating an independent Algeria would make the French more aware of the nature of our Commonwealth problems. I said that if the effort to enter the Common Market failed we should need to have ready an alternative policy, for example a closer union in some form of the Anglo-Saxon countries – Britain, Canada, Australia, New Zealand and the United States. The trouble was, said the P.M., that the economies of the 'white' Commonwealth countries were not really complementary to our own, but we should certainly have to give some thought to developments along these lines. We might well have to decide to cut ourselves off from Europe almost completely in politics and defence.

May 27, Sunday   *Rottingdean*
    Turning point for the Tories? I wonder.

The Gallup Poll in the *Telegraph*, and the National Opinion Poll in the *Mail*, both said on Monday that in a general election now the Tories would win again. In mid-week senior Ministers were on parade before the Tory women at the Albert Hall and performed with the vigour and assertiveness that is now the keynote – notably the Prime Minister himself with an attack on selfish employers and arrogant trade unions. He pulled out all the stops and had an ovation of unusual fervour. Yet the ever-loyal Knox Cunningham for once came back with inflections of doubt. The Press, however, was exceptionally favourable. An approving leader was even squeezed out of the *Telegraph*.

196

In a minute to the P.M. and a memorandum to Charles Hill I advocated, among other things, not only vigour and forthrightness in speeches but also that excitable backbenchers should be cuffed a bit (plus a reorganisation of the Ministerial information arrangements now that Charles Hill is so preoccupied with Housing and Local Government and Tony Barber with the Finance Bill).

On Friday before lunch I had forty minutes with the P.M. in his study and on the backbenchers point (note in the fawn leather notebook) he decided to think again about seeing the 1922 Committee next Thursday. He was already feeling annoyed about reports which implied that he had been 'summoned' to attend. He also made a note of my advocacy of Central Office fact sheets on immediate issues (e.g. nurses' pay, university grants) – one side of a single sheet making the essential points for distribution to Party members.

But at the centre of his thinking is the new economic policy package, including a tribunal to evaluate those professions and occupations which claim to be underpaid. The package began to take shape at last Sunday's meeting at Chequers, but the tribunal idea did not make much progress either in the Economic Policy Committee or, at first bite, in the Cabinet. I, too, think it has few presentational advantages and said so in my memorandum, but the P.M. is determined to persevere with it.

Certainly it will have to be accompanied by other action and there is some hope of this – abolition of resale price maintenance, for example, and a consumers' council.

We talked about how the package should be 'launched'. He has something up his sleeve and by degrees he began to pull it out – partly because I pressed the point about early consultation with Charles Hill and the need to get it into the co-ordination channel and away from the Treasury. He proposes to use Hailsham in some undefined way and there was even some talk of a separate, special and independent public relations arrangement. But eventually he seemed to agree that the evangelical fervour of Hailsham would need to be harnessed to the administrative and co-ordinating management of the Hill machinery.

He talked about the apparent inability of the Treasury to produce any convincing long-term policy. They had Cairncross, who was very good, and Armstrong, who was brilliant, and a few others, but they did not seem to be able to find time to think ahead. They could produce a perfectly adequate short-term policy to cope with an existing situation, but could not put it into a long-term context. And

Selwyn, who was a lawyer, did not seem to have time to do more than read his briefs. 'So you and I have to sit down and try and think something out. I am getting quite excited about it – but, then, I am an old man, of course.'

We talked also about the Common Market. I recapitulated the line we are taking about next weekend's de Gaulle talks and advocated resting on this rather than saying beforehand that there would be no communiqué and no briefing, as suggested at a P.M.–Home–Heath session at Chequers on Saturday. If then they found they *could* produce an agreed statement so much the better: but we *must* be able to back it up with briefing.

We talked about the Press, including the significance of Jacobson's move to the *Herald*. He seems to think that Jacobson is the man who has determined the crude anti-Macmillan campaign in the *Mirror*, but I say that I believe it to be Cudlipp. However, we shall see what Jacobson now does with the *Herald*. In the meantime the *Mirror* has stood away from its campaign – possibly a repercussion from a Macmillan letter of sympathy to Cudlipp about Eileen Ascroft's untimely death. Then there is the bitchiness of the *Telegraph* – despite Coote who is presumably a waning influence – which the P.M. thinks may be due principally to Lady Pamela. John Wyndham, whom I consulted subsequently, thinks it a waste of time to try to cultivate her. She thoroughly dislikes Uncle Harold and anyhow has less influence than most people believe: the trouble is that Michael Berry also dislikes Uncle Harold.

Another topic in my P.M. talk was the Pilkington report on broadcasting. Does it not mean two B.B.C.'s, asks the P.M., and what is the point of that?

For the rest, in a week of movement, I took Tommy Thompson to lunch at Whitehall Court (and agreed with him a piece for *Hardly Hansard* about Charles Hill wanting to give up the information chore – after talking to the latter); was given lunch at Verry's by Peter Hardiman Scott in appreciation of the help which he said I had given him on the North American trip; and summoned a Friday tea party of Alfred Richardson, Charles Birdsall, Jimmy Miller and Don Bickerton to talk about the frailties of Government policy and the information services (it produced some frank talking and some ideas which I must try to follow up).

On the domestic side there has been the great joy and relief of Annabel's return from Great Ormond Street with a clean bill of health. She is now back at school and full of vigour and cheerfulness after her ordeal.

June 3, Sunday   *Rottingdean*

Does Uncle Harold seriously contemplate the fall of the Government or his own fall? Twice this week – at lunch for Kenneth Young on Wednesday and when he saw Rees-Mogg on Friday – he quoted what he had said to the Queen at his Tuesday audience – that if he had to give up the administration she would at least know that it was to no party of revolution. 'The fac⁺ is that we have been too successful. There are no extremists. No one wants to overthrow the existing order. There is no bitterness. And, after all, that is what politics is about.' To Rees-Mogg he added, 'I hope you don't think that is too defeatist.'

The week has seen two developments which must worry him. First an angry Menzies – though the Menzies–Marshall statement at the end of the week about the 'agreement' with the Six on industrial imports from Australia, Canada and New Zealand had a pretty cool and sceptical reception. Secondly, a movement among Cabinet Ministers (plus the Chief Whip) against his 'New Approach'. 'This is not Conservatism,' says the Chief Whip in effect.

He *did* see the 1922 Committee and talked forthrightly about chattering to the Press and about loyalty ('a few who are disloyal riding on the backs of the majority'). But he hinted at the 'New Approach' and it was duly leaked and then hardened into a 'plan' by Douglas Clark in the *Express*. 'Why did you let him do it?' said Maudling to Tim Bligh: but, of course, it puts the doubters, including Maudling, on the spot. On the other hand – as I said in a note to him about presentation – leaks can only (a) inflate expectation, (b) render some items stale, and (c) alert the Opposition.

This has been the weekend of the visit to de Gaulle at the Chateau de Champs. There had been a natural disposition to see it as a momentous encounter in the context of British entry into Europe, but we succeeded in getting most people to see it rather as a continuation of the dialogue, without expectation of immediate or dramatic results. The disagreeable Joe Alsop[3] had contemplated a British double-cross of the U.S. in a nuclear deal with France: that, too, we succeeded in de-bunking.

The encounter went much better than the ambassadorial prophets had foretold. They put out a communiqué, in itself unusual for Macmillan–de Gaulle meetings, and French television news this evening put on it a very friendly gloss – clearly from the General himself since Philip had reported great affability and, at one point, a declaration by the General that he wished they might talk every week.

---

[3] American newspaper columnist.

But is this not rather too good? It hardly accords with the P.M.'s own assessment as given to Rees-Mogg – that though he has excellent personal relations with de Gaulle (probably no one knew him better because of the many hours they had spent together in Algerian days), the fact remained that the General strongly disliked the Anglo-Saxons. (One had but to read his books – and how beautifully they were written!) The question was which half of his mind would prevail – the half which wanted to put the Anglo-Saxons in their place or the half which saw himself at the bar of history.

When Rees-Mogg asked about domestic opposition to British entry, the P.M. made a face and said that perhaps, like Peel, he would win the country but lose the Party. But who would be the new Disraeli? Perhaps that was how Derek Walker-Smith saw himself?

June 9, Whit Saturday   *Rottingdean*

The Government continues to be buffeted. An award of four per cent by the arbitration tribunal on Civil Service pay hits perhaps harder than anything else to date at the incomes restraint policy. Labour won the Middlesbrough by-election, with the Tory only just pipping the Liberal for second place. ('Wonderful, wonderful,' says Mr. Gaitskell, and George Brown exults, 'This is the breakthrough, brothers!') But the West Derbyshire result the next day saw Aidan Crawley holding the seat for the Tories and there had to be a degree of re-thinking.

The P.M. showed some signs of strain mid-week. He was ratty at Cabinet on Thursday, I was told, until the Derbyshire result came through. And on a memo I sent him on Wednesday night about lunching Roger Wood, of the *Express*, he said he was beginning to doubt whether editors' lunches were worth the time and effort. 'These chaps seem friendly enough when they come but then there is renewed violence.'

I hope this is only a passing irritation. He must hang on – which is what he advised his backbenchers – and present a façade of equability and liveliness. He has been doing it extremely well on these private occasions and the effect must accumulate.

July 1, Sunday   *Rottingdean*

After a period of depression I am feeling more relaxed. Mainly I have been troubled by inaction on the information front by the Ministerial co-ordination team, Charles Hill and Tony Barber. As long as this was so I could hardly complain if, in planning his New

Approach, the P.M. should be turning to Macleod, Hailsham and Michael Fraser, as he did one weekend at Chequers. But this week I succeeded (I think) in persuading the two Ministers to adopt a more active stance (a session in Room 17 at the House, followed by gins on the Terrace).

The P.M. plans to launch the New Approach in an economic debate on the 30th. He has already trailed it, not only with the backbenchers but in a speech at Luton Hoo, which exposes it to the dangers of speculation and over-expectation, though Macleod has been inferring to the Lobby that no pronouncements are likely before the Party conference in the autumn.

Other reasons for a restored morale include a successful exercise on the Pilkington television report (which has awakened a noisy and diverting debate). Again, I had several stimulating encounters – a Reuters cocktail party for a party of Moscow-bound American editors (the home side included C. D. Hamilton, Pickering, Tyerman, Michael King, William Connor and Sidney Jacobsen); Saville Garner's farewell party for Ben Cockram; and lunch at Overtons with Kenneth Young, John Buxton and Bob Scott of the *Yorkshire Post*.

At the end of the week came Winston's fall (broken thigh) at Monte Carlo, which set the alarm bells ringing. An R.A.F. Comet was sent to fetch him, prompting a very late call from Bill Grieg who said that his editor was demanding to know on whose authority the Comet was sent. I thought it as well to see if I could really find out (knowing not least that the P.M. had been fussing about the arrangements, including the Press arrangements), and ended by being party to a midnight telephone conversation between the P.M. and Julian Amery before speaking to each of them separately. I think the P.M. rather liked being brought into it. At that time of night he tends to be lively without having anyone to share his liveliness with him. Also it pleased Bill Grieg to get an answer. The next morning I chased Aviation and the Air Ministry about the Press arrangements and then phoned the P.M. to tell him all about it which again pleased him. Fortunately, the arrangements worked well, and Winston, the indomitable (and puckish), seemed to enjoy being again the focal point of drama and excitement. I brought home for the weekend the Winston file, just in case (he is, after all, eighty-seven), but happily all the bulletins have been encouraging.

It has been an easy weekend – and a pleasant one, doing agreeable family things.

There now came the Cabinet re-shuffle which was to go into the history books because of its extent and seeming ruthlessness – the 'massacre' of July 13th. It was to prove but the first of a succession of dramatic and politically important events which were to follow each other without respite for fifteen months. In October 1963 they culminated in Harold Macmillan's own dramatic resignation because of sudden illness.

July 7, Saturday   *Rottingdean*

Events are gathering momentum. I am in them but not of them. A seat in the royal box. The P.M. has decided to attempt a major re-shuffle before the recess. Six are to go (says Tim). The key to it all is the replacement of Selwyn Lloyd as Chancellor of the Exchequer (he is to be seen next Thursday evening): presumably he can only become Lord Chancellor. And the others? My chief interest is whether they include Charles Hill. He is being almost ostentatiously vigorous at Housing. Kilmuir, Mills, Maclay – they seem obvious. Watkinson? Hare? Eccles? Erroll (probable).

The precise timing will be determined in relation to the announcement about the New Approach. And that appears to be lurching uncertainly. Yet following the Luton Hoo speech Iain Macleod has done so much talking that they will have to produce something – something more than something, indeed, for (as I warned) the Lobby boys are embarking on competitive speculation which is pushing expectations higher and higher. Dickinson and Carvell let themselves go on Friday with prophecies of a new golden age for house-owners and prospective house-owners. These are reflected in today's morning papers and will certainly get hotted up by the Sundays.

Charles Hill is counting on making a contribution to the launching – and that, not least, may keep him in, for performance and attitude on the New Approach must sway the P.M. in deciding who goes and who stays. Then, of course, the Common Market negotiations must come to a crunch in the next three or four weeks, with the Commonwealth Prime Ministers to give the pot a good stir in September. The opinion polls show strong trends against entry, but the battle is not seriously joined and for the moment the 'anti' proponents hold the field. Anthony Fell put on a vein-swelling performance in the House in attacking John Hare. One cannot think that when the chips go down people like this will count for much.

I had only one brief personal encounter with the P.M. during the week. He was then very amiable: highly satisfied with the three per cent settlement of the engineers' wage claim eighteen months after their last rise.

President Kennedy declared himself for U.S.–European inter-dependence in his Independence Day address. He is very consistent in saying the same things as the Prime Minister – after a due interval. Gratifying but frustrating since, in the role of Greeks, we must stay silent. Perhaps history will conclude that the greatest Macmillan achievement was to persuade the Americans into adopt-ing his thinking and acting on it. That plus taking us into Europe (if he succeeds).

July 22, Sunday   *Rottingdean*
Today's Sunday Press caps a dramatic ten days – probably as dramatic as any in British politics in peacetime – with newspaper stories all having the same broad theme. In headlines it appears as 'His Own Executioner?' (Peregrine Worsthorne in the *Sunday Telegraph*), 'Perils for the Premier' (James Margach in the *Sunday Times*), 'For Mac the Bell Tolls' (*Reynolds News* leader), and 'No more patronage so no more purges' (Mark Arnold-Forster in *The Observer*). On the news pages the main political story is Lord Avon's condemnation of the harsh treatment of Selwyn Lloyd. Pushed down page, but still there, is further speculation about a Butler–Macleod–Maudling ultimatum to the Prime Minister de-manding changes, this speculation having been set in train by Francis Boyd in *The Guardian* yesterday (that it came from him gave it credence), but angrily denied by Rab. He rang me yesterday to talk about it, to say he was denying it, to ask how we were handling it (John Groves, on duty, was also denying it), and to say that he hoped I did not think it would cause any disturbance at No. 10 for him to deny it.

For my part I have now reached the point where I cling without subtlety to the facts as I know them – and the facts as I know them do not support the story so I agreed that this could be the only line. Today Charles Hill rang to say that he, too, was getting calls about it: that he was protesting at getting them, but going on to say that he simply did not believe it.

He went on to tell me that during the week Rab had invited him to go along for a talk. He wanted no further involvement, however, and had found reasons for not going. Now Rab had pressed an invitation to see him at 5.30 tomorrow and said it was urgent. Something is surely brewing. To me Rab said that it had all been too upsetting for things to settle down easily.

Until these latest developments it had seemed that the motion of censure by the Opposition had served to consolidate the Tory ranks, at any rate until Thursday when the New Approach – 'the cat in the bag', to quote Macleod – is to be given an airing by the P.M. and will be found on examination to seem a rather tatty kitten. With the news from Brussels also not very good things are shaping for a further and bigger explosion.

But to go back to Thursday the 12th, when the button was pushed. In my note of the 7th I recorded that it had been decided to go ahead with the reconstruction before the recess, and that at least six Cabinet Ministers would go. Selwyn Lloyd was at the centre of it and an appointment had been made for him to see the P.M. at 6 p.m. on the 12th. It had also been decided that the announcement should be made on Monday, the 16th. On the morning of the 12th, however, the *Mail* (Walter Terry) led its front page with a story about 'Mac's Master Plan', including a major re-shuffle 'by the autumn', and mentioning enough about the names involved (though getting it wrong on Macleod) to suggest a leak. There had been forewarning in the sense that late on Wednesday night Gordon Grieg, of the *Express*, had rung to say that the Lobby was buzzing with rumours that there was to be an early re-shuffle: presumably he was checking up on the *Mail* story on its first appearance in the early editions. However, I rang Tim to alert him.

The *Mail* story was bound to revive the re-shuffle speculation which had died away after a front-page spree a few weeks ago. At Thursday morning's Lobby meeting the enquiry duly came, with Bob Carvel as the enquirer. Possibly he expected it to be ridiculed, but knowing that the announcement was timed for Monday I was in a quandary. Accordingly I had to temporise. I did so by recalling that when they had quizzed me some weeks ago on the same subject I had been prepared to put my money on the autumn: now, I said, I would probably hedge my bet. This was enough to set the alarm bells ringing, though they must have already been ringing in the Central Office and on the backbenches. The London evenings duly competed in sensational headlines, though neither anticipated immediate action. This, too, was the day of the Leicester North East by-election which all opinion reports forecast would be disastrous for the Tories.

For whatever accumulation of reasons – and the Chief Whip almost certainly had a decisive voice – it was decided to push the reconstruction through within twenty-four hours (i.e. a Friday evening announcement) instead of leaving it until Monday; but principally the purpose was to anticipate Sunday paper speculation, fortified by the likelihood of rumours sooner or later after Selwyn Lloyd had seen the P.M. at 6 o'clock.

The new intention was made known to me by Tim Bligh while

Selwyn was receiving his (seemingly) mortal wound in the Cabinet room. I pointed to the obvious practical difficulties, especially on a Friday when the Lobby men customarily dispersed during the afternoon, and said that the latest we could reasonably have the Lobby was 6.30 – of which I should have to give notice some hours ahead. But I said it could be done and supported the reasons for doing it, i.e. to avoid weekend speculation and leaks, taking note also that news of Winston Churchill's bronchial infection sounded ominous.

Of Selwyn Lloyd, Tim said that he had given him forewarning (though not saying when: I presume during the afternoon). He had taken it calmly, and recalled that a few days earlier the P.M. had asked him, 'Do you think the time has come for me to go?' which he had interpreted as meaning 'Don't you think the time has come for *you* to go?'

Even as we were talking in the Private Office, Selwyn Lloyd pushed open the door from the ante-room, having left the P.M. (about 6.15), and signalled Tim to go out to talk with him. That suspended our discussion for twenty or twenty-five minutes. On returning Tim reported that Selwyn had refused a viscountcy and has insisted on an exchange of letters (it had been thought that letters would not be possible because of the time and the numbers involved).

To get the measure of what was involved Tim then began to scribble down the people involved – Maudling for Chancellor, Manningham-Buller for Lord Chancellor ('But who else?'), Butler to give up the Home Office and be called First Secretary of State and 'act' as deputy Prime Minister, Brooke to the Home Office, Noble to succeed Maclay, Sandys to take over the Colonial Office as well as the Commonwealth Relations Office, Deedes to succeed Mills as Minister without Portfolio and to be given the job of information co-ordination. As to Charles Hill and Harold Watkinson, Tim put them on the list with queries, putting a square round Hill's name and saying, 'I'll fight all the way to keep him.' I produced reinforcing arguments – that his dismissal would be badly received, both because of popularity with the Lobby and the general belief that he is showing zest and determination at Housing. But we both knew it was really a lost cause.

For the rest – so far as the 12th was concerned – Charles Hill had reported after the morning Cabinet that he had detected a death wish among a number of his colleagues, including Selwyn Lloyd. He had absolutely no thought of his own departure, but Tim rang him late that night to tell him to hold himself ready for an interview with the P.M. on Friday. He was at my office first thing on Friday morning to ask if I knew what it signified. Tim had told him it might be neutral but could be worse. I said that it seemed clear that he should expect the worst.[4] He took it resolutely, of course, but said that he could not understand it: there had been occasions in the past when he thought he might go, but on this occasion it had not occurred to him. Indeed, he had earlier in the week sent in to the P.M. a preview of his Cabinet paper on housing policy, representing the crystallisation of his thinking and offering some original ideas: Tim had thought it a good paper and said so in his covering minute to the P.M. but it had come out initialled and without comment which both Tim and I recognised as ominous.

On Friday the Press were slow to cotton on to the fact that events were racing ahead, but death-watchers appeared at the door just before lunch after John Groves had stalled on the inevitable 'when' questions at the morning Lobby meeting. I had suggested that he should say that anything could happen on Friday the 13th and this was the line he took.

The comings and goings of Ministers at the front door were without intermission, though the watchers must have been puzzled by the appearance of Sir Charles Wheeler who had come to talk about the Leonardo. Only Rab and John Hare were spotted before lunch. John Hare left looking very downcast – or so it was thought – and the later editions of the evenings seized on this as evidence that he was being removed. In fact, he had come to be reassured that Selwyn's departure from the Treasury did not mean an inflationary economic policy: if it did, he said, he would wish to resign.

I spoke confidentially to Spenny Shew a little before 1 o'clock about calling a lobby meeting and we agreed that there would have to be a service message on the agency tapes at about 4: for the rest Spenny would spread the news orally of a meeting at 6.30 and avoid putting a notice on the board in the House.

Putting my guidance notes together could hardly have been a more haphazard procedure. Because of the rapidity of the entrances and exits, and the involvement of Tim Bligh, I could not get at either the P.M. or him. And the facts themselves could be pieced together only as they emerged. But we had a good number of the names and could assemble background about them, plus general

---

[4] He was succeeded as Minister of Housing and local Government by Sir Keith Joseph, and his responsibility for information co-ordination went to W. F. Deedes as Minister without Portfolio.

statistical background. Finally, I succeeded in pinning down the Chief Whip which proved invaluable.

With the girls (Esme and May only since Doris was on leave) playing their part with customary willingness, speed and efficiency, we got the notice ready in less than an hour so that John and I were able to walk more or less nonchalantly into the Lower Press Gallery promptly at 6.30 to confront the assembled Lobby (plus a few not strictly Lobby, including Trevor Smith). It took about twenty minutes only, with compliments freely dispensed both then and later, with a formal vote of thanks from the Lobby after issue of the second list on Monday and my telephone marathon on Sunday.

I did get into the P.M. for three or four minutes immediately before we left Admiralty House. He was slumped in his chair in the Cabinet room, but relaxed and very friendly. Norman Brook (not in the picture) also came in. The P.M. was mainly interested in what I proposed to say about Sandys taking on the C.O. as well as the C.R.O., and I had to undertake to let Norman Brook see my formula (a formula provided by Sandys with some editing by myself). The P.M. thought that Sandy's, with a vested interest, might have given it an angle of his own but Brook found no objection. For the rest he said something to the effect that, 'Of course, they will be saying I am an old man clinging like a limpet to power.' From Brook he sought an endorsement of his own enthusiasm for Boyle at Education. ('A bit difficult since I didn't know what he had done,' was Brook's comment afterwards.) Finally, as I left, he said, 'Don't look so worried, Harold,' to which I replied that what worried me was the time I now had left to get the announcement made.

In general Saturday's Press reaction was approval, tempered by misgivings about the speed, extent and ruthlessness of the purge (e.g. a *Mail* cartoon with Khruschev saying to his assembled colleagues that they should recognise that they had never had it so good). But Sunday's Press was sour, with almost the sole exception of Rees-Mogg in the *Sunday Times*. It seemed to have largely accepted the Opposition's interpretation (reasonable enough from the Opposition) of panic and desperation accelerated by the Leicester by-election. I said this to the P.M. when he rang me from Birch Grove early on Sunday afternoon, though he was inclined to dismiss it as 'not too bad', adding that Rees-Mogg had got it exactly right, and perhaps it was a good thing he had seen him recently.

His main purpose in ringing was to get my view on letters of appreciation to the departing Ministers, and to find whether it was feasible to issue them for the Monday morning papers, i.e. within the next three or four hours. I said I thought it was important to make clear that this was not just an afterthought in the light of Sunday Press comment and he ran through the kind of things he might say in the opening paragraphs of his letter to Kilmuir, and these, I felt, met my point (he had written personal letters to them all). The Chief Whip was going to Birch Grove at 5 to discuss the junior Ministers, and the P.M. rang me very shortly after to say the Chief Whip agreed about the letters. Quickly after that Tim (also at Birch Grove) rang me with the texts, and these I dictated to P.A. and Extel on a linked call.

This was no small incursion into my normal Sunday calls, which began with Harry Boyne at 2.45 and ended with Trevor Lloyd-Hughes at 10.20. At an earlier stage it had seemed likely that the second list of appointments would not be announced until Wednesday at least and I had said so to a number of my callers. So I had five or six ring-back calls to make when Tim came through to say that it was hoped to complete the list in time for a Monday announcement.

Monday morning's Press showed some return for my Sunday efforts, with the panic and desperation interpretation largely removed and much of what I had to say well reproduced, notably by David Wood in his weekly piece in *The Times* (which also had a satisfactory leader) and by Francis Boyd in *The Guardian*. But I was distressed by the pieces written in the *Mail* by Walter Terry (lead story) and Louis Kirby (main article on feature page).

For Monday's exercise on the second list we inevitably had the death-watchers from the beginning of the day (at the Horse Guards door as well as the front door), and the evening papers had a running commentary in successive editions. Compiling guidance was again a matter of my taking the initiative. A new title was being introduced for the Minister of Works but I proposed an amended formula to the Chief Whip which he accepted: and having got from him what he understood to be in the Prime Minister's mind I knocked together a piece of guidance which in the afternoon I was able to clear with the P.M. in the Cabinet room.

He was again apparently relaxed. He felt sure it had been right to issue the letters without delay, he said: it had been Dorothy's idea – women had an instinct about these things. He also thanked me for all I had done (re-inforcing a minute written on Sunday which, in effect, drew what little comfort was possible from the Sunday comment). We were again able to descend on the Lobby promptly at 6.30, and again, simply as an operation, it went without a hitch.

Late on Monday – just before 10.30 – I had a telephone call from

R. A. Butler. Its immediate purpose was not apparent but he began by saying, 'I haven't been in it at all. I feel quite calm about it all because it *is* a revolution. I feel my neck all the time to see if it is still there.' But then, quickly, 'I do understand the Prime Minister's motives and I am behind him. I know why he got rid of Selwyn after six years. But it wasn't done properly. My two friends became too emotional.' After that, back to his own problems. 'I have had to find a room. I have no staff. I have had to do it all myself. I have got the Air Council room in the Treasury. It is very dignified.' Finally some solicitude for me. 'How are you? You must take care of yourself,' and as a signing-off line, 'Well, there it is. Put it on the cuff of your excellent shirt.'

Tuesday's twist to the drama came with the Prime Minister's first appearance in the House following the massacre (the word most commonly used in stories and headlines). It was chilling and daunting, especially since it had been preceded by resounding cheers for Selwyn on taking his seat on the backbenches. This was the first clear indication that the changes – or at any rate the method of making them – had not pleased the backbenchers.

July 29, Sunday   *Rottingdean*

From Charles Hill, who had dinner with me at Whitehall Court on Tuesday, I heard that an effort had been made to persuade forty or fifty backbenchers to abstain on the censure motion tabled by the Opposition – in the hope that this would cause H. Macmillan to resign without actually bringing down the Government. But he – and all the others, it seems – would have none of it, and by Monday the effort had been abandoned. In the upshot the Tories rallied without exception and had a majority of ninety-eight, the maximum possible.

Charles still feels hurt. He has had his first bus ride for eleven years and found it dirty, uncomfortable and expensive. He has had three hundred letters – some quite unexpected (for example, a most unbureaucratic one from Dame Evelyn, with whom he had fought some stern battles on first going to Housing). One letter said it was sad but, of course, he had chosen to live in a menagerie and could not be surprised if he got scratched. But some he might have expected had *not* come. He said that in writing to the P.M. he had entered a further strong plea for a knighthood for me: for that I expressed gratitude again (and how much I owe him), but had to admit to scepticism, given mandarin attitudes.

We now have other things to think about.

From Brussels it is reported that the Common Market negotiations are likely to fail. The P.M. won't admit it, says Tim, but has
nevertheless included two qualifying phrases in his speech to the
1922 Committee.

With Norman Brook I have been involved this weekend in an
operation to sort things out following a total scoop by the *Sunday
Telegraph* on the new appointments at the head of the Civil Service
(Helsby as head of the Civil Service, Armstrong as Lee's successor
and Burke Trend as Brook's successor as Cabinet Secretary). It
started with a check call by James Margach at 7.30 p.m. on
Saturday and shattered my weekend yet again. I rang Brook to
warn him and then got involved in calls with Tim Bligh, the three
concerned, Fife Clark and Esme. Raphael at the Treasury had not
left a phone number and could not be raised. Brook decided that we
should have to announce the whole thing forthwith (including the
long explanation about the internal re-organisation at the Treasury).
How to do it became my business. It involved getting a No. 10 car to
fetch me from Rottingdean on Sunday morning, a meeting with
Brook and others at Admiralty House and then a dash back by train
to Brighton in time to pick up the afternoon calls from the Lobby
(had I not been available at Rottingdean we should have had the
wildest speculation since a strong rumour had been circulating at
the end of the week that H. Macmillan intended to resign during the
weekend).

Brook turned up for the meeting with both his private secretaries
(James Robertson and Douglas Tanner) plus a girl. Tanner and the
girl gave Esme some useful practical help in preparing the release,
and with the C.O.I.'s Mr. Margetts doing an efficient job we had
the announcement in Fleet Street before 2. Not that, in fact, the
story had caused any great ripples. James Margach reproduced
strongly in the *Sunday Times* the guidance I was able to give him,
and the B.B.C. have also done so today.

But Brook is putting together a list of all those who knew beforehand. I had told Bill Deedes (with subsequent authority) and was
half afraid that it might turn out to be an aberration on his part: but
when I rang him this afternoon he said that Kenneth Rose (whose
scoop it was) had told him as early as Tuesday that he was nursing
for Sunday his best-ever story. With Deedes I begin to establish a
more satisfactory relationship after a first week at arm's length.

August 4, Saturday   *Rottingdean*
Philip de Zulueta rang me this morning and from that and news
stories coming from Brussels it seems that the French have suc-

210

ceeded in sabotaging the E.E.C. negotiations. My own instinct is to hope that, if this really is so, we should make no bones about it: but Master will no doubt try to blur it, to play it long, to seek some new way through. I feel that the country in general has no enthusiasm for going into the European community (and especially being linked with the French), that it had accepted the need to make the effort and that if the effort fails there will be relief and a possible release of energy and determination of the kind we had after Dunkirk. There would then be a rallying to the standard and an opportunity for forthright leadership. But, alas, I don't see the P.M. choosing to play it that way: and perhaps true wisdom lies in refusing to be rebuffed given that the stakes are so high.

Yesterday we had another day of drama (if, by recent standards, lesser drama). With a mandate to keep the upsurge in defence expenditure within some kind of limits, Thorneycroft decided to recommend the axing of Blue Water. That something of the kind was under discussion inevitably leaked because of the departmental and industrial lobbies. Chapman Pincher is said to have had an anonymous letter on Monday through the *Express*, but if so he had made astonishingly little of it the following morning. The *Mail* then produced a banner about an attempt by Harold Watkinson (now with an electronics group) to intervene with Thorneycroft – successfully said the *Mail* (Stevenson Pugh and Angus Macpherson). Godfrey Hobbs got indignant about this, but I found that substantially it was true apart from the assumption that the intervention had been successful.

It then became evident that very wide issues of defence policy were involved, and a Defence Committee for Thursday evening became transmuted into a full Cabinet on Friday morning at a few hours' notice. I announced the meeting to Friday morning's Lobby, not making any mystery of the fact (apparent from the attendance) that it resulted from a wish to deal before the holidays with matters arising from the annual review of defence expenditure, including Blue Water. What I could not tell them was that Profumo – summoned back at short notice from a visit to the B.A.O.R. – had seen the Prime Minister before the Cabinet and that his resignation had become very much a possibility. ('The poor boy was nearly in tears,' reported the P.M.) Continuing into the afternoon the Cabinet decided to cancel Blue Water and Jack Profumo decided on second thoughts *not* to resign. So I managed to catch the 6 o'clock Brighton train.

September 5, Wednesday   *Rottingdean*
   It is 10.30 p.m. and tomorrow I return to the office after three
weeks' leave, broken by only two calls from John Groves. I am four
pounds heavier, feel relaxed and need no further conviction about
my ability to enjoy leisure. I return, however, with my schizo-
phrenic feelings unresolved. It remains love-hate, and I am still torn
on this vital issue of entry into Europe.

*Parallel with the negotiations for British entry elaborate arrange-
ments had been made for consultation with the Commonwealth
countries, especially to identify matters in which they felt their own
critical interests to be adversely affected. The Canadian Prime
Minister, Mr. Diefenbaker, was openly hostile, and among the others
there was at best grudging acquiescence, with attitudes depending
largely on the ability of the British negotiators in Brussels to obtain
concessions which would minimise the impact on U.K.-Common-
wealth trading patterns. With a meeting of the Commonwealth Prime
Ministers due in London in September it was clear that a critical point
would be reached, not least because each Prime Minister would have
to stand up and be counted in relation to his own domestic politics. It
was likely, therefore, that the meeting would produce rough talking,
whatever compromises might be possible behind the scenes. In the
U.K. the outcome of the conference would certainly influence
strongly attitudes within the Tory Party, traditionally Commonwealth in orientation, and so determine what was politically viable in
Government policy. In his memoirs Harold Macmillan writes, 'The
sense that we were now approaching a decisive stage in the great issue
filled us all with a feeling of romance and drama.'*

September 22, Saturday   *Rottingdean*
   A fortnight later and the high drama of the Commonwealth
Prime Ministers' conference has gone into the history books,
together with the broadcast on Thursday night when the P.M.
finally and publicly cast aside caution and reservations on U.K.
entry into Europe.
   On getting back to the office I found myself immediately
nominated for a central role. Press reporting and attitudes were
thought to be vital, and it had been decided that the normal rules of
Press briefing could not apply since there were fifteen visiting Prime
Ministers, each with critical national and political issues at stake.
There would, therefore, have to be a factual daily communiqué and
then every man for himself in briefing.
   Then there was the tug of war between Duncan Sandys and Ted

Heath. Sandys felt that the Prime Ministers would have to be offered some prospect of re-opening points of substance in the provisional agreements already reached. Heath felt that this was out of the question and that attention must be directed to those parts of the negotiation still to be completed. The P.M.'s answer was, 'Leave it all to Harold!' So, at any rate, Tim Bligh reports – Duncan stamping round the Cabinet room, jaw sticking out, and saying that he won't have any interference from the Foreign Office News Department: and nor, for that matter, will he have his own department doing it. So that was the wicket on which I had to bat. The official to carry the can if it went wrong.

But, of course, there is great strength when you have responsibility firmly and without challenge in your own hands: and Sandys made that clear at the initial briefing for the U.K. Press group (Commonwealth specialists plus) – Evans was the sole source of U.K. briefing and subsidiary briefings would be based on his instruction. I sat in accordingly at the plenary sessions: briefed the briefers (including Donald Maitland, of News Department, Heath's man) as soon as possible thereafter: and then dashed to the C.R.O. for a daily 6.30 briefing of the U.K. group.

Monday's opening speeches by the P.M. and Heath were obviously going to be crucial. I urged therefore that I should be allowed to use a summary of the P.M.'s speech at the first daily briefing (Heath did not speak from a text): and took the initiative by doing a summary at 6 a.m., dictating it to Admiralty House, and getting it cleared there and then by the P.M. I had it sent also to Sandys who made some peculiar amendments of a minor nature. But I had a firm base for the first day's briefing.

These were the only two speeches. Came the inevitable question, 'What sort of reception did they get?' To which my response in effect was, 'Well, you'd better get that from the other delegations, but for what it's worth they were both applauded, which in my experience is unusual at this kind of meeting.' It came out in exaggerated form in the headlines but at any rate the great British public knew that the Prime Minister had made a powerful speech, as it certainly was.

Then came Tuesday's onslaught, begun by Diefenbaker in the morning. 'Grumbling acquiescence' – to quote the P.M. – had been expected, but the cumulative effect of the day's speeches was shaking, probably for the Prime Ministers themselves as much as for anyone else. And most of the speeches were issued, with extensive verbatim extracts. At the end of the day Sandys could only counsel a philosophical reaction, which was clearly right. I described it as 'the day for doubts and reservations'. ('They won't use that,' said Sandys, but many of them did, not least Christopher Serpell, leading the B.B.C. television news).

Next morning the P.M. put a brave face on it. The Press, he thought, was not too bad and, in any case, it was accurate reporting. But Ted Heath, who had been pleased enough with the first day's reporting, now thought the Press was 'appalling', whatever its accuracy.

Wednesday's speeches brought little mitigation. When I sought Sandys' view he shrugged and said, 'You'll just have to look serene.' What I did was to underline the fact that though all the Prime Ministers had said they wanted a strong Britain at the centre of a strong Commonwealth none had suggested how we could do this if we deprived ourselves of the economic advantages of the Community.

With the large-scale issue of texts from the delegations the question now arose whether we should issue the full text of the P.M.'s opening speech. At a meeting at Marlborough House after the morning session R. A. Butler said that he thought it should be issued forthwith, and with the other Ministers not then dissenting this was decided. It seemed to me a doubtful proposition, however, partly because it would seem that we were rattled, and partly because we had to steer such a careful course in getting our views across without disturbing the development of a shamefaced mood in the Prime Ministers.

These misgivings also took root in Ted Heath's mind during lunch and he asked to see the P.M. at 3. I got in first (in the study) and advocated giving the speech to the Sunday papers, not for publication but for the guidance of leader writers and commentary writers. The earlier decision was then reversed and this new action authorised (it succeeded remarkably well: the three heavy Sunday papers could hardly have been more satisfactory, notably Rees-Mogg in the *Sunday Times*).

At this talk with the P.M. – before Ted Heath's arrival – I also argued that the time had come to begin a great positive campaign in the country to explain the arguments so forcefully set out in the opening speech. This I thought might be launched in the broadcast he had been invited to make by the B.B.C. next week: he could use it to distil the essence of the speech.

On the following morning (Thursday) a chance encounter with Heath, as we were both leaving Albany Chambers after breakfast, gave me a chance in the car (he gave me a lift) to take his view on the extent to which a positive campaign might prejudice the further negotiations in Brussels. He thought it would not do so to an embarrassing extent.

Since the plenary sessions had now given way to group discussions I was able that morning to spend some time at Admiralty House. The Chief Whip looked in to see me, and I found that he, too, was convinced that the boats were burnt and that the time had come to argue for Common Market entry without inhibitions: indeed, if they were going to lose the next election – and he thought they probably would – it would be entirely to Tory advantage to go down carrying the flag for a cause which could clearly be seen as bold, imaginative and forward-looking. I said also that I thought the Labour Party were getting themselves into an impossible position in which they might well be landed with an image of timid, parish-pump politicians, though I thought Gaitskell would be clever enough to see the danger in time to avert it.

With a Cabinet meeting that morning – though the P.M. went to Marlborough House to see Menzies and Ayub – Deedes had also returned to the scene after leave, and on the telephone I found that his thinking had developed in exactly the same way. At the end of the day Macleod rang me both about the broadcast and about Central Office ideas on turning the speech into a pamphlet, so here again one found the conviction that the time had come to move to a vigorous offensive.

By the end of the week the P.M. clearly took this view, and the Central Office were asked to prepare the first draft for the broadcast. In the meantime some of the heat had been taken out of the Prime Ministers' conference by the organisation of the group discussions. Moreover, the discussions were to extend to Saturday which would help to sort out the situation behind the scenes. The P.M. really did all he had to do when he went to Marlborough House on Thursday (the day he missed Cabinet to the discomfiture of those correspondents who had ignored guidance and written it up as a crisis Cabinet), and on Friday he had no engagements at all except a talk with Maudling. It seemed to me that the Press would think it peculiar if, after Thursday's activities, he simply stayed at Admiralty House and saw nobody, and I went up to see him in his bedroom to propose that he should go to Marlborough House for the second half of the morning and perhaps some of the afternoon. This he agreed to do, seeing Maudling (off to Washington for the annual meeting of the World Bank) at Marlborough House, and so I was spared trying to explain away a 'mystery'.

For the group discussions on Thursday and Friday, Sandys gave me useful background, and other background I collected from

Norman Brook (affable and helpful throughout) and Michael Cary and Angus Mackintosh in the Secretariat (it was fortunate that these two – both first-class and both uncomplainingly accessible despite the pressures on them – should have been the key official figures behind the scenes). My task was, of course, to reduce the temperature and the group discussions made this not too difficult.

Then came the Saturday plenary, with an arrangement that Sandys should see the U.K. Press group at 12.15 before a luncheon date with Makarios: this was to be his first meeting with the group since the conference opened and it was obviously important that he should not miss it, particularly if the Sundays were to be given the right angles. In the event the morning meeting dragged on and shortly after 12.15 Jack Howard-Drake came out with a message from Sandys to say that he thought it was 'hopeless' to get away for the briefing, and what did I think? I sent a message back saying he *must* see them, if only for fifteen minutes. Happily the meeting broke up on the stroke of 12.30 which meant he was able to give them twenty to twenty-five minutes. He did it very ably, though pitching his optimism somewhat high. Also his reference to the negative role of the Canadians had them hopping mad since inevitably it went back to them (both the Beaverbrook people and Patrick Keightley of *The Guardian* had close links with the Canadian delegation).

Indeed, they were so hopping mad that on Monday morning Diefenbaker asked for fifteen minutes with the P.M. immediately before the plenary session opened. He used it largely to complain about Duncan's briefing. The P.M. said that he didn't read the Press except for Flook, in which he had a publishing interest. Other Prime Ministers – certainly Menzies, since he referred to the 'highly imaginative London Press' – also did not like the Sunday Press and began to mutter about sinister British briefing.

On Monday (the 17th) there was another plenary, with the P.M. inviting further thoughts as a prelude to a summing-up speech by himself. Things went well in timing as he was able to get in his speech before lunch. Again I had prepared a summary and went in to see him in the chairman's room at Marlborough House before the afternoon session began. Rab was with him and they were sitting in the corner between the window and the door into the conference room. The P.M. (mellow after lunch) promptly launched into compliments about the Press briefing (he had done so similarly in my private meetings with him). I found this embarrassing and diverted his attention to the points I proposed to use from his speech and he agreed these.

Heath and Home came in while this was going on, and then

Sandys. We got on to the question of the broadcast. The P.M. wanted to get the Independent Television audience as well, if possible, and said that he was prepared to make separate appearances the following day. Rab protested that this would be too great a burden, but the P.M. took me on one side afterwards to say that he was not feeling in the least tired and could easily do both. But I, too, disliked the prospect, and to win time said I would take the view of Deedes.

A text for the B.B.C. broadcast had now appeared out of the Conservative Central Office. Philip de Zulueta and I both thought it appalling. At the end of the day I got down to doing a framework of my own, and Philip, characteristically, had a new text of his own ready by Tuesday morning – and a very good one, too, into which my few additional points fitted easily enough.

Monday night's briefing, on the basis of four points of principle from the P.M.'s speech, gave me plenty of substance, and we again had the initiative in Tuesday's papers.

The Tuesday briefing was another matter – in some ways the most difficult though I felt confident in handling it. The trouble was that, after a morning on foreign affairs, they had a session in the afternoon on the communiqué – a draft worked out by Brook and delegation officials, largely on the P.M.'s four points of agreement. This drafting exercise by the officials had begun at 10 the previous night and continued until 2 a.m., which disposed to some extent at least of Sandys' fears about leakage of the original British draft to the *Daily Express*. Sandys then proposed that when the Prime Ministers considered the draft they should be kept at it without break until they agreed – again largely because he feared Press leaks. But I said privately to the P.M. before he went in to take the session that I thought this would be a mistake: that if by 5.30 there seemed no prospect of agreeing a text quickly he should call it a day and remit to officials, on the grounds that (a) a two-hour session would be normal and could be presented as such, and (b) if they went on they would either produce a communiqué too late for effective handling in guidance, or fail to produce one at all, in which case there was a 'squabble' story laid on for the Press.

This procedure – discussion of ninety minutes and then a remission to officials – was, in fact, adopted, but when the meeting broke up the British side had been thrown into despair. The meeting had been a shambles, with demands beginning to pile up from each P.M. for a piece to suit his own particular purposes. For the P.M. himself a shopping-list communiqué could only be disastrous, and he had begun to talk gloomily of throwing his hand in.

From the bar Menzies sent him a message via Tim that it was always darkest before the dawn. Sandys proved unexpectedly forthcoming when I consulted him about a briefing line – it could be said plainly that the question lay between having a communiqué concentrating on general principles or one which amounted in effect to a shopping list. This I felt I should play gently, and I introduced it only after a fair amount of questioning, and in general took a matter-of-fact and quite-sure-it-will-come-out-all-right attitude.

But of course the mass circulation papers – prompted by briefing from other delegations – made it sensational, and it was a pretty gloomy meeting of Ministers (Sandys, Heath, Home) which assembled in the Cabinet room at 9.30 a.m. to plan tactics. But, astoundingly, Brook produced a draft agreed with delegation officials which largely met British requirements and which Brook felt would almost certainly be accepted by Prime Ministers. An alternative draft, in effect the shopping list, had also been prepared, but Brook said none of the officials had taken it very seriously.

And so it proved. When the Prime Ministers met in restricted session Tim came out at intervals to report progress, and it became clear that they had no intention of having even the semblance of a row.

We began accordingly to look at the practical problems of issuing the communiqué – a considerable physical task – and I sent in a message to ask if stencilling could go ahead with some of the first pages. That brought an assurance that the first three stood with only one minor amendment, and Tim appeared shortly afterwards to ask when I thought it could be issued. From the previous estimates of the admirable Angus Mackintosh I was prepared to say 2.15. A few minutes later I was summoned inside.

But the great men had reached the stage of saying nice things about Brook (P.M. and Diefenbaker, who also thanked the P.M. for his 'valuable services' as chairman), and after a clap for Brook they broke up, with the P.M. shaking hands at the door.

Earlier the P.M. had said to Tim that he wanted me, not Duncan Sandys, to 'go through the communiqué with the Press'. But this was out of the question. Sandys' briefing for the U.K. Press we had fixed for 3.30 and just before 3 I went to see him in his room at the C.R.O. (the first Minister's room I knew on entering the Civil Service: Cranborne was then its occupant before becoming Lord Salisbury). He could scarcely contain his jubilation. It was a miracle, he said, a miracle – with which I agreed but counselled caution in letting it seem that we were claiming a 'victory' over the other P.M.'s.

Now – Wednesday afternoon – we had to turn to the broadcast.

The P.M. had summoned a small meeting in the Cabinet room at 5 – Philip de Zulueta, Michael Fraser, George Hutchinson and myself. I was a few minutes late after the briefing and when I slipped in he was 'doing' the broadcast on the basis of Philip's draft (Fraser and Hutchinson looking pretty glum), with the tape machine switched on. The first part sounded very well, but the second half – as he tired – became too prolix and altogether it lasted twenty-five minutes. However, we now had a basic version in the can on which to work, with the advantage that the work would be fining down rather than re-writing. In fact, a couple of hours later, in bed after a rest, the P.M. dictated yet another and shorter version, and it was this which looked like holding the field when Thursday dawned.

I had arranged for Huw Wheldon to come in immediately after lunch. He had seen the drafts leading up to the overnight one: on seeing this he said at once that he vastly preferred the force and vitality of the first part of the draft dictated in the Cabinet room. I agreed, involved Philip, and as we stood discussing it in the ante-room the P.M. appeared at the psychological moment and took the point at once.

So Philip had to go away to 'marry' the two drafts. The hiatus the P.M. spent with Wheldon and myself in the inner drawing room. How absurd it was, said the P.M., to expect television to produce a constant succession of outstanding programmes when they had to be turned out so quickly and in such profusion: it was not expected that we should see outstanding books or plays produced with greater frequency than perhaps once a year – why then should it be thought that television could do any better?

In the event he did three runs of the broadcast (watched on the monitors in the drawing room by Lady D., little Mark Faber, Michael Fraser, George Hutchinson, Knox Cunningham, Philip and myself). The first ran to sixteen and a half minutes and was certainly adequate (though Mark went to sleep on the settee). The second improved on it, but he lost the thread at one point and also used the word 'Commonwealth' for 'Caribbean'. In the third he was excellent.

In my view this was his best broadcast to date, partly because he was saying things he really wanted to say and partly because he was determined to say them in the best possible way so that he didn't let himself stray from the script. Indeed, we had out of it a very good script and this was important.

It had a good Press, but with the political correspondents all in

Llandudno for the Liberal Party conference, and with the broadcast so late in the day (9.30, though the text was available at about 8), there could be little comment in depth, and its political significance – a burning of boats or, as Deedes said subsequently, the establishment of a new frontier – did not seem to be fully realised.

Then there was the business of a Gaitskell reply. About an hour after the broadcast Harman Grisewood rang me to say that Carleton Greene and he had felt that it was such a powerful and persuasive piece of pleading that Hugh had felt it necessary to agree forthwith to Gaitskell's immediate demand for a reply on the following night. I said that I thought that this raised a very important point of principle if the Prime Minister of the United Kingdom could not broadcast to the nation without having the Leader of the Opposition put up the following night to make a counter-statement with the advantage of the last word. I said also that in the discussions I had had with the B.B.C. they had made it clear that though a claim to reply could be expected from Gaitskell they did not contemplate conceding it until the following week, if at all. It was on this basis that the invitation had been considered and accepted. The point of principle, I said, I must of course leave to Ministers, but I could not hide the fact that I felt let down personally.

I then rang Deedes. He appeared to be taken aback by the force of the broadcast, especially in its later stages, and said that he could well understand that Gaitskell should demand and be given the right to reply. He recognised the point of principle, but looking at it in terms of political expediency he thought that Gaitskell's reply could only get him deeper into the mire, given present contentions in the Labour Party and the speed with which the reply would have to be drafted.

This was a prolonged conversation and at the end of it – 11.45 p.m. – I rang the P.M. His immediate reaction was to be philosophical, but I expressed my doubts and it became clear that he did not share the Deedes view that Gaitskell would fail to turn the opportunity to account. 'He's a very clever fellow: he will find all the weaknesses.' However, it would be a mistake to protest and we should just have to see how it turned out.

My own assessment is that inevitably it reduced the impact of the P.M.'s broadcast, if only by providing a competing focus of argument, but I don't think that Gaitskell entirely steered clear of the danger of being seen as a timid, dismal Jimmy (and certainly Jo Grimond, in winding up the Liberal conference, slammed him hard and effectively on this basis).

So ended a tense and dramatic fortnight. But when I said to the P.M. on the telephone that we seemed to have got through all the excitements pretty well he replied – with a note of relish in his voice – that even greater excitements lay ahead.

Earlier he had sent me a minute which said, 'I would like to thank you most warmly for the wonderful way in which you steered the Press guidance throughout the anxious weeks of the conference and after. I am indeed grateful to you.'

October 7, Sunday   *Rottingdean*

With Gaitskell allegedly feeling that he might be compelled at the Labour conference to repudiate any agreement reached by the Government for British entry into the Common Market (so Cecil King reported after lunching with him), the P.M. had the Private Office clearing the decks for resignation and an election. Ted Heath had said that if the Labour Party declared an intention to repudiate it would be impossible for him to continue to negotiate. So the P.M. by Tuesday night (Gaitskell to speak on Wednesday morning) had gone some way to deciding that with repudiation on Wednesday he would fly to Balmoral on Thursday with his resignation.

My own source, a later one (T. F. Thompson also after lunching with Gaitskell), said there seemed little likelihood of a repudiation, and on this basis I expressed scepticism about the alarm bells. In the event, Gaitskell did not mention repudiation in his speech, and the conference declared itself roundly against demanding an election now. He did, however, make a speech which all the commentators interpreted as strongly anti-entry (though reading the fine print afterwards one found many qualifications, loopholes and escape hatches). This 'anti' impression came out so strongly that the triumvirate – Macmillan, Butler, Macleod – at a meeting on Thursday night seriously weighed the pros and cons of an immediate election.

I saw the P.M. on Friday afternoon in the study. Rab, he said, had wanted an immediate election, but no one else. He himself was for going straight on (I said I felt sure that this was right). This, he said, was not an issue which Party political considerations should be allowed to dominate. People would think he was flapping. In his speech at the Conservative Party rally next Saturday he would make hardly any reference to Gaitskell. He would talk about the Common Market in the first part of the speech (developing his Commonwealth conference speech), and then go on to talk about the economic position with the theme of growth based on change

(*The Times* had published a leader on these lines which pleased him).

Today (Sunday) the Tory Party published their Common Market pamphlet over the P.M.'s signature, distilling the broad arguments for entry into Europe. It has a good Press this morning and W. F. Deedes will be delighted.

Meanwhile, on Wednesday, we had the one-day rail strike, plus the excitement of Mr. Marples's television exchange with Sidney Greene. Wednesday was a fine day and everyone enjoyed the strike, both the large proportion of London's working population who had a day's leave, and the rest who found London without crowds and traffic congestion an altogether more agreeable place. But Mr. Marples undoubtedly over-reached himself, and the Press was speculating about his future. Having established that the Prime Minister still had memories of July 13th and was unlikely to contemplate another sacking, I waxed philosophical in talking to the Lobby and others about it. But Ernie must really stop waving that admonitory finger and behaving as though the great British public did praiseworthy things solely for the blue eyes of E. Marples.

October 11, Thursday   *Rottingdean*

Tomorrow Dr. Butcher proposes to pull more varicose veins out of my left leg and I face ten to fourteen days of semi-crippledom. In anticipation I have taken two days leave to get various things done in the garden, in particular raking the lawns. Yesterday was Sussex October at its most splendid – climax to a spell of fine, warm weather.

Last Saturday we had Jim Hagerty[5] at Rottingdean for the day, with the likeable Bill Sheehan, his London man, plus Harry Boyne, at the end of the Labour Party conference in Brighton, and wife Margaret. To drag the great Hagerty away from the sophistication of the big city was something of an experiment, but the arrangements worked well and in a letter of thanks he described it as 'one of the most delightful days I have ever spent'.

I collected him and Bill Sheehan off the 11 o'clock Brighton train in a Brighton cab with a rubicund driver who by happy coincidence had just returned from working in Chicago. We drove round the sights before going through the Pavilion (exclamations of incredulity), and so to Rottingdean, walking up past the windmill to

---

[5] After ceasing to be President Eisenhower's Press Secretary he had joined the American Broadcasting Company and was visiting London on A.B.C. business.

inspect the village from Beacon Hill. After lunch I had hired Mr. Stevens with his big Vauxhall, and the men, plus Annabel, drove to see the beauties of East Sussex – Ditchling Beacon, Lewes, Alfriston, Beachy Head – and how lovely they were in that gentle autumn sunshine.

So back for tea and they all caught the 7.25 back to London. Memo: J. Hagerty doesn't like cold chicken; W. Sheehan doesn't like tongue; both like iced water with their meals (we failed to provide it); J. Hagerty dislikes heights (he had to sit down at Beachy Head).

In London I had lunch with Freddie Bishop (unhappy about our move towards Europe): had dinner at the Savoy at Tony Cole's party for John Russell, shortly to fly to Addis Ababa to become ambassador (a dozen, all male, in the Mikado room, with an exchange of bawdy stories over brandy and coffee between John and his successor, Michael Hadow): and accompanied the Prime Minister to a *Daily Mail* lunch at the Stafford Hotel (he scattered his thoughts freely, but would not be drawn about an election). On Wednesday his thoughts about 'change' duly emerged in George Murray's leader which caused him to ring me to say would I please draft him a letter to Bill Hardcastle and include some chaff about the leader.

This morning's debate on the Common Market at the Conservative Party conference at Llandudno saw the rout of the rebels led by Turton and Walker-Smith. One gets the impression that Tory morale is building up again, and that there is a more cheerful spirit abroad.

October 18, Thursday   *Rottingdean*

A more cheerful spirit? Rather more than that if the views of the political writers are to be accepted. At the end of the Party conference they were writing of jubilant and united Conservatives looking forward eagerly to yet another election victory. And for the Prime Minister himself acclaim for far-seeing policies. *The Observer*, for example, 'it is often difficult to decide whether to admire Mr. Macmillan's ambitious, statesmanlike ideas or to deplore his wily politician-like methods in pursuing them. It would be difficult, however, to ignore his spectacular success.' Then Colin Welch in the *Sunday Telegraph*, 'His speech was a grand one, elevated in sentiment, dignified in language, well delivered, remarkable for the comprehensive breadth and masterly ordering of its material.' And Rees-Mogg in the *Sunday Times* puts it all into a splendid, orderly perspective beginning in January 1961, 'At Llandudno one has been able to see the working out of a major strategy.'

Euphoria for the Tories, but now – totally without warning – Kennedy and Khruschev had become locked in a dramatic power confrontation over the building of Soviet missile sites in Cuba, and the possibility of nuclear war hung in the air. News of the crisis did not reach the Prime Minister until late on Sunday, October 21st. 'About 10 p.m.,' he writes in his memoirs, 'I was handed by the duty clerk an urgent message informing me that a serious crisis was rapidly developing between the United States and the Soviet Union.' At noon on Monday the American ambassador arrived with a long letter from the President, enclosing photographs of the missile sites under construction, and reported that the President was to make a public statement that evening announcing that the U.S. would establish an arms blockade on Cuba. The Soviet reaction to a blockade was unpredictable but the possibility had to be contemplated that it might lead to retaliatory action in Europe, and even to war. With the stakes so high the governments of America's allies in Europe needed to know that in supporting the American action they had the backing of their own public opinion. To convince public opinion of the reality of the Soviet threat nothing was more important than publication of explicit aerial photographs of the sites. Oddly, the Americans seemed to be slow in realising the critical importance of these photographs in convincing European public opinion, and urgent pressures had to be exerted to obtain their release. I added my own mite of pressure in a telephone call to Pierre Salinger. Release of the photographs helped to win wide acceptance of the need for decisive U.S. action, and in the critical days when the issue continued to hang in the balance the U.K. Government knew that it could count on broad public support for the Prime Minister's statement in the House that the Allies must not waver. The crisis ended on Sunday, October 28th, as suddenly as it had begun, when news came that the Soviet Union would dismantle the missile sites.

October 28, Sunday   *London*
   End of the Cuba crisis week and, in particular, of a dramatic weekend.
   I feel jaded and worn. 'It's like a wedding,' said the P.M., 'when there is nothing left to do but drink the champagne and go to sleep.' He had flopped down in a chair by the tape machine, with Tim, Philip de Zulueta and myself as audience. The captains and the kings had departed and this was the No. 10 family.

The captains and the kings – Rab and Alec Home in particular, plus Ted Heath, plus Harold Caccia,[6] plus (this morning) Thorneycroft[7] – had spent most of the last twenty-four hours in and out of Admiralty House. I was summoned from Rottingdean at 6.30 last night (Saturday) and got to Admiralty House at 8.40. The position then seemed to be that Kennedy had rejected a Cuba-Turkey deal and was hell-bent on destroying the missile sites. This carried the strong possibility of Soviet retaliation in Berlin or elsewhere, with the prospect of escalation into nuclear war.

The P.M. felt that he must intervene if it really looked like coming to that. He proposed to suggest immobilisation of the Thors in Britain in return for immobilisation of the Cuba missiles during a standstill period of negotiations at a London summit.

I got called in, first to the dining room (chairs pulled back from the table, with Ted still eating), and later to the drawing room to comment on the draft statement and advise on publication and briefing. I thought that an ambiguity existed in the phrase 'standstill and negotiations' and the point was accepted. Then, going over probable supplementaries with Alec Home while the others talked, I asked exactly how a London summit meeting would be handled. Home was already feeling that this particular part of the proposition had a Diefenbakerish flavour to it, and faced with the hard questions he suddenly decided that it ought to be erased and jumped up to say so to the P.M. The P.M. agreed without argument, and I had to run down and get the paragraph struck out when the draft was already being typed on the teleprinter to the White House.

Later, at about 11.30, when the group broke up, I expressed doubts about the appeasement flavour which some would see in the Thors proposition (the three Ministers – Butler, Home, Heath – with Caccia, at the top of the staircase) and found that this struck a chord. Fortunately Ormsby-Gore had said to Home on the telephone from Washington (the call being taken in the dining room) that we now had a little more time, and the group went away in agreement that the doubts could be mulled over before they re-assembled at 9 o'clock this morning to look at it all again in the light of comment from Kennedy.

During the night, however, a telephone exchange between Philip de Zulueta and Bundy[8] at the White House revealed strong

[6] Permanent Under-Secretary, Foreign Office.
[7] Minister of Defence.
[8] President Kennedy's Special Assistant for National Security Affairs.

American reservations – chiefly because, it was said, of the undesirability of extending the dispute into Europe if this could be avoided. So when the group came together – plus Thorneycroft – the Thors proposition was already virtually ruled out.

The P.M. retained a hankering to take the initiative on a summit meeting, but Caccia came up hard and strong against anything which might be construed as the British being the first to crack – developing, he told me later, the doubts I had expressed overnight.

So we ended with a mouselike message to Khruschev, appealing to him to take the course proposed by Kennedy, and this went off at noon – just in time for us to be able to claim that it had anticipated Khruschev's caving-in reply.

November 11, Sunday   *Rottingdean*
Wayland Young in *The Guardian* and Michael Foot in *Tribune* speculated on the lines of 'Did Britain waver?' but that was the extent of it. The American correspondents in London conducted a separate post mortem on why the British Press showed something less than wholehearted support.

Joe Fromm and Joe Harsch had me to lunch at the St. James's to get my angle. To over-summarise and over-simplify, I said that (a) it was asking a good deal to expect the British Press and public to jump immediately to attention, as if by reflex action, when the President of the United States confronted them overnight with the possibility of nuclear annihilation; and (b) it was Walter Lippmann who publicly advocated a Turkey-Cuba deal.

They mentioned, though lightly, the belief among the Americans that on Tuesday morning – the morning after Kennedy's broadcast – I had been less than wholehearted in talking about it to the Lobby. I said I had made clear our condemnation of Russian deception and emphasised the American view, no less than our own, that the affair should not be allowed to spill over to this side of the Atlantic if it could be avoided. I had also confirmed that there was no formal military commitment. Later, after the Cabinet meeting, H.M.G. had gone on record with a denunciation of Soviet action, and Lord Home had spoken forthrightly the same evening. Then on Thursday, when the House reassembled for prorogation, came the Prime Minister's unqualified declaration of support. All this they recognised as handsome: but they still felt that much of the British press had been lily-livered.

If storm clouds in international politics now seemed less threatening, they were gathering ominously in British domestic politics in the wake of the trial and conviction on spying charges of William Vassall, a junior civil servant who had been posted to the Admiralty following a period of service in the British embassy in Moscow. Spy stories rank high in news value, and the Press – or at least some sections of it – pressed hard as always to find stories within the story and to identify culprits. In particular, disagreeable allegations were made about the relationship between Vassall and Thomas Galbraith, who was now an Under-Secretary of State for Scotland but had been Civil Lord of the Admiralty when Vassall was serving there. It was the circulation of these allegations that prompted the Prime Minister to set up a judicial tribunal under Lord Radcliffe to look into the whole affair, although initially he had believed that an internal enquiry would be sufficient to establish why Vassall's espionage activities had not been detected at an earlier stage. In the meantime letters between Galbraith and Vassall were published as a White Paper, and these showed, in the words of the Annual Register, that though Galbraith might have 'suffered a socially pressing and plausible young colleague a trifle too gladly', there was no more to it than that. Galbraith insisted on resigning, however, partly to have freedom to take legal action against those who had libelled him. In setting up the Radcliffe tribunal the Prime Minister made it clear that he was determined not only that the truth should be searched out but also that 'the purveyors of lies should be punished. It was important that an incipient MacCarthyism should be stemmed without delay.' Many in Fleet Street were incensed by the decision to widen the tribunal's terms of reference in this way, but the extent to which this resentment (aggravated by the imprisonment of two journalists) was to sour relationships between the Prime Minister and the Press went beyond any expectations at the time. In particular it found expression in Press handling of the Profumo affair some months later. In his memoirs Harold Macmillan wrote of the last year of his administration being 'darkened by this cloud'.

November 11, Sunday   *Rottingdean*

Just when things appeared to be going better for the Government (including Maudling's measures on investment allowances and car purchase tax), the atmosphere has been soured by the consequences of the Vassall case.

For me it involved a special effort on Wednesday night to achieve effective presentation of the White Paper publishing the Galbraith letters, followed by the Galbraith resignation announced by the P.M. during Questions on Thursday. When the time of publication of the White Paper began to slip perilously late into the evening I got it agreed at an improvised meeting in my room (Chief Whip, Minister without Portfolio, Tim Bligh and Philip Woodfield) that I should have a quick meeting with the Lobby in order to read to them the gist of the short interim report and then let them have the full document direct from the presses – in effect, an oral final revise. It worked well and the Lobby thanked me formally on Thursday.

I lunched during the week with Douglas Clark, about to take over features at the *Sunday Express*, to his great satisfaction, not least because it will give him time to write a book on the Finnish winter war crisis in 1940: I offered to let him have my background note on the volunteers.

The P.M. put on one of his best parliamentary performances in opening Wednesday's debate on the motion to set up a tribunal. Most of us had been afraid that he would be too aggressive. As originally dictated during the weekend his speech had included some strongly vituperative passages after a measured and reasoned introduction: in particular he had a sentence on Wilson and Brown which would have put the House into turmoil. My fear was that in this form it would savour too much of the cornered man, lashing out in blind fury. I said so round the office and in particular to the Chief Whip. He took the same view, as also did W. F. Deedes, and (I am told) Macleod. The passages remained in the script but he did not use them.

In the early evening, feeling tired and triumphant, he drifted into the Private Office when I was there. I told him that I thought he had done it splendidly – exactly right in tone and temper – and he swept Tim Bligh, Philip Woodfield and myself into the Cabinet room to drink whisky and gossip. When I said that I was glad that he had not found it necessary to use the vituperative passages – the shots in his locker – he said that, well, it had been necessary to put them there in order to get them out of his system and he would have used them had he been barracked. It was remarkable, he went on to say, that the more experience he had in handling this kind of situation the more nervous he became beforehand: and the more drained of virtue he felt afterwards. Lloyd George had once said to him that this was the price of an effective parliamentary per-formance. But where did we go from here, he asked: and by degrees revealed that more was to come – that a woman at the C.O.I., earing £2500 a year, had shown Intels to the Yugoslavs (which wasn't very serious), but that another serious case also seemed likely to break soon. That was the significance of the reference he had made in the House to tightening the net and the possibility that the improved system, following the original Radcliffe report, would succeed in laying more of these people by the heels. I said that we had better, discreetly, put this thinking into circulation and he agreed.

Then the Press. 'I have made a lot of enemies in the Press today, Harold. But I am an old man and I don't really care.' (I question whether in fact he has made more Fleet Street enemies: several of the Lobby men have been expressing disgust about the excesses of the mass circulation papers, and this must reflect a degree of Fleet Street thinking.) He understood the pressures they were under, he went on to say, because at the moment they did not seem to be getting enough crime and sex to satisfy the need for sensationalism. Of course, it was all too easy to make the things one said or wrote privately sound silly or sinister. That morning, for example, he had rung and said, 'Send a young lady to my bedroom.' What could be made of that! Then, how did you recognise a homosexual? It was said that women could do so more easily than men. Would acceptance of the Wolfenden recommendations make blackmail more difficult? Probably not. It was not the avowed and complete homosexual who was vulnerable, but the man who did not go quite that far, who in part had a normal sexual life and felt ashamed of his aberrations.

So back to whether he should have played the hand differently, with the conclusion, 'I should have talked to Gaitskell in the first place. But it was during the recess and I wanted to get on with it.' Also Cuba had been at the centre of his thinking.

At this point, casting an eye at the clock on the mantelpiece, because of the Ikeda dinner at Claridges, he began loosening the laces of his shoes preparatory to changing, and we took our leave. While we gossiped he had rung Peter Carrington (one of the victims of speculation) and asked about the parallel debate in Lords. 'It went well with us. How did it go with you?'

Other items:

(1) Norman Brook is officially said to be 'progressing favourably'. I hope the medicos really mean it. To be thus struck down within months of retirement!

(2) We had the Lobby to drinks at Admiralty House. Government Hospitality mix strong drinks and some of the boys had to exercise great determination to take their leave with dignity. The P.M. did his customary soft-shoe shuffle while making his speech from in front of the fireplace. He had been fortunate, he said, in having Mr. Evans to look after things for him (making that languid gesture towards my shoulder): he knew that I had won their respect

and affection (applause in the parliamentary sense). Bill Grieg, as chairman, said that relations between No. 10 and the Lobby had never been better. John Dickinson said afterwards how glad he had been to hear all this said – a reminder that the P.M. rarely commits himself in public to any recognition of his spokesman. Which perhaps helps to explain why in an article in the current *Harpers* Anthony Lejeune says, in effect, that Evans is a nice enough chap, but has no influence on the formulation of policy and little on presentation.

November 25, Sunday   *Rottingdean*

Week of five by-elections, built up by the Press into a 'little general election' and a crucial test of the new-look Cabinet and of Macmillan's leadership.

As expected, the Tories lost Woodside (Glasgow), but by a much narrower margin than forecast. Unexpectedly, they lost South Dorset – the Hitchingbrooke seat – where the Tory vote was split by Sir Piers Debenham as an anti-Common Market candidate. Less open to explanation was 'skin-of-teeth' successes in the other three – all accounted safe Tory seats.

In sum a setback, especially coming at a moment when the Tories were telling themselves that they had found their way back to the winning trail. The Press exploded into sensational headlines, and the commentators had a field day explaining that the days of Macmillan are now numbered as the Party seek new and more vigorous leadership.

In a long leader *The Times* said, 'The country has moved close enough to a presidential form of government to mean that only a change of Prime Minister will persuade people that they are looking at a new Ministry' – a sentence picked up by James Margach in his weekend piece.

But all this I find sham and hollow. The Government has another two years left of its mandate. Only a loss of nerve could bring true crisis – or, for Macmillan, a palace revolution: and who could be an acceptable leader? Something to this effect is said today by the old war-horse Hugh Massingham, doing a come-back stint for the *Sunday Telegraph.*

Against this background Fleet Street sent a pack to Scotland to besiege the Home seat at Castlemains, where the P.M. and Lady Dorothy are spending this weekend. I had an anguished call from Ian Samuel last night (Saturday) asking if anything could be done to restrain the *Mail's* Ronnie Camp, who was being aggressive in demanding a statement from the P.M. about London rumours that

230

he was about to resign. I spoke to T. F. Thompson, but did so with reservations, both because it had not been possible on a rather difficult line to get details, and because anyhow one needs firm ground before complaining to a national newspaper about the behaviour of one of its representatives. Tommy duly rang Camp and reported him to be puzzled by the complaint, thinking he had done nothing offensive, and suggesting that maybe the Castlemains people were mixing him up with that rough and crude lot from the *Daily Express*.

I did stress to Samuel that the P.M. must *not* let himself be inveigled into saying anything, not only because a complaint to the *Mail*, or anyone else, must rest on refusal to accept an assurance that no statement would be made, but also because sending the hounds to Scotland really resulted from the P.M.'s own indiscretion in the past in letting himself be needled into making statements.

As to the P.M., I don't know at the moment how he *has* reacted. But on Thursday evening, when he saw the American correspondents, he put on a cheerful and unworried performance. The Chinese attack on the Indian frontier he described as a punitive expedition in the best imperialist tradition. Asked about the telephone line to the White House, he said that he had only one complaint – that the President sometimes forgot that 10 p.m. in Washington was 3 a.m. in London.

Talks with de Gaulle (Chateau de Rambouillet) and Kennedy (Bahamas) are in the offing during the ten days before Christmas. In Friday's *Mail* Dickie wrote a speculative piece about Kennedy–Macmillan talks during the Christmas recess, and this set everyone on the trail at a moment when nothing had been announced and there could be no categorical denial. I rang Pierre Salinger at the White House on Friday afternoon – the call went through in minutes and we had a very good line – and we agreed on spokesmanship. So far only Charles Douglas-Home (Alec Home's nephew) in the *Express* has suggested the Bahamas, and speculation on timing has generally anticipated after Christmas. There now lies ahead the usual internal intrigue and manoeuvring about who goes: but if Home and Rusk and their retinues don't go the spokesman will have to be Evans.

Footnote:
R. Camp's scoop from Lanarkshire turned out to be BERMUDA – 15 DECEMBER in banner headlines.

December 2, Sunday   *Rottingdean*

From Lady D. I had the inside story about the Camp episode. It amounted to a general *cri de coeur* against the siege of Castlemains and a wrecked weekend, focused on the wretched Ronnie because he handed in letters and was rough on the telephone with the Home daughter, Meriel (even the cook had to help in answering calls). The intervention from London did not help Lady D. because when the party went to church on Sunday morning, Camp insisted on waylaying her and apologising at length just when she wanted to talk to the parson and the old ladies. Her last view of him was as the train left Carstairs, with Ronnie hanging out of the window expressing Sassenach views about Scotland.

The by-election hysteria faded overnight, though in today's *Sunday Times* James Margach is surprisingly still in the groove with 'Whither Macmillan?' All the more peculiar because James was among those who saw a superlative performance by H. Macmillan at the annual Lobby lunch at the Savoy. Vigour, alertness, wit, timing, balance – it was all there. Rab was moved to send a note of congratulations – ruefully perhaps.

In essence it was the draft I did for him – but transmuted by Macmillan magic. He used my 'public antipathy and private affection' line and the 'commuters' companion' passage (from an idea by Lawrence Thompson out of lunch at the Reform), but then developed a brilliant piece of debunking of the stock allegations about nepotism ('perhaps you'd like to hear my wife's opinion of her new brother-in-law'). He wound up with a serious passage, dismissing such ephemeral issues as by-elections, unemployment and the Common Market in order to say that his greatest preoccupation at the moment was to see if true peace could be brought to the world in the wake of Cuba (giving a little encouragement, alas, to those pundits suspecting political gimmicks in Paris and the Bahamas).

To me he paid an extraordinarily handsome tribute. William Grieg, in the chair, had said that one thing they all owed to the Prime Minister was that he had put relations between No. 10 and the parliamentary journalists on such a firm and satisfactory basis. Picking up this reference the P.M. said that the present position was due to one man alone. 'No Prime Minister has been better served.'

One victim of the by-elections is likely to be Charles Hill. Macleod has said forthrightly that he cannot agree to Luton being vacated and must therefore oppose the proposed Hill appointment to the I.T.A. chairmanship. This is hard indeed, but they have him in a corner: unless he toes the line he won't get his peerage.

In a gossip over gins at the House, he asked how I should respond if offered an outside job. How firm should I be if the P.M. then wept on my shoulder and said he didn't want me to go? I wonder what the answer is to that?

After the Lobby lunch the P.M. stood on the pavement asking what had happened to Harold, but I had escaped too late from friendly interruptions (Geoffrey Cox, Fraser Wighton, Tommy Thompson) to join him in the car. Back at Admiralty House I was summoned to the study to talk about the Bahamas. 'You are coming, aren't you? I want you to come. You must come.' I say, 'Yes, of course, unless Home and Rusk go and it becomes a Foreign Office jamboree!' But Alec is *not* going, he says. That has been decided. At that moment, however, Philip de Zulueta was writing to Ormsby-Gore saying that the P.M. thought it would be a good thing for the Foreign Secretary to go unless the President particularly did not want Rusk with him.

After leaving the P.M. I encountered Maurice Macmillan in the ground floor ante-room. He, too, thought his father had done a splendid job at the Lobby lunch – certainly all the political people had been greatly impressed. This led us to a gossip about Prime Ministerial health and appearance and that misleading ivory complexion. When his father is feeling low, says Maurice, he likes to pretend that he is finished: it has become a family joke.

The forthcoming meeting with President Kennedy was now at the centre of No. 10's thinking and activities, its importance escalating as reports came from the United States about possible cancellation of the Skybolt missile project. The future of the British nuclear deterrent had been planned on the understanding that Skybolt would be available (using British warheads). Given Skybolt cancellation and U.S. unwillingness to reach an agreement about the Polaris submarine missiles, the U.K. would either have to give up an independent nuclear capability or accept the delay and expense involved in developing a new British missile.

December 8, Saturday   *Rottingdean*
Home is duly going (not Rusk, who has a major speaking engagement on the 19th). Though this will mean a News department presence the P.M. says that he still wants me to take responsibility for spokesmanship.

We are due to travel by R.A.F. Comet on Monday, the 17th,

which will give us four full days in the Bahamas – one to settle in, two for talks with Kennedy and one for talks with Diefenbaker. This will immediately follow the de Gaulle weekend, for which, as usual we shall leave spokesmanship to the embassy.

The P.M. had it in mind to mask the extent to which defence and Skybolt would feature in the Bahamas talks. (He will make an issue of Skybolt, if necessary, but it may have been brought to a head before then.) I sent him a note saying that I doubted if this was realistic, more particularly if Sir Solly Zuckerman[9] and Sir William Penney[10] went as well as Sir Robert Scott[11] – on which he concluded that perhaps they ought not to go.

During the week we have had the flurry caused by Acheson's speech at West Point, in which he referred to the British role in world affairs as 'almost played out'. The P.M. didn't spark immediately, but Chandos wrote to him the following day on behalf of the Institute of Directors, and brooding over it through Thursday night (the fog kept him at Admiralty House when he had intended to get down to Birch Grove) he had worked himself into a splendid anger by the morning. An unusually indignant minute was awaiting the private secretaries, together with a fierce letter to Acheson. 'They won't let me send it,' he told Chandos on the phone, 'but I shan't let them stop me.' But we did stop him. The second half of the letter threw acid at Acheson personally. I said that this would be a grave mistake and wreck the effect. Tim and Philip de Zulueta had an equally firm view. We had a meeting in the Cabinet room at 10 – Master in knickerbockers ready to shoot – to which Harold Caccia was summoned from the Foreign Office. But by then the second half had already been struck out and there was nothing to argue about. In its final form it was a good letter, and came out well both in television news (B.B.C. pictures of Philip of Spain, Louis XIV, Napoleon, the Kaiser and Hitler) and in the Press. Ormsby-Gore misfired by appearing to defend Acheson. At the 10 o'clock meeting the P.M. had become cheerful and relaxed. As I left he said, 'I suppose you're glad I kept it clean, Harold.'

The *Mail* produced an opinion poll during the week which showed Mac and the Tories in a strong decline: but it's difficult to get very much worked up about it when the election is still so far away – barring new developments.

---

[9] Chief Scientific Adviser, Ministry of Defence.
[10] Chairman, Atomic Energy Authority.
[11] Permanent Secretary, Ministry of Defence.

December 28, Friday   *Rottingdean*

Look back on Nassau.

With the Macnamara visit to London, followed by the NATO Council meeting, plus some peculiar spokesmanship at Defence ('2s. 6d. on Income Tax'), the Skybolt issue became inescapably identified as the main topic of the talks. We ended up with an enormous team. In addition to Alec Home with the Prime Minister, Duncan Sandys (already in the Bahamas at the beginning of a Caribbean tour) stayed on for the Indo-Chinese item on the second day, and Thorneycroft and a group of about eight top Service boffins flew out in a second R.A.F. Comet twelve hours after the P.M. That made three Comets, in fact, because a stand-by aircraft accompanied the Prime Minister's.

The P.M. made a departure statement at the airport on the basis of a draft I had done for him earlier in the morning (we took off at noon). On the Skybolt issue he maintained the line I had been taking – that undoubtedly Skybolt was running into technical and financial difficulties, but no less undoubtedly a way would be found through them with our transatlantic chums.

A Comet is sleek and beautiful, but not tremendously fast by current standards (about 420 m.p.h.): not tremendously big (so that the main cabin seemed overcrowded): and not capable of very long single hops (at any rate against the Atlantic westerlies so that we had to refuel at both the Azores and Bermuda). Then, also, we had five hours to wipe off on time difference so that although we arrived at 10.30 Nassau time this was 3.30 a.m. London time and 5 a.m. before we got to bed. Over-tired and with puzzled stomachs one then had a 'night' of only fitful sleep, having resisted the blandishments of the sleeping pills thoughtfully provided by Peggy Metcalfe. But Bahamas sunshine, flowers, palms and silver beaches, added to the millionaire setting of the Lyford Cay Club, compensated for tiredness – and with so much to do tiredness had to be forgotten, anyhow.

The President arrived at 11 a.m. (Tuesday, the 18th). Having my own car (driven by a friendly and sensible coloured Bahamanian, introducing himself as Joe), I arrived at the airport ahead of the P.M. and the Governor (my old friend and colleague from West African days, Robert Stapledon). I thus had an opportunity to talk to old acquaintances from the White House Press Corps, just arrived on the Press plane from Washington. This was fortunate since it led to the discovery that in an interview overnight with Bill Lawrence, of A.B.C., the President had virtually announced his intention to abandon Skybolt – and also his dislike of independent nuclear deterrents. No script was available, but Lawrence produced a newspaper containing the key passages and I tore out the page in order to present it to the Prime Minister when he arrived (leading to a confab – P.M., Tim Bligh and myself – on the tarmac in the hot sunshine as the President's plane taxied in: duly noted by the Press as evidence of the allegedly cool and strained atmosphere which they reported as apparent in the greetings).

Pierre Salinger travelled with the President. His three assistants (plus secretaries) had travelled in the Press plane so that, for all practical purposes, he had brought down the full panoply of the Press Secretary's office, in itself significant. On our side I had Michael Hadow,[12] of News Department, and his P.A., the placidly competent Angela, based in a suite at the Emerald Beach Hotel, with myself at the Lyford Cay Club. Pierre had originally booked himself at the hotel, but switched to the club when he found that I was there. This proved a good arrangement.

Cheerful, brisk, co-operative as ever, he and I agreed over beer that at joint briefings I should be in the chair, since the meeting was taking place on British soil, and that we should not let ourselves get drawn into cross-talk in front of the cameras, however great the provocation – but in so agreeing we were also recognising, of course, that for the first time we could be in disagreement on substance.

That this was not the normal 'cosy' occasion also became apparent in the early evening when the British correspondents were running round in little circles because Salinger had announced at a national briefing that the Congo was to be at the top of the agenda. Due expression had to be given to mystification and disbelief, and so the boys had another item to adduce as evidence of cross-purposes.

For my part I was sticking to the firmness of our intention to maintain an independent deterrent, with the implication that if we could not do a satisfactory deal we would go it alone. Prime Minister and President had met at 5 and word came out that all was far from well, with the President showing no disposition to make an offer on Polaris.

But for the time being this had to be pushed under the carpet, and the two great men, by arrangement, made separate appearances at parties organised for the Press – a Lyford Cay party at the swimming pool (Kennedy) and a beach barbecue party at the Emerald Beach (Macmillan). The barbecue party verged on the barbarous,

---

[12] Head of News Department, Foreign Office, 1962–65, and subsequently Ambassador to Israel and to Argentina.

and the P.M. had to sit through some folksy entertainment while gnawing at crayfish on a windy beach and hemmed in by the locals and by cameramen (plus lights). He dealt with it smoothly and in doing so made a hit with the Americans, if not with the British – though British disapproval did not matter a great deal since the time difference made it all too late for the London morning papers.

The time difference meant that to give Fleet Street correspondents a story we had to produce a briefing in the middle of each day – obviously difficult.

On Wednesday morning (the 19th) – the first session of formal talks – this represented a particular problem because a neat package could not be expected to emerge so quickly. When I talked to the P.M. briefly first thing in the garden at Bali-Hai he spoke darkly of rows and the possibility of his deciding not to go on with the talks if the Americans would not meet us – though as host he could not simply call for the Comet and fly home (an idea that clearly appealed to him and one with tempting political advantages), so that given this situation the ploy would have to be to ask Home to carry on with foreign affairs topics while he conferred with Thorneycroft and the defence boys on our next steps in defence policy.

He did agree, however, that I should ask Home to do a U.K. Press briefing at the club at 12.30, and Home faced up to the chore manfully, as he always does, so that at any rate we could make a gesture to keep the U.K. correspondents feeling that we wanted to help them.

In fact, the session finished at noon, with Kennedy striding up to Salinger and myself in the car park to say that he did not see that there was anything we could yet say and that he did not think there should be national briefings either.

But I didn't think we could accept this. We *had* to make a gesture to the U.K. group: it was too late to call off the arrangement with them, and, in any case, I doubted if we could be sure that the Americans would not brief privately. Home accepted this view against stiff opposition from Ormsby-Gore (as ambassador, understandingly sensitive about the President) and his own private secretary, Ian Samuel. He briefed accordingly in his sitting room at the club, and the correspondents went out of their way to say that they had found it helpful though at that stage he could give them nothing of real substance (even so it provided an opportunity to introduce the NATO concept).

What did emerge satisfactorily from their stories was British determination to retain an independent deterrent (the single theme

I had pumped into them in the club foyer while waiting for the fourteenth Earl). At the end of the first day we had little more to say at the first of the joint open briefings at the Emerald Beach, but with their stories already written, for better or for worse, the U.K. correspondents found this satisfactory rather than not.

. Joint briefings in the American manner are bound to be an ordeal for British spokesmen, unaccustomed to the battery of television and film cameras and the glare of the lights, but as on previous occasions when I have had to accept the White House formula I found the adrenalin running when the moment came.

It was not comforting all the same, when we climbed on to the dais for the first time, to find Randolph Churchill sitting immediately below, in beach shirt and crumpled yellow trousers, apparently spoiling for the row he customarily makes on these occasions. But if he had come to harass he stayed to cheer, including even a 'bravo', some helpful leading questions, and a complimentary handshake at the end.

It is something of a charade, of course. The real business is done at the national briefings. If the British spokesman performs competently and appears relaxed and confident it may help to form attitudes – perhaps significantly on occasion – but in the normal way it is more a question of flag flying than anything else. I was glad to get Randolph's approbation, and glad to get other compliments (both from British correspondents and from Michael Hadow and from Salinger through Hadow), but the British spokesman *ought* to be capable of these public performances, even if nurtured in the cloistered calm of non-attributable briefings.

So to Thursday and tough talking by the Americans at the morning session, trying to tie us up in a NATO formula with the British side trying to preserve the greatest possible measure of independent control. With an eye on the time difference I had hoped to see a conclusion by the end of the morning, opening up the possibility of Macmillan television interviews in the evening in time for the films to catch the overnight plane.

But when I again had a quick session with the P.M. before the day started I found that he contemplated submitting to the Cabinet overnight any formula that might be reached during the day. He agreed that I should need to say this, and that I should explain that the niceties lay in the terms and conditions on which Polaris could be obtained. For the rest, he thought we should make it clear that switching from one weapons system to another was not like switching from one club to another, or going into a shop to buy a new shirt. As to why we attached so much importance to having an independent deterrent, it was not a question of adding to the nuclear armoury against the Russians, but because without it we would be in no position to take an independent line on all the other issues in which we became involved round the world.

At breakfast in the club dining room there had been an opportunity to test the American temperature when Mac Bundy had waved to me to join their table – George Ball, Nitze, ambassadors Bruce and Thompson. At one point the conversation made it possible for me to ask lightly if the spokesmen were going to be able to say something worthwhile later in the day and had from Bundy a fairly emphatic 'Yes'. So it seemed they intended to reach a compromise.

By the end of the morning it had been agreed that the two Defence Ministers should go away and prepare during the afternoon a joint paper for final decision in the evening: and while they were doing this the Big Two proposed to talk about India in the President's house.

This left the delicate problem of midday briefing for the British correspondents without any certainty about the outcome. Home did it well enough, but without actually saying so he indicated that what was emerging was a Polaris-for-Skybolt deal against a NATO background. This led us quickly into trouble with the Americans, since Reuters (Pat Heffernan) filed it hard, with attribution to informed sources. I quickly had Salinger on the phone saying that the President wanted to discuss what should be done about it. Accordingly we found ourselves ushered into the afternoon meeting, bearing the Reuters tape. Alec Home rightly said he hadn't said anything as positive as that, with which I agreed. The Prime Minister put on an air of boredom and commented that the story said no more than that the Prime Minister and the President *hoped* to arrive at an agreement on these lines: and in the end there developed one of those corporate shrugs which left Pierre to do what he could about it.

I went through the motions of remonstrating with Pat Heffernan – and indeed the attribution was altogether too definite – but the plain fact was that the U.K. correspondents had acquired an accurate piece of news a jump ahead of the Americans and it was this that rankled. My worry was lest in doing so they should have upset the President and his team at a critical moment. In fact, Macnamara and Thorneycroft arrived at an agreed paper and the principals approved it quickly at the end of the Indian discussion so that there remained only the hurdle, for the British, of consulting the Cabinet.

The joint briefing I asked Salinger to chair, but quickly got drawn into cross-examination, not least in explaining the constitutional role of the Cabinet (with a word of commendation afterwards from Henry Brandon, with whom I spent half an hour going over the ground inch by inch: he put everyone else in the delegation similarly under the microscope in composing his 1400 words for the leader page of the *Sunday Times*).

The British correspondents, with an excellent story already filed, were afterwards content with a leisurely briefing from C. S. Pickard (Commonwealth Relations) on the Sino-Indian item.

That took us to Friday, the 21st, with only the morning for winding up before Diefenbaker arrived to join Macmillan and Kennedy for lunch (the Kennedy departure for Palm Beach and a Cuba victory holiday for himself and his staff was timed for 3.30).

Overnight I had worked out the principal questions with which I expected to be faced, assuming a Polaris agreement in a NATO setting – the next step, cost, precise NATO arrangements and the future of the R.A.F. given the switch to a submarine missile. On some I had already tackled the boffins and from them obtained the inevitably detailed and thrice-qualified answers. Fortunately at breakfast I was able to pin down Rob Scott and found him most admirably terse and lucid. Thus armed, I tackled the P.M. once again before the President arrived – but with the knowledge that the Cabinet had shown unhappiness and had proposed some re-wording, and also that the Chief Whip had sent a message of foreboding, suggesting that it would be better to have further consultations in London before clinching a deal. The significance of the proposed re-wording was not immediately apparent, and on the face of it there seemed no reason why it should be unacceptable to the Americans. Assuming agreement would be reached I tried out my answers on the P.M. and got his approval for them with only minor qualifications.

I also said that we ought now to decide on arrangements for subsequent briefing and television, taking into account not least that (a) *Panorama* wanted an interview during the early afternoon with the P.M., Home or Thorneycroft in that order of preference, and (b) Thorneycroft would be leaving for London in the afternoon and so would be the first Minister available in London for airport cross-examination by the Press and television. Having asked the other two to join us on the lower terrace, the P.M. said that he thought Peter ought to take the brunt of the Press briefing on the grounds that it would help to establish that this was an arrangement made for good, technical defence reasons and not for political reasons. Peter showed enthusiasm – 'I really believe that this is a good agreement and I can say so with conviction' – and that was that.

In the event, no difficulty was experienced about the re-wording proposed by the Cabinet, or about the communiqué itself, and I was able in mid-morning to pin Thorneycroft down, with Rob Scott, Solly Zuckerman and the boffins, to go through questions and answers finally.

So to the final joint briefing, with a scramble for the communiqué and a fifteen-minute wait while the agencies filed it. The briefing went through quickly and without difficulty, and all then went upstairs to the fifth-floor suites for the respective national briefings. Thorneycroft duly did it with enthusiasm and effect, with some brief but timely interventions by Alec Home.

That should have been that, but now came an agency message reporting that there had been a successful Skybolt firing. I should have joined the Diefenbaker lunch at Bali Hai, but found MacColl, Harris and Hodgson beating on the reception desk at the club in an effort to raise first me (unsuccessfully) and then Rob Scott (packing in his room). I went to his room to tell him what it was all about and he agreed to talk to them in the foyer. He did it with characteristic urbanity, forthrightness and mastery of the technicalities. But by then frenzied calls were coming from Michael Hadow on behalf of the other U.K. correspondents, and it seemed to me that the only answer was for Rob to dash to the hotel forthwith for a repeat performance. And this – splendid fellow – is what he did, though it made him considerably late for a lunch date in Nassau.

On the way he talked freely about his own misgivings about the agreement (of which I had already heard). At the centre was his feeling that the agreement would, in effect, put us in the Americans' pocket for the next decade.

This last-minute excitement over Skybolt meant that instead of lunch on the patio at Bali Hai with the great men I had club sandwiches in suite 532 at the Emerald Beach, and instead of looking at coral and fish through a glass-bottomed boat in the afternoon I did some shopping in Nassau before getting Joe to drive me circuitously to the airport.

On the aircraft we had six hours' work on the arrival statement and questions, and this, coupled with lost hours, refuelling in the small hours in torrential rain at the Azores, and the discomfort of the seats in the main cabin, meant that most of us arrived in London in a state of extreme fatigue. I had been worried about the P.M.'s performance in these circumstances, especially since he had shown irritability on the aircraft, but he thought it important enough to make a real effort and did it well, the only symptom of tiredness and nerves being a jumping right knee.

1963

'A year of destiny' — de Gaulle says no place for Britain — death of Hugh Gaitskell — collapse of E.E.C. negotiations — two journalists to prison — Profumo rumours and denial — Radcliffe Report on Vassall affair — Profumo thunderbolt — President Kennedy in Sussex — nuclear test ban treaty — Scandinavian sortie — Denning Report on Profumo affair — back to No. 10 — a stroke of providence

January 6, Sunday   *Rottingdean*

'It will be a year of destiny,' the P.M. tells me.

I had inserted myself into the Cabinet room to talk to him about the *Panorama* profile and the interview for *This Week* to mark his sixth anniversary.

He was in a very relaxed and buoyant mood – just back from shopping, a rare activity indeed, for a christening present for the new Hailsham baby, his god-daughter, and a personal present for Norman Brook, now on his feet again but retired as from the 1st. Because he is in so good a mood I get everything I want – but he is well aware, of course, of the need to pile on the presentational activity at this time. His January diary now includes major speeches at Birmingham and Liverpool, lunches for Michael Berry and Roger Wood (at last), dinner with the Thirty Club, a *Financial Times* boardroom lunch, drinks for the 'Young Turks', and the two television programmes next week (plus such excitements and opportunities as the recall of Parliament provides).

Last weekend he was tending to get into a state about the Polaris agreement, and to think that he might have to do a special broadcast. I advised against it and then pushed in a long minute on Sunday morning (dictated to No. 10 over the telephone) on the problems of presentation in 1963. Not least I looked at the position which would arise if the Common Market negotiations failed, drawing the conclusion that it could be turned to advantage. Everything now points to an election in the autumn, though the P.M. has called on the Chief Whip for a report on the latest moment at which an election could be held advantageously.

As to Polaris, Thorneycroft worked effectively on the group of backbenchers who came to cross-examine him, and the 'revolt' of Press speculation looks more than ever unlikely. I have been busy saying what a magnificent job the P.M. did in extracting the agreement from the reluctant Americans – and a new context presented itself with the inspired stories from Palm Beach about the President feeling that the Allies must be prepared to toe the American line. Also calling for quick action was a Chapman Pincher story alleging that a radio-lock on Polaris would ensure American control in any circumstances.

Later in the week guidance had to be devised to cope with speculation (correct) about proposals for increased social benefit rates, and about an allocation of Ministerial responsibility for the North-East (also correct).

Another encounter with Master during the week resulted from his agreeing to see Drew Middleton for valedictory drinks before he leaves for Paris as chief European correspondent. There had been no enthusiasm for the meeting because of Drew's sourness of recent years, but it went pleasantly enough and they parted on good terms.

When I went up to the study to announce that Drew had come, he was sitting in the armchair, dozing, with a rug round his knees and an open book on the rug. Ask him to the drawing room, he said, and jumped up to carry a tray with a whisky decanter and three goblets into the drawing room, with myself trailing behind with the siphon. When the talking began the P.M. at once showed himself in touch (how he fools us with his pretended ignorance and his bored questions) by talking about the dinner which the Garrick is laying on for Drew as a farewell gesture.

Mostly the talk is about non-political things – the economics of American newspapers, for example – but Drew reveals that he is writing a book comparing the British and American constitutional systems, and this causes the P.M. to speak of the 'courts' that have been built up round de Gaulle and Adenauer and the possibility that something similar could develop at the White House. In the U.K. one has the advantage of regular and inescapable contacts with Parliament. *Folie de grandeur* is hardly possible when you have to answer questions twice a week and also mix in the smoking room. Of Kennedy: 'He tires quickly. He is restless, very restless. His back seems to bother him.'

1963

But back to this year of destiny. 'It's going to be difficult, very difficult, but that makes it all the more exciting. At any rate it will be a year of destiny' – all in great good humour.

January 13, Sunday *Rottingdean*
'A good week,' says the P.M., looking back on the week of his sixth anniversary, thinking firstly of the success of his television interview with Kenneth Harris on *This Week*, but noting also the *Panorama* profile, plus no doubt some of the newspaper references, including a *Mail* leader and feature and an *Express* feature of quotes. Then, too, there was his Birmingham speech, which pleased him because he was moved to reprove the chairman for Birmingham's indifference to the wellbeing of their fellow-countrymen in less fortunate parts of the country. And again, the Hailsham appointment to undertake special responsibilities for the North-East had a generally good reception (though the *Telegraph* wrote a sadly sour and muddled leader).

We were both moved to think that there may now be an upward surge in the Government's fortunes, partly because some of the political writers may be feeling shamefaced. But, of course, the events must be there if advantage is to be taken of this developing psychological attitude. A new factor, still to be fully assessed, is the Gaitskell illness.

For me it was also a good week in the sense that right decisions were taken, right advice given and right arrangements made.

When Cyril Bennett originally rang about the possibility of an interview for *This Week* he did so on the basis of a beleaguered Prime Minister being given a chance to explain himself. I told him this would not do at all, but that a good opportunity to get an interview existed in the fact that the 10th was the sixth anniversary. So the approach was altered. I also settled for Kenneth Harris, and arranged for him to come in on Tuesday evening to go over the ground with the P.M., having first done it myself.

The recording was made on Wednesday morning before the P.M. left for Birmingham. Feeling a little out of sorts, as he tends to do in the morning, he performed more tersely and briskly than usual. 'Just as well I was feeling cross,' he said in the car afterwards. He had expected to do two or three recordings but I clinched the deal at the end of the first. Reward – apart from the success of the interview – a warmly worded letter of thanks from Cyril Bennett and a verbal commendation from Kenneth Harris on the telephone for my 'behaviour' (very imperial but he did it well). I had been worried by the kind of answer that the P.M. had in mind for the question on the July Cabinet reconstruction, and to get it right I got up at 3 a.m. to do a draft. On looking at it in the Cabinet room just before we left he said it was exactly right, and that was how it emerged.

For the rest, things worked out well with the Hailsham announcement (entirely a Lobby exercise), though we had to accelerate it by two hours when I became aware that the *Standard* (and possibly others) were sniffing round Hailsham's name.

I had several useful and agreeable meal engagements, including dinner with Carleton Greene, Harmon Grisewood and Donald Edwards at the Television Centre (fences mended after disagreements following the invitation to Gaitskell to reply the night after the Prime Minister's Common Market broadcast). Then there was lunch as one of Drew Middleton's guests for a valedictory occasion at the Garrick (Maudling, Heath, Callaghan, Caccia, the *Economist* diplomatic correspondent, A. N. Other, Godfrey Hobbs and myself – a peculiar assortment). Callaghan rather dampened the flow of conversation by trying too obviously to score party points. Caccia had the Congo on his mind – recall of Dobson from Elizabethville – and I advised robustness. Thirdly, lunch with the directors of Rediffusion to fill up the guest list after a board meeting, the other guests being Anthony Greenwood, an unidentified tycoon and the secretary of the Municipal and General Workers' Union. I sat next to Lord Swinton and we talked hard about West Africa to the boredom of those at our end of the table. At seventy-eight he is still alert and rasping – and wonderfully kind as ever to me personally. 'Well, old friend, are things really going well with you?' He was critical about the Government and Central Africa – 'What will they say if I line up with Bobbety?'[1] – and thought that Charles Hill should not be made chairman of I.T.A.

January 20, Sunday   *Rottingdean*

A week of drama – the de Gaulle Press conference declaring that Europe had no place for England, the subsequent uproar at Brussels with the other five fiercely indignant (for them the moment of truth as they see Europe through the eyes of de Gaulle), and finally the tragedy of Hugh Gaitskell's death on Friday night.

On de Gaulle we stood steady from the start, which probably frustrated his calculations that the British would walk out of the negotiations in a huff.

The death of Gaitskell took me back to London yesterday

[1] Lord Salisbury.

(Saturday) to complete the arrangements for the P.M.'s television tribute and to see him through it. The setting was a blizzard, in continuation of a month's Arctic weather. Even so he had elected to go to Lime Grove rather than cause the Outside Broadcast Unit to come to Admiralty House. The tribute he wrote largely himself, though Philip Woodfield set him going with an excellent first draft. The final version was too long and I took a hundred words out of it. He did it with great feeling and effect. It called for the nicest of judgments but he caught the mood exactly. He showed the same sensitivity in deciding that the House should adjourn on Tuesday as on the death of a former Prime Minister (there is no precedent for the death of a Leader of the Opposition who had not held office as Prime Minister). Further to credit was the authorising at very short notice of an R.A.F. aircraft to fetch George Brown from Manchester. This was Philip Woodfield's doing since the Prime Minister was out at dinner. He duly received Prime Ministerial approbation.

The broadcast gave me an evening in the Prime Minister's company, first at supper on Mrs. Bell's excellent coffee and sandwiches in the drawing room, in the car to and from Lime Grove, and at Lime Grove – in the make-up room and afterwards when Mrs. Wyndham-Goldie produced champagne and sandwiches.

He mused over the Gaitskell tragedy. It wasn't true that he had detested Gaitskell, as all the commentators said, though it *was* true that he found it difficult to warm to Gaitskell as he had done, for example, to Bevan. He liked Dora better as a person: he had a great admiration for her. It was terrible how the newspapers had given every detail of the progress of the illness. 'Don't let them behave like this when I die, will you, Harold.' A man should be allowed to die alone and in peace. 'Dorothy will keep them away.' Once again one had seen how things never happened as they were expected to happen: there was always some unexpected twist.

All this he had said when we were alone. In the relaxed mood that followed the broadcast – and further mellowed by champagne after whisky – he talked chiefly about fashions in speaking styles (with particular reference to Lloyd George, whom he rated a better speaker than Winston – beautiful voice, beautiful white hands, and a perfect sense of mood and timing), but again dwelt on the ghoulishness surrounding Gaitskell's illness and death. Why could they not wait at least a day or two before speculating about the succession? Then, turning to me, he asked, 'Who do you think they will put up for the succession if I die, Harold?' To which Harold could only answer, 'That's something I'm certainly not going to get drawn into.' To give Master the final line, 'That made you put on your Lobby face, didn't it?'

While he was being made up and waiting to go on, we talked about the role of Prime Minister – a theme of current debate and of a forthcoming *Gallery* programme. It was absolute nonsense, he said, to argue that we were moving towards a presidential system. That was about the point of evolution we had reached at the time of Charles II. The President had his own court. He appointed Ministers who were not elected, might be either Whig or Tory and might not even have met each other. He did not need to take the advice of his Cabinet. It had no collective responsibility. The only check on his power – as it had been with Charles II and his successors – was the need to go to the Legislature for funds. In the British system the Cabinet had collective responsibility. You could not ignore it. Even Winston had made sure that he could carry the Cabinet with him in major decisions. As for himself, had it escaped notice that before completing the agreement about Polaris with President Kennedy he had thought it necessary to put the agreement to the Cabinet. So, too, at Key West in 1960 when Vietnam was discussed with the President.

As to de Gaulle, the P.M. has a Party speech at Liverpool tomorrow. I looked at the draft and felt that it dealt too much with the fine points of the General's Press conference rather than making the broad statement that was now needed. This, said Philip de Zulueta, had been done deliberately to help Ted Heath tactically. In the car I had an opportunity of putting the point to the P.M. and he said that, indeed, he intended to have a passage in general terms. Then early this afternoon he rang me at Rottingdean to say that he had decided to make this an important passage – in effect, his vision of Europe to compare with that of de Gaulle – and would I trail it with the lobby accordingly. He had perhaps been influenced also by an article in the *Sunday Telegraph* this morning which says that, after all, the Prime Minister also could make speeches.

What else? 'Poor Dorothy' – at Birch Grove with a grandchild with a temperature of 104° and the roads, ice and snow bound to create hazards in getting to the hospital at East Grinstead.

More Macmillan thoughts on Gaitskell. The unwisdom of filling yourself with antibiotics to deal with minor illness. The wisdom of going to one of the big teaching hospitals, where everything was immediately available: that was what John Richardson had insisted on when it became necessary for him to have a gall bladder operation. Also, when you were recuperating, you could go into the general ward, with its splendid views over the Thames, and sit on the balcony talking to the chaps.

More on oratory. The old one-two-three technique to get laughs – the same point made in three different ways, like Charlie Chaplin on skates knocking down the old gentleman three times. Both Lloyd George and Winston did this. You should not make too many jokes, like Wilson did. There must be variations in tone and tempo.

Then a Winston story. After the war he went on making long speeches in the House, to which Attlee replied very effectively in dry, twenty-minute speeches. After one of these exchanges a Tory backbencher said to Winston in the smoking room, 'There's no doubt little Attlee is becoming a very good Commons speaker.' To which Winston retorted, 'I don't know if you have ever read Maeterlinck, Colonel, but if you do you will know that if you feed a grub with royal jelly for long enough it becomes a queen bee.' Then again on Winston – he was never allowed to develop the kind of megalomania one sees in some other leaders. Brendan Bracken and Randolph had seen to that. Randolph was quite capable of saying, 'Don't be silly, papa. You're talking rot.'

Speaking of Randolph, he rang me very late one night to talk about not letting the P.M. come back to London by road after his Birmingham speech, and to ask why there had not been a handout of the speech (Central Office business). But he was entirely amiable and proferred compliments on my Nassau performance: 'magisterial', he said (his current favourite word).

January 27, Sunday   *Rottingdean*

Unemployment over 800,000 – and this to coincide with disruption caused by the prolonged cold spell, the Skybolt–Polaris controversy (to be debated next Wednesday and Thursday), and the Common Market crisis (where, at the moment, we are in a good posture for a break if there *has* to be a break).

Yet all is not despair for the Tories. How different it will look in the autumn, their optimists are saying. There has been continuing speculation about the date of the election – stimulated by the P.M.'s recent references to uncertainty in industry because of fears of a Labour victory, plus the repercussions from Hugh Gaitskell's death and from Common Market developments. My own line is that anything said at the moment is just teasing, and that, for the rest, the 'natural' time is the autumn and that there will have to be good reasons for it *not* to be the autumn (while recognising that with circumstances critical and changing there *could* be good reasons).

At the end of the week, for the first time for a long time, the P.M. began to show signs of strain – chiefly because of next week's Polaris debate which he will both open and wind up. But he has gone to Chequers for three days, which should help him to unwind.

The debate has put into doubt his attendance at the Thirty Club dinner on Wednesday, which would be disappointing not only to the Club (and especially Tom Blackburn, this year's president) but also to me since it is an occasion largely of my own arranging. However, he left me to sort it out with the Chief Whip, and the show goes on – subject to third and fourth thoughts. On Thursday Blackburn lunched with me to work out the details. He is a sprightly sixty-five, with a declared admiration for H. Macmillan (Saturday's tribute to Gaitskell was 'magnificent'). But Blackburn admiration doesn't make any difference to Beaverbrook editorial policy. As to Friday's lunch for Roger Wood, editor of the *Express* – well, I'm not sure they found a wavelength, despite the supporting efforts of Iain Macleod, Edward Boyle, Martin Redmayne and myself. The shadows of the Vassall tribunal were too long and deep (Douglas Clark, bitter and resentful, and Percy Hoskins), Beaverbrook anti-Market policy (making it at this moment taboo for conversation between P.M. and editor) and the seeming lack of political depth of Roger Wood himself.

Earlier in the week I had been Barney Keelan's guest at the annual lunch of the Newspaper Conference, with George Brown as the principal speaker. Sitting next but one to him meant an introduction ('Oh yes, Evans the Leak'), and in the next sentence it was Christian names and an announcement that he would replace me with his brother-in-law, Maurice Hackett, of the C.O.I., when he became Prime Minister.

Walton A. (Tony) Cole died in his office at Reuters on Friday afternoon, which meant drafting and getting off a message from the P.M. He had his fiftieth birthday only two or three months ago. Too many fifty-year-olds are getting killed off. One feels depressingly vulnerable.

February 3, Sunday   *Rottingdean*

Collapse of the Common Market negotiations – yet the immediate mood is relief and cheerfulness, reflected alike in the Stock Exchange and in the House. Ted Heath had an ovation when he entered the House on Wednesday, and he performed with undiminished assurance. He had not intended to return until later in the day, or possibly Thursday, but at a ten-minutes-to-midnight meeting in the Prime Minister's room in the House on Tuesday he was persuaded by the P.M. and the Chief Whip on the telephone that this would be to miss the psychological moment. 'My dear old friend,' the P.M. said to him emotionally.

This was a meeting called chiefly to renew consideration of the text of the P.M.'s proposed broadcast – with Macleod, Maudling (who drifted in at the last moment), Deedes, the Chief Whip, Tim Bligh and myself. I had tried to keep out of this exercise, but was in the wrong spot at the wrong moment when the P.M. had Macleod and Deedes in with Burke Trend and Tim during the morning and I was commanded to attend. I had seen the P.M.'s dictated draft only a few minutes before, which was no basis for the 'say what you really think about it' approach of the P.M.

However, I said that (a) I thought our own conception of Europe should be declared in the opening passages, and (b) I thought the peroration lacked force. He accepted (a) and re-dictated a passage. On (b) I did a draft myself during the afternoon. When we met at night Macleod declared himself strongly in favour of my re-write. The P.M. at first said roundly that he didn't agree – he had been taken with the imagery of his final statement about icy winter moving into spring – but suddenly gave way. So the structure was decided and only polishing remained overnight and in the morning.

He was ready to record the broadcast by 7, but went through the text finally, with John Grist also present, in the drawing room. I then said that I thought the middle passages would need to be broken up into simpler and shorter sentences and made more colloquial, which he accepted, so that substitute pages had to be typed.

So to the first recording (in the first floor ante-room as usual), which we agreed would do well enough. But John Grist favoured a second run and I agreed, chiefly because the P.M. had rather muffed the final sentences, and also because the middle needed cutting (he accepted without discussion my proposal to remove one page completely). This second run I thought better for these two reasons, and so we settled for it.

Afterwards the P.M. still showed no signs of anything but good spirits, and he kept Grist, Craxton and myself talking round the dining room table over whiskies until after 9 (including developments of his piece about speaking techniques, with particular reference to Lloyd George, plus ways and means of revitalising the Queen's Christmas broadcast).

I went down to the hall to see him off to the House, and there he said, apropos of not feeling tired, 'John Richardson came to see me this morning. He said I have the blood pressure of a man of thirty.'

Then, in a conspiratorial whisper, 'I shan't chuck my hand in, you know . . . Anyhow, it wouldn't do any good if I did. Of course, if it would help that would be different.'

So from this, coupled with a minute to Maudling about the shape of the next *two* budgets, one concludes that H. Macmillan intends not to have an election before the spring of 1964 (or even the autumn?), and that he proposes to lead the Tories through it.

On Thursday he wound up the Polaris debate and did it splendidly, and though it took seventy minutes its success left him exhilarated where I had expected him to be exhausted. 'A remarkable parliamentary performance,' reported T. F. Lindsay in the *Telegraph*. Then, early on Friday, he went off to Rome for a two-night visit. What extraordinary resilience he has, mental and physical.

For my part I felt utterly drained by the end of the week, but this was partly due to being unwell, with a cold and stomach upset. Also I had been involved at the beginning of the week in the effort of drafting the speech he was to have delivered to the Thirty Club on Wednesday night – cancelled on Wednesday morning because of the broadcast. Macleod stepped into the breach, apparently did it very well and said he had enjoyed it, and Tom Blackburn felt in the end that his dinner had been a big occasion after all.

What else? I was in the Cabinet room with the P.M. when Diefenbaker came through from Ottawa, wishing to turn the E.E.C. situation to political advantage in the speech he was about to make in his House of Commons. 'Can't you say that this is a time for reflection and consideration?' asked the P.M. wearily. 'After all, if we proposed a free trade agreement you would have to turn it down, wouldn't you?' Then, with the end of the conversation, he slammed down the phone angrily.

February 10, Sunday   *Rottingdean*

Morale bumping along the bottom. It *could* be the head cold that has plagued me for the last ten days. But I don't think so. Primarily it must be the inept decision to cancel Margaret's weekend visit to Paris as a means of cocking a snook at the General. I did not know of the decision until the afternoon it was announced – suddenly announced because apparently the embassy wanted to stop the tickets being printed. There was opportunity neither to influence the decision nor to prepare a respectable explanation in an orderly way.

Here again was the blind spot that mars sophisticated cleverness. It followed the thoughtless use of quotations from a Gaitskell speech during the Polaris debate on the day of the memorial service

(Mrs. G. wrote angrily). The Margaret decision alarmed the Chief Whip and alarmed Deedes, who said it had aroused strong criticism among their colleagues. So we get some impetus for the rumours that are circulating about the desire for new leadership. But where is the crown prince?

In other evidence of lost grip, the effort has now been abandoned, says Tim, to produce new material for the P.M.'s opening speech in the Common Market debate tomorrow. Maudling stands away from contributing. Perhaps Reggie sees himself as the crown prince? He has at least one devoted follower – Bill Deedes – who cuts away his information co-ordination activities as completely as possible from No. 10. Macleod sent a note asking why the P.M.'s recent political speeches have lost their punch (hardly true of Liverpool), though the answer should really be sought in the Central Office. Confronted by Henry Fairlie in an unattributable interview the P.M. is prepared to analyse the problems of leadership at this moment ('They seem to expect us to be archbishops as well as politicians'), but not to explain what he proposes to do about them. So today we get disagreeable things in the Sunday Press, including a report that the annual conference of the Surrey Young Conservatives has called for more dynamic leadership.

And if Mac went, what of the public relations adviser – the man with Macmillan for six years. Either his advice could not have been very good or his voice went unheard (though, of course, there *was* 1959). We come back to the importance of the independent position of the adviser drawn from the Civil Service. 'As far as we are concerned,' says Bill Grieg as Lobby chairman, 'he can go on for another six years.' Personally gratifying but with little relevance to the situation as it could develop. However, doubts are not going to be allowed to emerge. An unruffled face will be presented to the world. And we shall have to see if things can be shaken up in No. 10.

February 17, Sunday   *Rottingdean*

My opening contribution to a shake-up took the form of a minute to the P.M. calling for formulation of a plan of action and propaganda, co-ordinated to cover a specific period and to produce a clear picture of vigour and decision, with speeches and documents stripped of verbiage. Method – Ministers to be required to report expected major events and speeches in their own field, plus ideas for intensification of activity, and the whole then to be co-ordinated under the Minister without Portfolio.

But in the meantime the drama has unfolded further, with the election of Harold Wilson as Labour leader and with the appearance in print of speculation about the resignation of Harold Macmillan.

John Dickinson opened the gates in the *Evening News* with a piece based, fairly enough, on the confusion of Tory opinion at this moment, but really triggered off (so, at least, says P.A.'s Mr. Stacpoole) by the opportunity he saw to steal a march on his sparring partner, Robert Carvel, absent for the day in the *Evening Standard* office writing a great profile of Harold Wilson. The Dickinson piece started quite low down in the early editions, but by the evening had been given a banner. Inevitably, most of the political correspondents of the dailies (except *The Times* and *Telegraph*) could not resist the pressure to write follow-up pieces, and so we had a spate of them on Thursday morning. Then the foreign correspondents and international agencies had to pick it up, and one had the inevitable calls from all and sundry on the basis of 'but if six papers say so it must be right'.

Well, does the No. 10 spokesman wash his hands of the whole thing – strictly having no role in the matter and no guidance or instructions? On the basis that I have responsibilities to both Harold Macmillan and to the Press, I volunteered to all with whom I can talk confidentially that if they wanted my personal guidance it was that the P.M. had no thought of giving up (remembering that aside in the hall – 'I'm not going to chuck my hand in'), and that the Party, whatever present unhappiness, could not resolve on a successor (based on conversations with Charles Hill – 'sullen acquiescence' – and with the Chief Whip – 'fluctuation but no more').

This advice went among others to Randolph Churchill (ringing as usual very late, slurred in speech, but friendly enough and 'thanks a million' at the end). So on the whole it got killed off even before the P.M.'s speech last night to the Young Conservatives annual conference, when he had a tremendous ovation, and gave a clear impression that the election was a long way off and his own disappearance as well.

This morning, as a result, my morale is no longer bumping along the bottom (though physically I continue very much under the weather and have been kept in bed).

On matters economic, we had in to see the P.M. the group led by David Howell (*Telegraph*). He talked to them for over two hours and did it very well – certainly they were unable to blind him with science – but he referred back to his experiences in publishing, housing and at Stockton with sufficient frequency for the intense

254

Nigel Lawson to say on his way out, 'Well, there it is. His thinking is rooted in Stockton and housing. All the rest is theory.' But I doubt if the others will necessarily have seen it like that. Not least, he pinned them down individually on the kind of budget they would put together on the assumption that a policy of expansion had been adopted.

February 24, Sunday   *Rottingdean*
In parallel to the proposed 'vigour' campaign – 'He keeps coming back to it,' says Tim – I have proposed setting up an independent organisation to harness and drive forward the feelings, now becoming more and more apparent, that the time has come for a moral and patriotic revival. On the basis of my minute the P.M. has asked me to do notes for his speech early in March to the Conservative Council. This task rests heavily on my tired brain: the continuing icy weather, coupled with head and chest cold, is making me feel incapable of intensive effort.

The truncated defence White Paper had a rough reception and prompted a piece of intensely vituperative writing by Anthony Sampson in today's *Observer* (despite a lunch during the week with Tim Bligh).

March 3, Sunday   *Rottingdean*
In myself more cheerful – the effect no doubt of sunshine which, out of the wind, gives one the first whiff of spring. Annabel and I had our first outings of lawn cricket and we had a fine bonfire. Everything is tinder dry. Snow still lies on the shaded side of the fences.

The Sundays today have returned to some extent to speculation about the P.M.'s future. Douglas Clark has it as lead story in the *Sunday Express* ('Macmillan's Gamble' – he is to wait and see after a bouncy budget and a cut in the dole queues). Ian Waller is on the front page of the *Sunday Telegraph* with a piece saying that 'uneasiness persists among the Conservative backbench M.P.'s over the leadership of the Prime Minister.' Harry Boyne, on the telephone this evening with his routine Sunday call, tells me that he has resisted pressure in the *Telegraph* office to do a follow-up piece since he does not accept the Waller premise. (This Boyne attitude is important, not simply because he rejects the Waller thesis, but because if he *did* give it a push the story would maintain impetus.)

In a weekend speech Martin Redmayne condemned very forthrightly those who complained of lack of leadership, and spoke of the P.M.'s 'guts and courage'. In the *Spectator* Henry Fairlie had a particularly well-argued article on leadership in a democracy in peace time. There are other signs, too, of a healthy reaction to the satirists and denigrators (I have included a passage about them in my draft for the P.M.). If now the Tory backbenchers would show loyalty and determination the situation could quickly look very different. But the key to it all is the budget. Government, H. Macmillan, R. Maudling and all the leadership contenders are involved in it, and the P.M. has said just this to Maudling.

As to the backbenchers, contempt and anger made themselves apparent when I attended a meeting with Macleod, Thorneycroft, Deedes, Profumo, Redmayne and Fraser to talk about presentation of the decision to go ahead with a more centralised direction of defence policy. This, incidentally, was substantially leaked in a story in the *Birmingham Post* by Cecil Melville, but no national paper followed it up. Deedes and I produced a long list of questions on which spokesmanship would be necessary.

Beware the Ides of March. Trouble was now piling on trouble. Simmering beneath the surface and now about to come into the open was the Keeler affair. Meanwhile, the Radcliffe tribunal was continuing the public hearings begun in January, and journalists were being questioned about the accuracy and sources of stories they had written about Vassall and Galbraith. Two of them – Reginald Foster of the Daily Sketch and Brendan Mulholland of the Daily Mail – refused to disclose sources and were committed to prison, Foster for three months and Mulholland for six.

March 10, Sunday   *Rottingdean*
Mulholland and Foster to prison, and an uproar in the *Mail* and *Sketch*. Some comment looks at the Lobby system, and London Letter in *The Guardian* got so far as mentioning the 'suggestion' that the Lobby might 'withhold its confidence' from the Government and Opposition alike. George Lockhead, this year's chairman of the Press Gallery, also reported that some late-night talk in the bar advocated withdrawing the invitation to the P.M. to be the Gallery's principal guest at the annual dinner at the end of May. I doubt if this will come to anything, though the tribunal report is yet to come.

Speculation about the Tory Party chairmanship was launched by Bob Carvel, trailing Heath, Lloyd and Hailsham. John Dickinson followed with Home (on present form, in fact, it looks like being Amory – but not until the end of April).

The P.M.'s speech to the Tory Central Council was adjudged a notable success – but it was Home not Macmillan who took the Evans' approach.

The *Sunday Telegraph* today has an opinion poll showing sixty-two per cent thinking Macmillan should retire, and seventy-five per cent thinking Wilson would do a good job. Among Tories, forty-five per cent are shown as in favour of the P.M.'s retirement, fifty against and five undecided.

Charles Hill lunched with me during the week. He has written 35,000 words of his memoirs. On government publicity he said that it was no good people (for example, Michael Heseltine) bellyaching about Deedes. Who did the Ministerial job didn't matter much. Neither did it make much difference that with the Deedes appointment the emphasis had been put on the Party propaganda machine.

I saw the P.M. only twice during the week and then briefly. He was friendly and considerate as ever. One meeting was a casual one in the hall when he was talking to Rab and Burke Trend. He broke off to come and speak to me with the news that he had seen an old friend of mine last night and brought his warm greetings – Philip Swinton. Swinton, he said, was one of the cleverest men he had known: it was unfortunate that he had alienated so many people by arrogance and impatience: had it not been for that . . . He had heard that Harold Wilson had not pleased the Press Gallery at their monthly luncheon meeting by giving them so much politics – to which I could add Trevor Smith's similar report of the Wilson meeting with the Commonwealth Correspondents' Association.

March 16, Saturday   *Rottingdean*

Chief excitement of the week has been Fleet Street's attempts to link Profumo with the Keeler girl (she failed to appear in the shooting case against her Jamaican boy friend) without exposing themselves to libel actions. The *Express* decided to chance its arm with a story by Ian Aitken saying categorically that Profumo had offered his resignation for personal reasons, and that the P.M. had refused to accept it because of the work going forward on the re-organisation of defence. First inkling came from Douglas Haig who rang at about 9 on Thursday night to say he had reason to believe that 'one of the public prints' was going to run a story about Profumo offering to resign and what about it? On the form as checked before leaving Admiralty House I could say confidently that it wasn't true, and a check with T. J. Bligh confirmed that there had been no later developments. So, as the calls came in from then until 12.30, I could dispose of them quickly and categorically. Just after 12.30 the Chief Whip came through from the House to say that

Profumo was with him and what did I think about Admiralty House denying on the record that a resignation had been offered. 'Not on your life,' I told him, for all the obvious reasons – and anyhow it had already been done non-attributably. Should then Profumo, on reaching his besieged house (he had been speaking in the Army Estimates debate) say 'No comment'. But no less obviously a direct on-the-record denial had to come from him as the person principally involved.

Then there was the non-event of the alleged 'most sensational' new evidence in the Vassall case – effectively reduced to its proper proportions in a statement by the Attorney-General. I was summoned to the Cabinet room yesterday to comment on the draft of the statement. It's rather much to have a text thrust under your nose for comment without full knowledge of the background. I picked on 'will deal' and said the nuance was wrong, the Chief Whip agreeing. So we changed it to 'will refer'. From the emphasis the word gets in reports I am sure this was right. The P.M. shrugged and said he didn't see the difference but . . . This morning he rang me, primarily to criticise the *Yorkshire Post*. Yesterday it had not only led the news page but also written a leader about the alleged new evidence: this morning it makes no mention of the statement from the Attorney-General's office. While we were talking he suddenly said, 'But you have courage and guts.' Since the precise context wasn't clear I felt as much mystified as gratified.

Anthony Craxton, of B.B.C. television, came in one evening to discuss the Queen's Christmas broadcast, which he produces. This stemmed from the concern the P.M. feels about the increasing ineffectiveness of the broadcast. I did not regard myself as involved, but put up the usual overnight minute, offering comment and ideas (chiefly to suggest that as the circumstances had changed so drastically since royal broadcasts began thirty years ago the pattern might be broken and a new pattern created by having two broadcasts – a Commonwealth broadcast sent out in advance and one to the U.K. live on the afternoon of Christmas Day). In the event, the discussion flagged a little and Craxton appealed to me so that I developed this kind of thinking. But something less drastic will emerge.

The P.M. is agreeably informal on these occasions. He puts his feet on the edge of the table and tips back his chair. From time to time you get a silence while he turns over in his mind some particular thought – and suddenly you become aware of the loudness of the tick of the Cabinet room clock.

On Monday morning he rang me from Birch Grove and said,

inter alia, that Margach got it about right – a significant reference to Jimmy's Sunday article on the leadership. He talked also about his successful speech on Friday to the Conservative Central Council in the context of drawing necessary lessons. He noted, rightly, that 'I looked rather well and young.'

March 24, Sunday   *Rottingdean*

Wigg and other Labour M.P.'s brought the Profumo gossip into the open late on Thursday during the debate on the imprisoned journalists, and Profumo made a personal statement in the House on Friday morning. It was explicit and seems to have been accepted as (almost) the last word.

But the *Sketch* on Saturday had a headline 'Lucky John Profumo' ostensibly attached to a story about his 10-1 winner at the races: it was coupled on the front page, however, with an attack on his record as Secretary of State for War. It lends support to the thought now going the rounds (and expressed by Paul Johnson in the *New Statesman*) that political journalists and others in Fleet Street have accumulated bitter feelings against the Prime Minister and that this will be reflected in their writing (if so, a poor commentary on their approach to the responsibilities of which they make so much). The P.M. is aware, of course, of the importance of trying to mend fences (perhaps a frank and conciliatory speech at the Parliamentary Press Gallery dinner on May 24th?).

For rather different reasons he has half made up his mind to embark on a series of open Press conferences, and I am commanded to marshal the pros and cons. I sent back an immediate minute saying, 'Yes – providing you give them genuine news: and if you give them genuine news what about Parliament?' Then on Friday, when I took him to the C.O.I. to record a message for Australian television about the F.B.I. trade campaign, we really ran through it all in the car and on the stairs of Admiralty House when we got back. We'd certainly better get the Radcliffe tribunal report out of the way first.

Among many callers during the week was Anthony Howard. With Richard West he has been commissioned to write a book on the lines of *The Making of the President*. Rumour says that Wilson intends to build up a group of 'whizz kids' on the White House model if he gets in, and one suspects that Howard is as much interested in assessing the feasibility of doing this as in getting material for his book. His reaction to my account of the organisation at No. 10 was to say, 'Well, without wishing to be personal, it's pretty lightweight isn't it?'

March 31, Sunday   *Rottingdean*
   Waiting for Maudling. With the Tory candidate losing her deposit
at Swansea, the confusion on Enahoro and the impending dissolution of the Central African Federation (fiery personal attack on the
P.M. by Sir Roy Welensky in the *Sunday Express* in an interview
with Douglas Clark, wiping off old scores with this and a Crossbencher attack), all now depends on the budget. If it fails to revive
the Party, it seems inevitable that the senior backbenchers will get
together to decide on a successor and to convey a demand to the
P.M. that he should go. This is confirmed by Charles Hill, who
(with Mrs. Hill) stayed with us at Rottingdean last night prior to a
luncheon speaking engagement in Brighton today. Selwyn Lloyd
clearly sniffs blood (and is perhaps additionally piqued by a direct
warning from the P.M. that in his report on the Party organisation
he should lay off public criticism of the chairman). This weekend he
has followed up earlier speeches growling about inflation with a call
for a Commonwealth Economic Development Council to parallel
Neddy.
   I duly minuted in detail to the P.M. about open Press conferences, making it clear that I saw the project as full of hazards
unless we could organise a flow of genuine news and unless he could
be direct and positive in his answers. That this is what the Press and
public are looking for was demonstrated this week by reaction to
the Beeching report, even though it proposed wholesale closings of
lines and stations. But it was bold, clear, incisive – and this is in
harmony with the mood of the country.

April 7, Sunday   *Rottingdean*
   Mild disappointment seemed to be the broad verdict of the Press
on the budget, while yet recognising its merits and finding difficulty
in faulting it. Tax cuts totalled £269 million, of which some £180
million went to easing the burden on income tax payers in the lower
ranges, coupled with abolition of Schedule A and the halving of
stamp duty. But I think Rees-Mogg gets it right in today's *Sunday
Times* when he says that this is a good budget and a good budget
ripens like a good cheese. He also assumes, like most other political
writers, that there will be another budget before the election.
   The P.M. was well satisfied when I talked to him for twenty
minutes in the Cabinet room on Friday just before he left for
Cardiff. 'You can see now why we had to have a new Chancellor.'
   He was bubbling over with good spirits, though he had been
working all morning on the Cardiff speech. In part it reflected his
feeling that the speech was a good one (as it was, though it didn't

260

get satisfactory Press coverage). Having taken me into the Cabinet room he went to the drinks cupboard and produced sherry (for me) and ginger ale for himself. 'Don't you think I look slimmer?' he wanted to know. He thought that giving up alcohol for Lent helped to get his weight down: he had been getting too fat. I said that it had not occurred to me that he was in the least fat (true enough for he carries himself so well). Giving up alcohol, he went on, was for religious reasons, of course, but it was also a useful piece of self-discipline.

Then to Cecil King, who wants to come and see him about Vassall and the feelings in Fleet Street against him. We agree that as soon as the tribunal report is out of the way he must mend his fences with the Press. He will make a careful and balanced speech in the tribunal debate, and then there will be the Parliamentary Press Gallery dinner at the end of May. I say that I hope Carrington will *not* pursue a libel action against Douglas Clark and the *Express*. Honour should be satisfied with the apology at the tribunal (and assuming, of course, that the tribunal report will be satisfactory from his point of view): if he then sued it would seem vindictive and would make fence-mending more difficult. The P.M. agreed and said that though he could not very well do anything about it at the moment he would talk to Carrington later.

He went on to speak of Carrington as an honourable man in whose word he had absolute confidence. He hoped that this would prove no less true of Profumo, and that indeed there had been nothing of a scandalous nature in his relationship with Christine Keeler.

I raised the question of his conducting a television tour of the reconstructed No. 10 before we went back (now tentatively fixed for the last week in September). He would very much like to do it, he said, and that, I hope, will put an end to the bureaucratic stuffiness I have been facing in the Ministry of Works and in John Hewitt (such an exceptionally nice person that I'm sorry to find myself at logger-heads with him).

The Chief Whip consulted me about the Press attitude and relationship to Lord Poole, under consideration for the Party chairmanship. I don't think it would work. But Tim tells that the P.M. was seeing Macleod today with the idea of talking him into giving up Leadership of the House, but staying as Party chairman, with Poole as Deputy. And who then, asks Tim, do I think would become Leader? 'Why, Henry Brooke, of course.' Collapse of Bligh.

It was a week in which I felt quick-tongued. At any rate I had successful talking occasions with the Association of Industrial Editors (monthly lunch at the Criterion), and with Joe Fromm, Joe Harsch and Tom Lambert at lunch at the Connaught, plus a good meeting as guest of Ernest Atkinson's group of London provincial editors at the Reform. Charles Beauclerk[2] came to lunch with me at Whitehall Court. Because of his impending dukedom he isn't getting the succession to Barbara Fell's job at the C.O.I. He is thinking of dabbling in politics, he says, as a Liberal peer. The present duke is eighty-eight. He settled the family wealth on Charles in return for a cash payment.

April 21, Sunday   *Rottingdean*
An Easter holiday for ten days (Midlands and Cornwall), and John Groves found No. 10 hard going.

The P.M. firmly declared at the 1922 Committee lunch that he proposed to lead the Tories at the election. Then, after all the juggling over the Party chairmanship, he hit on the compromise of making Oliver Poole joint chairman with Iain Macleod. So the air is cleared, and both announcements have had a good Press.

Publication of the Radcliffe report lies ahead. That should also help to clear the air. It offers no censure on the Press – simply takes the allegations and shows them to be false. But it doesn't really explain how Vassall was allowed to get away with it. Now we have a new security row over the C.N.D. *Spies for Peace* pamphlet.

April 28, Sunday   *Rottingdean*
Monday evening heart-to-heart with P.M. and Poole.

Poole wants the open Press conference. He accepts the risks, but says that the Tories won't make up lost ground without taking risks. Subsequently, he and I talked separately in the waiting room, and he added that he did not think the P.M. performs well enough either on the platform or in the House, and is only just adequate on television. On his mettle in question and answer, however, it is another matter. Hence support for the Press conference. At least we agreed that it would have to be a genuine Press conference and not a television show with the Press as extras, in the presidential manner. Poole proposes to get a film of a Kennedy conference through A.T.V. for us to study (*that* won't stay secret). He also embarks on a long explanation, without apology, about his criticisms in his talk to the I.P.U. of political reporting in the British Press (I

[2] Director, Films Division, Central Office of Information. Later thirteenth Duke of St. Albans.

had drawn attention to it in the memorandum I did after seeing Denis Hamilton).[3] Finally, he thinks that the P.M. and the administration generally have been too evasive – more candour will be necessary.

The exercise of publishing the Radcliffe tribunal report went well, and I pleased the editors of the *New Statesmen*, *Economist*, *Spectator* and *Statist* by agreeing that, exceptionally, they should have final revises. But we shall need to have a row with the two London evenings. Both broke the Morrison rules, and the *Standard* also broke the approach embargo by an interview with Rennell's daughter. As to reaction – much as I had expected. There is hope that it will have cleared the air – but the debate lies ahead, Mulholland and Foster remain in prison, and Carrington and Galbraith may well sue.

In other respects, events at last begin to move the way of the Tories (apparently). The P.M. made a bouncing speech at Glasgow on Friday, a new mood is evident, and the massive meeting of Ministers at Chequers at the weekend adds to the impression of action and buoyancy, as well as contributing to the Opposition's uncertainties about the timing of the election. We are now in the realms of double and treble bluff. The theory goes that the Tories are hinting at a spring election so that Labour will conclude that they really mean to have it in October and will trigger off their campaign and expenditure prematurely.

This week also saw the Macmillan–Kennedy approach to K. on nuclear tests, and I had a lively session with the American group about Washington speculation that it was all being done for Macmillan's political benefit. K. gave the ambassadors little joy and it seems unlikely that anything will develop – but it is now caught up in the wider speculation about K.'s future.

Add the Alexandra–Angus Ogilvy wedding (an occasion of great charm), and altogether it was a quick-moving week. I had to tackle it minus John Groves, taking his share of Easter leave.

I am invited to be the Guinea Club's guest of honour on June 18th, which flatters and pleases when one remembers the distinction of their list. With that and the P.M.'s speeches to the Variety Club, Press Gallery and Foreign Press Association I have a wearing time ahead in drafting.

[3] At a private meeting of the International Press Union Lord Poole was widely reported to have said that Lobby correspondents were not the kind of people who could – to quote from *The Times* – 'be invited by political hostesses to weekends in country houses'.

May 12, Sunday   *Rottingdean*

On Tuesday the P.M. had a splendid day with the success of his speeches – in entirely different idiom – to the Variety Club and in opening the Radcliffe tribunal debate.

At the Variety Club a record attendance gave him a standing ovation, and the gossip columnists used up their most shining adjectives in Wednesday's dailies. It also had a full television showing late on Tuesday, and long excerpts in radio programmes. All excellent publicity at the right moment – plus an audience drawn from the whole of the entertainment world left with impressions of a lively and witty Macmillan. Immensely satisfying for me, too, since I had first persuaded him to go, and then written ninety per cent of the text – a repetition of the B.B.C. television dinner success (as Joe Illingworth recalled in the *Yorkshire Post*'s London Letter, speculating about the member of the Prime Minister's staff who must have 'tell-tale square eyeballs').

But Tuesday's triumphs were blanketed at the end of the week by Tory losses in the local elections. If not catastrophic, they equalled the most pessimistic forecasts (a two and a half per cent increase in the Tory Gallup Poll rating could not be regarded as adequate compensation). The commentators now conclude that there is virtually no prospect of an autumn election. This seems to be in line with the P.M.'s own thinking.

Last Sunday, when *The Queen* had their team at Birch Grove to take colour pictures between church and lunch, Betty, Annabel and I were invited to lunch. It did not give much time for official gossip, but enough for him to tell me that he was planning an entirely new routine for the next year. He would be taking off time from Cabinet (the Lord Chancellor could preside) in order to concentrate on the things that really needed doing. He was being provided with two brand new speech writers, to be taken on the strength of the Central Office, and he would probably re-organise the No. 10 office under a chief of staff 'to work with you and Tim Bligh'.

This last idea looked rather different later in the week when Tim was deputed to put me in the picture after further meetings with Poole and Macleod. Their thought had been to bring a Minister into No. 10 as chief of staff – and Enoch Powell was the man they had in mind. But on realistic examination (with Tim brought into the consultation) they decided that it wasn't really an arrangement that would work (of course not!), and that they'd better do the best with what they've got. So Tim is to be chief of staff: there will be an inner steering committee meeting at 10 a.m. on Tuesdays, comprising P.M., Macleod, Poole, Bligh and (as necessary) Evans;

and Evans is to have oversight of planning the P.M.'s diary.

In the discussions leading to these conclusions, says Tim, the P.M. said he leaned heavily on me and that he intended to 'take care' of me, recognising that the Civil Service would have nothing to offer me. Well, let's see how it works out. To Tim I said that I thought the Chief Whip must surely be brought into the steering committee. As to the diary, John Wyndham may be sensitive (but I did begin by intercepting a Hewitt minute on an invitation from Cambridge).

The family Birch Grove visit went well. The P.M. applied his conversational charm to Betty at lunch, and Annabel (not banished to the nursery with the grandchildren) behaved impeccably – but announced with satisfaction in the drawing room after lunch that her teeth were chattering (Lady D. has the central heating turned off on May 1st).

Charles Hill had me to lunch at the Reform, seeking some thoughts on the information chapter of his book, plus advice on whether to opt for a life or hereditary peerage (he has been told that he can have either in the Birthday Honours, and also that he will get the I.T.A. chairmanship immediately thereafter: in fact, at the end of last week, the formal offer of the chairmanship was held back because, it seems, Wilson is threatening that if C. Hill is appointed, and if Labour comes in, they will throw him out). On the assumption that the way was now clear, Charles was pressing me to join him at the I.T.A. early next year. On the peerage point, I said that though an hereditary peerage still had a greater prestige value (Watkinson will get one), it was a declining prestige with Lords reform imminent, and a life peerage would seem right for Charles Hill in the eyes of most people: but, of course, it was essentially a matter to be resolved in the family.

Kenneth Young, editor of the *Yorkshire Post*, lunched with me during the week. With an intellect and a beard, he represented a duty engagement, but he is stimulating company and I enjoyed it. I hope he did. His book on Balfour has had a good success (though priced at three guineas), but he is now having copyright trouble with some letters from a third person which he used from the Balfour collection.

May 19, Sunday   *Rottingdean*

First meeting of the steering group (Tim dubs it the Sedan Committee) saw me in for an hour with my paper on presentation, and in particular the P.M.'s role at the centre. I had advocated, among other things, more positive use of Question Time. The Chief

Whip thought stooge questions were always too apparent, but I pressed for, at any rate, a more positive approach and something for the Press to report. Perhaps a quotable sentence could always be held ready.

As it turned out, Question Time that afternoon was the liveliest and best for a long time, with the P.M. scoring heavily over Wilson – but the quoted sentence was improvised! Perhaps it was only a flash in the pan because a sense of occasion existed from the first appearance of Winston since his accident last June (and how moving it was!). Also the opening question was on Queen Frederika and here the Tory backbenchers were ready to cheer.

For my part, I had two speeches to prepare – for the unveiling by the Prime Minister of the Lobby chairman's notice board, and for the Press Gallery dinner. I find that if I have time for my subconscious to sort it out, the draft eventually flows, though I probably have to be prepared to wake at intervals through one night to jot down great thoughts and telling phrases. At any rate, both drafts went in before the weekend, and that gives me a nice sense of relief. Next is the speech for the Foreign Press Association dinner.

My other activities during the week included lunch with T. F. Thompson at the Boulestin. He is now the *Mail*'s political editor and not assistant editor, which he regards as a demotion. He tried unsuccessfully for a silver handshake to match Bill Hardcastle's golden one. Paradoxically, he thinks he might now exercise more influence, since Mike Randall has less political knowledge and interest than had Hardcastle. I agreed that another editor's lunch for the Prime Minister would be welcomed and it is now arranged – obviously encouraging against the background of the Mulholland affair.

I was also a guest at the massive dinner given by Henry Luce at the Hyde Park Hotel. Not really my milieu for it turned out to be primarily an occasion for newspaper and magazine tycoons to mark the first meeting of the *Time-Life* board outside the U.S. I sat at Paul Hoffman's table, on his left, and heard about his U.N. aid programme – an agreeable man, described by Luce as 'a do-gooder but not too bad all the same'. Luce, having got a captive audience of British V.I.P.s, gave them half an hour of the facts of publishing life, but without grace or wit.

Then there was the job of persuading Jocelyn Stevens to remove from his Macmillan profile a few too-well-remembered quotes, as also a quote from me (used in his opening line) quoting in turn the P.M.'s 'how very shy-making'. I am used in the article as a kind of stooge, but since the effect of the article as a whole is favourable to the P.M., and since this is a device that helps to make it readable, I decided that I must put up with it. Stevens is a formidable young man, more especially because his ruthlessness is masked by charm and humour.

For the rest, the P.M. agreed to see Ronald Butt, now promoted to his own signed weekly column in the *Financial Times*; I was able to offer some thoughts to help Graham Cawthorne with his Macmillan obituary (being rewarded with a slice of currant tart); and I went to the Institute of Journalists to give an experimental briefing to the Commonwealth Correspondents' Association, finding myself reasonably fluent (though I doubt if this is the kind of thing they want).

At Chequers this weekend the P.M. has had Ormsby-Gore and others. This has helped to bring to a head rumblings which began with a mischievous piece in *The Times* by Louis Heren from Washington about alleged White House–Admiralty House 'differences' now interpreted by Crossman on the front page of today's *Sunday Mirror* as a deliberate snub by Kennedy. It was predictable – and I did predict it – as long as Kennedy chose for some mysterious reason not to have it announced that he will be coming to London on June 28th–29th during his European tour. The Americans have been putting into circulation hints about not wishing to prejudice a meeting with de Gaulle by announcing a Macmillan meeting in advance. No doubt, after the weekend, I shall hear what lies behind it all.

May 26, Sunday   *Rottingdean*
The Queen article was published this week, and had the unexpected bonus of a two-page spread in the *Mirror* of all papers. 'Do you think they are trying to be friendly?' asks the P.M. 'Did Stevens ask if he could do this? How much is he getting for it?' To which I say (a telephone conversation), 'Whatever they paid him, the Tory Central Office would have had to pay a good deal more for comparable publicity.' Insolent perhaps, but I felt nettled. Later, of course, he had seen its value and took a more philosophic view of the 'vulgarity'.

John Wyndham says that at his clubs they are saying that, of course, it is all those clever young men at No. 10: that really the P.M. is old and tired, but the young men are writing these brilliant speeches and putting him across in an imaginative way. You can't win.

The answer is that he *is* in splendid form, that he has entered into the spirit of battle and that he is taking his public appearances seriously (which includes listening to advice).

But he did not use much of the draft I had done for the Parliamentary Press Gallery dinner – a draft which he had accepted and put into psalm form almost untouched. But on the night it went into his pocket and he did perfectly well without it. Afterwards he went upstairs for nearly an hour and impressed the boys with his zest and good spirits. I missed it because Betty and I had to catch the Brighton train at 11. The speeches were better than usual (George Lockhead and T. F. Lindsay did well for the journalists, Nabarro less well for the politicians). We went as guests of James and Rona Margach, with the Robinson (*Times*) family at the same table.

The P.M. also did well with his Albert Hall speech to the Tory women. But the Gallup Poll at the end of the week did not reflect the feeling in Westminster that the Tories are pulling up fast.

The American group, at the end of a session with the P.M. on Thursday, would probably have disagreed with Gallup – though three rounds of double whiskies might have imparted a roseate hue. The P.M. talked to them for nearly an hour and a half and talked very well. Sydney Grusom was looking for trouble when he asked the P.M. what he thought of the Grusom piece on a Kennedy–Macmillan meeting. He duly collected it in the form of a devastatingly friendly, 'Oh, it was rot.'

Earlier in the week the P.M. talked to Ronald Butt for seventy minutes in the study, chiefly about matters nuclear when Ronald wanted to talk about matters European. Then the conscientious Ronald tied himself into introspective knots on what he might and might not legitimately use in his recently instituted Friday column – and not only that but also whether he was justified in reproducing someone else's views without attribution. He sent in a piece, which the P.M. thought very civil and which we agreed certainly did no damage.

I felt unduly tired and depressed at the end of the week. Being in the fifties doesn't help. However, the sun has shone brilliantly through the weekend, and with the sights and scents of early summer I now feel healed.

On Tuesday, at his steering committee, the P.M. said he wanted to have 'a jolly good talk about propaganda', so will I please be available. One thing I can talk about is a B.B.C. idea, conveyed by Mrs. Wyndham-Goldie, when she lunched with me at Whitehall Court, that in July–August they should do interviews in depth with the three political leaders. The P.M. could do well out of this –

given the right interviewer (I would settle for John Freeman, though I suggested an American) plus time to deploy his thinking (say, forty-five minutes).

June 2, Whit Sunday   *Rottingdean*

P.M. and Lady Dorothy to Scotland for ten days, leaving Rab to look after the day-to-day running of the government. After the Foreign Press Association dinner, returning to Admiralty House in the car, the P.M. said he felt as excited as a child at the thought of setting off for Scotland the next evening.

He had another success with his speech – enhanced by contrast with the insensitive and aggressive platitudes of George Brown. It was a piquant conjunction, since the evening before Brown had given to the agencies a vitriolic passage attacking the P.M. ('frankly, he lied') for his performance in the Enahoro debate (generally recognised as a notable parliamentary achievement). Robert Scott (*Yorkshire Post*) had rung me late to read the passage to me and ask (without expecting a positive reaction) if the P.M. might issue a counter-blast. I assured him there would be no counter-blast. Then I rang the P.M. to tell him what was coming and to advise that he should be seen to treat it with amused contempt. The outburst can have done harm only to Brown (and possibly to the Labour Party, as was apparent from the significant non-reporting by the *Herald* and the *Mirror*).

In the Enahoro debate the P.M. had been prepared to play it quietly, but in the car on the way to the *Mail* editorial lunch at the Stafford Hotel I said that I thought it might be a good occasion for 'bashing'. And bash he did – brilliantly, aided by the readiness of the Opposition to be led by the nose.

Mike Randall, the new editor, was host at the *Mail* lunch. Vere Harmsworth was there again, plus Redhead, the joint managing director. With Mulholland still in prison it would seem to be a significant gesture. The P.M. was in good form. In making the point that, even if the Tories were defeated, he would be able to assure the Queen when he handed in the seals of office that she ruled a nation in which no deep or bitter divisions existed, he was pressed to define where the difference *did* lie between Tories and Socialists. People were either doers or managers, he said. Tories were doers. They created wealth. Socialists, like bureaucrats, were managers. They created nothing. They planned only how to use the wealth that others had created.

He also talked about the nuclear tests problem, as he had done to Ronald Butt and to the Americans – its unreality when one had only to explode nuclear bombs in ships sunk off the American coast to cause a devastating tidal wave. Or why not use bacteria? At one point he was asked to comment on an assertion by Aubrey Jones. This he dismissed by asking, 'Who is Aubrey Jones? Do you know, Harold?' To which, as stooge, I dutifully responded, 'Goodness knows. Some Opposition politician I think.'

At the 10 a.m. Tuesday meeting we had our 'good talk about propaganda', and I made progress with the Wyndham-Goldie and tour of No. 10 projects.

On Monday afternoon Tim Bligh and I called on Sir Michael Adeane and Richard Colville at the Palace to talk about the Queen's Christmas broadcast. Adeane had shown some resentment when the topic had first been broached on the telephone, but he could not have been more friendly and agreeable when the moment came. This was my first meeting with him, though over the years I have called on Richard Colville (a little farther along the corridor) four or five times. His room has two large windows looking towards Green Park. Between them is a very, very gloomy painting, with a fat white dog standing out from the surrounding blackness. In the fireplace – an old-fashioned grate – the Palace footmen display an ancient art with decoratively cut paper.

The Palace tries each year to get some freshness into the broadcast, says Adeane, and women have been drawn into the drafting, but the limits are so circumscribing, of course. Television has ruined the whole thing. The Queen is gay and relaxed beforehand, but in front of the cameras she freezes and there is nothing to be done about it. One thing she won't have at any price – the idea of the family grouped round the fireside.

Tim and I are content to have had this part of the topic opened up, and we concentrate rather on the narrower problem of stopping the B.B.C. from broadcasting the message on radio at 9 a.m. on Christmas Day, six hours ahead of the television broadcast. Adeane agrees that we should pursue the B.B.C. on this point, and comes out to the car to see us off.

With the P.M. in such good form – and with this generally recognised in Westminster and Fleet Street – it was disconcerting to find a *Telegraph* Gallup Poll during the week (and also an *Express* poll) recording a setback to the upward movement of recent months. Just how long is the lag between Westminster and the constituencies?

June 9, Sunday   *Rottingdean*

Out of the clear blue sky came the Profumo thunderbolt to destroy that leisurely Whit weekend one had so fondly anticipated.

Today the Sunday papers write unanimously of a crisis for the Prime Minister (and, to a lesser degree, for the Chief Whip). It is fair enough. In a scrambled phone call today Tim Bligh tells that, (a) the Chief Whip feels he must resign; (b) the P.M. (from Gleneagles) says the Chief Whip shouldn't but if he does then he, too, will go; (c) Thorneycroft says he will want to raise the matter in Cabinet; (d) Heath says he thinks it has all been very badly handled; (e) Brooke says he will support the P.M. but thinks he ought to have been consulted more; (f) Hailsham is thought to be strongly critical and Powell likely to be so. For the rest, Macleod is in the States (will he come back for Wednesday's Cabinet?), and Butler was fully consulted and fully concurred in the decision that Profumo must resign.

Organising the announcement of the resignation, I had the problem of a scattered Lobby (a substantial number on a Northern Ireland jaunt), but by a stroke of good fortune the Conservative Central Office were having their briefing on the Selwyn Lloyd organisation report and I was able through that contact to summon all available Lobby men to Admiralty House at 6. I had prepared a pretty full background note and it did not leave much scope for further questions at the time.

I had more the following morning at the Birthday Honours Lobby, particularly on the security aspects, but was inhibited in my answers by the P.M.'s wish that I should not say that an 'enquiry' was proceeding. (The P.M. has asked the Lord Chancellor to make an investigation and had told Mr. Wilson so, but he does not want to be pinned down to a formal enquiry from which a formal published report would be expected – though, in fact, the Lord Chancellor will probably submit a report in publishable form.)

There can be no doubt that the Prime Minister's future lies in the balance. Against the wider background, there will be a strong temptation to the Party to jettison him, and to put the election off as long as possible in the hope of recovery under a new leader.

June 23, Sunday   *Rottingdean*

A fortnight later.

The Prime Minister returned overnight from Scotland on Sunday, June 9th. That brought him back to Admiralty House shortly after 8 a.m. on Monday.

The first task was to try to persuade him to let me announce the Lord Chancellor's enquiry forthwith. But he was as keen to see me as I was to see him, and I had an immediate summons to the Cabinet room. We started with a piece about the beauty and symbolism of Iona. He then embarked on a full rehearsal of what he would say in the debate a week later (the Chief Whip came in half way through). I was heartened and reassured to find that most of the misunderstandings in circulation could be met, in particular that Profumo had *not* been under surveillance in 1961 and that the warning Norman Brook gave to Profumo about Ward had *not* been reported to the P.M.

But, he says, what do we do in the meantime? One thing we must do almost within the hour, I suggest, is to let the Lobby know about the Lord Chancellor's enquiry. This he accepts – as does the Chief Whip – without argument. I then ask about publication of the report, assuming it will be available within the next forty-eight hours. On the one hand it is for question whether we should anticipate the debate, but on the other we should take care against being accused of allowing rumours and speculation to continue unchecked. This is left blurred. So I go away to prepare my piece for the Lobby, not promising publication but telling them that a copy of the report will go to Wilson. What I can't really explain satisfactorily to them is why the enquiry was not announced earlier – certainly after the Profumo resignation. The plain fact was that the Prime Minister had not wanted it to get inflated – to be seen for more than it was: and then, when he was in Scotland, it had been difficult to talk it out with him.

Looking back, had I been put under more pressure (for example, by the *Sunday Times* who, says Denis Hamilton, tackled every available Minister, including Macleod in Washington, for some counter line, but failed to do the obvious and come to me) I might either have made an issue of it in No. 10 or taken my own decision. In fact, I had given enough guidance for it to emerge in Friday morning's papers that some form of 'study' of the documents was being undertaken.

I had also to explain to the Lobby that an early call by Hailsham had nothing to do with Profumo. This was quite a morsel for them to swallow, but they did. I was aided by being able to say that I thought the reason might become apparent later in the day. This was the announcement that Hailsham was to be the Prime Minister's special representative for the talks in Moscow on a nuclear tests ban agreement. It meant another desperate rush but I just made it for the 4 o'clock Lobby. As I was leaving the office at the end of the day with my weekend bag, Hailsham appeared in the ante-room and quipped, 'I see you've got your bag packed', to which I could at least reply, 'Yes, may I come with you?'

Judging by the television and radio news bulletins the announcement of the enquiry had an immediate steadying effect after the eruption in the Sunday Press. In addition to all this I had also had to make time to take a look at arrangements for the President's visit in three weeks time.

On Tuesday, the 11th, the chief developments were virtual completion of the Chancellor's report and the summoning of a group of senior colleagues to discuss it in the early evening. Enoch Powell, it emerged, had qualms because of the meeting of the five Ministers with Profumo in the early hours of March 22nd. If they knew of a letter from Profumo to Keeler, he wonders, and especially if they knew it began with 'Darling', how could they have been so gullible: and if five of them assisted with the drafting did it not become a Government statement rather than a personal statement? But he seems uncertain about where all this leads him. The meeting apparently found the report reassuring, but made proposals for improved presentation. The amended document had then to be got ready for Wednesday's Cabinet meeting.

I had a brief encounter with a beaming R. A. Butler as he was going into the evening meeting – 'Oh, Harold, how *are* you standing up to things?' Then, alas, like everyone else where Rab is concerned, I found myself speculating about the reasons for this bonhomie.

On Wednesday, the 12th, the Cabinet duly met and looked reasonably solid. Enoch Powell made his points, but seemed to find the explanations acceptable and did not press the matter to an issue. To make quite sure the Prime Minister, in effect, made him stand up and be counted by saying that, of course, if the judgment of the five Ministers were to be challenged there would be no option but for him (the Prime Minister) to resign. All the five would then do so, says Deedes, who was one of them. The P.M. further made it clear that there was no question of his resigning before the debate, whatever might happen thereafter: he was not the man to go down without defending himself in person against the attacks made on his honour.

With this background, we could steer the evening papers with some confidence against expectation of drama or resignations after the Cabinet. They wrote it too hard, of course, and this may have been a factor in a counter-story, fed to Henry Fairlie (who had most of the *Express* front page to splash it) and David Wood, in *The*

Times, saying that, in fact, not only Enoch Powell, but also Edward Boyle, Keith Joseph and Henry Brooke remained dissatisfied, and that the second Cabinet on Thursday would prove to be critical (it was designed, in fact, to cross the t's and dot the i's of the report).

Knocking this down late on Wednesday night was virtually impossible, but Joseph came out with a 'nonsense' reaction in time for the later editions, and Henry Brooke (from the Channel Islands) issued an indignant denial which caught the last editions.

Events proved our assessment and guidance right, and those few papers which stood firm (notably the *Mail*) had the last laugh – the *Mail* to the extent of a front-page story 'exposing' the plot, attributed to a prominent ex-Minister (Nigel Birch was generally said to be responsible, though David Wood subsequently denied having got it from him). The *Telegraph* came out of it badly, their totally contradictory headlines in successive editions being duly noted in the radio Press summary on Thursday morning.

As to *The Times*, whatever the source, the Wood article looked like the second arm of a pincer, the first arm being a leader calling for a Powell resignation as a means of bringing Macmillan down. This manoeuvre was generally seen as a follow-up to a massive leader earlier in the week saying that the Tories under Macmillan had brought the country to a low ebb in every respect and must go.

Enoch Powell could, of course, have killed off the uncertainties at any time but did not do so until a speech on Saturday afternoon – in the event perhaps more helpful that way since it seemed to suggest that this reputedly puritanical and fanatical Minister had duly wrestled with his conscience and reached a clear verdict. At any rate, this speech, plus Hailsham on television (an explosive, moody interview with 'young Mackenzie'), plus Poole, plus our consistent guidance about the Prime Minister's confidence in his ability to meet the allegations, had the effect of inducing a different mood in the Sunday Press.

But much goes on behind the scenes. There are rumours that Birch has fifty anti-Macmillan rebels lined up to abstain. And what are Lord Poole's motives? Certainly not simply to sustain the Prime Minister but to preserve the Party even if it means pushing Macmillan out. He and the Chief Whip have said to the Prime Minister, in effect, that he will need to go before the next session of Parliament.

On the morning of Sunday, the 16th, I had a longish telephone call at home from the Prime Minister, saying that he thought the Press was better, and that it had clearly been worthwhile seeing

Rees-Mogg (I had fed him in late on Friday after hearing that he wished to write a balancing article). He also canvassed the thought that a pattern could be discerned pointing to a conspiracy to discredit and pull down the system. Then he rehearsed his speech again, declaring that he must be judged on grounds of good faith, justice and prudence. He said that he particularly wanted me to see the draft first thing in the morning. ('You are clever. You will bring an objective view to it.') He also discussed the speech he is to make in opening the annual conference of the Commonwealth Press Union. I had done a draft and he asked, 'Why should I be nice to them?' – meaning the Press generally – but I say that in fact the draft is carefully balanced while still maintaining the 'mending fences' line.

On Monday, the 17th, I duly turned up early at Admiralty House and obtained a copy of the draft of the debate speech as it had emerged from the weekend's thinking. By the time the P.M. rang me I had already given comments to Philip Woodfield, making one point of substance (the discrepancy in dates, as between August and December 1961, when Profumo was said to have abandoned his affair with Christine Keeler) and six or seven drafting points designed to remove sentences or phrases which might be seen as having a *double entendre* and raise a snigger.

Shortly after 10 we left for the Stationers' Hall for the Common-wealth Press Union conference (too early, as it turned out, Howsden having been a little too pessimistic about the state of the traffic). As we left Admiralty House it was to face that great battery of cameras and reporters which has maintained an hour-by-hour vigil since the P.M. returned from Scotland.

In the car, there and back, I heard again of the possibility that underlying the whole business is a conspiracy to pull down the system – Opposition no less than Government – with statements by Ward's young ladies implicating eight or ten Ministers and many besides. Of himself, he said that it had not broken his spirit but for the time being he has lost his zest – adding that no doubt it will come back again.

Then the debate. Alas, the loss of zest is all too obvious. The substance is good, but the manner weary and dispirited: and here and there he tried to interpolate and lost the thread. By contrast both Wilson and Brown are crisp and confident. Then Macleod winds up ineffectively – and gets black marks in the Press Gallery (for example, from an unusually angry Margach) for being seen too obviously to be trying to keep his own nose clean, without much regard to the Prime Minister. Half way through the debate the

Chief Whip sounded the alarm. The majority, he feared, would be down to sixty. In fact, it was sixty-nine.

Afterwards the small group of private secretaries, with John Groves and myself, sat around the private office in the House, drained and melancholy, but attempting the customary banter, aided by the antics of John Wyndham who makes a pantomime of going away in the rain. The Chief Whip came in and told me that there had been eighteen abstentions – but the Whips got even that wrong for it turned out to be twenty-seven.

On Tuesday – despite headlines like MAC: THE END (*Mail*) – there is a sense of anticlimax and the job of running the country begins to take pride of place again. The Prime Minister had a very good Question Time – a quite different Macmillan from the day before. And the Guinea Club entertained Harold Evans who, with the aid of asides from Lord Hill of Luton, managed to roll them in the aisles in a speech prepared at odd moments during the preceding twenty-four hours.

On Wednesday (19th) I talked to the P.M. on the telephone at the beginning of the morning. He talked about 'this strange battle of nerves'. Some of the wiser heads were now seeing the dangers. If they forced him out now there would be a sharp division in the Party and in the country for ten years. They would strongly resent it if he was driven out now by a lot of little crooks. He must get all the scandal cleared up before he went. It looked as though there was a plot to destroy the system. If they got one side down they would start on the other. It was like the position in the Third Republic in France which ended in the collapse of the State. 'That has got to be stopped – even if it is one's last effort.'

But we were quickly back to crisis – this time unrealised by the world at large. On Thursday morning I arrived at Admiralty House to be greeted by Tim Bligh with a warning that at the 11.30 Lobby I should almost certainly have to announce a Ministerial resignation. The Minister's name was being linked with the 'headless man' in the Argyll affair six years ago. He was *not* the headless man, but he had been involved with the lady and apparently felt that he must expiate the indulgence by resignation now – regardless of the political consequences.

Incredibly, it did not seem to be realised what these consequences must almost certainly be. So I said that I wished my voice to be heard formally – and that what I had to say was that if this resignation went forward it would bring down, not only the Prime Minister, but also the Government. But, said Tim, if you perform an operation and leave the scalpel in the wound you have to get it out. I retort that if you do re-open the wound you kill the patient. Well, says Tim, the patient will die if you leave it in.

The Cabinet had been summoned for 10 to consider the Prime Minister's draft statement to be made in the afternoon about the setting up of a judicial enquiry under Lord Denning. Here again I called for my voice to be heard formally, saying that the statement should make it clear beyond doubt that the enquiry was not aimed at the Press and that it should not refer to the possible existence of a conspiracy. Would the Cabinet be told of the proposed resignation, I asked. Goodness knows, said Tim, in effect, at which I could only express astonishment: how could they be allowed to go solemnly through the draft statement without being told of this further bombshell which would entirely alter the situation and affect everyone of them? But by now they had assembled.

While the meeting proceeded, and having found that my assessment coincided with that of John Groves, I returned to the Private Office to see what opportunities existed for ramming it home. Fortunately, Tim had come out of the meeting, and we had an impromptu meeting round his desk, joined by Philip Woodfield and Philip de Zulueta. The situation had now changed a little in that the Minister had decided that he would announce his resignation in a personal statement in the House (cheek by jowl with the Prime Minister's enquiry statement!), rather than have it announced to the Lobby this morning. Philip Woodfield, it seemed, had expressed identical views to mine to the Chief Whip overnight. The quick-witted Philip de Z. for once missed the point. No one, he argued, could possibly take seriously a resignation on grounds so quixotic. But that, I said, was precisely the point. No one would accept that this was the real reason. It would be seen as another Minister getting out from under as Profumo had done, because worse was to come – i.e. that he was involved in the Keeler affair, as rumour alleged. Moreover, this was happening just at the moment when public opinion was moving in support of the Prime Minister. Public goodwill would be totally dissipated: the Cabinet would be disrupted: the backbenchers thrown into even greater disorder: and the Opposition and the Press inspired to an even greater hue and cry.

Tim then went back into Cabinet. The meeting lasted only an hour, and W. F. Deedes came immediately to my room. After they had discussed the statement, it seems, the Minister had declared his intention to make a personal statement on Friday morning (the Profumo procedure precisely) and there was no further discussion. To Deedes I repeated my belief that this spelt the fall of the

Government. He had not seen it quite like that, though greatly shaken, but he accepted the likelihood of this being a correct judgment and went off.

A little later I went to the Private Office to check the position with Tim Bligh. Things were now on an even keel, he said. The Minister had agreed that he should *not* resign, but that the P.M. should ask Denning to look into the allegations against him. Macleod, added Tim, was now ringing round the Cabinet to tell them of the changed intention. At this moment the Prime Minister came into the Private Office from the Cabinet room and, seeing me, called me in with Tim. He started talking about the Wilson meetings, but I chipped in to say that if the resignation business leaked it would bring the Government down – he agreed – and speed was therefore the essence in letting members of the Cabinet know of the changed situation: was it sufficient to leave to Macleod the job of ringing round the whole Cabinet? Some of them might start talking, or doing something dramatic in the way of cancelling engagements. So Tim went to check on progress.

Nothing did leak – and so the situation was saved within a hairsbreadth of disaster at a moment when the tide had begun to turn. (What would have been the effect, for example, on the dramatic meeting of the 1922 Committee later in the day, when Derek Walker-Smith put the wild men into retreat with hardly a counter-blow?)

At the end of the day Philip Woodfield filled in the details as he had seen them overnight – the Chief Whip saying that a head must fall if his backbenchers were to be assuaged, Philip arguing as I had done, the Chief Whip refusing to listen, the Prime Minister seeing the dangers but feeling that he could on no account let the Chief Whip resign.

Deedes also had some details to fill in. After leaving me, he had found Macleod and one or two others still in conclave in the ante-room. To them he had repeated my belief about the consequences. Macleod had then gone to the waiting room to write a note to the Prime Minister – still in the Cabinet room with the Minister. Deedes believed that it was this note that had changed the situation, but Tim Bligh's version said that the Minister had already volunteered the alternative procedure.

With the Denning enquiry in train, the Profumo affair came out of the headlines for the time being, though the political commentators continued to speculate about 'whither Macmillan'. Other events now drew attention, notably the visit of President Kennedy to Britain in

July, when he stayed with the Macmillans as a house guest at Birch Grove. In August the Prime Minister paid official visits to Finland and Sweden. Then came the signing in Moscow of the nuclear test ban treaty, and with it general tribute to the part played by the persuasion and persistence of Harold Macmillan over a long period.

July 7, Sunday . *Rottingdean*

Looking back on a fortnight's events.

The leadership issue took a new turn when the Prime Minister was interviewed by Alastair Burnet on I.T.N. on the eve of the Kennedy visit. He gave the interview in Wolverhampton immediately before a Party rally (thunderous reception but the interview took the headlines). The interview had been arranged before the Profumo crisis broke, as a stock item in the programme for a provincial visit. The B.B.C. had not asked for an interview but the local I.T.V. company did and then asked I.T.N. to take it on. I.T.N. rightly sought to make all possible capital out of it by sending Alastair Burnet, their political correspondent, to ask sharp questions.

On the leadership issue the Prime Minister had already declared his attitude at Bromley the previous Saturday ('neither panic nor obstinacy'), and he had not intended to take it further. But Alastair Burnet quoted his declaration to the 1922 Committee in April that 'all being well, and given health and strength', he would lead the Party into the general election. Was it possible, asked Burnet, that he might retreat from this? For a Prime Minister to forecast resignation is tantamount to resignation tomorrow. So he had little option but to repeat the April words and stand by them.

The exchange caused great excitement among the political correspondents, who seized on it as a carefully calculated challenge to the rebellious Tory backbenchers.

He rather enjoyed the commotion. I saw him the following afternoon in the V.I.P. tent at Gatwick as we waited for Kennedy. He came towards me smiling mischievously and I said quickly, 'You didn't really mean it to come out like that, did you?' To which he said, 'Of course not,' and went on to explain just why he had to play it the way he did. It had not turned out too badly, we agreed, though no doubt he could not leave it like that.

In fact, it wasn't a very clever arrangement. Since it was a Party occasion I did not hear about the interview until Friday afternoon, and I then exploded, but there was nothing I could do about it because he was then on the train. It is incredible that these situations are not foreseen and prepared for.

Equally I felt that on the Party side they had made a mistake in inviting Eldon Griffiths to join the speech-writing team, beginning with an evening at Chequers. One cannot hide this kind of appointment, and to give such an *entrée* to a working journalist – correspondent of an American news magazine moreover – is asking for trouble. But Poole wanted it and that was that.

It brought complications almost immediately for twenty-four hours later the New York office of *Newsweek* went into a frenzy about an alleged worse-than-ever security scandal in London – based, they claimed, on an unchallengeable security source in Washington. Eldon, in a state of excitement, pursued the allegation with me and everyone else but drew blanks all round. He then remembered the story of Wigg's 'further dossier' and went running off to him. He managed to reveal to Wigg that he had recently seen the Prime Minister without revealing that it was as a newly appointed speech writer. Wigg concluded that Eldon had been to tell the P.M. about Philby and that this was the first the British Government knew about Philby as the third man in the Burgess and Maclean case. So I found myself acting as adviser to Eldon. What he had to say and stick to, I suggested, was the fact that he had at no time discussed this or any other security matter with the P.M. For the time being there has been no further *Newsweek* commotion, but the matter is unlikely to rest there.

Meanwhile, I am assured by what should be an unimpeachable authority that the allegation is unfounded. In accepting this assurance (and acting on it in guidance) I made it clear that if I found that I had been let down then I, too, would resign – and, in present circumstances, who knows, this also could have critical consequences.

Ted Heath made the Philby statement on Monday, and to my horror I found the Prime Minister again involved – as the Foreign Secretary who in 1955 told the House that no evidence had been brought forward against Philby. Had I known this I would have sought some other means of handling it. But Heath was convinced that had a statement not already been volunteered it would be raised in the foreign affairs debate on Tuesday and Wednesday. There is now the issue of Marcus Lipton's personal statement in 1955 retracting his allegations against Philby in the light of the assurances in the House. Perhaps this won't come to anything but, as one Labour Shadow Minister is quoted as saying, 'If there were only one piece of banana skin in the whole of Britain, Mac would step on it.'

The *Newsweek* episode raises again the question of whether there is a conspiracy to destroy the system, more especially since the timing seemed significant in relation to the Kennedy visit. The original *Newsweek* story said that a tearful Macmillan had rung Kennedy to say that in the light of these developments he could not expect Kennedy to come to England after all (there is a naivety here which tells against the conspiracy theory).

As to the Kennedy visit, all went well, and in the subsequent foreign affairs debate the Prime Minister made a winding-up speech which won general acclaim. It is now being argued that he has pinned all his hopes on a test ban agreement and the Hailsham mission: if it comes off, then either he can retire in full glory – or refuse to get out, knowing that he can go over the heads of the backbenchers.

During the President's visit we had two full on-the-record Press conferences at the Metropole in Brighton – Saturday night at 8.30 and Sunday at 1.30. To get there from Birch Grove Pierre Salinger and I were ferried by R.A.F. helicopter. I had expected a tough session on Saturday night, with cross-examination by the White House Press Corps about British attitudes on everything under the sun, and had been to some pains in preparation. In the event, it was surprisingly un-difficult.

The Sunday conference, based on the communiqué, was more exacting, and I found it exhausting. I was exhausted by then, anyhow, not least because of a late-night dinner in Brighton for Pierre Salinger, Kilduff, Bob Manning, Mrs. Kennedy's Press Secretary (a charmer, along for the ride, she said, though she had been given a role), and Lucy Jarvis of C.B.S., determined to do for Buckingham Palace what she had done for the Kremlin. We had dinner in the Metropole's Starlit Room, which helped to enhance the reputation of swinging Britain in the Sixties.

As usual when the British are hosts, I chaired the Press conferences, and that as usual meant being at the receiving end of virtually all the questions. Pierre showed no disposition to accept questions and was monosyllabic when he did. On one occasion he simply passed the microphone to Bob Manning to deal with a question to the American side on British Guiana (a sensitive subject following a *Times* story on Saturday morning), without having taken the precaution of briefing Bob so that I had to rescue him. Dealing with an aggressive question on Kennedy's late arrival at Gatwick I got a round of applause for a quick-thinking reply which sounded wittier than it was (the first time, said Lucy Jarvis, that she had heard applause for an official spokesman).

To take questions for half an hour on a communiqué seen very little in advance can hardly fail to be an ordeal. Immediately before leaving Birch Grove I pinned down Home and Thorneycroft in the study and collected their thinking on interpretation of the passage on the mixed-manned force: we also exchanged briefing notes with Bundy. But this was all one had. To say that is perhaps misleading. Spokesmanship is based, of course, on sustained acquaintance with subjects and objectives.

As on previous occasions, Pierre Salinger proved agreeable and businesslike. I took an opportunity to say to him that, after all, the British were probably the best allies the U.S. had got. He paused before answering, and then said he did not think anyone in Washington questioned that. On techniques of spokesmanship, he said that he was convinced that non-attributable briefings had much greater importance than the attributable conferences which are so much part of the American pattern (this at a time when, for my part, I have had reason to feel that there would be advantages on occasion for the No. 10 spokesman to be on the record).

When the President arrived Pierre and I helicoptered from Gatwick to the Isle of Thorns (what *is* the origin of that?) and then joined the tea party in the drawing room at Birch Grove – two low tables, with Lady Dorothy presiding at one (with the President) and the P.M. at the other. I inserted Pierre next to the P.M. – in sparkling form – and afterwards Pierre commented on the re-juvenated Macmillan in comparison with his seeming weariness at Nassau. At Lady D.'s table were also the Maurice Macmillans, with son Alexander standing behind and studying the President with rapt concentration.

Lady D. was not too much preoccupied with the President's visit to seek my aid in taking two orange-coloured posters about Birch Grove open day to the Metropole and Grand for display on their notice boards. On the helicopter journeys from Birch Grove there were splendid views of Rottingdean (duly photographed) and the coastal stretch from Peacehaven to Brighton (landing on Brunswick Lawns at Hove).

At the end of the visit I had a note from the P.M. thanking me for 'a very fine job', another inscribed photograph from the President (in recognition of 'the major role' I had played in the success of the visit as the Americans saw it), sundry pleasant compliments from the Lobby men and the American correspondents, and a notable boost to my morale from Bill Howsden who declared that it was a privilege to drive someone who had done such a wonderful job (he slipped in to one of the briefings)!

But Robin Day and *Panorama* did a debunking piece on official spokesmen (to Salinger, 'Why do you think they come all this way when you and Harold Evans are only able to give them crumbs?' followed by a carefully selected and truncated extract from the first joint briefing). However, on the Beaverbrook theory that any publicity is good publicity, I suppose I must not grumble.

As it happened, I had an unexpected opportunity to get back at *Panorama* when the great Mrs. Wyndham-Goldie invited me to lunch at Lime Grove, and had David Wheeler, editor of *Panorama*, and John Grist, editor of *Gallery*, as her other guests. Ted Heath and I, she declared, were the only two people she had ever felt convinced were 'right' for television. An extraordinary thing to be said of the diffident and inarticulate Evans – though it is true that when sufficiently frightened by microphones, cameras and a large audience I become articulate and may look self-assured.

July 14, Sunday   *Rottingdean*
In a dither about whether to go with the P.M. to Sweden and Finland at the beginning of August, not least since Michael Hadow, head of News Department, has a yen to go and it really means more to him than to me. I eventually asked the P.M. forthrightly if he wished me to go. His answer: 'Oh yes, certainly I want you to come. It may be our last trip. We can have some fun.'

This was one indication of his thinking about the leadership issue. Another came when he told me, 'I am not going to think about the future until we get back from Finland. That will be time enough. We can then do it quickly and calmly.' Then again, after the Henry Fairlie interview (from which Fairlie deduced that the P.M. had no intention of going on), he rang me to compare notes. The ambivalence of it did not worry him, he said. There *was* ambivalence for the time being. Both he and the Party must have time to think it out.

In the interview with Fairlie he was extremely candid about the Profumo affair. At one point, he said, it had been touch and go: only the support of his dear wife and his staff at No. 10 had seen him through it: but he had then decided that even if there had been a majority of only five in the Profumo debate he would have carried on. 'I wasn't going to have the British Government pulled down by the antics of a whore.'

Though it did not matter in the event, Fairlie cheated. His interview was sought and given on the basis of discussion of the things that matter, and he submitted quotations he proposed to use. The interview was given secondary treatment, however, and all the emphasis was put on personal impressions, given splash treatment on the *Express* front page, with extensive quotations which had *not* been submitted.

At the end of the week we had a nonsense about a Russian official who defected some eighteen months ago. It leaked in the *Telegraph* that he was in this country, and the D-notice machinery was put into motion in such a way as to give the impression that it had just happened and to alert the whole of the British Press. I had then, on Friday morning, to try and sort out the mess, ending in a meeting with the P.M., Home and Brooke in the Cabinet room.

But the great issue at the moment is the negotiation with the Russians in Moscow on a test ban agreement, the Hailsham–Harriman mission having left today. It begins with expectations of success, based on indications of K.'s wish to do serious business, at any rate on a partial ban. The apparent total breakdown today of the 'theological' talks between the Russians and Chinese in Moscow would also seem to point that way. If the negotiation leads to substantial agreement the prospect opens up of a Moscow summit (Kennedy prefers Moscow) in September (so much for that holiday in Jersey). What then of the Tory leadership?

The Baron Hill of Luton had his 'introduction party' at the Lords on Wednesday. Following an hilarious lunch, the new baron performed the initiation ceremonies with due dignity and resonance of voice. He complained, however, of the cocked hat borrowed for the occasion. 'The bloody thing's too small.'

July 21, Sunday   *Rottingdean*

In Moscow the test ban talks went forward 'reasonably nicely' (Hailsham), and Mr. K. made a forthcoming speech at the same time as he sent the Chinese packing (the 'war fanatics').

I saw the P.M. only two or three times, including an exercise in colour photography for the *Sunday Times* magazine. It involved Lady Dorothy and also the 'loyal staff', peculiarly grouped in the drawing room by the artistic Mr. Ward, standing with his camera on a kitchen chair.

July 28, Sunday   *Rottingdean*

Macmillan's week.

The test ban treaty was initialled in Moscow late on Thursday and at 11 o'clock that night we had the emotional moment of the Prime Minister's statement in the House. The initialling had been ex-pected on Wednesday, but the Americans began to quibble over words and there came a moment on Thursday afternoon when it seemed that the cup might be snatched away. There was a flurry of

White House–Admiralty House communication, including a Kennedy–Macmillan call (Kennedy initiative, which in the circumstances sounded ominous), but all came out well.

This was an event which will surely merit a place in the history books – and rank as a true Macmillan achievement. It was he – with his sense of history – who read the signs aright in Russia and saw the opportunities: who coaxed and prodded the Americans: who argued the case with Khruschev: and finally took the initiative which led to the Kennedy–Macmillan approach. He had persisted, moreover, despite the collapse of the Paris summit. Looking back to the speech he then made in the House I found a passage which reiterated his determination to continue with the policies which at that moment seemed discredited and shattered.

So let no one – even *The Times* with its cheap and ungenerous sentence about the third man – try to belittle this historic achievement. Nor begrudge the good fortune which brought him this triumph at a psychological moment in his own political battle. His true stature is now seen again – and the pygmies of the 1922 Committee were reduced to *their* stature when he met them at 6 o'clock on Thursday, half an hour after the initialling. At one stage he had not accepted the desirability of making a statement in the House himself. Why shouldn't Heath do it, he asked. But I put in a note saying that it was now necessary for him to be seen back in the centre of the stage: otherwise Washington and Hailsham would steal all the thunder.

After the statement I went back to Admiralty House with him in the car. Although it was so late there was a small group of people at the gates of Palace Yard. A flash bulb went, and someone shouted, 'Well done.' He thought it had been wise to mention Eisenhower in the statement, he said: it would perhaps help Kennedy to get the backing he would need in getting the treaty ratified.

At Admiralty House two *Express* photographers were waiting (by arrangement), plus a *Mail* photographer (crabbing the *Express* exclusive while already having an exclusive *Mail* picture from earlier in the day). He swept them all inside and spent five minutes at the foot of the staircase going through the routines they wanted. He then gave them whiskies in the ante-room, the five of us sitting at the round table behind the screen. 'You know Mr. Evans, don't you? He's the boss.'

In the car after the Reform Club lunch the P.M. speculated about what fun it would be to resign forthwith now that the treaty is in the bag. What then of all the 'little crooks'? But he won't, of course. There is still too much to be done in following it up.

If hearing nice things said is the yardstick I, too, had a good week – Lord Swinton writing to say that it would have warmed my heart to hear how enthusiastically old friends in the Lobby spoke of me when he dined with them on Monday: Wilson at the Nyere dinner on Tuesday saying that he thought I did a marvellous job: the Prime Minister telling Ernest Atkinson's group at lunch on Friday, 'Of course, he's been wonderful'; and David White, on the same occasion, telling me that his hard-boiled editor, James Holburn, thinks his visits to London from Glasgow are worth while if he has a talk with Evans.

We have a Jersey holiday booked in September. A new complication is the condition of my left leg which will need a further operation. How I detest these vein afflictions: my whole being revolts. Today, the 28th, is the eighth anniversary of Timothy's death in Italy. He would be fourteen and a half. Here is the greatest of my afflictions, though from it I have derived strength.

August 4, Sunday   *Rottingdean*

End of summer term, thank goodness – and with the P.M. jauntily and firmly back in the saddle: to the extent that the political correspondents are getting back to speculation about Cabinet changes.

His television interview on Thursday with Kenneth Harris went as well as we could have hoped and its timing was precisely right. 'Confident', 'buoyant', 'relaxed' – these were the adjectives – and that the right effect was achieved can be seen from Maurice Wiggins's comment in today's *Sunday Times*, 'He didn't actually *say* much, perhaps, but he presented an attractive picture of a man rooted in family loyalties and the immemorial decencies of life as most of us like to live it.'

The interview was recorded in the early evening – we went to Aldwych at 7. The first run had a poor start. Asked how long he hoped to remain Prime Minister, the P.M. retorted, 'Can *you* tell *me* when we shall have a general election?' which not only threw Kenneth back on his haunches but was not clever in itself. Once they had got going, however, it flowed extremely well in the general pattern I had outlined. When he came off the set the P.M. declared, 'I'm not going to do it again,' and went off to the upper floors to drink with the tycoons as represented by Sir Edwin Herbert and Tom Brownrigg.

But I was less sure, and took the views of Cyril Bennett, Peter Morley and Brian Connel. All agreed in thinking that the bad start merited a second run which would at least provide a choice. 'But he won't do it,' said Bennett, to which I replied brashly, 'Yes he will if I put enough pressure on him.' Bold words to be put immediately to the test. Upstairs – Master behind a drink – I was discomfited to find Herbert and Brownrigg telling him how splendid it had been, and what a good effect was achieved by the hesitancy and evasion at the start because it was 'natural'. When I expressed doubt, however, the P.M. immediately took it seriously, we had a quick conference apart from the others, and he put down his drink and made for the door.

So it was done again – started well and ran just as smoothly as the first. Brownrigg said loudly that of course it was my business but he would have no hesitation in choosing the first. But when I said 'No' he could get no support. The P.M. also felt that the second run had been better, and on the way back to drinks upstairs he was ready to say exactly why – that what he had to say about the test ban and the economy contained nothing new, but what he had to say about his own position would attract attention: so I was absolutely right to make him do it again and he was extremely grateful.

August 18, Sunday   *Rottingdean*
We came back on Tuesday from our week in Finland and Sweden. It had significance to the extent of being the first visit by a western leader, but the talks with President Kekkonen and Prime Minister Erlander were essentially exercises in goodwill. So the visit had a greater element of sightseeing and relaxation than we normally expect. Even so it was inescapably strenuous, with many speeches, two Press conferences, two television interviews, a day's drive to look at factories at Valkeakoski in Finland, and the long drive to Harpsund (the Swedish Chequers) from Stockholm.

Also, for my part, I went with accumulated tiredness. I had my hot and troublesome left leg: and with an outbreak of eczema on my chin and neck I felt like pulling out at the last moment and would have done so but for the magically effective antibiotic ointment prescribed by Dr. Yeardsley. After several days of non-stop activity, lack of sleep (not least the difficulty of getting acclimatised to 3 a.m. dawns), over-eating and over-drinking I felt in no shape to enjoy the Swedish festivities. In fact, I enjoyed the Harpsund dinner excessively well, and that finished me off.

There can have been no confrontation of Prime Ministers when inhibitions were so completely cast aside. Crayfish and schnapps set the party going. This was the opening day of the short Swedish crayfish season, and dinner was preceded by a traditional crayfish party, held in a hut facing the main entrance to Harpsund across the drive. Traditional means schnapps and beer, a chorus for each new crayfish, and arranging the heads round the edge of each plate as a tally of achievement. The early choruses – begun at the end of the table by Lars Berquist (what better qualification for a Press Secretary?) – caught the visitors by surprise, but to put them at their ease the new Foreign Minister, Tors Nilsson, launched on 'My Bonny lies over the ocean', followed by 'Little Brown Jug'. Honour was then satisfied and the Swedes could roar out their choruses without fear of embarrassing the British.

Even so, when we returned to the house for the main dinner (after rowdy poses for the photographers) Mr. Erlander had lurking fears that it had all gone rather far and asked anxiously, 'I hope you don't think we have been too informal.' 'Oh no,' I could tell him. 'Its the best party we have had in years of travelling.'

Harpsund lacks space, and dinner was served at three small tables, each of about eight. On my right I had the Swedish ambassador in London (proud possessor of a flambuoyant Italian wife), and on my left the newspaper tycoon who owns *Dagens Nyheter*. Also at this table – the Prime Minister and Alec Home. I ought to remember the conversation, since it was lively and fast moving, but I don't.

A moving little speech was made by Erlander. Then, after a short period of brooding, H. Macmillan suddenly shot to his feet and capped it with an analysis of why the British and the Swedes felt instinctively at one – because we shared trusteeship for the culture and religion inherited from Greece and Israel. Speaking of their wish to make the visit as informal and friendly as possible, Erlander said that informality was difficult to organise, of course, and it had not always been easy to distinguish between organised informality and disorganised formality (a reference, no doubt, to the chaos when we arrived, the great men being whisked away while everyone else had to scramble – a moment when tour experience becomes useful).

After the Harpsund dinner four or five of us had a forty-minute night drive to the small town hotel where we were staying (including the admirable Mr. Astrom, political head of the Swedish Foreign Office, wearing a splendidly incongruous tight-fitting cloth cap with his dinner jacket). At the hotel the girls (plus John Richardson, Charles Thompson and their Swedish mentors) were also having a gay party, so that we had an agreeable climax to a riotous evening (John Richardson said afterwards that I did not stop talking for an hour and a quarter – a bit much even for an official spokesman). But I paid the price. Not for years had a hotel room pitched and swayed so convulsively, and for me Sunday was the palest of days. However, I enjoyed the visit to the Drottningholm theatre (or at any rate contrived not to go to sleep).

Fortunately, Monday was a day of escape, since the great men flew off to the south to lunch with the King and Queen of Sweden. This made it possible for me to have a restful day at the embassy and the Grand Hotel, preparing a dossier for the Press conference preceding Tuesday's departure. It also gave me a chance to go shopping, which meant N.K., Stockholm's Harrods, and the irresistible attraction of Jonah carved into a glass whale. The price was 250 kroners and I had to borrow from Sheila Strachan since there was no time to get to the embassy.

The Press conferences in Helsinki and Stockholm were unsatisfactory in that both were 'hogged' by the travelling correspondents, especially the Americans, and that the questions were chiefly aimed at British politics and the Prime Minister's own future. Also he was himself bad-tempered about doing them, particularly in Helsinki, where he behaved in a peevish and grumpy manner. Yet measured in space and headlines in the British Press they had a not unsatisfactory result.

After the Stockholm conference was over he became cheerful. 'Well, that was rollicking, wasn't it? Goodness knows what they will make of it.' But for me they are worrying occasions and leave me depressed.

In Helsinki, after the ambassador's garden party, he let himself be cornered by four or five British and American correspondents, including Charles Douglas-Home and Eric Sewell. He talked about the burdens of being Foreign Secretary and so set Fleet Street off on a spree of speculation about the future of Alec Home (shades of 'enough is enough'). It came back to me in Stockholm, from Eric Sewell in particular. He demanded a quote, either from Home or from a spokesman. He also wrote to Home (staying at the Grand), who felt half inclined to give them an interview – 'They are quite nice fellows.' I explained, however, that new hares would then be set running, and he agreed that as spokesman I should say (a) it wasn't his practice to comment on rumours of this kind, and (b) as from myself, that his reaction had been to say, 'It sounds like the silly season.' And that, in fact, largely disposed of it.

This was my only real encounter with Home, who joined us late from Moscow, where he had been for the signing of the test ban treaty. I don't think he quite knows what to make of me. Nor I of him. But his private secretary, Oliver Wright (large, rugged, black-browed, D.F.C.),[4] has a warm admiration for him, as does 'Bill' Easton, the P.A., who is always in the entourage – and they should know.

I had one opportunity for a long talk with the P.M. when he took me into the ambassador's garden at Helsinki for a deck-chair gossip before lunch. One thought he floated in the form of a query. Would we ever get a really egalitarian society without doing away with the public schools? This linked with a John Richardson thought about education for girls (in relation to his own daughter, now nearly twenty, and to Annabel): the social cachet of the school, he felt, now mattered less than the university, so the objective should be to find a school with a good academic record.

I saw a fair amount of John Richardson, which is an agreeable feature of these tours. He lent me a pair of braces for my tails; gave me the name of the top veins man; said you had to judge a G.P. by the degree of interest and assiduity he showed; and invited me to address the St. Thomas's students society.

For the rest:

(1) The military tramp, tramp, tramp of the marching waiters at the President's banquet in Helsinki.

(2) Helsinki seems little changed, except for the admirable Palace Hotel, where I had a splendid suite on the ninth floor, overlooking the harbour: but there is massive high-rise building on the periphery of the city.

(3) It seemed doubtful if having been a volunteer in the winter war now rated merit in Finland, but when it emerged that I *had* been a volunteer I found myself hailed as a hero in the later, alcoholic stages of the ambassador's dinner.

(4) Unable to sleep in Stockholm because of the early dawn, I took successful colour photographs of the royal palace, across the water from the hotel window, at 3.30 a.m.

(5) *Express–Mail* rivalry did not prevent Douglas-Home and Sewell from being personally on excellent terms (perhaps neither dare let the other out of his sight?): at any rate they had a sauna together in Helsinki and reported the effect as a bout of hysterical laughter.

(6) The Finns have the excellent Max Jacobssen as head of the political department of their Foreign Office – an experienced and sophisticated spokesman (plus English wife).

(7) Mr. Erlander's newly appointed Press Secretary, Lars

---

[4] Later Private Secretary to the Prime Minister, 1964–66, and ambassador to Denmark.

Berquist, took a turn round the Harpsund garden to cross-examine me about how we did it in London, and I have engineered an official visit for him.

(8) We had reindeer and raspberries at most meals in Finland. The Finnish Prime Minister, the young Mr. Karjalainen, gave us our best meal of the tour, when we had neither.

(9) The Swedes all speak fluent English – including my driver, recently returned from U.N. service in the Congo.

September 29, Sunday   *Rottingdean*

For three weeks (two and a half in Jersey) I neither thought nor talked politics (except at lunch with the Lieutenant-Governor, 'Bobby' Erskine) and I returned rejuvenated. But now, a week later – the Denning week – I badly need this weekend's respite.

Tim Bligh produced the news on Monday morning that the P.M. had at last taken the great decision – he would retire in January at the end of his seven years. The decision would be announced in his speech at the Party conference. This, said Tim, was the most secret of secrets, not known to any of the colleagues. Except, of course, that the *Yorkshire Post* had it as their lead story that morning!

Later in the day, when I went to see the P.M. to sell him the idea of a radio broadcast on the Denning report, he referred to the *Yorkshire Post*. Without saying directly that the story was accurate he speculated about its source. Fleet Street at first ignored the story, but on Friday the two London evenings appear to have tapped the same source (Central Office?) and speculated about January or February.

But to Denning. I had to try and digest it at odd moments on Monday. The narrative read well from the P.M.'s point of view, but then came Chapter XXIII, in particular paragraph 286, and in particular the sentence ending 'they did not succeed'. W. F. Deedes had been charged with organising presentation, under a general instruction that, since Wilson was accepting radio and television invitations, Ministers should be willing to do so as well, rather than reserving comment for the debate. Macleod and Hailsham had been selected as the instruments. It seemed to me, however, that the P.M. had to speak for himself – also that if the headlines on Friday were to be taken from Wilson only the P.M. could do it. There were invitations in from independent television but I felt that television should be left to others and that the answer lay in reviving the earlier invitation from radio's *Ten O'Clock*. This would give the P.M. the advantage of the last word.

I argued the case to him in the Cabinet room on Monday evening.

He at first pulled a mouth, but then began to see the attractions and suddenly became enthusiastic – so enthusiastic that I suggested we should at any rate sleep on it. In the morning he charged me to take the view of a Ministers' meeting under Macleod (Chief Whip, Attorney-General, Solicitor-General, W. F. Deedes). Macleod reacted against it, but the others saw advantages and they returned a verdict that it had 'a narrow margin of advantage'.

In the meantime *Ten O'Clock*'s George Camacho had come up with a renewed invitation so that I had no need to prompt it. Nor did I have to press very hard for it to be agreed that there should be one interviewer only, that this should be Peter Hardiman-Scott, and that we should be told of the proposed area of questioning.

On presentation generally, I forecast to the Ministers that the Press would focus on 'they did not succeed'. Something would also be made of the revelation, I suggested, of the Home Secretary's responsibilities for M.I.5 and of the 1952 directive. This latter aspect had not really clicked with them: at any rate neither at this meeting, nor at one the following day, was Brooke present.

In the event this expectation proved right, though at the Deedes Lobby meeting before publication the questioning focused almost exclusively on the Home Secretary aspect – to a misleading extent since this was not the aspect on which editorial comment principally seized. Had the Lobby followed a Wilson red herring from earlier in the afternoon?

Headlines and reporting were more disagreeable than had been feared. Editorial comment, if not understanding, was less aggressive, with some exceptions, notably *The Times* and the *Mirror* which, in their respective styles, questioned whether Denning had indeed disposed of all scandalous rumour. The *Telegraph*, characteristically, put the story in the worst possible light for the Prime Minister, to the extent of a tendentious headline saying that Macmillan and his Ministers had 'failed' – quoting 'failed' with the implication that this was the Denning word whereas, in fact, it was the Boyne word. How sad it is that Harry Boyne is now so anti-Macmillan.

From the headlines the impression was undoubtedly given of Macmillan in the dock, so that the decision to broadcast on Thursday night became all the more important. He did it live from Admiralty House – from Knox Cunningham's small room overlooking the courtyard – and did it well so that he *did* get Friday's headlines. The Sunday papers were also left with food for thought. Macleod rang enthusiastically as soon as it was over, and Friday's *Standard* had a leader headed 'MAC'S NIGHT'.

Early on Monday the P.M. rang from Chequers to thank me. At least we now had some consolation for a miserable week.

The broadcast was the P.M.'s last official act at Admiralty House. When he left late at night to drive to Chequers he was leaving Admiralty House for good, since this week the office is moving back into No. 10. Tomorrow morning I shall be installed in my new room at No. 10. It will be good to be back. In the not very distant future I shall have to move on to some other job, but before this happened I wanted to be back at No. 10 and to have completed seven years as the Prime Minister's adviser.

October 6, Sunday   *Rottingdean*

The Prime Ministerial soul-searching went on throughout the week, with second, third and fourth thoughts about whether he ought to pack up after all.

He returned from Chequers on Wednesday morning, and since he had no engagements until noon I contrived to encounter him going into the Cabinet room and went in with him. We quickly reached the topic of what he should say at Blackpool. There were three possibilities, he said – to say nothing, to say he intended to lead them into the general election (Operation Limpet), or to announce that he intended to begin taking 'the appropriate steps' (what are they?) to hand over the leadership. He felt he *must* say something. As to Limpet, he had no particular wish to go on – it would really mean another two or three years. No doubt he could make the effort to fight another election, if he had to, but not if he was going to be sniped at from behind. And anyhow he did not see why he should be used as a scapegoat.

So we came to the appropriate steps. He produced the draft of what he might then say and asked me to read it. I said I thought this would be the right decision. This was the moment to go – especially when, in New York in the United Nations, Alec Home had been able to make a speech about a transformation in East–West relations. History would see that this had been achieved largely because of the foresight, courage and persistence of H. Macmillan. Then again, what could the future offer if he stayed? Almost certainly electoral defeat. If he went now it would be with inter-national prospects brighter and with the economy strong at home.

As to the draft, I said that I thought a bald announcement that he intended to go did not adequately reflect his declared attitude of basing his decision on what he judged to be the best interests of the Party as well as the country. The succession issue had not been resolved, and it might be held against him that he had walked out regardless of what might follow, even to the extent of major controversy between contending groups. Should he not include a sentence which made it clear that though his judgment said the time had come to take the appropriate steps he would do so only if the Party seemed ready for this? He took the point – though believing that the ranks would close behind a new man, once declared – and asked me to put up an alternative draft for these sentences, which I did later.

On the succession, he posed the dilemma – Maudling (a respectable Wilson) or Hailsham, the man with fire but erratic and impulsive? He doubted if Rab would be the right choice but what did I think. To that I said, why not? – if they anticipated defeat in the election and if the dog fight among the younger men could not be resolved?

On my personal problems – 'How old are you, Harold, my dear friend?' – he thought that a job outside the Civil Service would be the best move (I mentioned the Charles Hill proposal). For my impending veins operation, we agreed that towards the end of the week after Blackpool would probably be the least inconvenient moment: the dust would fly for several days but after that we should be moving towards the re-assembly of Parliament and the debate on the Address, which would be more or less routine. So I am likely to go into St. Thomas's on the 17th or 18th.

I saw him a second time on Friday morning when I went up to his bedroom on the second floor. Like the old bedroom, it has windows looking across St. James's Park, but the rooms have been re-designed. He was in bed, wearing his old brown cardigan over his pyjamas – patched at the elbows and threadbare. He had seen Poole and Martin Redmayne the previous evening and now appeared to have decided firmly on the appropriate steps. He appeared also to have moved towards thinking that Hailsham should be the successor.

But even now doubts seemed to linger. On scope for new achievement, he handed me a telegram from Alec Home which showed prospects for a deal with the Russians, including not least (from the U.K. point of view) dropping the mixed-manned force and reduction of conventional forces in Europe. 'Well, *there* is something,' he said. Then, too, Tony Barber had told him of the disgust in the north with attacks on him arising from the Profumo affair.

Meanwhile, at their conference in Scarborough, the Labour Party were putting on a demonstration of confidence and unity which impressed the political writers. Their deputies in London involved me in a long discussion on the Tory leadership – from which they drew such inferences as political inclination pleased them about the absence of a clear view inside the Tory Party.

This was at a meeting in my new, larger and splendid room at No. 10 (splendid, at any rate, until one saw the Whips' quarters in No. 12). With my windows almost flush with the Downing Street pavement I feel vulnerable to the aggrieved taxpayer with half a brick or a milk bottle. But Chief Superintendent Gilbert, of Cannon Row, says his men will divert the sightseers to the opposite pavement.

The new No. 10 looks very much – in the main rooms – as it always did, but most of the staff have better accommodation. The notable exception is the Private Office which comprises the same two small poky rooms which the private secretaries traditionally occupy at No. 10, not at all comparable with the grandly pro-portioned room they occupied at Admiralty House.

But the new splendour for the Press Secretary seems unlikely to be mine for long. Apart from other considerations, after seven years, I feel I have had enough. I hope that subjective feeling does not lie behind my advice to Prime Minister Macmillan.

October 13, Sunday   *Rottingdean*

The week that Providence took a hand.

When I got back on Monday the P.M. had virtually decided on Operation Limpet. This had followed a talk at Chequers on Sunday night with Alec Home (back from the U.N. twenty-four hours earlier) though it is at least open to doubt whether this had not been his intention throughout. Reasoning – that since the Party could not agree on a successor he must be prepared to respond to the call of duty; they must not be able to say that he had left them to a dog fight. This intention he proposed to announce to the Cabinet on Tuesday, in terms of his willingness to continue provided his doctors assured him that he was capable of the physical effort. Of his ability to mount the moral effort he felt confident.

This was the position late on Monday. But at 8 o'clock the next morning – day of the Cabinet meeting – Tim Bligh rang me with news that during the night Master had suffered a prostate obstruc-tion, that a doctor had been summoned at 5 a.m., that it might mean a quick operation, that Master pinned his hopes on carrying on without an operation, and that he proposed to take the Cabinet as planned and to make his announcement as planned about carrying on.

I contrived to be on the scene when he came down the stairs to go into the Cabinet meeting. Maurice was with him. He walked slowly and looked tired, but it would not have been apparent to anyone not in the picture that he had just been through a physical ordeal, involving great pain. It had been arranged that the doctor should return with a consultant at 1 o'clock. In the meantime, medicine and tablets had been prescribed. Goodwin took them to the chemists with the name of T. J. Bligh on them, and I found Tim a little later, in the Private Office, reading the instructions and measuring out the doses (prompting me to clap him on the back and say, 'One private secretary in his time . . .').

At that stage the Cabinet were proceeding with normal business. I had buttonholed Maurice by the tape machine when he left his father. He was hailing the night's developments as an opportunity for his father to retire with honour. Why should he go on, it would probably kill him, and at the end he would have no thanks. The Tory Party gave nothing, and the backbenchers had behaved abominably – sentiments I could but echo.

But the P.M. was now delivering his pronouncement to the Cabinet about carrying on subject to a medical report. He was in pain and discomfort, and a message came out to ask the doctors to come earlier if they could. He raised the subject of the leadership at about noon (the secretariat having withdrawn), and then left them, saying that he would ask Mr. Butler to continue the discussion. It had been thought that having completed this discussion they would return to normal business, but Michael Cary and two others were not asked to go back and the discussion went on for about an hour. The upshot: a message that if he should decide to carry on they would give him unanimous support (but it was clear that other possibilities had been thoroughly discussed).

When the Cabinet dispersed they still had no idea of the drama behind the scenes. The consultant's examination made it clear (to Lady D. and Tim at any rate) that an operation would be necessary very quickly, but a final decision was reserved for the evening when John Richardson would have returned from Windermere. In the meantime, the P.M. went on trying to delude himself that it would be possible for him to go to Blackpool to address the rally on Saturday.

Earlier he and Lady D. had invited the staff (including some of the ex-staff like Freddie Bishop and David Stephens) to a back-to-No. 10 house-warming party at 6.30. As I went up the stairs just after 6.30 the P.M. was coming from the study, and I took it on myself to squeeze his elbow sympathetically. He had a good colour and his manner was brisk and cheerful. It was all a stroke of Providence, he said. It gained time. He could pull out with honour if the doctor's verdict went that way – no one would be able to say that he had run away. But for the moment he was feeling much better, and there was a chance that they would be able to get him through Blackpool.

Ten minutes later the doctors had assembled. Ten minutes after that Tim came to look for me in the party. The decision – an operation immediately, subject to the necessary medical examination. The P.M. would go to hospital at 9 o'clock (in just over an hour's time). The operation would be on Thursday morning.

So there was now the question of an announcement. In fact, I had anticipated events and prepared a draft, including a background note setting out the sequence of events vis-à-vis the Cabinet. But the key question would clearly be, 'Does this mean that the Prime Minister will resign?'

On my way to the study to see the P.M. I met Martin Redmayne who showed signs of wanting to join the discussion. Tim was not prepared to concede this without asking the P.M. – still upstairs – a reflection of the feeling that had been building up that the Chief Whip and Lord Poole had been unduly harassing the P.M. to declare his intention to retire. But the P.M. came down the stairs from the second floor with John Richardson, and swept us all into the study.

He was in his dressing gown (red and blue facings) over pale blue pyjamas and the old brown cardigan, plus black slippers. I told him what I proposed to say in the announcement, and then posed the critical question I would have to answer, 'Does this mean the P.M. will resign?' Was it unfeeling? Walking up and down by the windows, in the half light of the table lamp, he threw up his arms in a dramatic gesture. 'Of course, I am finished. Perhaps I shall die. You can say it is quite clear that I shall be unable to fight the election.' I asked, did he *really* want that to be said. He said 'Yes', and so I went away to re-jig the draft.

As I was leaving, Rab appeared at the study door. I told him of the intention to issue the announcement as soon as the P.M. was in hospital – i.e. about 9.30 – and its purport. On the point about not being able to fight the election, he seemed rather surprised and said that surely this was going rather far, but shrugged his shoulders.

One of the Garden Room girls typed the re-jigged draft for me, but it went into the Private Office instead of coming back to me in the waiting room. I found the private secretaries, plus Michael Cary, all discussing it, with Burke Trend now joining in. We all felt that it would be better, if possible, not to declare the inability to fight the election and the draft was amended again and sent back for re-typing. I had then to discuss it with the P.M.

By this time, fully dressed, he was having supper in the small dining room with Lady D., John Richardson and Tim, and I took the draft to him there. I was pressed to join them at supper, but said I had to organise issue of the announcement and the subsequent briefing, and anyhow I never ate much in the evening. So I sat in an armchair at the Prime Minister's right while he looked at the draft. As always he responded with an almost immediate verdict. 'That's exactly right. They can draw their own conclusions.'

So just after nine he left in John Richardson's Jaguar. At 19.25 John Groves and I started telephoning to an unsuspecting Fleet Street. Since I had packed into the announcement all the salient facts and background, none of the subsequent enquirers, though numerous, could really produce a new question. By 11 they had begun to leave us alone as interest now focused on reaction in Blackpool, and I left No. 10 at about 11.15.

There remained for decision on Wednesday the question of just what should be said to the Party conference, when and by whom. Tim Bligh took to the hospital in the morning a draft letter to the Queen, designed to catch the courier leaving at the end of the morning for Scotland. He took also a draft letter, announcing resignation, for Alec Home to read to the conference in Blackpool on Thursday afternoon. Alec Home went to the hospital at the same time. It was agreed with him that he should motor to Blackpool after the ceremonies involved in ratification of the test ban treaty early on Thursday. He would then be able to read the letter to the conference at the end of its day's business.

This left me with twenty-four hours in which to keep the secret of the intended resignation from the Lobby 2nd XI (the 1st XI being in Blackpool). The first intention had, in fact, been to hold the announcement back until Friday morning after Hailsham had declared his intention to become Mr. Hogg, but the advice had come from Blackpool to do it as soon as Lord Home arrived. In thus determining the timing in relation to Hailsham's declaration, the P.M.'s support for Hailsham became clear, prompted largely, one assumes, by Lord Poole and the Chief Whip on an assessment of the type of leadership most likely to win the election and very little else (here I reveal prejudice). With the change in timing, however, the Hailsham announcement was seen as an immediate consequence to the Macmillan announcement, and with Hailsham supporters staging what looked like a Nuremburg rally (plus baby to admire), the Establishment (and some others) reacted with curled lips.

So a Home lobby built up, and the reluctant Alec found himself having to contemplate being drafted. On Friday morning he agreed to be drafted (reports Tim, who joined Rab in Blackpool), provided Quintin did not proceed with his candidature. But Quintin, having opted to be Mr. Hogg, wasn't playing; it would have made him look too, too silly. So they have all returned to London with the dilemma unresolved, and with Dilhorne charged with collecting Cabinet voices.

In opting for Hailsham, the P.M. was proceeding on the assumption that Home was not in the field. He has now to swap horses – embarrassing when Julian Amery and others had whispered his support for Quintin, and when Randolph Churchill has distilled it in the *News of the World* (other Randolph activities included pinning a Q.H. badge on Rab's lapel and sending him a telegram before his rally speech).

Amid the excitement, I have now to think also about my own future. Charles Hill wants me to become head of information and research at the I.T.A., but I must first be clear about my Civil Service prospects. If Hailsham came in it might be necessary for me to go quickly. With Rab or Home I could probably go in my own time. Two Lobby men have been perceptive enough and friendly enough to send me personal notes – Barney Keelan and Mark Arnold-Forster.

But to end cheerfully – the announcement that Macmillan was to go brought some degree of measured assessment of his place and achievement. How vastly different it looks from the cheap, carping and often vicious criticism of recent months. It has been aided by the generously worded personal message from Kennedy about the test ban treaty (a message sent without knowledge of his illness or intention to resign). I issued it on Thursday morning in the breathing space before the announcement in Blackpool. The *Mail* splashed it. *The Times* hid it away in a one-sentence reference in an obscure report.

October 27, Sunday   *Rottingdean*

A fortnight which has seen the exit of Macmillan, the entry of Home (now Sir Alec Douglas-Home), and a baronetcy for Evans.

The week of enquiry within the Party about the leadership produced a consensus which pointed with apparent firmness to Home (the Chief Whip has since made a speech in which he asserts this categorically). By Wednesday the Home trend was clear, and on Thursday morning it was formally confirmed to the Prime Minister at the hospital by the various counters of heads.

But a final flurry was to come.

The Prime Minister had arranged with the Palace for his resignation to be taken there by Tim Bligh at 9.30 on Friday morning, its acceptance to be announced by the Palace at 10.30. The Queen then proposed to visit Uncle Harold in hospital. Following her consultation with him it was expected that she would call on Lord Home to try and form a government.

I had hinted to the Lobby that Home might be the choice as early as the Wednesday afternoon meeting with them, but the Rab supporters were so active that the Lobby did not take the lead. On Thursday the P.M. became worried lest the choice of Home should fall too unexpectedly on an astonished world, and said that I should virtually firm it up in the afternoon. I did not go quite as far as this, but gave it another push. Some of the first edition headlines in Friday's papers duly came out hard on Home, notably the *Mail* (T. F. Thompson had spoken to me during the evening). What W. F. Deedes and I feared then duly happened. There was a midnight assembly of a small group of dissenting Cabinet Ministers, apparently trying to push Rab into revolt. Inevitably this became known and the *Express* had a dramatic headline in its later editions – '1 A.M. CABINET REVOLT'. More sedately *The Times* declared, 'THE QUEEN MAY SEND FOR MR. BUTLER TODAY'.

This new development had to be assessed by the Prime Minister very early on Friday. Home rang him at the hospital, and said in essence that if his selection would mean a split and not unification then its whole purpose became abortive. The P.M. argued that he should not let himself be ousted at the last minute by a *putsch* which went against the undoubted consensus. So he decided to go ahead.

Rab had simultaneously told Dilhorne that he thought the latter should now call a meeting to check on the latest feelings of Cabinet colleagues. Dilhorne said that he would not do so unless H. Macmillan approved. H. Macmillan didn't approve and there was no meeting. This exchange probably gave rise to subsequent stories that Macmillan had refused to take a telephone call from Rab. But no such call was made.

Nor, as some papers reported, was there an acceleration by Macmillan of his resignation. In fact, Tim Bligh went to the Palace half an hour *later* than had been intended, but the Palace announcement appeared at 10.30 as planned. The situation was left in some doubt, however, because Home did not kiss hands on appointment, but only accepted the task of trying to form an administration. This left scope for some further coming and going among the rebels, who emerged as Rab, Maudling, Macleod, Powell and Boyle. Hailsham wavered for a time but then opted to accept a Home appointment. These comings and goings went on all through Friday. The show-down came on Saturday morning. Rab then accepted the Foreign Office, and that, in effect, was that. Some interplay continued between Maudling, Boyle, Macleod and Powell, but it ended with only Macleod and Powell standing out.

On Saturday morning Home had made enough progress to decide that, if necessary, he would go ahead without Rab. But Rab proved persuadable. I met him coming from the Cabinet room, beaming after several black-brow'd days. He asked if I did not think it right that he should accept the Foreign Office, and then went on to congratulate me on my baronetcy, announced the day before.

We had a whirlwind weekend getting the Cabinet list completed for announcement on Sunday afternoon. This gave me an absurdly short time to assemble my speaking notes. I did it mainly by going to see Ted Heath at the Foreign Office to get *his* line, and then checking it with Alec Home in the Cabinet room, with only ten minutes to go before the Lobby meeting. He had not really thought how it should be presented (no wonder, poor man), and started by talking about the Godber appointment. He reacted quickly, how-ever, and I emerged with a tolerable line (scribbled in pencil).

The launching of A. Home had begun the night before with his broadcast on appointment (I had agreed to the installation of cameras in No. 10 on Friday in readiness for the moment and the man, whenever it and he came). He did this extremely well, with a splendid punch line – 'No stunts – just straight talking.' He went over it with me earlier in the afternoon. It was not as taut then and I persuaded him to take out references to 'simple' words, phrases like 'factory, farm and field', and allusions which conjured visions of 'I' and 'the people' (but Harold Wilson still picked on enough in this vein to allege that it revealed an attitude of mind).

Then on Monday he agreed to accept further invitations from both television networks to be interviewed. He did them excellently, with a minimum of preparation – if anything resenting my arrange-ments for a preliminary discussion about the areas of questioning. Both were done at No. 10, and at last we got some sensible co-operation between the two networks in sharing technical facilities. I warned him that he must be prepared to counter the Wilson dismissal of him as 'the 14th Earl'. Oh well, he said in effect, I shall refer to him as 'the 14th Mr. Wilson'. I made sure accordingly that Kenneth Harris asked the right question: astonishingly they had not intended to tackle him about the fourteenth Earl criticisms.

Requests for interviews also came in from the *Mail* and the *Express*. This was clearly a case of both or neither. He agreed to both. Initially, however, he did not realise that they were on-the-record interviews, and I was then caught up in some last-minute persuasion. Again he performed admirably, though better with Ian Aitken than with Walter Terry, partly because he was getting tired and partly because Walter did not quite get his wavelength. Then he agreed to answer some written questions from Randolph Churchill for the *News of the World* (and to see him briefly and socially as well). Add a conference by Lady Home for the women writers, and by Thursday, when the House assembled for prorogation, we found that all the Tory M.P.'s loved the Homes and that the great Macleod–Powell rebellion had fizzled out.

During the week I went to see H. Macmillan in hospital. He was in a very small room (when the Queen came they took him to the Matron's room), but brisk and cheerful, with only occasional references to his dotage. Chiefly he talked about why Rab had never made the final ascent. Quite simply it was because ultimately the fire and determination were lacking. He also browsed over the old problem of No. 10 organisation without really seeing an answer (or at any rate revealing it to me). Tim came in for high praise, particularly for his courage. He had one complaint, he said. Within twenty-four hours of his ceasing to be Prime Minister, the Post Office had taken out his line to No. 10. Now he was having to pay a penny halfpenny a call, so please would I call him rather than wait for him to call me.

Earlier, while in the throes of king-making, he had rung me four times – twice on the Thursday morning – because he thought the Press was 'bad'. It wasn't, but I pinned it down to that bloody man Cassandra saying that his illness had all been contrived. For goodness sake, I argued, he must know that Cassandra had been attacking him venomously for seven years, that these attacks no longer attracted any credence, that it was politics anyhow, and why on earth let a man like Cassandra upset him at a moment when he really ought to be concentrating on things that really mattered. He took it well. Later Lady Dorothy wrote a letter of protest to Hugh Cudlipp. At least they printed it, though without embroidery or prominence.

The resignation honours list caused a great commotion at the top of the Civil Service because of the knighthoods for Tim Bligh and

Philip de Zulueta and the baronetcy for me. Honours for civil servants, it was contended, should not be allowed to disturb the delicate traceries of the mandarin pattern. Mainly the pressure came against the nomination of Tim Bligh for a K.B.E. A baronetcy for Evans – the first to be offered to a serving civil servant – was obviously to be deplored, but at least Evans could be regarded as a joker in the pack whereas Bligh was within the hierarchy of the administrative service. Attempts at arm twisting failed, however, and the list went ahead. I had, in fact, been offered the choice of being put forward for either a baronetcy or a knighthood. Among those from whom I sought advice was Sheila Minto. She was forthright – a baronetcy took precedence so why on earth the dithering? Since, with Timothy's death, the hereditary aspect did not enter into it I had no need to ponder on this point. On the other hand, hereditary honours are clearly on their way out, and the prospect of being one of the last of the bold, bad baronets had strong attractions. So a baronetcy it was.

SIXTEEN MONTHS LATER

'Jane Parson. Cocktails 6.30 p.m.' What would William Hickey make of this strange gathering at a terraced house in Pimlico? A new Cliveden set? The Macmillans. The Homes. Normanbrook, Bishop and Bligh. Evans. The 'in' group of No. 10's Young Ladies. Cover for some deep political plot? A move to restore Macmillan to No. 10, with the support of Normanbrook and Evans, shrewdly installed within the two broadcasting systems.

Perhaps, indeed, Uncle Harold *would* be ready to be drafted. Sitting on one arm of an armchair, with myself on the other, and Tim Bligh joining in he admitted to missing the battle. It was very nice down there at Birch Grove, of course, being so well looked after by Dorothy, but he got a little fed up being surrounded by women (three have been installed in the cottage behind the house to research for his book). The book itself was making him look to the past, of course, and he was taking great care not to seem to get into Alec's way. That was why he was so glad to retain the chairmanship of Macmillans. It brought him up to London twice a week and kept him in touch with people. That and Oxford. But might not a situation be developing when a coalition government could be set up? He might then come back. He could take a life peerage which could be arranged in a matter of hours. A coalition government would perhaps be the best way of tackling our economic problems – problems which remained exactly the same however differently they might be described and however differently the remedies might be presented (though one thing was certain – you could not have your foot on the accelerator and the brake at the same time). This was the main trend of his thinking.

He took some swipes at the journalists who tried to write in detail about the events of the leadership fortnight. Most of it, he said, was just gossip. This business of the supposed telephone call from Rab, for example. There were only two telephones at the hospital on which he *could* have taken a call. One was down the corridor and how could he have got out of bed and gone down the corridor with a tube in his abdomen? The other was the official line at the side of his bed, and no attempt to make a call could be traced on that phone.

About his book – the first volume had not been too difficult because it was based on what he remembered. It was something out of his own mind. But now every fact and every date had to be checked. It was strange that little interest had been shown in Lloyd George, in some ways a greater man than Churchill, but probably interest would revive. People tended to turn away from the immediate past but to become interested when events had become more remote – for example, the recent surge of interest in the 1914–18 war.

And there we had to become sociable again.

BIBLIOGRAPHY

Clive Bigham, *The Prime Ministers of Britain 1721–1921* (John Murray, 1922)

Hector Bolitho, *No. 10 Downing Street 1660–1900* (Hutchinson, 1957)

Benjamin J. Bradlee, *Conversations with Kennedy* (Quartet Books, 1976)

Lord Butler, *The Art of the Possible* (Hamish Hamilton, 1971)

Ronald Butt, *The Power of Parliament* (Constable, 1967)

Viscount Cilcenning, *Admiralty House* (Country Life, 1960)

Randolph Churchill, *The Fight for the Tory Leadership* (Heinemann, 1964)

Robin Day, *Television. A Personal Report* (Hutchinson, 1961)

Lord Egremont, *Wyndham and Children First* (Macmillan, 1968)

Henry Fairlie, *The Life of Politics* (Methuen, 1968)

Nigel Fisher, *Iain Macleod* (Deutsch, 1973)

Basil Fuller and John Cornes, *No. 10 Downing Street* (Paul, 1936)

C. L. Graves, *Life and Letters of Alexander Macmillan* (Macmillan, 1910)

John Gunther, *Inside Europe Today* (Harper & Brothers, 1961)

Lord Hailsham, *The Door Wherein I Went* (Collins, 1975)

Lord Hill, *Both Sides of the Hill* (Heinemann, 1964)

Lord Home, *The Way the Wind Blows* (Collins, 1976)

Thomas Hughes, *Memoir of Daniel Macmillan* (1882)

George Hutchinson, *The Last Edwardian at No. 10* (Quartet Books, 1980)

Clive Irving, Ron Hall, Jeremy Wallington, *Scandal '63* (Heinemann, 1963)

The Earl of Kilmuir, *Political Adventure* (Weidenfeld & Nicolson, 1964)

Anthony King and Anne Sloman, *Westminster and Beyond* (Macmillan, 1973)

Bernard Levin, *The Pendulum Years* (Jonathan Cape, 1970)

Harold Macmillan, *Riding the Storm 1956–1959* (Macmillan, 1971)

Harold Macmillan, *Pointing the Way 1959–1961* (Macmillan, 1972)

Harold Macmillan, *At the End of the Day 1961–1963* (Macmillan, 1973)

James Margach, *The Abuse of Power* (W. H. Allen, 1978)

Reginald Maudling, *Memoirs* (Sidgwick and Jackson, 1978)

R. J. Minney, *No. 10* (Cassell, 1963)

David Nunnerley, *President Kennedy and Britain* (Bodley Head, 1972)

Earl of Oxford and Asquith, *Fifty Years of Parliament* (Cassell, 1926)

Marjorie Ogilvy-Webb, *The Government Explains* (Allen & Unwin, 1965)

Sir Charles Petrie, *The Powers behind the Prime Ministers* (Macgibbon & Kee, 1958)

Pierre Salinger, *With Kennedy* (Jonathan Cape, 1967)

Anthony Sampson, *Macmillan. A Study in Ambiguity* (Penguin, 1966)

Theodore Sorensen, *Kennedy* (Hodder & Stoughton, 1965)

The Earl of Swinton (with James Margach), *Sixty Years of Power* (Hutchinson, 1966)

Colin Seymour-Ure, *The Press, Politics and the Public* (Methuen, 1968)

Jeremy Tunstall, *The Westminster Lobby Correspondents* (Routledge & Kegan Paul, 1970)

Index

INDEX

Lobby correspondents, 13, 22–3, 35–7,
45–58, 64, 119, 127, 130, 137, 140, 152, 156,
164–7, 182–3, 189, 202, 204, 205–8, 226,
228–30, 232, 246, 256, 263, 266, 271–2, 276,
286, 292, 301
Lockhead, George, 256, 268
Louw, Eric, 102–4, 141
Low, Toby (later Lord Aldington), 156
Luce, Henry, 266
Lusaka, 97–9
Lyttelton, Oliver – see Chandos, Lord

Macaulay, Lord, 63, 68
McLachlan, Donald, 186
Maclean, Donald, 280
Maclay, John Scott, 202, 205
Macleod, Iain, 107–8, 124, 133–4, 137–41,
159–60, 163–8, 171, 175, 178, 182, 185, 201,
203–4, 215, 221, 228, 232, 250–3, 256,
261–2, 264, 271–2, 275, 278, 291–2, 301
MacColl, René, 88, 96, 98–9, 111, 241
Mackenzie, Robert, 42, 44, 274
Mackintosh, Angus, 216, 218
Macmillan, Alexander, 282
Macmillan, Lady Dorothy, 21–2, 73, 88, 92,
97, 99–100, 102, 106, 123–4, 126, 131, 149,
172, 180, 208, 219, 230, 232, 247–8, 265,
269, 282–4, 296, 298, 302–3
Macmillan, Sir Frederick, 154
Macmillan, Harold: and Finnish Aid Bureau,
19–20; as Under-Secretary of State for the
Colonies, 18; as Minister Resident at Allied
Headquarters in North West Africa, 29–30,
122; becomes Prime Minister, 13; expects
short administration, 18; working style and
organisation at No. 10, 21–2, 24, 31–2, 38,
72–3, 172, 302; and foreign affairs, 29–30,
72, 113; and security services, 65–6, 69; and
public relations and 'image', 27–8, 45–7;
and the Press, 63–71, 98, 111, 137, 139, 140,
159, 163, 171, 190, 194, 198, 200, 229, 247,
275, 302; and the Lobby correspondents,
57–8; and television, 42–4, 82; and speech
drafting, 38–42, 193; 'enough is enough'
incident, 52–4; 'little local difficulties'
(resignation of three Treasury Ministers),
73; first Commonwealth tour (India,
Pakistan, Ceylon, Singapore, New
Zealand, Australia), 72–4; visits Soviet
Union, 73, 74–9; General Election victory
(October 1959), 87; second Commonwealth tour (Ghana, Nigeria, Central
African Federation, High Commission
Territories and South Africa), 72, 87–107;
and problems of Central African
Federation, 97, 101, 107, 134–5,
138–9; failure of East-West summit in

Paris, 113–15; appoints Lord Home as
Foreign Secretary, 115–17; moves from
No. 10 to Admiralty House, 118, 126;
addresses United Nations General
Assembly, 120–3; John F. Kennedy
becomes U.S. President, 127–8; party for
civil service colleagues, 131; and struggle
for control of Odhams Press, 136–7; and
Commonwealth Prime Ministers'
conference (March 1961) (withdrawal of
South Africa), 141–3; third Common-
wealth tour (Trinidad, Barbados, Antigua,
Jamaica) and first meeting with President
Kennedy (Key West) followed by talks in
Washington, 72, 143–9; speech at
Massachusetts Institute of Technology,
147; approach to E.E.C. membership, 150;
visit of Yuri Gagarin, 151–2; announces
U.K. application for E.E.C. membership,
156; upsets Lobby correspondents, 156–7;
'No war about Berlin', 159; Iain Macleod
appointed Leader of the House and
Chairman of the Conservative Party in
succession to R. A. Butler, 159–60, 163,
165–8; surprised by reactions to B.B.C.
television anniversary speech, 170, 175;
speaks at Press Club, 171; entertains
General and Madame de Gaulle at Birch
Grove House, 172–5; called upon to resign
by Sir Harry Legge-Bourke, 181, 183–4;
railway settlement (February 1962), 185–6;
appoints R. A. Butler to take special
responsibility for Central African
Federation, 189; Liberals capture
Orpington, 188–9, 190; visits
New York–Washington–Ottawa–Toronto,
191–5; supports election of U Thant as
U.N. Secretary-General, 194; plans
economic 'package' ('The New
Approach'), 197, 199, 201–3; visits General
de Gaulle at Chateau de Champs, 199, 200;
reconstructs Cabinet (July 1962) (criticised
as a 'massacre'), 201–9; cuts in defence
expenditure, 211; Commonwealth Prime
Ministers conference to discuss proposed
British membership of E.E.C., 212–18;
television broadcast on U.K. application to
join E.E.C., 219–20; Cuba missile crisis,
224–6; Vassall spy case (Radcliffe Tribunal
set up), 227–9; Skybolt–Polaris talks with
President Kennedy at Nassau, 233–42;
forecasts 'a year of destiny' (1963), 243,
245; General de Gaulle opposes British
entry into E.E.C., 246, 248; death of Hugh
Gaitskell, 246–8; Press speculation about
Conservative leadership, 254–5; two
journalists to prison for refusal to disclose

313